Get the eBook FREE!

(PDF, ePub, Kindle, and liveBook all included)

We believe that once you buy a book from us, you should be able to read it in any format we have available. To get electronic versions of this book at no additional cost to you, purchase and then register this book at the Manning website.

Go to https://www.manning.com/freebook and follow the instructions to complete your pBook registration.

That's it!
Thanks from Manning!

Apache Pulsar in Action

DAVID KJERRUMGAARD
FOREWORD BY MATTEO MERLI

MANNING
SHELTER ISLAND

For online information and ordering of this and other Manning books, please visit
www.manning.com. The publisher offers discounts on this book when ordered in quantity.
For more information, please contact

Special Sales Department
Manning Publications Co.
20 Baldwin Road
PO Box 761
Shelter Island, NY 11964
Email: orders@manning.com

Manning Publications Co.
20 Baldwin Road
PO Box 761
Shelter Island, NY 11964

Development editor:	Karen Miller
Technical development editors:	Alain Couniot
Review editor:	Adriana Sabo
Production editor:	Keri Hales
Copy editor:	Christian Berk
Proofreader:	Melody Dolab
Technical proofreader:	Ninoslav Čerkez
Typesetter:	Gordan Salinovic
Cover designer:	Marija Tudor

ISBN 9781617296888

Printed in the United States of America

To my father, who promised to read this book even if he can't understand a word of it. May your heart be filled with pride every time you tell your friends that your son is a published author.

To my mother, who believed in me when no one else did and worked so hard to ensure that I had every opportunity in life to succeed. Your hard work, faith, and tenacity have been a source of inspiration for me. Thank you for passing these traits down to me, as they have been the foundation of all my achievements including this book.

brief contents

contents

foreword

Apache Pulsar in Action is the missing guide that will walk you through your journey with Apache Pulsar. It is a book that I'd recommend to anyone, from developers starting to explore pub-sub messaging, to someone with messaging experience, up to experienced Pulsar power users.

The Apache Pulsar project was started at Yahoo! around 2012 with the mission of experimenting with a new architecture that would be able to solve the operational challenges of existing messaging platforms. This was also a time when some significant shifts in the world of data infrastructure were starting to become more visible. Application developers started to look more and more at scalable and reliable messaging as the core component for building the next generation of products. At the same time, companies started to see large-scale real-time streaming data analytics as an essential component and business advantage.

Pulsar was designed from the ground up with the objective of bridging these two worlds, pub-sub messaging and streaming analytics, that are too often isolated in different silos. We worked toward creating an infrastructure that would represent a next generation of real-time data platforms, where one single system would be able to support all the use cases throughout the entire life cycle of data events.

Over time, that vision has expanded further, as can be clearly seen from the wide range of components described in this book. The project has added support for lightweight processing with Pulsar Functions, the Pulsar IO connectors framework, support for data schema, and many other features. What has not changed is the ultimate goal of creating the most scalable, flexible, and reliable platform for real-time data, and allowing any user to process the data stored in Pulsar in the most convenient form.

I have known and worked with this book's author, David Kjerrumgaard, for several years. Throughout this time, I've seen his passion for working with the Pulsar community. He is always able to help users make sense of technical issues, as well as to show them how Pulsar fits into the bigger picture of solving their data problem.

I particularly appreciate how *Pulsar in Action* is able to seamlessly mix the theory and abstract concepts with the clarity of practical step-by-step examples, and how these examples are rooted in common use cases and messaging design patterns that will surely resonate with many readers. There is truly something for everyone, and everyone will be able to get acquainted with all the aspects and the possibilities that Pulsar offers.

—MATTEO MERLI
CTO AT STREAMNATIVE
CO-CREATOR AND PMC CHAIR OF APACHE PULSAR

preface

Back in 2012, the Yahoo! team was looking for a global, geo-replicated platform that could stream all of Yahoo!'s messaging data between various apps such as Yahoo Mail and Yahoo Finance. At the time, there were generally two types of systems to handle in-motion data: message queues that handled mission-critical business events in real-time, and streaming systems that handled scalable data pipelines at scale. But there wasn't a platform that provided both capabilities that Yahoo required.

After vetting the messaging and streaming landscape, it became clear that existing technologies were not able to serve their needs, so the team at Yahoo! started working on building a unified messaging and streaming platform for in-motion data named Pulsar. After 4 years of operation across 10 datacenters processing billions of messages per day, Yahoo! decided to open source its messaging platform under the Apache license in 2016.

I first encountered Pulsar in the fall of 2017. I was leading the professional services team at Hortonworks focused on the streaming data platform known as Hortonworks Data Flow (HDF) that comprised Apache NiFi, Kafka, and Storm. It was my job to oversee the deployment of these technologies into a customer's infrastructure and help them get started developing streaming applications.

The greatest challenge we faced when working with Kafka was helping our customers administer it properly, and specifically determining the proper number of partitions for a given topic to achieve a proper balance of speed and efficiency while allowing for future data growth. Those of you that are familiar with Kafka are painfully aware of the fact that this seemingly simple decision has a profound impact on the scalability of your topics, and the process of changing this value (even from 3 to 4) necessitates a rebalancing process that is slow and results in the rebalancing topic being unavailable for reading or writing during the entire process.

This rebalancing requirement was universally disliked by all the customers who were using HDF, and rightfully so, because they saw it as a clear impediment to their ability to scale the Kafka cluster as their data volumes grew. They knew from experience just how difficult it was to scale their messaging platform up and down. Even worse was the fact that we could not simply "drop in" a few more nodes to add computing capacity to our customer's existing cluster without also reconfiguring the topics to use them by assigning more partitions to the existing topics to have the data redistributed onto the recently added nodes. This inability to horizontally scale out their streaming capacity without manual (or heavily scripted) intervention was in direct conflict with most of our customers' desires to move their messaging platforms to the cloud and capitalize on the elastic computing capability the cloud provides.

That is when I discovered the Apache Pulsar platform and found its claim to be "cloud-native" especially appealing because it addressed both scalability pain points. While HDF had allowed my customers to get started quickly, they found it difficult to manage and not architected to run in the cloud. I realized that Apache Pulsar was a much better solution than what we were currently offering to our customers and tried to convince our product team to consider replacing Kafka with Pulsar in our HDF product. I even went so far as to write connectors that allowed it to work with the Apache NiFi component of our stack to facilitate that adoption, but to no avail.

When I was approached by the original developers of Apache Pulsar in January of 2018 and offered the opportunity to join a small start-up called Streamlio, I immediately jumped at the chance to work with them. Pulsar was a young project back then, having just been placed into the Apache incubation program, and we spent the next 15 months working to get our fledgling "podling" through the incubation process and promoted to top-level project status.

This was during the height of the streaming data hype, and Kafka was the dominant player in the space, so naturally everyone considered the terms interchangeable. The consensus was that Kafka was the only data-streaming platform available. I knew better from my prior experiences and took it upon myself to relentlessly evangelize what I knew to be a technologically superior solution—a lonely voice shouting in the proverbial wilderness.

By the spring of 2019, the Apache Pulsar community had experienced tremendous growth in terms of contributors and users, but there was a profound lack of reliable documentation on the technology. So, when the prospect of writing *Apache Pulsar in Action* was first proposed to me, I immediately seized upon it as an opportunity to address the glaring need within the Pulsar community. While I was never able to convince my colleagues to join me in this endeavor, they were an invaluable source of guidance and information throughout the process and have used this book as a means of transferring some of their knowledge to you.

This book is targeted to individuals who are brand new to Pulsar, and is a combination of the information I gathered while working directly with the project founders when they were actively developing Pulsar, along with experience gained from working directly with organizations that have adopted Apache Pulsar in production.

It is intended to provide guidance over the stumbling blocks and pitfalls that others have encountered during their journeys with Pulsar. Above all, this book will give you the confidence to develop stream processing applications and microservices employing Pulsar using the Java programming language. Even though I have chosen to use Java for most of the code samples throughout the book due to my familiarity with the language, I have also created a similar set of code using Python and have uploaded it to my GitHub account for those of you who prefer coding in that language.

acknowledgments

In the order of nature, we cannot render benefits to those from whom we receive them, or only seldom. But the benefit we receive must be rendered again, line for line, deed for deed, cent for cent, to somebody.

—Ralph Waldo Emerson

I want to take this opportunity to thank everyone who contributed in some way to making this book a reality and to acknowledge the fact that I never would have been able to take on such an enormous project without those who helped lay the foundations for it. In the spirit of Emerson, please consider this book my way of paying forward all the knowledge and encouragement you have given me.

I would be remiss if I didn't start this list with the very first person who introduced me to the wonderful world of coding at the very young age of 6: my elementary school principal, Mr. Rodgers, who decided to put me in front of a computer rather than in detention for not paying attention during first-grade math class. You introduced me to the pure creative joy of coding and set me on a lifelong path of learning.

I also want to acknowledge the development team at Yahoo! that created Pulsar: you wrote an amazing piece of software and contributed it to the open source community for the rest of us to enjoy. Without you this book wouldn't be possible.

I want to acknowledge all my former colleagues at Streamlio, especially Jerry Peng, Ivan Kelly, Matteo Merli, Sijie Guo, and Sanjeev Kulkarni for serving as Apache PMC Members on either Apache Pulsar, Apache BookKeeper, or both. Without your guidance and commitment, Pulsar wouldn't be where it is today. I also want to thank my former CEO, Karthik Ramasamy, for helping me grow the Apache Pulsar community while working for him at Streamlio: I really appreciate your mentorship.

I want to thank all my former colleagues at Splunk for your efforts on getting Apache Pulsar integrated into such a large organization and for helping us promote its adoption across the organization. When presented with a new technology, you stepped up to the plate and did everything you could to make that effort a success. I want to give a special thank you to the connectors team, particularly Alamusi, Gimi, Alex, and Spike.

I'd also like to thank the reviewers who took time from their busy lives to read my manuscript at various stages of its development. Your positive feedback was a welcomed reassurance that I was on the right track and lifted my spirits when the writing process had worn me down. Your negative feedback was always constructive and provided a fresh perspective on the material that only a fresh set of eyes can provide. This feedback was invaluable to me and ultimately resulted in the book being much better than it would have been without you. Thank you all: Alessandro Campeis, Alexander Schwartz, Andres Sacco, Andy Keffalas, Angelo Simone Scotto, Chris Viner, Emanuele Piccinelli, Eric Platon, Giampiero Granatella, Gianluca Righetto, Gilberto Taccari, Henry Saputra, Igor Savin, Jason Rendel, Jeremy Chen, Kabeer Ahmed, Kent Spillner, Richard Tobias, Sanket Naik, Satej Kumar Sah, Simone Sguazza, and Thorsten Weber.

To all the online reviewers, thank you for taking the time to provide valuable feedback to me via Manning's online forum—especially Chris Latimer, and his uncanny knack for finding all the misspellings and grammatical errors that Microsoft Word could not. All future readers owe you a debt of gratitude.

Last, and certainly not least, I want to thank my editors at Manning, especially Karen Miller, Ivan Martinović, Adriana Sabo, Alain Couniot, and Ninoslav Čerkez. Thank you for working with me and for being patient when things got rough. It was a long process, and I couldn't have done it without your encouragement. Your commitment to the quality of this book has made it better for everyone who reads it. Thanks as well to all the other folks at Manning who worked with me on the production and promotion of the book. It was truly a team effort.

about this book

Apache Pulsar in Action was written as an introduction to the stream processing world and to help you become familiar with the terminology, semantics, and considerations one must take when adopting the stream processing paradigm while coming from a batch-processing background. It starts with a historical review of the evolution of messaging systems over the past 40 years and shows how Pulsar sits at the top of this evolutionary cycle.

After a brief introduction to common messaging terminology and a discussion of the two most common message consumption patterns, it covers the architecture of Pulsar from a physical perspective focusing on its cloud-native design, as well as from its logical structuring of data and its support for multi-tenancy.

The remainder of the book is focused on how you can use Pulsar's built-in computing platform known as Pulsar Function to develop applications using a simple API. This is demonstrated by implementing an order-processing use case: a fictional food delivery microservices application based solely on Pulsar Functions, complete with a delivery time estimation machine learning model deployment.

Who should read this book

Apache Pulsar in Action is primarily intended for Java developers who have an interest in working with streaming data, or microservice developers who are looking for an alternative message-based framework that can be used for event sourcing. DevOps teams who are looking to deploy and operate Pulsar within their organizations will find this book useful as well. One of the primary criticisms of Apache Pulsar is an overall lack of documentation and blog posts available online, and although I fully expect that to change in the near future, I hope that this book will help fill that gap in the interim and will benefit anyone wanting to learn more about stream processing in general and Apache Pulsar in particular.

How this book is organized: A roadmap

This book consists of 12 chapters that are spread across three different parts. Part 1 starts with a basic introduction to Apache Pulsar and where it fits in the 40-year evolution of messaging systems by comparing it to and contrasting it with the various messaging platforms that have come before it:

- Chapter 1 provides a historical perspective on messaging systems and where Apache Pulsar fits into the 40-year evolution of messaging technology. It also previews some of Pulsar's architectural advantages over other systems and why you should consider using it as your single messaging platform of choice.
- Chapter 2 covers the details of Pulsar's multi-tiered architecture, which allows you to dynamically scale up the storage or serving layers independently. It also describes some of the common message consumption patterns, how they are different from one another, and how Pulsar supports them all.
- Chapter 3 demonstrates how to interact with Apache Pulsar from both the command line as well as by using its programming API. After completing this chapter, you should be comfortable running a local instance of Apache Pulsar and interacting with it.

Part 2 covers some of the more basic usage and features of Pulsar, including how to perform basic messaging and how to secure your Pulsar cluster, along with more advanced features such as the schema registry. It also introduces the Pulsar Functions framework, including how to build, deploy, and test functions:

- Chapter 4 introduces Pulsar's stream native computing framework called Pulsar Functions, provides some background on its design and configuration, and show you how to develop, test, and deploy functions.
- Chapter 5 introduces Pulsar's connector framework that is designed to move between Apache Pulsar and external storage systems, such as relational databases, key-value stores, and blob storage such as S3. It teaches you how to develop a connector in a step-by-step fashion.
- Chapter 6 provides step-by-step details on how to secure your Pulsar cluster to ensure that your data is secured while it is in transit and while it is at rest.
- Chapter 7 covers Pulsar's built-in schema registry, why it is necessary, and how it can help simplify microservice development. We also cover the schema evolution process and how to update the schemas used inside your Pulsar Functions.

Part 3 focuses on the use of Pulsar Functions to implement microservices and demonstrates how to implement various common microservice design patterns within Pulsar

Functions. This section focuses on the development of a food delivery application to make the examples more realistic and addresses more-complex use cases including resiliency, data access, and how to use Pulsar Functions to deploy machine learning models that can run against real-time data:

- Chapter 8 demonstrates how to implement common messaging routing patterns such as message splitting, content-based routing, and filtering. It also shows how to implement various message transformation patterns such as value extraction and message translation.

- Chapter 9 stresses the importance of having resiliency built into your microservices and demonstrates how to implement this inside your Java-based Pulsar Functions with the help of the resiliency4j library. It covers various events that can occur in an event-based program and the different patterns you can use to insulate your services from these failure scenarios to maximize your application uptime.

- Chapter 10 focuses on how you can access data from a variety of external systems from inside your Pulsar functions. It demonstrates various ways of acquiring information within your microservices and considerations you should take into account in terms of latency.

- Chapter 11 walks you through the process of deploying different machine learning model types inside of a Pulsar function using various ML frameworks. It also covers the very important topic of how to feed the necessary information into the model to get an accurate prediction

- Chapter 12 covers the use of Pulsar Functions within an edge computing environment to perform real-time analytics on IoT data. It starts with a detailed description of what an edge computing environment looks like and describes the various layers of the architecture before showing how to leverage Pulsar Functions to process the information on the edge and only forward summaries rather than the entire dataset.

Finally, two appendices demonstrate more advanced operational scenarios including deployment within a Kubernetes environment and geo-replication:

1. Appendix A walks you through the steps necessary to deploy Pulsar into a Kubernetes environment using the Helm charts that are provided as part of the open source project. It also covers how to modify these charts to suit your environment.

- Appendix B describes Pulsar's built-in geo-replication mechanism and some of the common replication patterns that are used in production today. It then walks you through the process of implementing one of these geo-replication patterns in Pulsar.

About the code

This book contains many examples of source code both in numbered listings and in line with normal text. In both cases, source code is formatted in a `fixed-width font` `like this` to separate it from ordinary text. Sometimes code is also **in bold** to highlight code that has changed from previous steps in the chapter, such as when a new feature adds to an existing line of code.

In many cases, the original source code has been reformatted; we've added line breaks and reworked indentation to accommodate the available page space in the book. In rare cases, even this was not enough, and listings include line-continuation markers (➥). Additionally, comments in the source code have often been removed from the listings when the code is described in the text. Code annotations accompany many of the listings, highlighting important concepts.

This book is first and foremost a programming book designed to be used as a hands-on guide for learning how to develop microservices using Pulsar Functions. Therefore, I have provided multiple source code repositories that I often refer to throughout the course of the book. I encourage you to download the code from the publisher's website at https://www.manning.com/books/apache-pulsar-in-action, or from my personal GitHub account:

- This GitHub repository contains the code examples for chapters 3 through 6 as well as chapter 8: https://github.com/david-streamlio/pulsar-in-action
- The code for the food delivery microservices application can be found in the following GitHub repository: https://github.com/david-streamlio/GottaEat
- The code for the IoT Analytics application discussed in Chapter 12 can be found here: https://github.com/david-streamlio/Pulsar-Edge-Analytics
- For those of you looking for Python-based examples, you can find them in the following repository: https://github.com/david-streamlio/pulsar-in-action-python

Other online resources

Need additional help?

- The Apache Pulsar project website, https://pulsar.apache.org, is a good source of information about the configuration settings of various components of the Apache Pulsar software, as well as various cookbooks on how to implement specific features of the software, and it will have the most current information.
- The Apache Pulsar Slack channel, apache-pulsar.slack.com, is an active forum where members of the Apache Pulsar community from around the world meet to exchange advice, share best practices, and provide troubleshooting advice to people who are experiencing problems with Pulsar. It is a great place to go for advice if you get stuck.
- In my current capacity as a Developer Advocate, I will continue to develop additional educational content including blog posts and code examples that will be made readily available online at my company's website, streamnative.io.

liveBook discussion forum

Purchase of *Apache Pulsar in Action* includes free access to a private web forum run by Manning Publications where you can make comments about the book, ask technical questions, and receive help from the author and from other users. To access the forum, go to https://livebook.manning.com/#!/book/apache-pulsar-in-action/discussion. You can also learn more about Manning's forums and the rules of conduct at https://livebook.manning.com/#!/discussion.

Manning's commitment to our readers is to provide a venue where a meaningful dialogue between individual readers and between readers and the author can take place. It is not a commitment to any specific amount of participation on the part of the author, whose contribution to the forum remains voluntary (and unpaid). We suggest you try asking the author some challenging questions lest his interest stray! The forum and the archives of previous discussions will be accessible from the publisher's website as long as the book is in print.

about the author

 **DAVID KJERRUMGAARD** is a committer on the Apache Pulsar project and serves as a Developer Advocate for StreamNative with a focus on educating developers about Apache Pulsar. He was formerly the Global Practice Director at Hortonworks, where he was responsible for the development of best practices and solutions for the professional services team, with a focus on Streaming technologies including Kafka, NiFi, and Storm. He has both a BS and MS in computer science and mathematics from Kent State University.

about the cover illustration

The figure on the cover of *Apache Pulsar in Action* is captioned "Cosaque," or a Cossack man. The illustration is taken from a collection of dress costumes from various countries by Jacques Grasset de Saint-Sauveur (1757–1810), titled *Costumes civils actuels de tous les peuples connus*, published in France in 1788. Each illustration is finely drawn and colored by hand. The rich variety of Grasset de Saint-Sauveur's collection reminds us vividly of how culturally apart the world's towns and regions were just 200 years ago. Isolated from each other, people spoke different dialects and languages. In the streets or in the countryside, it was easy to identify where they lived and what their trade or station in life was just by their dress.

The way we dress has changed since then and the diversity by region, so rich at the time, has faded away. It is now hard to tell apart the inhabitants of different continents, let alone different towns, regions, or countries. Perhaps we have traded cultural diversity for a more varied personal life—certainly for a more varied and fast-paced technological life.

At a time when it is hard to tell one computer book from another, Manning celebrates the inventiveness and initiative of the computer business with book covers based on the rich diversity of regional life of two centuries ago, brought back to life by Grasset de Saint-Sauveur's pictures.

Part 1

Getting started with Apache Pulsar

Enterprise messaging systems (EMS) are designed to promote loosely coupled architectures that allow geographically distributed systems to communicate with one another by exchanging messages via a simple API that supports two basic operations: publish a message and subscribe to a topic (read messages). Over the course of their 40+ year history, enterprise messaging systems have given rise to several important distributed software architectural styles, including

- Remote-procedure-call (RPC) programming, using technologies such as COBRA and Amazon Web Services, which enables programs developed in different languages to directly interact with one another.
- Messaging-oriented middleware (MOM) programming for enterprise application integration, as exemplified by Apache Camel, which allows different systems to exchange information using a common message format using XML or a similar self-describing format.
- Service-oriented-architecture (SOA), which promotes a modular programming-by-contract style that allowed applications to be composed of services that were combined in a specific way to perform the necessary business logic.
- Event-driven-architecture (EDA), which promotes the production and detection of and reaction to individual changes in state, referred to as events, and writing code that detects and reacts to these individual events. This style was adopted in part to address the need to process continuous streams of internet-scale data, such as server logs and digital events like clickstreams.

The EMS plays a key role in each of these architectural styles, as it serves as the underlying technology that allows these distributed components to communicate with one another by storing the intermediate messages and distributing to all the intended consumers in a timely manner. The key differentiator between communication via an EMS and some other network-only-based communication mechanisms is that an EMS is designed to guarantee message delivery. If an event is published to an EMS, it will be stored and forwarded to all the intended recipients, as opposed to a HTTP-based inter-microservices call that can be lost in the event of a network failure.

These retained messages on an EMS have also proven to be valuable sources of information for organizations, which they can analyze to extract more business value. Consider the treasure trove of information on customer behavior that a company's click stream provides them. Processing these types of data sources is referred to as *stream processing* because you are literally processing an unbounded stream of data. This is why there is great interest in processing these streams with analytical tools, such as Apache Flink or Spark.

The first part of this book provides an evolutionary overview of the EMS with a focus on the core capabilities that were added at each evolutionary step. Having this background will help you better understand how various messaging systems compare with one another by knowing each generation's strengths and weaknesses and the capabilities the next generation added along the way. At the end, I hope you understand why Apache Pulsar is an evolutionary step forward in the EMS lineage and worthy of your consideration as a critical piece of your company's infrastructure.

Chapter 1 provides a basic introduction to Apache Pulsar and where it fits in the 40-year evolution of messaging systems by comparing it to and contrasting it with the various messaging platforms that have come before it. Next, chapter 2 dives into the details of Pulsar's physical architecture and how its multitiered architecture allows its storage and computing layers to scale independently of one another. It also describes some of the common message consumption patterns, how they are different from one another, and how Pulsar supports them all. Finally, chapter 3 demonstrates how to interact with Apache Pulsar from both the command line as well as by using its programming API. After completing this chapter, you should be comfortable running a local instance of Apache Pulsar and interacting with it.

Introduction
to Apache Pulsar

This chapter covers

- The evolution of the enterprise messaging system
- A comparison of Apache Pulsar to existing enterprise messaging systems
- How Pulsar's segment-centric storage differs from the partition-centric storage model used in Apache Kafka
- Real-world use cases where Pulsar is used for stream processing, and why you should consider using Apache Pulsar

Developed by Yahoo! in 2013, Pulsar was first open sourced in 2016, and only 15 months after joining the Apache Software Foundation's incubation program, it graduated to top-level project status. Apache Pulsar was designed from the ground up to address the gaps in current open source messaging systems, such as multi-tenancy, geo-replication, and strong durability guarantees.

The Apache Pulsar site describes it as a distributed pub–sub messaging system that provides very low publish and end-to-end latency, guaranteed message delivery, zero data loss, and a serverless, lightweight computing framework for stream data processing. Apache Pulsar provides three key capabilities for processing large data sets:

- *Real-time messaging*—Enables geographically distributed applications and systems to communicate with one another in an asynchronous manner by exchanging messages. Pulsar's goal is to provide this capability to the broadest audience of clients via support for multiple programming languages and binary messaging protocols.
- *Real-time compute*—Provides the ability to perform user-defined computations on these messages inside of Pulsar itself and without the need for an external computational system to perform basic transformational operations, such as data enrichment, filtering, and aggregations.
- *Scalable storage*—Pulsar's independent storage layer and support for tiered storage enable the retention of your message data for as long as you need. There is no physical limitation on the amount of data that can be retained and accessed by Pulsar.

1.1   Enterprise messaging systems

Messaging is a broad term that is used to describe the routing of data between producers and consumers. Consequently, there are several different technologies and protocols that have evolved over the years that provide this capability. Most people are familiar with messaging systems such as email, text messaging, and instant messaging applications, including WhatsApp and Facebook Messenger. Messaging systems within this category are designed to transmit text data and images over the internet between two or more parties. More-advanced instant messaging systems support Voice over IP (VoIP) and video chat capabilities as well. All of these systems were designed to support person-to-person communication over ad hoc channels.

Another category of messaging system that people are already familiar with is video on demand streaming services, such as Netflix or Hulu, that stream video content to multiple subscribers simultaneously. These video streaming services are examples of one-way broadcast (one message to many consumers) transmissions of data to consumers that subscribe to an existing channel in order to receive the content. While these types of applications might be what comes to mind when using the terms *messaging systems* or *streaming*, for the purposes of this book, we will be focusing on enterprise messaging systems.

An *enterprise messaging system* (EMS) is the software that provides the implementation of various messaging protocols, such as data distribution service (DDS), advanced message queuing protocol (AMQP), Microsoft message queuing (MSMQ), and others. These protocols support the sending and receiving of messages between distributed systems and applications in an asynchronous fashion. However, asynchronous communication wasn't always an option, particularly during the earliest days of distributed computing when both client/server and remote procedure call (RPC) architectures were the dominant approach. Prime examples of RPC were the simple object access protocol (SOAP) and representational state transfer (REST) based web services that interacted with one another through fixed endpoints. Within both of these styles, when a process wanted to interact with a remote service, it needed to first determine the service's remote location via a discovery service and then invoke the desired method remotely, using the proper parameters and types, as shown in figure 1.1.

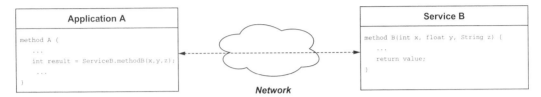

Figure 1.1   Within an RPC architecture, an application invokes a procedure on a service that is running on a different host and must wait for that procedure call to return before it can continue processing.

The calling application would then have to wait for the called procedure to return before it could continue processing. The synchronous nature of these architectures made applications based upon them inherently slow. In addition, there was the possibility that the remote service was unavailable for a period of time, which would require the application developer to use defensive programming techniques to identify this condition and react accordingly.

Unlike the point-to-point communication channels used in RPC programming, where you had to wait for the procedure calls to provide a response, an EMS allows remote applications and services to communicate with one another via an intermediate service rather than directly with one another. Rather than having to establish a direct network communication channel between the calling/receiving applications over which the parameters are exchanged, an EMS can be used to retain these parameters in message form, and they are guaranteed to be delivered to the intended recipient for processing. This allows the caller to send its request asynchronously and await a response from the service they were trying to invoke. It also allows the service to communicate its response back in an asynchronous manner as well by publishing its result to the EMS for eventual delivery to the original caller. This decoupling promotes asynchronous application development by providing a standardized, reliable intra-component communication channel that serves as a persistent buffer for handling data, even when some of the components are offline, as you can see in figure 1.2.

An EMS promotes loosely coupled architectures by allowing independently developed software components that are distributed across different systems to communicate with one another via structured messages. These message schemas are usually defined in language-neutral formats, such as XML, JSON, or Avro IDL, which allows

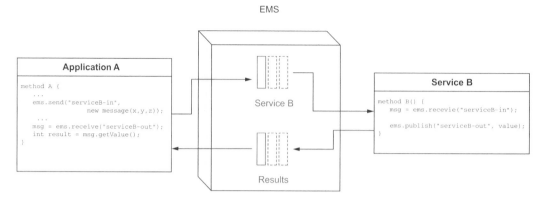

Figure 1.2   An EMS allows distributed applications and services to exchange information in an asynchronous fashion.

the components to be developed in any programming language that supports those formats.

1.1.1   *Key capabilities*

Now that we have introduced the concept of enterprise message systems and provided some context for the types of problems they have been used to solve, let's further refine the definition of what an EMS is, based upon the capabilities it provides.

ASYNCHRONOUS COMMUNICATION

Messaging systems allow services and applications to communicate with one another in a non-blocking manner, meaning that the message sender and receiver are not required to interact with the messaging system (or one another) at the same time. A messaging system will retain the messages until all of the intended recipients consume it.

MESSAGE RETENTION

Unlike network-based messaging in which the messages only exist on the network, such as RPC, messages published to a messaging system are retained on disk until they are delivered. Undelivered messages can be held for hours, days, or even weeks, and most messaging systems allow you to specify the retention policy.

ACKNOWLEDGMENT

Messaging systems are required to retain messages until all of the intended recipients receive it; therefore, a mechanism by which the message consumers can acknowledge the successful delivery and processing of the message is required. This allows the messaging system to purge all successfully delivered messages and to retry message delivery to those consumers who have not yet received it.

MESSAGE CONSUMPTION

Obviously, a messaging system isn't particularly useful if it doesn't provide a mechanism by which the intended recipients can consume messages. First and foremost, an

EMS must guarantee that all the messages it receives get delivered. Oftentimes, a message might be intended for multiple consumers, and the EMS must maintain the information along with which messages have been delivered and to whom.

1.2 Message consumption patterns

With an EMS, you have the option of publishing messages to either a topic or a queue, and there are fundamental differences between the two. A topic supports multiple concurrent consumers of the same message. Any message published to a topic is automatically broadcast to all of the consumers who have *subscribed* to the topic. Any number of consumers can subscribe to a topic in order to receive the information being sent—like any number of users can subscribe to Netflix and receive their streaming content.

1.2.1 Publish–subscribe messaging

In publish and subscribe messaging, producers publish messages to named channels, known as *topics*. Consumers can then subscribe to those topics to receive the incoming messages. A publish–subscribe (pub–sub) message channel receives incoming messages from multiple producers and stores them in the exact order that they arrive. However, it differs from message queuing on the consumption side because it supports multiple consumers receiving each message in a topic via a subscription mechanism, as shown below in figure 1.3.

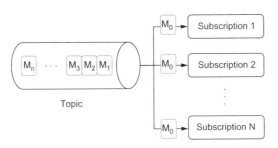

Figure 1.3   **With pub–sub message consumption, each message is delivered to each and every subscription that has been established on the topic. In this case, message M_0 was delivered to subscriptions through N inclusive.**

Publish–subscribe messaging systems are ideally suited for use cases that require multiple consumers to receive each message or those in which the order in which the messages are received and processed is crucial for maintaining a correct system state. Consider the case of a stock price service that can be used by a large number of systems. Not only is it important that these services receive all the messages, but it is also equally important that the price changes arrive in the correct order.

1.2.2 Message queuing

Queues, on the other hand, provide first in, first out (FIFO) message delivery semantics to one or more competing consumers, as shown in figure 1.4. With queues, the messages are delivered in the order they are received, and only one message consumer receives and processes an individual message, rather than all of them. These are perfect for queuing up messages that represent events that trigger some work to be performed, such as orders into a fulfillment center for dispatch. In this scenario, you want each order processed just once.

Message queues can easily support higher rates of consumption by scaling up the number of consumers in the event of a high number of backlogged messages. To ensure that a message is processed exactly once, each message must be removed from the queue after it has been successfully processed and acknowledged by the consumer. Due to its exactly-once processing guarantees, message queuing is ideal for work queue use cases.

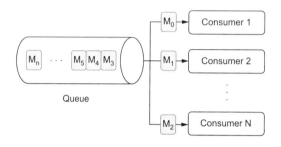

Figure 1.4   With queue-based message consumption, each message is delivered to exactly one consumer. In this case, message M_0 was consumed by consumer 1, M_1 by consumer 2, etc.

In the event of consumer failures (meaning no acknowledgment is received within a specified timeframe), the message will be resent to another consumer. In such a scenario, the message will most likely be processed out of order. Therefore, message queues are well suited for use cases where it is critical that each message is processed exactly once, but the order in which the messages are processed is not important.

1.3   *The evolution of messaging systems*

Now that we have clearly defined what constitutes an EMS along with the core capabilities it provides, I would like to provide a brief historical review of messaging systems and how they have evolved over the years. Messaging systems have been around for decades and have been effectively used within many organizations, so Apache Pulsar isn't some brand-new technology that emerged on the scene but rather another step in the evolution of the messaging system. By providing some historical context, my hope is that you will be able to understand how Pulsar compares to existing messaging systems.

1.3.1   *Generic messaging systems*

Before I jump into specific messaging systems, I wanted to present a simplified representation of a messaging system in order to highlight the underlying components that all messaging systems have. Identifying these core features will provide a basis for comparison between messaging systems over time.

As you can see in figure 1.5, every messaging system consists of two primary layers, each with its own specific responsibilities that we will explore next. We will examine the evolution of messaging systems across each of these layers in order to properly categorize and compare different messaging systems, including Apache Pulsar.

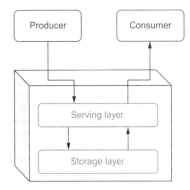

SERVING LAYER

The serving layer is a conceptual layer within an EMS that interacts directly with the message producers and consumers. Its primary purpose is to accept incoming messages and route them to one or more destinations. Therefore, it communicates via one or more of the supported messaging proto-

Figure 1.5 Every messaging system can be separated into two distinct architectural layers.

cols, such as DDS, AMQP, or MSMQ. Consequently, this layer is heavily dependent on network bandwidth for communication and CPU for message protocol translation.

STORAGE LAYER

The storage layer is the conceptual layer within an EMS that is responsible for the persistence and retrieval of the messages. It interacts directly with the serving layer to provide the requested messages and is responsible for retaining the proper order of the messages. Consequently, this layer is heavily dependent on the disk for message storage.

1.3.2 *Message-oriented middleware*

The first category of messaging systems is often referred to as message-oriented middleware (MOM), which was designed to provide inter-process communication and application integration between distributed systems running on different networks and operating systems. One of the most prominent MOM implementations was IBM WebSphere MQ, which debuted in 1993.

The earliest implementations were designed to be deployed on a single machine that was often located deep within the company's datacenter. Not only was this a single point of failure, it also meant that the scalability of the system was limited to the physical hardware capacity of the host machine because this single server was responsible for handling all client requests and storing all messages, as shown in figure 1.6. The number of concurrent producers and consumers these single-server MOM systems could serve was limited by the bandwidth of the network card, and the storage capacity was limited by the physical disk on the machine.

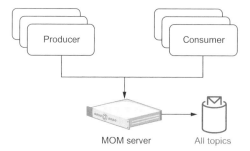

Figure 1.6   Message-oriented middleware was designed to be hosted on a single server and therefore hosted all of the message topics and handled requests from all clients.

To be fair, these limitations were not limited to just IBM, but are rather a limitation of all messaging systems that were designed to be hosted on a single machine, including RabbitMQ and RocketMQ, among many others. In fact, this limitation wasn't limited to just messaging systems of this era, but rather was pervasive across all types of enterprise software that were designed to run on one physical host.

CLUSTERING

Eventually these scalability issues were addressed though the addition of clustering capabilities to these single-server MOM systems. This allowed multiple single-service instances to share the processing of the messages and provide some load balancing, as shown in figure 1.7. Even though the MOM was clustered, in reality it just meant that each single-service instance was responsible for serving and storing messages for a subset of all the topics. A similar approach, called *sharding*, was taken by relational databases during this period to address this scalability issue.

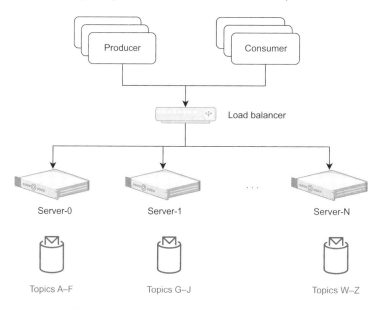

Figure 1.7   Clustering allowed the load to be spread across multiple servers instead of just one. Each server in the cluster was responsible for handling only a portion of the topics.

In the event of topic "hot-spots," the unlucky server assigned that particular topic could still become a bottleneck or potentially run out of storage capacity as well. In the event that any one of these servers in the cluster were to fail, it would take all of the topics it was serving down with it. While this did minimize the impact of the failure on the cluster as a whole (i.e., it continued to run) it was a single point of failure for the particular topics/queues it was serving.

This limitation required organizations to meticulously monitor their message distribution in order to align their topic distribution to match their underlying physical hardware and ensure that the load was evenly distributed across the cluster. Even then, there was still the possibility that a single topic could be problematic. Consider the scenario where you work for a major financial institution, and you want a single topic to store all the trade information for a particular stock and provide this information to all the trade desk applications within your organization. The sheer number of consumers and volume of data for this one topic could easily overwhelm a single server that was dedicated to serving just that topic. What was needed in such a scenario was the ability to distribute the load of a single topic across multiple machines, which, as we shall see, is exactly what distributed messaging systems do.

1.3.3　*Enterprise service bus*

Enterprise service buses (ESB) emerged during the early part of this century when XML was the preferred message format used for implementing service-oriented architecture (SOA) applications using SOAP-based web services. The core concept of ESBs was the *message bus*, as shown in figure 1.8, which served as a communication channel between all applications and services. This centralized architecture is in direct contrast to the point-to-point integration previously used by other message-oriented middleware.

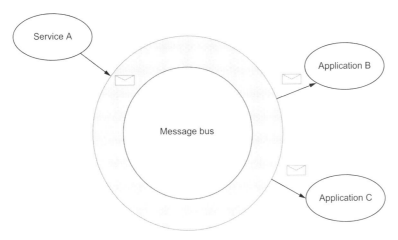

Figure 1.8　The core concept of ESBs is the use of a message bus in order to eliminate the need for point-to-point communication. Service A merely publishes its message to the bus, and it is automatically routed to applications B and C.

With an ESB, each application or service would send and receive all its messages over a single communication channel, rather than having to specify the specific topic names they wanted to publish and consume from. Each application would register itself with the ESB and specify a set of rules used to identify which messages it was interested in, and the ESB would handle all of the logic necessary to dynamically route messages from the bus that matched those rules. Similarly, each service was no longer required to know the intended target(s) of its messages beforehand and could simply publish its messages to the bus and allow it to route the messages.

Consider the scenario where you have a large XML document that contains hundreds of individual line items within a single customer order, and you want to route only a subset of those items to a service based upon some criteria within the message itself (e.g., by product category or department). An ESB provided the capability to extract those individual messages (based on the results of an XQuery) and route them to different consumers based on the content of the message itself.

In addition to these dynamic routing capabilities, ESBs also took the first evolutionary step down the road of *stream processing* by emphasizing the capabilities to process the messages inside the messaging system itself, rather than having the consuming applications perform this task. Most ESBs provided message transformation services, often via XSLT or XQuery, which handled the translation of message formats between the sending and receiving services. They also provided message enrichment and processing capabilities into the message system itself, which up until that point had been performed by the applications receiving the messages. This was a fundamentally new way of thinking about messaging systems that had previously been used almost exclusively as a transportation mechanism.

One could argue that the ESB was the first category of EMS to introduce a third layer to the basic architecture of messaging systems, as shown in figure 1.9. In fact, today most modern ESBs support more advanced computing capabilities, including process choreography for managing business process flows, complex event processing for event correlation and pattern matching, and out-of-the-box implementations of several enterprise integration patterns.

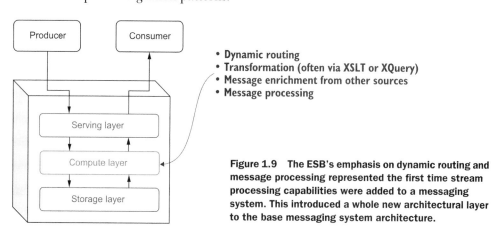

Figure 1.9   The ESB's emphasis on dynamic routing and message processing represented the first time stream processing capabilities were added to a messaging system. This introduced a whole new architectural layer to the base messaging system architecture.

The ESB's other significant contribution to the evolution of the messaging system was its focus on integration with external systems, which forced messaging systems to support a wide variety of non-messaging protocols for the first time. While ESBs still fully support AMQP and other pub–sub messaging protocols, a key differentiator of ESB was its ability to move data onto and off of the bus from non-message-oriented systems, such as email, databases, and other third-party systems. In order to do this, ESBs provided software development kits (SDKs) that allowed developers to implement their own adapters to integrate with their system of choice.

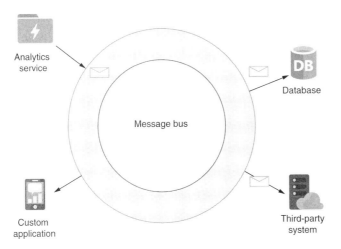

Figure 1.10 ESBs supported the integration of non-message-based systems into the message bus, thereby expanding the messaging capabilities beyond applications and into third-party applications, such as databases.

As you can see in figure 1.10, this allowed data to be more readily exchanged between systems, which simplified the integration of a variety of systems. In this role, the ESB served as both the message-passing infrastructure as well as the mediator between the systems that provided the protocol transformation.

While ESBs undoubtedly pushed the EMS forward with these innovations and features and are still very popular today, they are centralized systems that are designed to be deployed on a single host. Consequently, they suffer from the same scalability issues as their MOM predecessors.

1.3.4 *Distributed messaging systems*

A distributed system can be described as a collection of computers working together to provide a service or feature, such as a filesystem, key-value store, or database, that acts as though they are running on a single computer to the end user. That is to say, the end user isn't aware of the fact that the service is being provided by a collection of machines working together. Distributed systems have a shared state, operate concurrently, and are able to tolerate hardware failures without affecting the availability of the system as a whole.

When the distributed computing paradigm started becoming widely adopted, as popularized by the Hadoop computing framework, the single-machine constraint was lifted. This ushered in an era where new systems were developed that distributed the processing and storage across multiple machines. One of the biggest benefits of distributed computing is the ability to scale the system horizontally, simply by adding new machines to the system. Unlike their non-distributed predecessors that were constrained to the physical hardware capacity of a single machine, these newly developed systems could now leverage the resources from hundreds of machines easily and cost effectively.

As you can see in figure 1.11, messaging systems, just like databases and computation frameworks, have also made the transition to the distributed computing paradigm as well. Newer messaging systems, with Apache Kafka being the first and, more recently, Apache Pulsar, have adopted the distributed computing model in order to provide the scalability and performance required by modern enterprises.

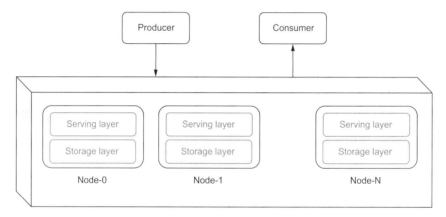

Figure 1.11 **Within a distributed messaging system, several nodes act together to behave as a single logic system from the perspective of the end user. Internally, the data storage and message processing are distributed across all the nodes.**

Within a distributed messaging system, the contents of a single topic are distributed across multiple machines in order to provide horizontally scalable storage at the message layer, which is something that was not possible with previous messaging systems. Distributing the data across several nodes in the cluster also provides several advantages, including redundancy and high availability of the data, increased storage capacity for messages, increased message throughput due to the increased number of message brokers, and the elimination of a single point of failure within the system.

The key architectural difference between a distributed messaging system and a clustered single-node system is the way in which the storage layer is designed. In the previous single-node systems, the message data for any given topic was all stored together on the same machine, which allowed the data to be served quickly from a local disk. However, as we mentioned earlier, this limited the size of the topic to the capacity of the local disk on that machine. Within a distributed messaging system, the data is distributed across several machines within the cluster. This distribution of data across multiple machines allowed us to retain messages within an individual topic that exceeded the storage capacity of an individual machine. The key architectural abstraction that makes this distribution of data possible is the *write-ahead log*, which treats the contents of a message queue as a single append-only data structure that messages can be stored in.

As you can see in figure 1.12, from a logical perspective, when a new message is published to the topic, it is appended to the end of the log. However, from a physical perspective, the message can be written to any server within the cluster.

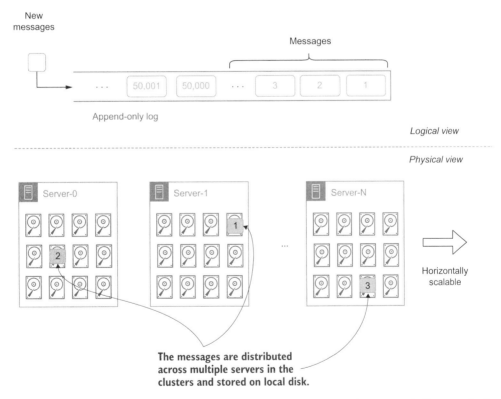

Figure 1.12 The key architectural concept underlying distributed messaging systems is the append-only log (aka the write-ahead log). From a logical perspective, the messages within a topic are all stored sequentially, but are stored in a distributed fashion across multiple servers.

This provides distributed messaging systems with a far more scalable storage capacity layer than the previous generations of messaging systems. Another benefit of the distributed messaging architecture is the ability of more than one broker to serve the messages for any given topic, which increases the message production and consumption throughput by spreading the load across multiple machines. For example, messages published to the topic shown in figure 1.12 would be handled by three separate servers, each with its own write path to disk. This would result in a higher write rate, since the load is spread across multiple disks rather than just a single disk, as it was in the previous generation of messaging systems. There are two distinct approaches taken when it comes to how the data is distributed across the nodes in the cluster: partition-based and segment-based.

PARTITION-CENTRIC STORAGE IN KAFKA

When using the partition-based strategy within a messaging system, the topic is divided into a fixed number of groupings known as partitions. Data that is published to the topic is distributed across the partitions, as shown in figure 1.13, with each partition receiving a portion of the messages published to the topic. The total storage capacity of the topic is now equal to the number of partitions in the topic times the size of each partition. Once this limit is reached, no more data can be added to the topic. Simply adding more brokers to the cluster will not alleviate this issue because you will also need to increase the number of partitions in the topic, which must be performed manually. Furthermore, increasing the number of partitions also requires a rebalance to be performed, which, as I will discuss, is an expensive and time-consuming process.

Within a partition-centric storage-based system, the number of partitions is specified when the topic is created, as this allows the system to determine which nodes will be responsible for storing which partition, etc. However, predetermining the number of partitions has a few unintended side effects, including the following:

- A single partition can only be stored on a single node within the cluster, so the size of the partition is limited to the amount of free disk space on that node.
- Since the data is evenly distributed across all partitions, each partition is limited to the size of the smallest partition in the topic. For instance, if a topic is distributed across three nodes with 4 TB, 2 TB, and 1 TB of free disk, respectively, then the partition on the third node can only grow to 1 TB in size, which in turn means all partitions in the topic can only grow to 1 TB as well.
- Although it isn't strictly required, each partition is usually replicated multiple times to different nodes to ensure data redundancy. Therefore, the maximum partition size is further restricted to the size of the smallest replica.

In the event that you run into one of these capacity limitations, your only remedy is to increase the number of partitions in the topic. However, this capacity expansion process requires rebalancing the entire topic, as shown in figure 1.14. During this rebalancing process, the existing topic data is redistributed across all of the topic partitions in order to free up disk space on the existing nodes. Therefore, when you add a

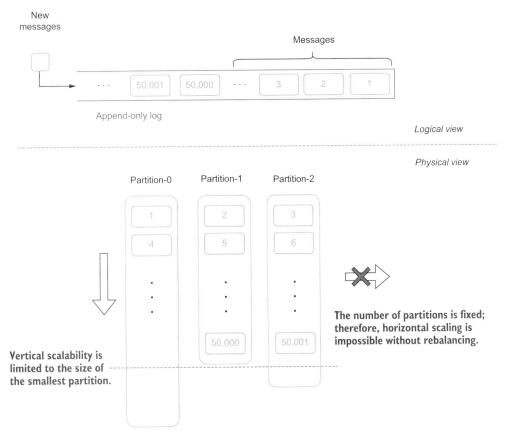

Figure 1.13 Message storage in a partition-based messaging system

fourth partition to an existing topic, each partition should have approximately 25% of the total messages once the rebalancing process has completed.

This recopying of data is expensive and error prone, as it consumes network bandwidth and disk I/O directly proportional to the size of the topic (e.g., rebalancing a 10 TB topic would result in 10 TB of data being read from disk, transmitted over the network, and written to disk on the target brokers). Only after the rebalancing process has completed can the previously existing data be deleted and the topic resume serving clients. Therefore, it is advisable to choose your partition sizing wisely, as the cost to rebalance cannot be easily dismissed.

In order to provide redundancy and failover for the data, you can configure the partitions to be replicated across multiple nodes. This ensures that there is more than one copy of the data available on disk even in the event of a node failure. The default replica setting is three, which means that the system will retain three copies of each message. While this is a good trade-off in terms of space for redundancy, you need to account for this additional storage requirement when you size your Kafka cluster.

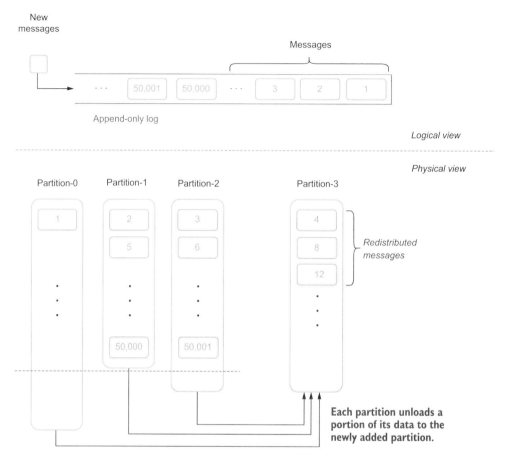

Figure 1.14   Increasing the storage capacity of a partition-based topic incurs the cost of rebalancing, in which a portion of the data from the existing partitions is copied over to the newly added partition(s) in order to free up disk space on the existing nodes.

SEGMENT-CENTRIC STORAGE IN PULSAR

Pulsar relies upon the Apache BookKeeper projects to provide the persistent storage of its messages. BookKeeper's logical storage model is based on the concept of boundless stream entries stored as a sequential log. As you can see in figure 1.15, within Book-Keeper each log is broken down into smaller chunks of data, known as segments, which in turn are comprised of multiple log entries. These segments are then written across a number of nodes, known as bookies, in the storage layer for redundancy and scale.

As you can see from figure 1.15, the segments can be placed anywhere on the storage layer that has sufficient disk capacity. When there isn't sufficient storage capacity in the storage layer for new segments, new nodes can be easily added and used immediately for storing data. One of the key benefits of segment-centric storage architecture is true horizontal scalability as segments can be created indefinitely and stored

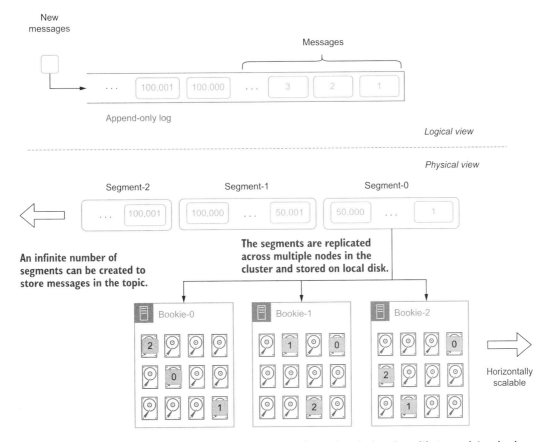

Figure 1.15 Message storage in a segment-centric messaging system is done by writing a predetermined number of messages into a "segment" and then storing multiple replicas of the segment across different nodes in the storage layer.

anywhere, unlike partition-centric storage which imposes artificial limitations to both vertical and horizontal scaling based on the number of partitions.

1.4 Comparison to Apache Kafka

Apache Kafka and Apache Pulsar are both distributed messaging systems that have similar messaging concepts. Clients interact with both systems via topics that are logically treated as unbounded, append-only streams of data. However, there are some fundamental differences between Apache Pulsar and Apache Kafka when it comes to scalability, message consumption, data durability, and message retention.

1.4.1 Multilayered architecture

Apache Pulsar's multilayered architecture completely decouples the message-serving layer from the message-storage layer, allowing each to scale independently. Traditional distributed messaging technologies, such as Kafka, have taken the approach of co-locating data processing and data storage on the same cluster nodes or instances. That design choice offers a simpler infrastructure and some performance benefits due to reducing the transfer of data over the network, but at the cost of a lot of tradeoffs that impact scalability, resiliency, and operations.

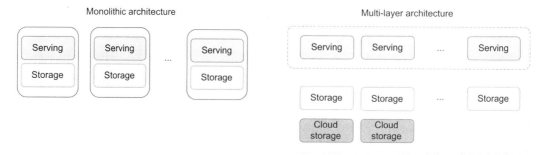

Figure 1.16   Monolithic distributed architectures co-locate the serving and storage layers, while Pulsar uses a multilayer architecture that decouples the storage and serving layers from one another, which allows them to scale independently.

Pulsar's architecture takes a very different approach—one that's starting to gain traction in a number of cloud-native solutions and that is made possible in part by the significant improvements in network bandwidth that are commonplace today: namely the separation of compute and storage. Pulsar's architecture decouples data serving and data storage into separate layers: data serving is handled by stateless *broker nodes*, while data storage is handled by *bookie nodes*, as shown in figure 1.16. This decoupling has several benefits, including dynamic scalability, zero downtime upgrades, and infinite storage capacity upgrades, just to name a few. Further, this design is container-friendly, making Pulsar the ideal technology for hosting a cloud-native streaming system.

DYNAMIC SCALING

Consider the case where we have a service that is CPU-intensive and whose performance starts to degrade when the requests exceed a certain threshold. In such a scenario, we need to horizontally scale the infrastructure to provide new machines and instances of the application to distribute the load when the CPU usage goes above 90% on the current machine. Rather than relying on a monitoring tool to alert your DevOps team to this condition and having them perform this process manually, it would be preferable to have the entire process automated.

Autoscaling is a common feature of all public cloud providers, such as AWS, Microsoft Azure, Google Cloud, and Kubernetes. It allows autoscaling of the infrastructure horizontally based on resource utilization metrics, such as CPU/memory, without any human interaction. While it is true that this capability is not exclusive to Pulsar and can be leveraged by any other messaging platforms to scale up during high traffic conditions, it is much more useful in a multitiered architecture such as Pulsar's for two reasons we will discuss.

Pulsar's stateless brokers in the serving layer also enable the ability to scale the infrastructure down once the spike has passed, which translates directly into cost savings in a public cloud environment. Other messaging systems that use a monolithic architecture cannot scale down the nodes due to the fact that the nodes contain data on their attached hard drives. Removal of the excess nodes can only be done once that data has been completely processed or has been moved to another node that will remain in the cluster. Neither of these can be performed in an automated fashion easily.

Secondly, in a monolithic architecture, such as Apache Kafka, the broker can only serve requests for data that is stored on an attached disk. This limits the usefulness of autoscaling the cluster in response to traffic spikes, because the newly added nodes to the Kafka cluster will not have any data to serve and, therefore, will not be able to handle any incoming requests to read existing data from the topics. The newly added nodes will only be able to handle write requests.

Lastly, in a monolithic architecture such as Apache Kafka, horizontal scaling is achieved by adding new nodes that have both storage and serving capacity, regardless of which metric you are tracking and responding to. Therefore, when you scale up your serving capacity in response to high CPU usage, you are also scaling up your storage capacity whether you actually need additional storage or not and vice-versa

AUTO-RECOVERY

Before you move your messaging platform into production, you will need to understand how to recover from various failure scenarios, starting with a single node failure. In a multitiered architecture such as Pulsar, the process is very straightforward. Since the broker nodes are stateless, they can be replaced by spinning up a new instance of the service to replace the one that failed without a disruption of service or any other data replacement considerations. At the storage layer, multiple replicas of the data are distributed across multiple nodes, which can be easily replaced with new nodes in the event of a failure. In either scenario, Pulsar can rely on cloud-provider mechanisms, such as autoscaling groups, to ensure that a minimum number of nodes are always running. Monolithic architectures, such as Kafka, will suffer again from the fact that newly added nodes to the Kafka cluster will not have any data to serve and, therefore, will only be able to handle incoming write requests.

1.4.2 *Message consumption*

Reading messages from a distributed messaging system is a bit different from reading them from a legacy messaging system, as distributed messaging systems were designed to support a large number of concurrent consumers. The way in which the data is consumed is driven in large part by the way it is stored inside the system itself, with both partition-centric and segment-centric systems having their own unique way of supporting pub–sub semantics for consumers.

MESSAGE CONSUMPTION IN KAFKA

Within Kafka, all consumers belong to what is referred to as a *consumer group*, which forms a single *logical subscriber* for a topic. Each group is composed of many consumer instances for scalability and fault tolerance, so if one instance fails, the remaining consumers will take over. By default, a new consumer group is created whenever an application subscribes to a Kafka topic. An application can leverage an existing consumer group by providing the group.id as well.

According to the Kafka documentation, "The way consumption is implemented in Kafka is by dividing up the partitions in the log over the consumer instances so that each instance is the exclusive consumer of a 'fair share' of partitions at any point in time" (https://docs.confluent.io/5.5.5/kafka/introduction.html). In layman's terms, this means that each partition within a topic can only have one consumer at a time, and the partitions are distributed evenly across the consumers within the group. As shown in figure 1.17, if a consumer group has less members than partitions, then some consumers will be assigned to multiple partitions, but if you have more consumers than partitions, the excess consumers will remain idle and only take over in the event of a consumer failure.

One important side effect of creating exclusive consumers is that within a consumer group, the number of active consumers can never exceed the number of partitions in the topic. This limitation can be problematic, as the only way of scaling data consumption from a Kafka topic is by adding more consumers to a consumer group. This effectively limits the amount of parallelism to the number of partitions, which in turn limits the ability to scale up data consumption in the event that your consumers cannot keep up the topic producers. Unfortunately, the only remedy to this is to increase the number of topic partitions, which as we discussed earlier, is not a simple, fast, or cheap operation.

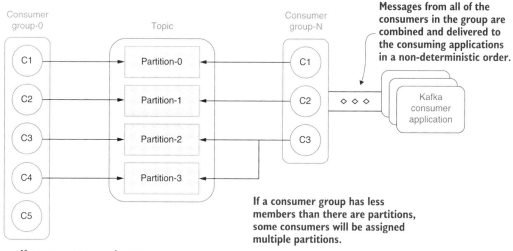

Figure 1.17   Kafka's consumer groups are closely tied to the partition concept. This limits the number of concurrent topic consumers to the number of topic partitions.

You can also see in figure 1.17 that all of the individual consumers' messages are combined and sent back to the Kafka client. Therefore, message ordering is not maintained by the consumer group. Kafka only provides a total order over records within a partition, not between different partitions in a topic.

As I mentioned earlier, consumer groups act as a cluster to provide scalability and fault tolerance. This means they dynamically adapt to the addition or loss of consumers within the group. When a new consumer is added to the group, it starts consuming messages from partitions previously consumed by another consumer. The same thing happens when a consumer shuts down or crashes; it leaves the group, and the partitions it used to consume will be consumed by one of the remaining consumers. This shuffling of partition ownership with a consumer group is referred to as *rebalancing*, and can have some undesirable consequences, including the potential for data loss if consumer offsets aren't saved before the rebalancing occurs.

It is very common to have multiple applications that need to read data from the same topic. In fact, this is one of the primary features of a messaging system. Consequently, topics are shared resources among multiple consuming applications that may have very different consumption needs. Consider a financial services company that streams in real time stock market quote information into a topic named "stock quotes" and wants to share that information across the entire enterprise. Some of their business-critical applications, such as their internal trading platforms, algorithmic trading systems, and customer-facing websites, will all need to process that topic data as quickly as it arrives. This would require a high number of partitions in order to provide the necessary throughput to meet these tight SLAs.

On the other hand, the data science team may want to feed the stock topic data through some of their machine learning models in order to train or validate their models using real stock pricing data. This would require processing the records in exactly the order they were received, which requires a single partition topic to ensure global message ordering.

The business analytics team will develop reports using KSQL that join the stock topic data with other topic(s) based on a particular key, such as the stock ticker, which would benefit from having the topic partitioned by the ticker symbol.

Efficiently providing the stock topic data for these applications with such vastly different consumption patterns would be difficult, if not impossible, given how to dependent the consumer groups are tied to the partition number, which is a fixed decision that cannot be easily changed. Typically, in such a scenario, your only realistic option is to maintain multiple copies of the data in different topics, each configured with the correct number of partitions for the application.

1.4.3   *Data durability*

Within the context of messaging systems, the term *data durability* refers to the guarantees that messages that have been acknowledged by the system will survive even in the event of a system failure. In a distributed system with many nodes, such as Pulsar or

Kafka, failures can occur at many levels; therefore, it is important to understand how the data is stored and what durability guarantees the system provides.

When a producer publishes a message, an acknowledgment is returned from the messaging system to indicate that the message on the topic was received. This acknowledgment signals to the producer that the message is safe, and that the producer can discard it without worrying about it getting lost. As we shall see, the strength of these guarantees is much greater in Pulsar than Kafka.

DATA DURABILITY IN KAFKA

As we discussed earlier, Apache Kafka takes a partition-centric storage approach to message storage. In order to ensure data durability, multiple replicas of each partition are maintained within a cluster to provide a configurable level of data redundancy.

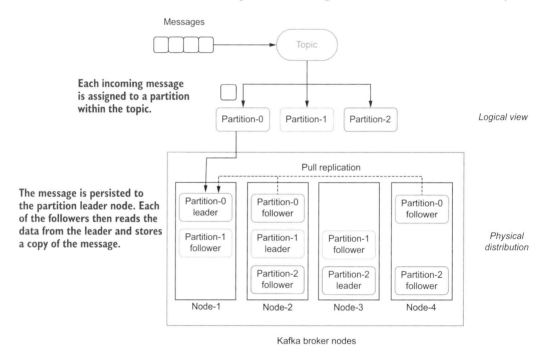

Figure 1.18   Kafka's partition replication mechanism

When Kafka receives an incoming message, a hashing function is applied to the message to determine which of the topic's partitions the message should be written to. Once that has been determined, the message contents are written to the page cache (not the disk) of the partition *leader replica*. Once the message has been acknowledged by the leader, each of the *follower replicas* are responsible for retrieving the message contents from the partition leader in a pull manner (i.e., they act as consumers and read the messages from the leader), as shown in figure 1.18. This overall approach is what is referred to as an *eventually consistent strategy* in which there is one node in a distributed system that has the most recent view of the data, which is eventually communicated to other nodes until they all achieve a consistent view of the data. While this approach has the advantage of decreasing the amount of time required to store an incoming message, it also introduces two opportunities for data loss; first, in the event of a power outage or other process termination event on the leader node, any data that was written to the page cache that had not been persisted to local disk will be lost. The second opportunity for data loss is when the current leader process fails and another one of the remaining followers is selected as the new leader. In the leader failover scenario, any messages that were acknowledged by the previous leader but not yet replicated to the newly elected leader replica will be lost as well.

By default, messages are acknowledged once the leader has written it to memory. However, this behavior can be overridden to withhold the acknowledgment until all of the replicas have received a copy of the message. This does not impact the underlying replication mechanism in which the followers must pull the information across the network and send a response back to the leader. Obviously, this behavior will incur a performance penalty, which is often hidden in most published Kafka performance benchmarks, so you are advised to do your own performance testing with this configuration in order to get a better understanding of what the expected performance will be.

The other side effect of this replication strategy is that only the leader replica can serve both producers and consumers, as it is the only one guaranteed to have the most recent and correct copy of the data. All of the follower replicas are passive nodes that cannot alleviate any of the load from the leader during traffic spikes.

DATA DURABILITY IN PULSAR

When Pulsar receives an incoming message, it saves a copy in memory and also writes the data to a write-ahead log (WAL), which is forced onto disk *before* an acknowledgment is sent back to the message publisher, as shown in figure 1.19. This approach is modelled after traditional database atomicity, consistency, isolation, and durability (ACID) transaction semantics, which ensures that the data is not lost even if the machine fails and comes back online in the future.

The number of replicas required for a topic can be configured in Pulsar based on your data replication needs, and Pulsar guarantees that the data that has been received and acknowledged by a quorum of servers before an acknowledgment is sent to the producer. This design ensures that data can only be lost in the highly unlikely event of simultaneous fatal errors occurring on all bookie nodes to which the data was written. This is why is it recommended to distribute the bookie nodes across multiple regions and use rack-aware placement policies to ensure a copy of the data is stored in more than one region or data center.

More importantly, this design eliminates the need for a secondary replication process that is responsible for ensuring that the data is kept in sync between replicas and eliminates any data inconsistency issues due to any lag in the replication process.

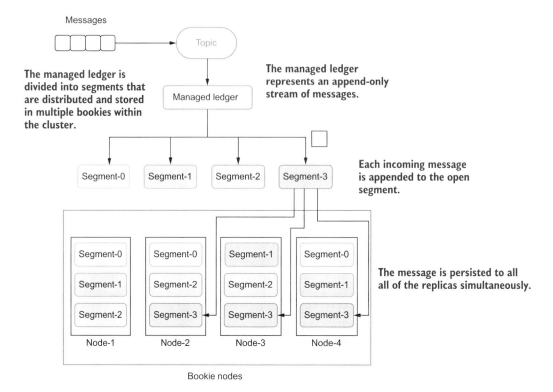

Figure 1.19   Pulsar's replication occurs when the message is initially written to the topic.

1.4.4   *Message acknowledgment*

Within a distributed messaging system, failures are to be expected. In a distributed message system such as Pulsar, both the consumers consuming the messages and the message brokers serving the messages can fail. When such a failure occurs, it is imperative to resume consumption from exactly the point where the consumers left off once everything recovers to ensure that messages aren't skipped or reprocessed. This point from which the consumer should resume consumption is often called the topic *offset*. Kafka and Pulsar take different approaches with respect to maintaining these offsets, which have a direct impact on data durability.

MESSAGE ACKNOWLEDGMENT IN KAFKA

The resume point is referred to as the consumer offset in Apache Kafka, which is controlled entirely by the consumer. Typically, a consumer increments its offset in a sequential manner as it reads records from the topic to indicate message acknowledgment. However, keeping this offset solely in the consumer's memory is dangerous. Therefore, these offsets are also stored as messages in a separate topic named __consumer_offsets. Each consumer commits a message containing its current position into that topic at periodic intervals, which is every five seconds if you use Kafka's auto-commit capability. While this strategy is better than keeping the offsets solely in memory, there are consequences to this periodic update approach.

Consider a single-consumer scenario where automatic commits occur every five seconds and a consumer dies exactly three seconds after the most recent commit to the offset topic. In this case, the offset read from the topic will be three seconds old, so all the events that arrived in that three-second window will be processed twice. While it is possible to configure the commit interval to a smaller value and reduce the window in which records will be duplicated, it is impossible to completely eliminate them.

The Kafka consumer API provides a method that enables committing the current offset at a point that makes sense to the application developer rather than based on a timer. Therefore, if you really wanted to eliminate duplicate messaging processing, you could use this API to commit the offset after every successfully consumed message. However, this pushes the burden of ensuring accurate recovery offsets onto the application developer and introduces additional latency to the message consumers who now have to commit each offset to a Kafka topic and await an acknowledgment.

MESSAGE ACKNOWLEDGMENT IN PULSAR

Apache Pulsar maintains a ledger inside of Apache BookKeeper for each subscriber that is referred to as the cursor ledger for tracking message acknowledgments. When a consumer has read and processed a message, it sends an acknowledgment to the Pulsar broker. Upon receipt of this acknowledgment, the broker immediately updates the cursor ledger for that consumer's subscription. Since this information is stored on a ledger in BookKeeper, we know that it has been fsynced to disk and multiple copies exist across multiple bookie nodes. Keeping this information on disk ensures that the consumers will not receive the message again even if they crash and restart at a later point in time.

In Apache Pulsar, there are two ways that messages can be acknowledged: selectively or cumulatively. With cumulative acknowledgment, the consumer only needs to acknowledge the last message it receives. All the messages in the topic partition up to and including the given message ID will be marked as acknowledged and will not be redelivered to the consumer again. Cumulative acknowledgment is effectively the same as offset update in Apache Kafka.

The differentiating feature of Apache Pulsar over Kafka is the ability of consumers to acknowledge messages individually (i.e., selective acknowledgment). This capability is critical in supporting multiple consumers per topic because it allows for message redelivery in the event of a single consumer failure.

Let's consider the single-consumer failure scenario again where the consumer individually acknowledges messages after it has successfully processed them. During the time leading up to the failure, the consumer was struggling to process some of the messages while successfully processing others. Figure 1.20 shows an example where only two of the messages (4 and 7) were successfully processed and acknowledged.

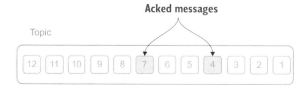

Figure 1.20   Individual message acknowledgment in Pulsar

Given the fact that Kafka's offset concept treats consumer groups' offsets as a high-water mark that marks the point up to which all messages are considered acknowledged, in this scenario the offset would have been updated to seven, since that is the highest number message ID that was acknowledged. When the Kafka consumer is restarted on that topic it would start at message 8 and continue onward, skipping messages 1–3, 5, and 6, making them effectively lost because they are never processed.

Under the same scenario with Pulsar's selective acks, all of the unacknowledged messages would be redelivered, including messages 1–3, 5, and 6, when the consumer is restarted, thereby avoiding message loss due to consumer offset limitations.

1.4.5   *Message retention*

In contrast to legacy messaging systems, such as ActiveMQ, messages are not immediately removed from distributed messaging systems after they have been acknowledged by all consumers. These legacy systems took such an approach as a way to immediately reclaim as much of the local disk capacity as possible, since it was a constrained resource. While distributed messaging systems such as Kafka and Pulsar have alleviated this constraint to some degree by horizontally scalable message storage, both of these systems still provide a mechanism for reclaiming disk space. It is important to understand exactly how automated message deletion is handled by both systems, as it can lead to accidental data loss if not properly configured.

MESSAGE RETENTION IN KAFKA

Kafka retains all messages published to a topic for a configurable retention period. For instance, if the retention policy is set to seven days, then for the seven days immediately after a message has been published to the topic, it is available for consumption. Once the retention period has elapsed, the message will be discarded to free up space. This deletion occurs regardless of whether or not the message has been consumed and acknowledged. Obviously, this presents the opportunity for data loss in the event that the retention period is less than the time it takes for all consumers to consume the message, such as a long-term outage of the consuming system. The other drawback to this time-based approach is that there is a high probability that you will be retaining messages much longer than necessary (i.e., after they have been consumed by all relevant consumers), which is an inefficient use of your storage capacity.

MESSAGE RETENTION IN PULSAR

In Pulsar, when a consumer has successfully processed a message, it needs to send an acknowledgment to the broker so that the broker can discard the message. By default,

Pulsar immediately deletes all messages that have been acknowledged by all the topic's consumers and retains all unacknowledged messages in a message backlog. In Pulsar, messages can only be deleted after all the subscriptions have already consumed it. Pulsar also allows you to keep messages for a longer time even after all subscriptions have already consumed them by configuring a message retention period, which I will discuss in more depth in chapter 2.

1.5 Why do I need Pulsar?

If you are just getting started with messaging or streaming data applications, you should definitely consider Apache Pulsar as a core component of your messaging infrastructure. However, it is worth noting that there are several technology options that you can choose from, many of which have become entrenched in the software community. In this section, I will attempt to bring to light some of the scenarios in which Apache Pulsar shines above the rest, as well as clear up some common misconceptions about existing systems and point out some of the challenges users of these systems face.

Within adoption cycles there are often several misconceptions about the entrenched technology that are perpetuated throughout the user community for a multitude of reasons. It is often an uphill battle to convince yourself and others that you need to replace a technology that sits at the very core of your architecture. It was not until we had the benefit of hindsight that we saw that our traditional database systems were fundamentally incapable of scaling to meet the demands imposed by our ever-increasing data and that we needed to rethink the way we stored and processed data with a framework such as Hadoop. Only after we had transitioned our business analytics platforms from traditional data warehouses to Hadoop-based SQL engines, such as Hive, Tez, and Impala, did we realize that those tools had inadequate response times for the end users who were used to subsecond response times. This gave rise to the rapid adoption of Apache Spark as the technology of choice for big data processing.

I wanted to highlight these two recent technologies to remind us that we cannot let our affinity for the status quo blind us to issues lurking within our core architectural systems and put forth the notion that we need to rethink our approach to messaging systems, as the incumbent technologies in this space, such as RabbitMQ and Kafka, suffer from key architectural flaws. The team that developed Apache Pulsar at Yahoo! could have easily chosen to adopt one of the existing solutions, but after careful consideration they decided not to do so because they needed a messaging platform that provided capabilities that weren't available in the existing monolithic technologies that we will discuss in the following sections.

1.5.1 Guaranteed message delivery

Because of the data durability mechanism within the platform that we have already covered, Pulsar provides guaranteed message delivery for applications. If a message successfully reaches a Pulsar broker, it will be delivered to all of the topic consumers.

To provide such a guarantee requires that non-acknowledged messages are stored in a durable manner until they can be delivered to and acknowledged by consumers. This mode of messaging is commonly called persistent messaging. In Pulsar, a configurable number of copies of all messages is stored and synced on disk.

By default, Pulsar message brokers ensure that incoming messages are persisted to disk on the storage layer before acknowledging receipt of the message. These messages are kept in Pulsar's infinitely scalable storage layer until they are acknowledged, thereby ensuring message delivery.

1.5.2 *Infinite scalability*

In order to better understand the scalability of Pulsar, let's look at a typical Pulsar installation. As you can see from figure 1.21, a Pulsar cluster is composed of two layers: a stateless serving layer, which is made up of a set of brokers for handling client requests, and a stateful persistence layer, which is made up of a set of bookies for persisting the messages.

This architectural pattern, which separates the storage of the messages from the layer that serves the messages, differs significantly from traditional messaging systems which have historically chosen to co-locate these two services. This decoupled approached has several advantages when it comes to scalability. For starters, making the brokers stateless allows you to dynamically increase or decrease the number of brokers to meet the demands of the client applications.

SEAMLESS CLUSTER EXPANSION

Any bookies that are added to the storage layer are automatically discovered by the brokers, which will then immediately begin to utilize them for message storage. This is unlike Kafka, which requires repartitioning the topics to distribute the incoming messages to the newly added brokers.

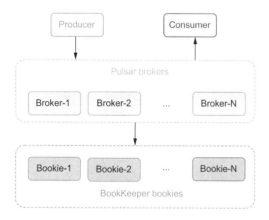

Figure 1.21   A typical Pulsar cluster

UNBOUNDED TOPIC PARTITION STORAGE

Unlike Kafka, the capacity of a topic partition is not limited by the capacity of any smallest node. Instead, topic partitions can scale up to the total capacity of the storage layer, which itself can be scaled up by simply adding additional bookies. As we discussed earlier, partitions within Kafka have several limitations on their size, whereas no such restrictions apply to Pulsar.

INSTANT SCALING WITHOUT DATA REBALANCING

Because message serving and storage are separated into two layers, moving a topic partition from one broker to another can happen almost instantly and without any data rebalancing (recopying the data from one node to the other). This characteristic is crucial to many things, such as cluster expansion and fast failure reaction to broker and bookie failures.

1.5.3 *Resilient to failure*

Pulsar's decoupled architecture also provided enhance resiliency by ensuring that there is no single point of failure within the system. By isolating the serving and storage layers, Pulsar is able to limit the impact of a failure within the system while making the recovery process seamless.

SEAMLESS BROKER FAILURE RECOVERY

Brokers form the stateless serving layer in Apache Pulsar. The serving layer is stateless because brokers don't actually store any message data locally. This makes Pulsar resilient to broker failures. When Pulsar detects that a broker is down, it can immediately transfer the incoming producers and consumers to a different broker. Since the data is kept in a separate layer, there is no need to recopy data as you would in Kafka. Because Pulsar doesn't have to recopy the data, the recovery happens instantly without sacrificing the availability of any of the data on the topic.

Kafka, in contrast, directs all client requests to the leader replica, so it will always have the latest data. The leader is also responsible for propagating the incoming data to the other followers in the replica set, so the data will eventually be available on those nodes in the event of a failure. However, due to the inherent lag between the leader and the replica, data can be lost before it is copied over.

SEAMLESS BOOKIE FAILURE RECOVERY

The stateful persistence layer utilized by Pulsar consists of Apache BookKeeper bookies to provide segment-centric storage, as we mentioned previously. When a message is published to Pulsar, the data is persisted to disk on all N replicas before it is acknowledged. This design ensures that the data will be available on multiple nodes and, thus, will survive N-1 node failures before the data is lost.

Pulsar's storage layer is also self-healing, and if there is a node or disk failure that causes a particular segment to be under-replicated, Apache BookKeeper will automatically detect this and schedule a replica repair to run in the background. The replica repair in Apache BookKeeper is a many-to-many fast repair at the segment level, which is a much finer granularity than recopying the whole topic partition, which is required in Kafka.

1.5.4   *Support for millions of topics*

Consider a scenario in which you want to model your application around some entity, such as a customer, and for each one of these you want to have a different topic. Different events would be published for that entity; the customer is created, places an order, makes a payment, returns some items, changes their address, etc.

By placing these events in a single topic, you are guaranteed to process them in the correct chronological order and can quickly scan the topic to determine the correct state of the customer's account, etc. However, as your business grows you will need support for millions of topics, and traditional messaging systems cannot support this requirement. There is a high cost associated with having many topics, including increased end-to-end latency, file descriptors, memory overhead, and recovery time after a failure.

In Kafka, as a rule of thumb you should keep your total number of topic partitions in the hundreds if you care about latency performance. There are several guides for how to restructure your Kafka-based applications in order to avoid hitting this limitation. If you don't want a platform limitation affecting your application design with respect to how you structure your topics, then you should consider Pulsar.

Pulsar has the ability to support up to 2.8 million topics while continuing to provide consistent performance. The key to scaling the number of topics lies in how the underlying data is organized in the storage layer. If the topic data is stored in dedicated files or directories, as it is in traditional messaging systems such as Kafka, then the ability to scale will be limited because the I/O will be scattered across the disk as the number of topics increases, which leads to disk thrashing and results in very low throughput. In order to prevent this behavior, messages from different topics are aggregated, sorted, and stored in large files and then indexed in Apache Pulsar. This approach limits the proliferation of small files that leads to performance problems as the number of topics increases.

1.5.5   *Geo-replication and active failover*

Apache Pulsar is a messaging system that supports both synchronous geo-replication within a single Pulsar cluster and asynchronous geo-replication across multiple clusters. It has been deployed globally in more than 10 data centers at Yahoo! since 2015 with full 10 x 10 mesh replication for mission critical services, such as Yahoo! Mail and Finance.

Geo-replication is a common practice used to provide disaster recovery capabilities for enterprise systems by distributing a copy of the data to different geographical locations. This ensures that your data, and the systems that rely upon it, will be able to withstand any unforeseen disasters, such as natural disasters. The geo-replication mechanisms used in different data systems can be classified as either synchronous or asynchronous. Apache Pulsar allows you to easily enable asynchronous geo-replication using just a few configuration settings.

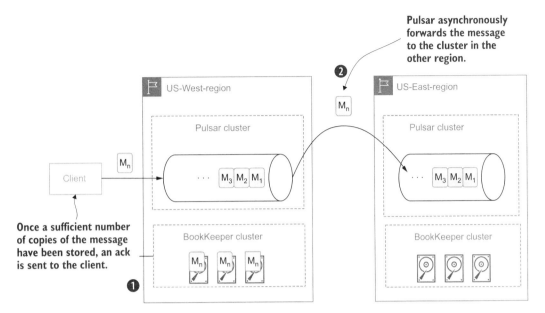

Figure 1.22 When using asynchronous geo-replication in Apache Pulsar, the message is stored locally within the BookKeeper cluster running in the same region that receives the message. The message is asynchronously forwarded in the background to the Pulsar cluster in the other region.

With asynchronous geo-replication, the producer doesn't wait for an acknowledgment from the other data centers that they have received the message. Instead, the producing client receives an acknowledgment immediately after the message has been successfully persisted within the local BookKeeper cluster. The data is then replicated from the source cluster to the other data centers in an asynchronous fashion, as shown in figure 1.22.

Asynchronous geo-replication provides lower latency because the client doesn't have to wait for responses from the other data centers. However, it also results in weaker consistency guarantees due to asynchronous replication. Since there is always a replication lag in asynchronous replication, there is always some amount of data that hasn't been replicated from source to destination.

Synchronous geo-replication is a bit more complicated to achieve with Apache Pulsar than asynchronous, as it requires some manual configuration to properly ensure that a message will only be acknowledged when a majority of the data centers have issued a confirmation that the message data has been persisted to disk. While I will save the details of exactly how synchronous geo-replication can be achieved with Apache Pulsar for appendix B, I can tell you that it is made possible due to Pulsar's two-tiered architecture design and the ability for an Apache BookKeeper cluster to be composed of both local and remote nodes, particularly ones in different geographical regions, as shown in figure 1.23.

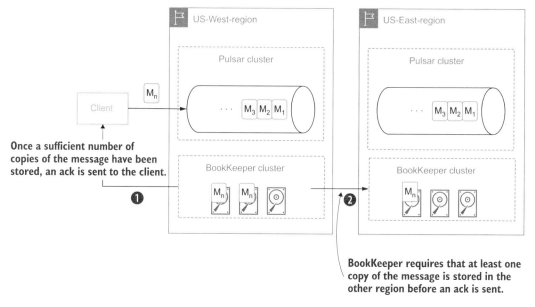

Figure 1.23   You can exploit BookKeeper's ability to use remote nodes in order to achieve synchronous geo-replication to ensure that a copy of the message is stored in the remote region.

Synchronous geo-replication provides the highest availability, where all of your physically available data centers form a global logical instance for your data system. Your applications can run everywhere at any data center and still be able to access the data. It also guarantees stronger data consistency between different data centers, which your applications can easily rely on without any manual operations involved when data center failures occur.

Unlike other messaging systems that rely on external services, Pulsar offers geo-replication as a built-in feature. Users can easily enable replication of message data between Pulsar clusters in different geographical regions. Once replication is configured, data is continuously replicated to the remote clusters without any interaction on the part of the producers or consumers. I cover to how configure geo-replication in greater detail in appendix B.

1.6   Real-world use cases

If you are a product manager whose product includes a requirement for operating on massive amounts of data to deliver a meaningful new experience or dataset to your users in real time, then Apache Pulsar is the key to unlocking the real-time potential of your data. The beauty of Pulsar is that there are several specific scenarios in which it can excel. Before we dive further into the technical details, it might be informative to discuss at a high level some of the use cases in which Pulsar has already been proven.

1.6.1 Unified messaging systems

You are probably familiar with the mnemonic "keep it simple, stupid," which is often used to remind architects that there is great value in simple designs and solutions. A system that comprises fewer technologies is easier to deploy, maintain, and monitor. As mentioned earlier, there are two common messaging patterns, and until now, if you wanted to support both messaging styles within your infrastructure, you were required to deploy and maintain two completely different systems.

As a bilingual job board, Zhaopin.com has one of the largest selections of job vacancies in China, including both prominent local and foreign companies. The company has over 2.2 million clients and average daily page views of over 68 million. As the company grew, the challenges of maintaining two separate messaging systems, RabbitMQ for queuing and Apache Kafka for pub–sub, became increasingly difficult. By replacing them both with a single unified messaging platform based on Apache Pulsar, they were able to reduce their operational overhead, infrastructure footprint, and ongoing support costs by half, while meeting their requirements of high durability, high throughput, and low latency.

1.6.2 Microservices platforms

Narvar provides a supply chain management and customer care platform for e-commerce customers around the world, including order tracking and notifications and seamless returns and customer care. Narvar's platform helps retailers and brands by processing data and events to ensure timely and accurate communication with their customers to 400 million consumers worldwide.

Prior to Apache Pulsar, Narvar's platform had been built using a variety of messaging and processing technologies over time—from Kafka to Amazon SQS, Kinesis Streams to Kinesis Firehose, and RabbitMQ to AWS Lambda. As its traffic grew, it became apparent that the growing amount of DevOps and developer support required to maintain and scale these systems was unsustainable. Many of them were not containerized, making infrastructure configuration and management burdensome and requiring frequent manual intervention.

Systems like Kafka—while reliable, popular, and open source—had significant maintenance overhead as they scaled. Increasing throughput required increasing partitions, tuning consumers, and a large amount of manual intervention by developers and DevOps. Similarly, cloud-native solutions like Kinesis Streams and Kinesis Firehose were not cloud-agnostic, making it hard to decouple the choice of cloud solutions from functionality and making it difficult to leverage technologies in other clouds and to support customers who needed to run on other public clouds.

Narvar decided to transition its microservice-based platform over to Apache Pulsar because like Kafka, Pulsar was reliable, cloud-agnostic and open source. Unlike Kafka, Pulsar entailed very little maintenance overhead and scaled with minimal manual intervention. Pulsar was containerized and built on Kubernetes from the outset, making it much more scalable and maintainable. Most importantly for Narvar was

Pulsar Functions, which allowed Narvar to develop microservices that consumed and processed the incoming events directly on the messaging system itself, eliminating the need for expensive Lambda functions or standing up additional services.

In a microservices architecture, each microservice is designed as an atomic and self-sufficient piece of software. These independent software components run as multiple processes distributed across multiple servers. A microservices-based application requires the interaction of multiple services via some sort of inter-process communication. The two most commonly used communication protocols are HTTP request/response and lightweight messaging. Pulsar was a perfect candidate for providing the lightweight messaging system that supports asynchronous messaging required by Narvar.

1.6.3   *Connected cars*

A major North American auto manufacturer has built a connected car service based on Apache Pulsar that collect data from computing devices within its 12 million connected vehicles. Billions of pieces of data are collected daily and used to provide real-time visibility and remote diagnostics across the world. This data is then used to provide better insights into how vehicles are performing and to identify potential problems before they occur, so the manufacturer can provide customers with proactive alerts.

1.6.4   *Fraud detection*

As China's largest mobile payment platform, Orange Financial must analyze 50 million transactions per day for financial fraud on behalf of it 500 million registered users. Orange Financial faces threats from financial fraud every day, including identity theft, money laundering, affiliate fraud, and merchant fraud. The company runs thousands of fraud detection models against each transaction to combat these threats in its risk management system.

The company was seeking a solution that would unify the data store, computing engine, and programing language for decision development in its risk control system. From an end-user perspective, the fraud detection scanning could not impact the latency of the applications; therefore, they needed a platform that allowed them to process the data as quickly as possible. Apache Pulsar allowed the transactional data to be accessed directly in the messaging layer and processed in parallel using Pulsar Functions, thereby reducing the processing latency introduced from having to move the data to a secondary system for processing.

While some of the fraud detection processing has been offloaded to the Pulsar functions framework, Orange Financial was still able to leverage its more complex fraud detection algorithms that were developed in Spark, using Pulsar's built-in connector for the Spark computing engine. This allows the company to choose the best processing framework for its models on a case-by-case basis.

Additional resources

Pulsar has a vibrant and growing community and graduated from the Apache Incubator in August of 2018. Current documentation for the project can be found on the official project website at http://pulsar.apache.org.

Other resources for information on Apache Pulsar include blogs (such as http://mng.bz/PXE9 and https://streamnative.io/blog) and tutorials (such as http://mng.bz/J600). Lastly, I would be remiss if I didn't mention the Apache Pulsar slack channel, apache-pulsar.slack.com, which I and several of the project committers monitor on a daily basis. The heavily used channel contains a wealth of information for beginners and a concentrated community of developers who are actively using Apache Pulsar on a daily basis.

Summary

- Apache Pulsar is a modern messaging system that provides both high-performance streaming and traditional queuing messaging.
- Apache Pulsar provides a lightweight computing engine, Pulsar Functions, which allows developers to implement simple processing logic that is executed against each message and published to a given topic.
- The benefits of Pulsar's decoupled storage and serving layers include infinite scalability and zero data loss.
- Specific use cases where Pulsar has been used in production include IoT analytics, inter-microservice communication, and unified messaging.

Pulsar concepts and architecture

This chapter covers

- Pulsar's physical architecture
- Pulsar's logical architecture
- Message consumption and the subscription types provided by Pulsar
- Pulsar's message retention, expiration, and backlog policies

Now that you have been introduced to the Pulsar messaging platform and how it compares to other messaging systems, we will drill down into the low-level architectural details and cover some of the unique terminology used by the platform. If you are unfamiliar with messaging systems and distributed systems, then it might be difficult to wrap your head around some of Pulsar's concepts and terminology. I will start with an overview of Pulsar's physical architecture before diving into how Pulsar logically structures messages.

2.1   *Pulsar's physical architecture*

Other messaging systems consider the cluster the highest level from an administrative and deployment perspective, which necessitates managing and configuring each cluster as an independent system. Fortunately, Pulsar provides an even higher level of abstraction known as a *Pulsar instance*, which is comprised of one or more Pulsar clusters that act together as a single unit and can be administered from a single location, as shown in figure 2.1.

One of the biggest reasons for using a Pulsar instance is to enable geo-replication. In fact, only clusters within the same instance can be configured to replicate data amongst themselves.

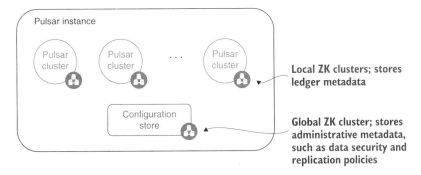

Figure 2.1   A Pulsar instance can consist of multiple geographically dispersed clusters.

A Pulsar instance employs an instance-wide ZooKeeper cluster called the *configuration store* to retain information that pertains to multiple clusters, such as geo-replication and tenant-level security policies. This allows you to define and manage these policies in a single location. In order to provide resiliency to the configuration store, each of the nodes within the Pulsar instance's ZooKeeper ensemble should be deployed across multiple regions to ensure its availability in the event of a region failure.

It is important to note that the availability of the ZooKeeper ensemble used by the Pulsar instance for the configuration store is required by the individual Pulsar clusters to operate even when geo-replication is enabled. When geo-replication is enabled, if the configuration store is down, messages published to the respective clusters will be buffered locally and forwarded to the other regions when the ensemble becomes operational again.

2.1.1   *Pulsar's layered architecture*

As you can see in figure 2.2, each Pulsar cluster is made up of a stateless serving layer of multiple Pulsar message *broker instances*, a stateful storage layer of multiple Book-Keeper *bookie instances*, and an optional routing layer of multiple Pulsar proxies. When hosted inside a Kubernetes environment, this decoupled architecture enables your DevOps team to dynamically scale the number of brokers, bookies, and proxies to meet peak demand and to scale down to save cost during slower periods. Message traffic is spread across all the available brokers as evenly as possible to provide maximum throughput.

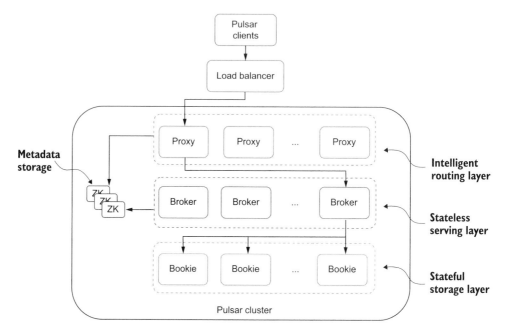

Figure 2.2   A Pulsar cluster consists of multiple layers: an optional proxy layer that routes incoming client requests to the appropriate message broker, a stateless serving layer consisting of multiple brokers that serve client requests, and a stateful storage layer consisting of multiple bookies that retains multiple copies of the messages.

When a client accesses a topic that has not yet been used, a process is triggered to select the broker best suited to acquire ownership of the topic. Once a broker assumes ownership of a topic, it is responsible for handling all requests for that topic, and any clients wishing to publish to or consume data from the topic need to interact with the corresponding broker that owns it. Therefore, if you want to publish data to a particular topic, you will need to know which broker owns that topic and connect to it. However, the broker assignment information is only available in the ZooKeeper metadata and is subject to change based on load rebalancing, broker crashes, etc. Consequently, you cannot connect directly to the brokers themselves and hope that you are communicating with the one you want. This is exactly why the Pulsar proxy was created—to act as an intermediary for all the brokers in the cluster.

THE PULSAR PROXY

If you are hosting your Pulsar cluster inside of a private and/or virtual network environment, such as Kubernetes, and you want to provide inbound connections to your Pulsar brokers, then you will need to translate their private IP addresses to public IP addresses. While this can be accomplished using traditional load balancing technologies and techniques such as physical load balancers, virtual IP addresses, or DNS-based load balancing that distributes client requests across a group of brokers, it is not the best approach for providing redundancy and failover capabilities for your clients.

The traditional load-balancer approach is not efficient, as the load-balancer will not know which broker is assigned to a given topic and instead will direct the request to a random broker in the cluster. If a broker receives a request for a topic it isn't serving, it will automatically reroute the request over to the appropriate broker for processing, but this incurs a nontrivial penalty in terms of time. This is why it is recommended to use the Pulsar proxy instead, which acts as an intelligent load balancer for Pulsar brokers.

When using the Pulsar proxy, all client connections will first travel through the proxy, rather than directly to the brokers themselves. The proxy will then use Pulsar's built-in service discovery mechanism to determine which broker is hosting the topic you are trying to reach and automatically route the client request to it. Furthermore, it will cache this information in memory for future requests to streamline the lookup process even more. For performance and failover purposes, it is recommended to run more than one Pulsar proxy behind a traditional load balancer. Unlike the brokers, Pulsar Proxies *can* handle any request, so they can be load balanced without any issue.

2.1.2 *Stateless serving layer*

Pulsar's multi-layered design ensures that message data is stored separately from the brokers, which guarantees that any broker can serve data from any topic at any time. This also allows the cluster to assign ownership of a topic to any broker in the cluster at any time, unlike other messaging systems that co-locate the broker and the topic data they are serving. Hence, we use the term "stateless" to describe the serving layer, since there is no information stored on the brokers themselves that is necessary to handle client requests.

The stateless nature of the brokers not only allows us to dynamically scale them up and down based on demand, but also makes them cluster-resilient to multiple broker failures. Lastly, Pulsar has an internal load-shedding mechanism that rebalances the load amongst all the active brokers based on the ever-changing message traffic.

BUNDLES

The assignment of a topic to a particular broker is done at what is referred to as the *bundle* level. All the topics in a Pulsar cluster are assigned to a specific bundle with each bundle assigned to a different broker, as shown in figure 2.3. This helps ensure that all topics in a namespace are evenly distributed across all the brokers.

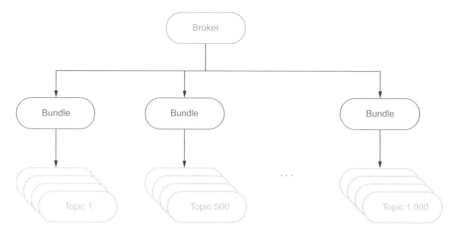

Figure 2.3 **From a serving perspective, each broker is assigned a set of bundles that contain multiple topics. Bundle assignment is determined by hashing the topic name, which allows us to determine which bundle it belongs to without having to keep that information in ZooKeeper.**

The number of bundles created is controlled by the `defaultNumberOfNamespace-Bundles` property inside the broker configuration file, which has a default value of 4. You can override this setting on a per-namespace level when you create the namespace by providing a different value when you create the namespace using the Pulsar admin API. In general, you want the number of bundles to be a multiple of the number of brokers to ensure that they are evenly distributed. For instance, if you have three brokers and four bundles, then one of the brokers will be assigned two of the bundles, while the others only get one each.

LOAD BALANCING
While the message traffic might initially be spread as evenly as possible across the active brokers, several factors can change over time, resulting in the load becoming unbalanced. Changes in the message traffic patterns might result in a broker serving several topics with heavy traffic, while others aren't being utilized at all. When an existing bundle exceeds some preconfigured thresholds defined by the following properties in the broker configuration file, the bundle will be split into two new bundles with one of them being offloaded to a new broker:

- `loadBalancerNamespaceBundleMaxTopics`
- `loadBalancerNamespaceBundleMaxSessions`
- `loadBalancerNamespaceBundleMaxMsgRate`
- `loadBalancerNamespaceBundleMaxBandwidthMbytes`

This mechanism identifies and corrects scenarios when some bundles are experiencing a heavier load than others by splitting these overloaded bundles in two. Then one of these bundles can be offloaded to a different broker in the cluster.

LOAD SHEDDING

The Pulsar brokers have another mechanism to detect when a particular broker is overloaded, and automatically have it shed or offload some of its bundles to other brokers in the cluster. When a broker's resource utilization exceeds the preconfigured threshold defined by the `loadBalancerBrokerOverloadedThresholdPercentage` property in the broker configuration file, the broker will offload one or more bundles to a new broker. This property defines the maximum percentage of the total available CPU, network capacity, or memory that the broker can consume. If any of these resources cross this threshold, then the offload is triggered.

The bundle selected is left intact and assigned to a different broker. This is because the load shedding process solves a different problem than the load balancing process does. With load balancing, we are correcting the distribution of the topics across the bundles because one of them has much more traffic than the others, and we are attempting to spread that load out across all the bundles.

Load shedding, on the other hand, corrects the distribution of the bundles across the brokers based on the number of resources required to service them. Even though each broker can be assigned the same number of bundles, the message traffic handled by each broker could be dramatically different if the load is unbalanced across the bundles.

To illustrate this point, consider the scenario where there are 3 brokers and a total of 60 bundles with each broker serving 20 bundles each. Furthermore, 20 of the bundles are currently handling 90% of the total message traffic. Now, if most of these bundles happen to be assigned to the same broker, it could easily exhaust that broker's CPU, network, and memory resources. Therefore, offloading some of these bundles to another broker will help alleviate the problem, whereas splitting the bundles themselves would only shed approximately half of the message traffic, while leaving 45% of it still on the original broker.

DATA ACCESS PATTERNS

There are generally three I/O patterns in a streaming system: *writes*, where new data is written to the system; *tailing reads*, where the consumer is reading the most recently published messages immediately after they have been published; and *catch-up reads*, where a consumer reads a large number of messages from the beginning of the topic in order to catch up, such as when a new consumer wants to access data beginning at a point much earlier than the latest message.

When a producer sends a message to Pulsar, it is immediately written to Book-Keeper. Once BookKeeper acknowledges that the data was committed, the broker stores a copy of the message in its local cache before it acknowledges the message publication to the producer. This allows the broker to serve tailing read consumers directly from memory and avoid the latency associated with disk access.

It becomes more interesting when looking at catch-up reads, which access data from the storage layer. When a client consumes a message from Pulsar, the message will go through the steps shown in figure 2.4. The most common example of a catch-up read

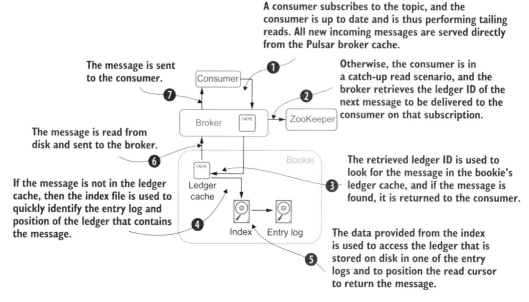

A consumer subscribes to the topic, and the consumer is up to date and is thus performing tailing reads. All new incoming messages are served directly from the Pulsar broker cache.

The message is sent to the consumer. ❼

❶

Otherwise, the consumer is in a catch-up read scenario, and the broker retrieves the ledger ID of the next message to be delivered to the consumer on that subscription. ❷

The message is read from disk and sent to the broker. ❻

If the message is not in the ledger cache, then the index file is used to quickly identify the entry log and position of the ledger that contains the message. ❹

The retrieved ledger ID is used to look for the message in the bookie's ledger cache, and if the message is found, it is returned to the consumer. ❸

The data provided from the index is used to access the ledger that is stored on disk in one of the entry logs and to position the read cursor to return the message. ❺

Figure 2.4   Message consumption steps in Pulsar

is when a consumer goes offline for an extended period and then starts consuming again, although any scenario in which a consumer is *not* directly served from the broker's in-memory cache would be considered a catch-up read, such as topic reassignment to a new broker.

2.1.3 *Stream storage layer*

Pulsar guarantees message delivery for all message consumers. If a message successfully reaches a Pulsar broker, you can rest assured it will be delivered to its intended target. In order to provide this guarantee, all non-acknowledged messages must be persisted until they can be delivered to and acknowledged by consumers. As I mentioned earlier, Pulsar uses a distributed write-ahead log (WAL) system called Apache BookKeeper for persistent message storage. BookKeeper is a service that provides persistent storage of streams of log entries in sequences called ledgers.

LOGICAL STORAGE ARCHITECTURE

Pulsar topics can be thought of as infinite streams of messages that are stored sequentially in the order the messages are received. Incoming messages are appended to the end of the stream, while consumers read messages further up the stream based on the data access patterns that I discussed earlier. While this simplified view makes it easy for us to reason about a consumer's position within the topic, such an abstraction cannot exist in reality due to the space limitations of storage devices. Eventually this abstract infinite stream concept must be implemented on a physical system where such a limitation exists.

Apache Pulsar takes a dramatically different approach from traditional messages systems, such as Kafka, when it comes to implementing stream storage. Within Kafka, each stream is separated into multiple replicas that are each stored entirely on a broker's local disk. The great thing about this approach is that it is simple and fast because all writes are sequential, which limits the amount of disk head movement required to access the data. The downside to Kafka's approach is that a single broker must have sufficient storage capacity to hold the partition data, as I discussed in chapter 1.

So how is Apache Pulsar's approach different? For starters, each topic is *not* modeled as a collection of partitions, but rather as a series of segments. Each of these segments can contain a configurable number of messages, with the default being 50,000. Once a segment is full, a new one is created to hold new messages. Therefore, a Pulsar topic can be thought of as an unbounded list of segments with each containing a subset of the messages, as shown in figure 2.5, which shows both the logical architecture of the stream storage layer and how it maps to the underlying physical implementation.

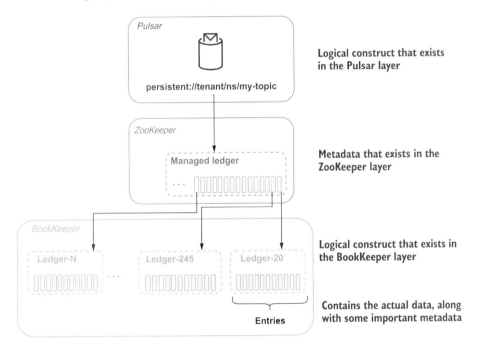

Figure 2.5   The data for a Pulsar topic is stored as a sequence of ledgers inside the BookKeeper layer. A list of these ledger IDs is stored inside a logical construct known as a managed ledger on ZooKeeper. Each ledger holds 50,000 entries that store a copy of the message data. Note that persistent://tenant/ns/my-topic will be discussed as a concept later in the book.

A Pulsar topic is nothing more than an addressable endpoint that is used to uniquely identify a specific topic within Pulsar and is analogous to a URL in the sense that it is merely used to uniquely identify the resource that the client is attempting to connect to. The topic name must be decoded by the Pulsar broker to determine the storage location of the data.

Pulsar adds an additional layer of abstraction on top of BookKeeper's ledgers, known as managed ledgers, that retains the IDs of the ledgers that hold the data published to the topic. As we can see in figure 2.5, when data was first published to topic A, it was written to ledger-20. After 50,000 records had been published to the topic, the ledger was closed and another one (ledger-245) was created to take its place. This process is repeated every 50,000 records to store the incoming data, and the managed ledger retains this unique sequence of ledger IDs inside of ZooKeeper.

Later, when a consumer attempts to read the data from topic A, the managed ledger is used to locate the data inside of BookKeeper and return it to the consumer. If the consumer is performing a catch-up read starting at the oldest message, then it would first get all the data from ledger-20, followed by ledger-245, and so on. The traversal of these ledgers from oldest to youngest is transparent to the end user and creates the illusion of a single sequential stream of data. Managed ledgers allow this to happen and retain the ordering of the BookKeeper ledgers to ensure the messages are read in the same order they were published.

BookKeeper physical architecture

In BookKeeper, each unit of a ledger is referred to as an entry. These entries contain the actual raw bytes from the incoming messages, along with some important metadata that is used to track and access the entries. The most critical piece of metadata is the ID of the ledger to which it belongs, which is kept in the local ZooKeeper instance, so the message can be retrieved quickly from BookKeeper when a consumer attempts to read it in the future. Streams of log entries are stored in append-only data structures, known as ledgers, as shown in figure 2.6.

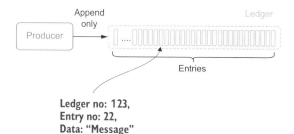

Figure 2.6   In BookKeeper, incoming entries get stored together as ledgers on servers known as bookies.

Ledgers have append-only semantics, meaning that entries are written to a ledger sequentially and cannot be modified once they've been written to a ledger. From a practical perspective, this means

- A Pulsar broker first creates a ledger, then appends entries to the ledger, and finally closes the ledger. There are no other interactions permitted.
- After the ledger has been closed, either normally or because the process crashed, it can then be opened only in read-only mode.
- Finally, when entries in the ledger are no longer needed, the whole ledger can be deleted from the system.

The individual BookKeeper servers that are responsible for the storage of ledgers (more specifically, fragments of ledgers) are known as bookies. Whenever entries are written to a ledger, those entries are written across a subgroup of bookie nodes known as an ensemble. The size of the ensemble is equal to the replication factor (R) you specify for your Pulsar topic and ensures that you have exactly R copies of the entry saved to disk to prevent data loss.

Bookies manage data in a log-structured way, which is implemented using three types of files: journals, entry logs, and index files. The journal file retains all of the BookKeeper transaction logs. Before any update to a ledger takes place, the bookie ensures that a transaction describing the update is written to disk to prevent data loss.

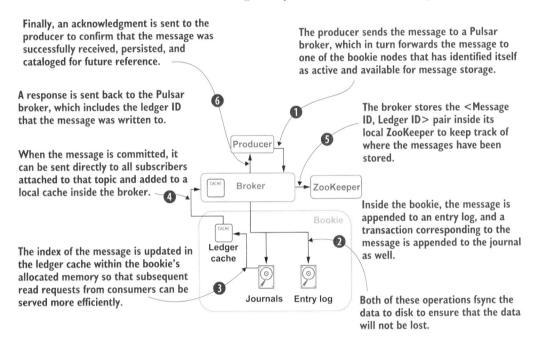

Finally, an acknowledgment is sent to the producer to confirm that the message was successfully received, persisted, and cataloged for future reference.

A response is sent back to the Pulsar broker, which includes the ledger ID that the message was written to.

When the message is committed, it can be sent directly to all subscribers attached to that topic and added to a local cache inside the broker.

The index of the message is updated in the ledger cache within the bookie's allocated memory so that subsequent read requests from consumers can be served more efficiently.

The producer sends the message to a Pulsar broker, which in turn forwards the message to one of the bookie nodes that has identified itself as active and available for message storage.

The broker stores the <Message ID, Ledger ID> pair inside its local ZooKeeper to keep track of where the messages have been stored.

Inside the bookie, the message is appended to an entry log, and a transaction corresponding to the message is appended to the journal as well.

Both of these operations fsync the data to disk to ensure that the data will not be lost.

Figure 2.7   Message persistence steps in Pulsar

The entry log file contains the actual data written to BookKeeper. Entries from different ledgers are aggregated and written sequentially, while their offsets are kept as pointers in a ledger cache for fast lookup. An index file is created for each ledger, which contains several indexes that record the offsets of data stored in entry log files. The index file is modelled after index files in traditional relational databases and allows for quick lookups for ledger consumers. When a client publishes a message to Pulsar the message will go through the steps shown in figure 2.7 to persist it to disk within a BookKeeper ledger.

By distributing the entry data across multiple files on different disk devices, bookies are able to isolate the effects of read operations from the latency of ongoing write operations, allowing them to handle thousands of concurrent reads and writes.

2.1.4   *Metadata storage*

Lastly, each cluster also has its own local ZooKeeper ensemble that Pulsar uses to store cluster-specific configuration information for tenants, namespaces, and topics, including security and data retention policies. This is in addition to the managed ledger information we discussed earlier.

ZOOKEEPER BASICS

According to the official Apache website, "ZooKeeper is a centralized service for maintaining configuration information, naming, providing distributed synchronization, and providing group services" (https://zookeeper.apache.org), which is an elaborate way of saying it is a distributed data source. ZooKeeper provides a decentralized location for storing information, which is crucial within distributed systems, such as Pulsar or BookKeeper.

Apache ZooKeeper solves the fundamental problem of achieving consensus (i.e., agreement) that virtually every distributed system must solve. Processes in a distributed system need to agree on several different pieces of information, such as the current configuration values and the owner of a topic. This is a problem particularly for distributed systems due the fact that there are multiple copies of the same component running concurrently with no real way to coordinate information between them. Traditional databases are not an option because they introduce a serialization point within the framework where all the calling services would be blocked waiting for the same lock on a table, which essentially eliminates all the benefits of distributed computing.

Having access to a consensus implementation enables distributed systems to coordinate processes in a more effective manner by providing a compare-and-swap (CAS) operation to implement distributed locks. The CAS operation compares the value retrieved from ZooKeeper with an expected value and, only if they are the same, updates the value. This guarantees that the system is acting based on up-to-date information. One such example would be checking that the state of a BookKeeper ledger is *open* before writing any data to it. If some other process has closed the ledger, it would be reflected in the ZooKeeper data, and the process would know not to proceed with the write operation. Conversely, if a process were to *close* a ledger, this information would be sent to ZooKeeper so that it could be propagated to the other services, so they would know it is *closed* before they attempted to write to it.

The ZooKeeper service itself exposes a file-system-like API so that clients can manipulate simple data files (znodes) to store information. Each of these znodes forms a hierarchical structure similar to a filesystem. In the following sections, I will examine the metadata that is retained within ZooKeeper along with how it is used and by whom so that you can see for yourself exactly why it is needed. The best way to do this is by using the `zookeeper-shell` tool that is distributed along with Pulsar, as shown in the following listing, to list all the znodes.

Listing 2.1 Using the ZooKeeper-shell tool to list the znodes

Starts the ZooKeeper shell

Lists the children znodes under the root level node

```
/pulsar/bin/pulsar zookeeper-shell
ls /
[admin, bookies, counters, ledgers, loadbalance,
   managed-ledgers, namespace, pulsar, schemas, stream, zookeeper]
```

The output of all the znodes used by Pulsar

As you can see in listing 2.1, there are a total of 11 different znodes created inside ZooKeeper for Apache Pulsar and BookKeeper. These fall into one of four categories based on what information they contain and how it is used.

CONFIGURATION DATA

The first category of information is configuration data for tenants, namespaces, schemas, etc. All this information is slow-changing information that is only updated through the Pulsar administration API when a user creates or updates a new cluster, tenant, namespace, or schema and includes such things as security policies, message retention policies, replication policies, and schemas. This information is stored in the following znodes: /admin and /schemas.

METADATA STORAGE

The managed ledger information for all of the topics is stored in the /managed-ledgers znode, while the /ledgers znode is used by BookKeeper to keep track of all the ledgers currently stored across all the bookies within the cluster.

Listing 2.2 Inspecting the managed ledger

The managed ledger tool allows you to look up the ledgers by topic name.

```
/pulsar/bin/pulsar-managed-ledger-admin print-managed-ledger -
   managedLedgerPath /public/default/persistent/topicA
   --zkServer localhost:2181

ledgerInfo { ledgerId: 20 entries: 50000 size: 3417764 timestamp: 1589590969679}
ledgerInfo { ledgerId: 245 timestamp: 0}
```

This topic has two ledgers: one with 50K entries that is closed and another open one.

As you can see in listing 2.2, there is another tool called pulsar-managed-ledger-admin that allows you to easily access the managed ledger information that is used by Pulsar to read and write the data to and from BookKeeper. In this case, the topic data is stored on two different ledgers: ledgerID-20, which is closed and contains 50,000 entries, and ledgerID-245, which is currently open and where the incoming data will be published.

DYNAMIC COORDINATION BETWEEN SERVICES

The remaining znodes are all used for distributed coordination across the systems, including /bookies, which maintains a list of the bookies registered with the Book-Keeper cluster, and /namespace, which is used by the proxy service to determine which broker owns a given topic. As we can see in the following listing, the /namespace znode hierarchy is used to store the bundle IDs for each namespace.

Listing 2.3   Metadata used to determine topic ownership

```
/pulsar/bin/pulsar zookeeper-shell    <──── Starts the ZooKeeper shell
ls /namespace
[customers, public, pulsar]   <──── There is one znode per tenant.
ls /namespace/customers
[orders]                  <──── There is one znode per namespace.
ls /namespace/customers/orders
[0x40000000_0x80000000]                                  <─┐
get /namespace/customers/orders/0x40000000_0x80000000      │ There is one znode
{"nativeUrl":"pulsar://localhost:6650",                    │ per bundle_id.
    "httpUrl":"http://localhost:8080","disabled":false} <─┘
```

As you'll recall from our earlier discussion, the topic name is hashed by the proxy to determine the bundle name, which in this case is 0x40000000_0x80000000. The proxy then queries the /namespace/{tenant}/{namespace}/{bundle-id} znode to retrieve the URL for the broker that "owns" the topic.

Hopefully, this gives you some more insight into the role ZooKeeper plays inside a Pulsar cluster and how it provides a service that can be easily accessed by nodes that have been dynamically added to the cluster, so they can quickly determine the cluster configuration and start handling client requests. One such example would be the ability of newly added brokers to start serving data from a topic by referencing the data in the /managed-ledgers znode.

2.2   Pulsar's logical architecture

Like other messaging systems, Pulsar uses the concept of topics to denote message channels for transmitting data between producers and consumers. However, the way in which these topics are named is different in Pulsar than in other messaging systems. In the following sections, I will cover the underlying logical structure that Pulsar uses for storing and managing topics.

2.2.1   Tenants, namespaces, and topics

In this section we will cover the logical constructs that describe how data is structured and stored inside the cluster. Pulsar was designed to serve as a multi-tenant system, allowing it to be shared across multiple departments within your organization by providing each its own secure and exclusive messaging environment. This design enables a single Pulsar instance to effectively serve as the messaging platform-as-a-service across your entire enterprise. The logical architecture of Pulsar supports multitenancy via a hierarchy of tenants, namespaces, and, finally, topics, as shown in figure 2.8.

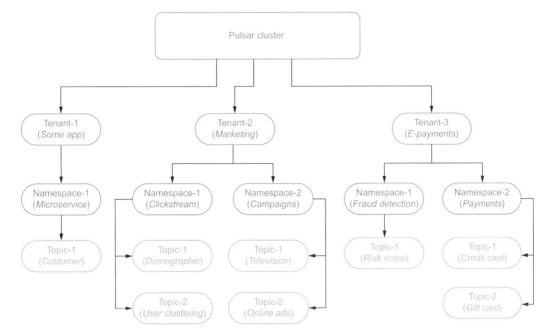

Figure 2.8   Pulsar's logical architecture consists of tenants, namespaces, and topics.

TENANTS

At the top of the Pulsar hierarchy sit the tenants, which can represent a specific business unit, a core feature, or a product line. Tenants can be spread across clusters and can each have their own authentication and authorization scheme applied to them, thereby controlling who has access to the data stored within. They are also the administrative unit at which storage quotas, message time to live, and isolation policies can be managed.

NAMESPACES

Each tenant can have multiple *namespaces*, which are logical grouping mechanisms for administering related topics via policies. At the namespace level, you can set access permissions, fine-tune replication settings, manage geo-replication of message data across clusters, and control message expiry for all the topics in the namespace.

Let's consider how we would structure Pulsar's namespace for an e-commerce application. To provide isolation for the sensitive incoming payment data and limit access to only members of the finance team, you may configure a separate tenant named E-payments, as shown in figure 2.8, and apply an access policy that restricts full access to only members of the finance group so they can perform audits and process credit card transactions.

Within the E-payments tenant you might create two namespaces: one named payments that will hold the incoming payments, including credit card payments and gift card redemptions, and another named fraud detection, which will contain those transactions that are flagged as suspicious for further processing. In such a deployment, you would limit the user-facing application to write-only access to the payments namespace, while granting read-only access to the fraud detection application, so it can evaluate them for potential fraud.

On the fraud detection namespace you would configure write access for the fraud detection application, so it can place potentially fraudulent payments into the "risk score" topic. You would also grant read-only access to the e-commerce application to the same namespace, so it can be notified of any potential fraud and react accordingly, such as by blocking the sale.

TOPICS

Topics are the only communication channel type available in Pulsar. All messages are written to and read from topics. Other messaging systems support more than one communication channel type (e.g., topics and queues that are differentiated by the type of message consumption they support). As I discussed in chapter 1, queues support first in, first out exclusive message consumption, while topics support pub–sub, one-to-many message consumption. Pulsar makes no such distinction and, instead, relies on various subscription types to control the message consumption pattern.

In Pulsar, non-partitioned topics are served by a single broker, which is responsible for receiving and delivering all the messages for the topic. Therefore, the throughput of a single topic is bound by the computing power of the broker serving it.

PARTITIONED TOPICS

Pulsar also supports the notion of partitioned topics that can be served by multiple brokers, which allows for much higher throughput as the load is distributed across multiple machines. Behind the scenes, a partitioned topic is implemented as N internal topics, where N is the number of partitions. The distribution of partitions across brokers is handled automatically by Pulsar, effectively making the process transparent to the end user.

Implementing partitioned topics as a series of individual topics allows a user to increase the number of partitions without having to rebalance the entire topic. Instead, internal topics are created for the new partitions and will be able to receive incoming messages immediately without impacting the other internal topics at all (e.g., consumers will still be able to read/write messages to the existing partitions without interruption).

From a consumer perspective, these is no difference between partitioned topics and normal topics. All consumer subscriptions work exactly as they do on non-partitioned topics. But there is a big difference in what happens when a message is published to a partitioned topic. The message producer is responsible for determining which internal topic the message is ultimately published to. If the message has a value in its key meta-data field, then the producer will hash that value to determine which topic to publish to. This ensures that all messages with the same key get stored in the same topic and will be in the order in which they were published.

When publishing a message without a key, the producer should be configured with a routing mode that specifies how to route messages across the partitions in the topic. The default routing mode is called RoundRobinPartition, which as the name implies, publishes messages across all partitions in round-robin fashion. This approach evenly distributes the messages across the partitions, which maximizes the publish through-put. Alternatively, you could use the SinglePartition routing mode, which ran-domly selects a single partition to publish all its messages into. This approach can be used to group messages from a specific producer together to maintain message order-ing when you don't have a key value. You can also provide your own routing imple-mentation as well if you need more control over message distribution across your partitioned topic.

Let's look at the message flow depicted in figure 2.9 in which the producer is con-figured to use the RoundRobinPartition publish mode. In this scenario, the producer connects to the Pulsar proxy and expects back the IP address of the broker assigned to the topic it is writing to. The proxy, in turn refers to the local metastore for this infor-mation and discovers that the topic is partitioned and needs to translate the specified partition number into the name of the internal topic that is serving that partition.

In figure 2.9, the producer's round-robin routing strategy determined that the message should be published to partition number 3, which is implemented as internal

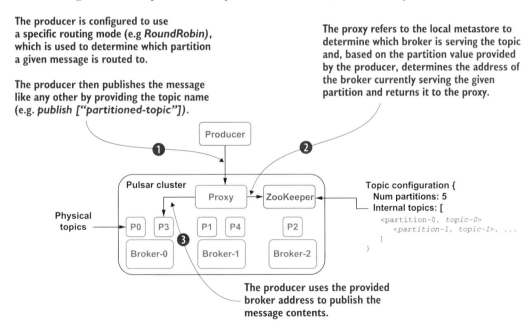

The producer is configured to use a specific routing mode (e.g *RoundRobin*), which is used to determine which partition a given message is routed to.

The producer then publishes the message like any other by providing the topic name (e.g. *publish ["partitioned-topic"]*).

The proxy refers to the local metastore to determine which broker is serving the topic and, based on the partition value provided by the producer, determines the address of the broker currently serving the given partition and returns it to the proxy.

The producer uses the provided broker address to publish the message contents.

Figure 2.9   Publishing to a partitioned topic

topic p3. The proxy can also determine that internal topic p3 is currently being served by broker-0. Therefore, the message is routed to that broker and written to the p3 topic. Since the routing mode is round robin, a subsequent call by the same producer will result in the message being routed to the p4 internal topic on broker-1.

2.2.2 Addressing topics in Pulsar

The hierarchical structure of Pulsar's logical layer is reflected in the naming convention of endpoints used to access topics within Pulsar. As you can see in figure 2.10, each topic addressed within Pulsar contains both the tenant and namespace to which it belongs. The address also contains a persistency prefix that indicates whether the message contents are persisted to long-term storage or they are only retained in the bookie's memory space. If a topic name is created with a prefix of `persistent://`, then all messages that have been received but not yet acknowledged will be stored on multiple bookie nodes, and thus, can survive broker failures.

Pulsar also supports non-persistent topics, which retain all unacknowledged messages in the broker memory. Non-persistent topic names begin with the `non-persistent://` prefix to indicate this behavior. When using non-persistent topics, brokers immediately deliver messages to all connected subscribers without persisting them.

(non-)persistent://tenant/namespace/topic-name

Figure 2.10   Topic addressing scheme in Pulsar

When using non-persistent delivery, any form of broker failure, or disconnecting a subscriber from a topic, results in all in-transit messages being lost on the (non-persistent) topic. This means that the topic subscribers will never be able to receive those messages even if they reconnect. While non-persistent messaging is usually faster than persistent messaging because it avoids the latency associated with persisting the data to disk, it is only advisable to use it if you are certain that your use case can tolerate the loss of messages.

2.2.3 Producers, consumers, and subscriptions

Pulsar is built on the publish–subscribe (pub–sub) pattern. In this pattern, producers publish messages to topics. Consumers can then subscribe to those topics, process incoming messages, and send an acknowledgment when processing is complete.

A producer is any process that connects to a Pulsar broker, either directly or via the Pulsar proxy, and publishes messages to a topic, while a consumer is any process that connects to a Pulsar broker to receive messages from a topic. When a consumer has successfully processed a message, it needs to send an acknowledgment to the broker so the broker knows that it has been received and processed. If no such acknowledgment is received within a preconfigured timeframe, the broker will redeliver it to consumers on that subscription.

When a consumer connects to a Pulsar topic, it establishes what is referred to as a *subscription*, which specifies how messages will be delivered to a group of one or more consumers. There are four available subscription modes in Pulsar: exclusive, failover, key-shared, and shared. Regardless of the subscription type, messages are delivered in the order they are received.

Information about these subscriptions is retained in the local Pulsar ZooKeeper metadata and includes the http addresses of all the consumers, among other things. Each subscription also has a cursor associated with it that represents the position of the last message which was consumed and acknowledged for the subscription. To prevent message redelivery, these subscription cursors are retained on the bookies to ensure they will survive any broker level failures.

Pulsar supports multiple subscriptions per topic, which allows multiple consumers to read data from a topic. As you can see in figure 2.11, the topic has two different subscriptions: Sub-A and Sub-B. Consumer-A connected to the topic first and is operating in exclusive consumer mode, which means that all the messages in the topic will be consumed by Consumer-A. Thus far, Consumer-A has only acknowledged the first four messages, so its cursor position for the subscription, Sub-A is currently set to 5.

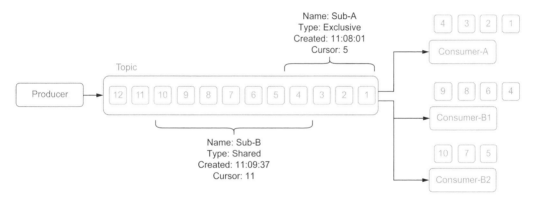

Figure 2.11 Pulsar supports multiple subscriptions per topic, which allows multiple consumers to read the same data. Consumer-A has consumed the first four messages on the exclusive subscription named Sub-A, whereas messages 4 through 10 have been distributed across the two consumers on the shared subscription named Sub-B.

The subscription named Sub-B was created after the first three messages were produced; therefore, none of those messages were delivered to the consumers for that subscription. It is a common misconception that any subscriptions created on a topic will start at the very first message for that topic, which is why I chose to illustrate that point here and show that you will only receive messages that are published to the topic *after* you subscribe to it.

We can also see that, since Sub-B is operating in shared mode, the messages have been distributed across *all* the consumers in the group with each message only being processed by a single consumer in the group. You can also see that Sub-B's cursor is farther ahead than Sub-A's cursor, which is not uncommon when you distribute the messages across multiple consumers.

2.2.4   *Subscription types*

In Pulsar, all consumers use subscriptions to consume data from a topic. Subscriptions are just configuration rules that define how messages are delivered to consumers of a given topic. Pulsar subscriptions can be shared across multiple applications, and in fact, most subscription types are designed specifically for that usage pattern. Pulsar supports four different types of subscriptions: exclusive, failover, shared, and key-shared, as shown in figure 2.12.

A Pulsar topic can support multiple subscriptions concurrently, allowing you to use a single topic to serve applications with vastly different consumption patterns. It is also important to point out that different subscriptions on the same topic don't have to be of the same subscription type. This allows you to use a single topic to serve both queuing and streaming use cases simultaneously.

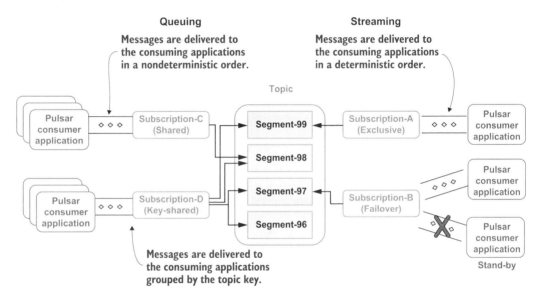

Figure 2.12   Pulsar's subscription modes

Each of Pulsar's subscription types serve a different type of use case, so it is important to understand them in order to use them properly. Let's revisit the scenario where a financial services company that streams stock market quote information in real time into a topic named `stock quotes` wants to share that information across the entire enterprise and see how each of these subscription modes would be used for the same use cases.

EXCLUSIVE

An exclusive subscription only permits a single consumer to the messages for that subscription. If any other consumer attempts to subscribe to a topic using the same subscription, an exception will be thrown, and it won't be able to connect. This mode is used when you want to ensure that each message is processed exactly once and by a known consumer.

Within our financial services organization, the data science team would use this type of subscription to feed the stock topic data through their machine learning models to train or validate them. This would allow them to process the records in exactly the order they were received to provide a stream of stock quotes in the proper time sequence. Each model would require its own exclusive subscription, as shown in figure 2.13, to receive its own copy of the data.

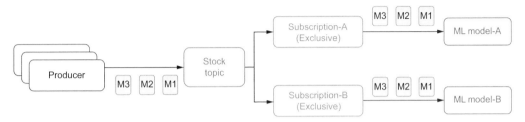

Figure 2.13   An exclusive subscription permits only a single consumer to consume the messages.

FAILOVER SUBSCRIPTIONS

Failover subscriptions allow multiple consumers to attach to the subscription, but only one consumer is selected to receive the messages. This configuration allows you to provide a failover consumer to continue processing the messages in the topic in the event of a consumer failure. If the active consumer fails to process a message, Pulsar automatically fails over to the next consumer in the list and continues delivering the messages.

This type of subscription is useful when you want single processing semantics with high availability of the consumers. This is useful if you want your application to continue processing messages in the event of a system failure and another consumer to take over if the first consumer were to fail for any reason. Typically, these consumers are spread across different hosts and/or data centers to ensure that the application can survive multiple outages. As you can see in figure 2.14, Consumer-A is the active consumer, while Consumer-B is the standby consumer that would be the next in line to receive messages if Consumer-A disconnected for any reason.

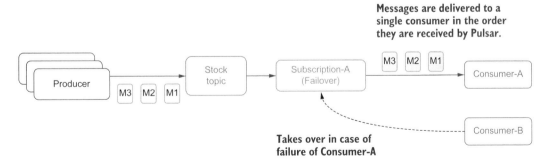

Figure 2.14   A failover subscription has only one active consumer at a time, but it permits multiple standby consumers.

One such example would be if the data science team from our financial services company had deployed one of their models using data from the `stock quotes` topic that generates market volatility scores that are combined with scores from other models to produce an overall recommendation for the trading team. It would be critical that exactly one instance of this model remain up and always running to help the trading team make informed trading decisions. Having multiple instances running and generating recommendations could skew the overall recommendation.

SHARED SUBSCRIPTIONS

Shared subscriptions also allow multiple consumers to attach to the subscription; each of which can actively receive messages, unlike failover subscriptions that support only one active consumer at a time. Messages are delivered in a round-robin fashion to all the registered consumers, and any given message is delivered to only one consumer, as shown in figure 2.15.

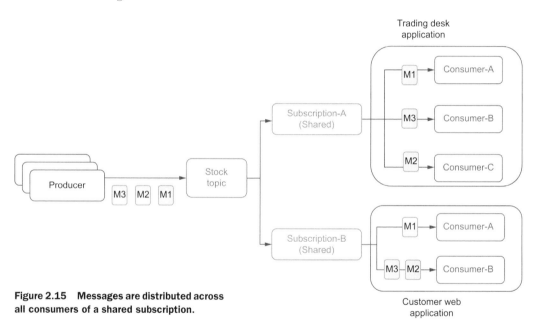

Figure 2.15   Messages are distributed across all consumers of a shared subscription.

This subscription type is useful for implementing work queues, where message ordering isn't important, as it allows you to scale up the number of consumers on the topic quickly to process the incoming messages. There are no upper limits on the number of consumers per shared subscription, which allows you to scale up consumption by increasing the number of consumers beyond some artificial limit that is imposed by the storage layer.

Within our fictitious financial services organization, the business-critical applications, such as our internal trading platforms, algorithmic trading systems, and customer facing website would all benefit from such a subscription. Each of these applications would use their own shared subscription, as shown in figure 2.15, to ensure that they each received all the messages published to the stock topic.

KEY-SHARED SUBSCRIPTIONS

The key-shared subscription also permitted multiple concurrent consumers, but unlike the shared subscription which distributes the messages in a round-robin manner amongst the consumers, it adds a secondary key index, which ensures that messages with the same key get delivered to the same consumer. This subscription acts as a distributed GROUP BY in SQL, where data with similar keys is grouped together. This is particularly useful in cases where you want to presort the data prior to consumption.

Consider the scenario of the business analytics team needing to perform some analytics on the data in the stock topic. By having using a key-shared subscription, they are assured that all the data for a given ticker symbol will be processed by the same consumer, as depicted in figure 2.16, making it easier for them to join this data with other data streams.

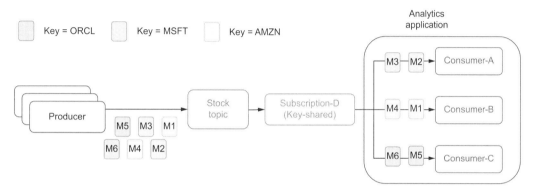

Figure 2.16 Messages are grouped together by the specified key in a shared-key subscription.

In summary, exclusive and failover subscriptions allow only one consumer per topic partition per subscription, which ensures that messages are consumed in the order they are received. They are best applied to streaming use cases where strict ordering is required.

Shared subscriptions, on the other hand, allow multiple consumers per topic partition. Each consumer within the subscription receives only a portion of the messages published to a topic. Shared subscriptions are best for queuing use cases, where strict message ordering is not required but high throughput is.

2.3 *Message retention and expiration*

As a messaging system, Pulsar's primary function is to move data from point A to point B. Once the data has been delivered to all the intended recipients, the presumption is that there is no need to keep it. Consequently, the default message retention policy in Pulsar does exactly that: when a message is published to a Pulsar topic, it will be stored until it has been acknowledged by all the topic's consumers, at which point it will be deleted. This behavior is controlled by the `defaultRetentionTimeInMinutes` and `defaultRetentionSizeInMB` configuration properties in the broker configuration file, which are both set to zero by default to indicate that no acknowledged messages should be retained.

2.3.1 *Data retention*

However, Pulsar also supports namespace-level retention policies that allow you to override this default behavior for situations where you want to retain the topic data for a longer period, such as if you want to access the topic data at a later point in time via the reader interface or SQL.

These retention policies dictate how long you retain messages in persistent storage after they have been acknowledged as consumed by all the known consumers. Acknowledged messages that are not covered by the retention policy will be deleted. Retention policies are defined by a combination of size and time limits and are applied on a per-topic basis to every topic in that namespace. For instance, if you specify a size limit of 100 GB, then up to 100 GB worth of data will be retained in each topic within that namespace, and once this size limit is exceeded, messages will be purged from the topic (from oldest to newest) until the total data volume is under the specified limit again. Similarly, if you specify a time limit of 24 hours, then acknowledged messages for all the topics in the namespace will be retained for a maximum of 24 hours based on the time they were received by the broker.

The retention policies require you to specify both a size and a time limit, which are applied independently of one another. Thus, if a message violates either of these limits, it will be removed from the topic, regardless of whether or not it complies with the other policy.

If you specify a retention policy with time limit of 24 hours and a size limit of 10 GB for the `E-payments/refunds` namespace, as shown in listing 2.4, then when either of the specified policy limits are reached, the data is deleted. Therefore, it is possible for messages that are less than 24 hours old to be deleted if the total volume exceeds 10 GB.

Listing 2.4   Setting various Pulsar retention policies

```
./bin/pulsar-admin namespaces set-retention E-payments/payments \
  --time 24h \
  --size -1          ◁───┤ Retains all messages less than 24 hours
                          │ old with no restriction on the size

./bin/pulsar-admin namespaces set-retention E-payments/fraud-detection \
  --time -1 \
  --size 20G         ◁───┤ Retains up to 20 GB of messages
                          │ with no restriction on the time

./bin/pulsar-admin namespaces set-retention E-payments/refunds \
  --time 24h \
  --size 10G         ◁─── Retains up to 10 GB of messages less than 24 hours old
```

```
./bin/pulsar-admin namespaces set-retention E-payments/gift-cards \
  --time -1 \
  --size -1            ◁──── Retains an infinite number of messages
```

It is also possible to set infinite size or time by specifying a value of -1 for either of those settings when you create the retention policy and providing it for both settings, effectively creating an infinite retention policy for the namespace. Therefore, be careful when using that policy, as the data will never be removed from the storage layer; be sure you have sufficient storage capacity and/or configure periodic offloading of the data to tiered storage.

2.3.2 Backlog quotas

Backlog is the term used for all the unacknowledged messages in a topic that must be stored on bookies until they are delivered to all the intended recipients. By default, Pulsar retains all unacknowledged messages indefinitely. However, Pulsar supports namespace-level backlog quota policies that allow you to override this behavior to reduce the space consumed by these unacknowledged messages in situations where one or more of the consumers goes offline for an extended period due to a system crash.

These backlog quotas are designed to solve a very specific situation in which the topic producers have sent more messages than the consumer can possibly process without falling even further behind. Under these circumstances, you would want to prevent the consumer from getting so far behind that it will never catch up. When this situation occurs, you need to consider the timeliness of the data that the consumer is processing and ensure that the consumer abandons older, less-recent data in favor of more recent messages that can still be processed within the agreed upon SLA. If the data in your topic becomes "stale" by sitting there for an extended period, then implementing a backlog quota will help you focus your processing efforts on only the more recent data by limiting the size of the backlog.

Figure 2.17   Pulsar's backlog quota allows you to dictate what action the broker should take when the volume of unacknowledged messages exceeds a certain size. This prevents the backlog from growing so large that the consumer is processing data that is of little or no value.

Unlike the message retention policies I discussed in the previous section, which are intended to extend the lifespan of acknowledged messages inside a Pulsar topic, these backlog quota policies are designed to reduce the lifespan of unacknowledged messages.

You can limit the allowable size of these message backlogs by configuring a backlog policy that specifies the maximum allowable size of the topic backlog and the action to take when this threshold is exceeded, as shown in figure 2.17. There are three distinct options for the backlog retention policy, which dictate the behavior the broker should take to alleviate the condition:

- The broker can reject inbound messages by sending an exception to the producers to indicate that they should hold off sending new messages by specifying the `producer_request_hold` retention policy.
- Rather than requesting that the producers hold off, the broker will forcibly disconnect any existing producers when the `producer_exception` policy is specified.
- If you want the broker to discard existing, unacknowledged messages from the topic, then you should specify the `consumer_backlog_eviction` policy.

Each of these provide you with three very different approaches to handling the situation shown in figure 2.17. The first one, `producer_request_hold`, would leave the producer connected but throw an exception to slow it down. This policy would be applicable in a scenario where you want the client application to catch the thrown exception and resend the message at a later point. So, it would be best to use this policy when you don't want to reject any messages sent from the consumer, and the clients will buffer the rejected messages for a period of time before resending them.

The second policy, `producer_exception`, would forcibly disconnect the producer entirely, which would stop the messages from getting published and would require the producer code to detect this condition and reconnect. With this policy there is the distinct possibility of losing messages sent from the client producers during the period they are disconnected. This policy is best used when you know the producers aren't capable of buffering messages (e.g., they are running inside a resource-constrained environment, such as an IoT device), and you don't want Pulsar's inability to receive messages to cause the client application to crash.

The last policy, `consumer_backlog_eviction`, does not impact the functionality of the producer whatsoever, and it will continue to produce messages at the current rate. However, older messages that haven't been consumed will be discarded, resulting in message loss.

2.3.3   *Message expiration*

As we already discussed, Pulsar retains all unacknowledged messages indefinitely, and one of the tools we must use to prevent these messages from backing up is backlog quotas. However, one of the downsides of backlog quotas is that they only allow you to make your decision on whether to keep a message based on the total space consumed by the topic's unacknowledged messages. As you'll recall, one of the primary reasons for backlog quotas was to ensure that the consumer was ignoring stale data in favor of more recent data. Therefore, it would make more sense if there was a way to enforce exactly that based on the age of messages themselves. This is where message expiration policies come into play.

Pulsar supports namespace-level time-to-live (TTL) policies that allow you to have messages automatically deleted if they remain unacknowledged after a certain period of time. Message expiration is useful in situations where it is more important for the application consuming the data to be working with more recent data, rather than a complete history. One such example would be driver location data being displayed for users of a ride-sharing application while their driver is en route. The customer is more interested in the most recent location of the driver than they are in where the driver was five minutes ago. Therefore, driver location information that is older than five minutes would no longer be relevant and should be purged to allow the consumers to process only the more recent data, rather than trying to process messages that are no longer useful.

Listing 2.5 Setting backlog quota and message expiration policies

```
./bin/pulsar-admin namespaces set-backlog-quota E-payments/payments \
--limit 2G
--policy producer_request-hold    ⟵  Defines a backlog quota with a size limit of
                                      2 GB and producer_request_hold policy

./bin/pulsar-admin namespaces set-message-ttl E-payments/payments \
--messageTTL 120              ⟵  Sets the message TTL to 120 seconds
```

A namespace can have both a backlog quota and a TTL policy associated with it to provide even finer control over the retention of unacknowledged messages stored inside a Pulsar topic, as shown in listing 2.5.

2.3.4 *Message backlog vs. message expiration*

Message retention and message expiration solve two fundamentally different problems. As you can see in figure 2.18, message retention policies only apply to acknowledged messages, and those messages that fall within the retention policy are retained. Message expiration only applies to unacknowledged messages and is controlled by the TTL setting, meaning any messages that are not processed and acked within that timeframe are discarded and not processed.

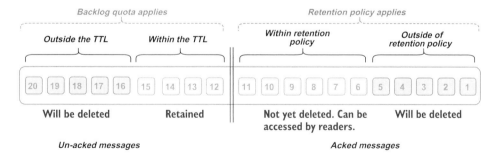

Figure 2.18 The backlog quota applies to messages that have not been acknowledged by all subscriptions and is based on the TTL setting, while the retention policy applies to acknowledged messages and is based on the volume of data to retain.

Message retention policies can be used in conjunction with tiered storage to support infinite message retention for critical datasets you want to retain indefinitely for backup/recovery, event sourcing, or SQL exploration.

2.4   *Tiered storage*

Pulsar's tiered storage feature allows older topic data to be offloaded to more cost-effective long-term storage, thereby freeing up disk space inside of the bookies. To the end user, there is no difference between consuming a topic whose data is stored inside Apache BookKeeper or one whose data is on tiered storage. The clients still produce and consume messages in the same way, and the entire process is handled transparently behind the scenes.

As we discussed earlier, Apache Pulsar stores topics as an ordered list of ledgers that are spread across the bookies in the storage layer. Because these ledgers are append-only, new messages are only written to the final ledger in the list. All the previous ledgers are sealed, so the data within the segment is immutable. Because the data is immutable, it can be easily be copied to another storage system, such as cloud storage.

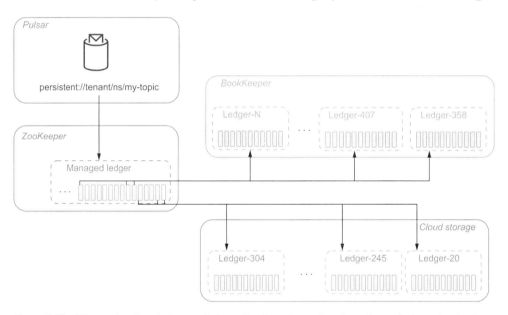

Figure 2.19   When using tiered storage, ledgers that have been closed can be copied over to cloud storage and removed from the bookies to free up space. The managed ledger entries are updated to reflect the new location of the ledgers, which can still be read by the topic consumers.

Once the copy is complete, the managed ledger information can be updated to reflect the new storage location of the data, as shown in figure 2.19, and the original copy of the data stored in Apache BookKeeper can be deleted. When a ledger is offloaded to an external storage system, the ledgers are copied to that storage system one by one, from oldest to newest.

Apache Pulsar currently supports multiple cloud storage systems for tiered storage, but I will focus on using AWS in this section. Please consult the documentation for more details on how to use other cloud vendors' storage systems.

AWS OFFLOAD CONFIGURATION

The first steps you need to perform are to create the S3 bucket you will be using to store the offloaded ledgers and to ensure that the AWS account you are going to use has sufficient permissions to read and write data to the bucket. Once those are completed, you will need to modify the broker configuration settings again, as shown in the following listing.

Listing 2.6 Configuring AWS tiered storage in Pulsar

You will need to add the AWS-specific settings to tell the Pulsar where to store the ledgers inside of S3. Once these settings are added, you can save the file and restart the Pulsar brokers for the changes to take effect.

AWS AUTHENTICATION

For Pulsar to offload data to S3, it must authenticate with AWS using a valid set of credentials. As you may have already noticed, Pulsar doesn't provide any means of configuring authentication for AWS. Instead, it relies on the standard mechanisms supported by the `DefaultAWSCredentialsProviderChain`, which searches for AWS credentials in various predefined locations.

If you are running your broker on an AWS instance with an instance profile that provides credentials, Pulsar will use these credentials if no other mechanism is provided. Alternatively, you can provide your credentials via environment variables. The easiest way to do this is to edit the conf/pulsar_env.sh file and export the environment variables `AWS_ACCESS_KEY_ID` and `AWS_SECRET_ACCESS_KEY` by adding the statements shown in the following listing.

Listing 2.7 Providing AWS credentials via environment variables

```
# Add these at the beginning of the pulsar_env.sh
export AWS_ACCESS_KEY_ID=ABC123456789
export AWS_SECRET_ACCESS_KEY=ded7db27a4558e2ea8bbf0bf37ae0e8521618f366c

# or you can set them here instead.
PULSAR_EXTRA_OPTS="${PULSAR_EXTRA_OPTS} ${PULSAR_MEM} ${PULSAR_GC}
```

```
-Daws.accessKeyId=ABC123456789
-Daws.secretKey=ded7db27a4558e2ea8bbf0bf37ae0e8521618f366c
-Dio.netty.leakDetectionLevel=disabled
-Dio.netty.recycler.maxCapacity.default=1000
-Dio.netty.recycler.linkCapacity=1024"
```

You only need to use one of the two methods shown in listing 2.7. Both options work equally well, so you can take your pick. However, both methods pose a security risk, as these AWS credentials will be visible in the process if you run a linux `ps` command. If you would prefer to avoid that scenario, you can store your credentials in the traditional location for AWS credentials files, `~/.aws/credentials` (shown in listing 2.8), which can be modified to have read-only permissions for the user account that will be launching the Pulsar broker (e.g., root). However, this approach does require you to store your unencrypted credentials on disk, which introduces some security risks, so it is not recommend for production use.

Listing 2.8   Contents of the ~/.aws/credentials file

```
[default]
aws_access_key_id=ABC123456789
aws_secret_access_key=ded7db27a4558e2ea8bbf0bf37ae0e8521618f366c
```

CONFIGURING OFFLOAD TO RUN AUTOMATICALLY

Simply because we have configured the managed ledger offloader does not mean that the offloading will occur. We still need to define a namespace-level policy to have the data offloaded automatically once a certain threshold is reached. The threshold is based on the total volume of data that a Pulsar topic has stored in the BookKeeper storage layer.

Listing 2.9   Configuring automatic offloads to tiered storage

```
/pulsar/bin/pulsar-admin namespaces set-offload-threshold \
-size 10GB \
E-payments/payments
```

You can define a policy such as the one shown in listing 2.9, which sets a threshold of 10 GB for all topics in the namespace. Once a topic reaches 10 GB of storage, an offload of all closed segments is triggered. Setting the threshold to zero will cause the broker to offload ledgers as aggressively as it can and can be used to minimize the amount of topic data stored on BookKeeper. Specifying a negative value for the threshold effectively disables automatic offloading entirely and can be used for topics with tight SLA response times that cannot tolerate the additional latency required to read data from tiered storage.

Tiered storage should be used when you have a topic for which you want to retain the data for a very long time. One example would be clickstream data for a customer-facing website. This information should be retained for a long period of time in case you want to perform user behavioral analytics on your customer's interactions in order to detect patterns of behavior.

While tiered storage is often used in conjunction with topics that have retention policies that encompass enormous amounts of data, there is no such requirement. It can, in fact, be used with any topic.

Summary

- We discussed the logical structure of Pulsar's address space in order to support multitenancy.
- We discussed the difference between message retention and message expiration in Pulsar.
- We discussed the low-level details of how Pulsar stores and serves messages.

Interacting with Pulsar

This chapter covers

- Running a local instance of Pulsar on your development machine
- Administering a Pulsar cluster using its command-line tools
- Interacting with Pulsar using the Java, Python, and Go client libraries
- Troubleshooting Pulsar with its command-line tools

Now that we have covered the overall architecture and terminology of Apache Pulsar, let's start using it. For local development and testing, I recommend running Pulsar inside a Docker container on your own machine, which provides an easy way to get started with Pulsar with a minimal amount of time, effort, and money. For those of you who would prefer to use a full-size Pulsar cluster, you can refer to appendix A for more details on how to install and run one inside a containerized environment, such as Kubernetes. In this chapter, I will walk you through the process of sending and receiving messages programmatically using the Java API, starting with the process of creating a Pulsar namespace and topic using Pulsar's administrative tools.

3.1 Getting started with Pulsar

For the purposes of local development and testing, you can run Pulsar on your development machine within a Docker container. If you don't already have Docker installed, you should download the community edition (https://www.docker.com/community-edition) and follow the instructions for your operating system. For those of you unfamiliar with Docker, it is an open source project for automating the deployment of applications as portable, self-contained images that can be run from a single command. Each Docker image bundles all the separate software components necessary to run an entire application together into a single deployment. For example, the Docker image for a simple web application would include the web server, database, and application code—in short, everything the application needs to run. Similarly, there is an existing Docker image that includes a Pulsar broker as well as the necessary ZooKeeper and BookKeeper components.

Software developers can create Docker images and publish them to a central repository known as Docker Hub. You can specify a tag when uploading an image that uniquely identifies it. This allows people to quickly locate and download the desired version of the image to their development machines.

To start the Pulsar Docker container, simply execute the command shown in listing 3.1, which will download the container image and start all the necessary components. Note that we have specified a pair of ports (6650 and 8080) that will be exposed on your local machine. You will use these ports to interact with the Pulsar cluster later in the chapter.

Listing 3.1 Running Pulsar on your desktop

```
docker pull apachepulsar/pulsar-standalone   ←── Pull down the latest version from DockerHub.

docker run -d \                                      Configure port forwarding for these ports.
  -p 6650:6650 -p 8080:8080 \   ←────────────────┘   Retain the data on a local drive.
  -v $PWD/data:/pulsar/data \   ←────────────────────
  --name pulsar \                         ←────────── Specify the name of the container.
 apachepulsar/pulsar-standalone   ←────┐
                                        └── The tag for the standalone image
```

If Pulsar has successfully started, you should be able to locate INFO-level messages in the log file of the Pulsar container indicating that the messaging service is ready, like those shown in the following listing. You can access the Docker log files via the `docker log` command, which allows you to locate any issues if your container fails to start.

Listing 3.2 Verifying that the Pulsar cluster is running

```
$docker logs pulsar | grep "messaging service is ready"

20:11:45.834 [main] INFO  org.apache.pulsar.broker.PulsarService -
➥ messaging service is ready
```

```
20:11:45.855 [main] INFO  org.apache.pulsar.broker.PulsarService -
```
➡ messaging service is ready, bootstrap service port = 8080,
➡ broker url= pulsar://localhost:6650, cluster=standalone

These log messages indicate that the Pulsar broker is up and running and accepting connections on port 6650 of your local development machine. Therefore, all the code examples in this chapter will use the `pulsar://localhost:6650` URL to send and receive data from the Pulsar broker.

3.2   Administering Pulsar

Pulsar provides a single administrative layer that allows you to administer the entire Pulsar instance, including all the subclusters, from a single endpoint. Pulsar's admin layer controls authentication and authorization for all tenants, resource isolation policies, storage quotas, and more, as shown in figure 3.1.

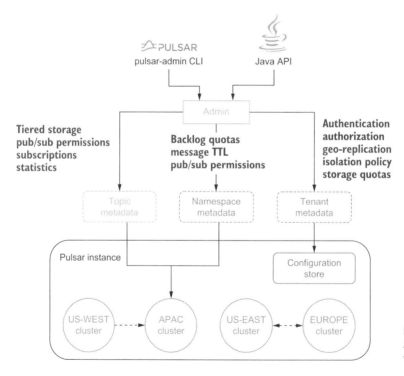

Figure 3.1
Administrative
view of Pulsar

This administrative interface allows you to create and manage all the various entities within a Pulsar cluster, such as tenants, namespaces, and topics, and configure their various security and data retention policies. Users can interact with this administrative interface via the `pulsar-admin` command-line interface tool or programmatically via a Java API, as shown in figure 3.1

When you start a local standalone cluster, Pulsar automatically creates a *public tenant* with a namespace named `default` that can be used for development purposes. However, this is not a realistic production scenario, so I will demonstrate how to create a tenant and namespace.

3.2.1 *Creating a tenant, namespace, and topic*

Pulsar provides a command-line interface (CLI) tool called `pulsar-admin` inside the bin folder of your Pulsar installation, which in our case is inside the Docker container. Therefore, to use this command line tool, you must execute the command inside the running Docker container. Fortunately, Docker provides a method for doing just that via its `docker exec` command. Just like the name implies, this command executes the given statement inside the container itself, rather than on your local machine. You can start using the `pulsar-admin` CLI by issuing the sequence of commands shown in the listing that follows to create a topic named `persistent://manning/chapter03/example-topic` that we will use in throughout the chapter.

Listing 3.3 `pulsar-admin` commands

List all the clusters in the Pulsar instance.

```
docker exec -it pulsar /pulsar/bin/pulsar-admin clusters list
"standalone"

docker exec -it pulsar /pulsar/bin/pulsar-admin tenants list
"public"
"sample"

docker exec -it pulsar /pulsar/bin/pulsar-admin tenants create manning

docker exec -it pulsar /pulsar/bin/pulsar-admin tenants list
"manning"
"public"
"sample"

docker exec -it pulsar /pulsar/bin/pulsar-admin namespaces
➥ create manning/chapter03

docker exec -it pulsar /pulsar/bin/pulsar-admin namespaces list manning
"manning/chapter03"

docker exec -it pulsar /pulsar/bin/pulsar-admin topics create
➥ persistent://manning/chapter03/example-topic

docker exec -it pulsar /pulsar/bin/pulsar-admin topics list manning/chapter03
"persistent://manning/chapter03/example-topic"
```

List all the tenants in the Pulsar instance.

Create a new tenant named manning.

Confirm that the new tenant was created.

Create a new namespace named chapter03 under the manning tenant.

List the namespaces under the manning tenant.

Create a new topic.

List the topic inside the manning/chapter03 namespace.

These commands barely scratch the surface of what you can do with the `pulsar-admin` tool, and I highly recommend that you refer to the online documentation (https://pulsar.apache.org/docs/en/pulsar-admin) for additional details on the CLI tool and all of its features. We will revisit the `pulsar-admin` CLI tool later in the chapter to retrieve some performance metrics from the cluster after we have published some messages.

3.2.2   *Java Admin API*

Another way in which you can administer the Pulsar Instance is via the Java Admin API, which provides a programmable interface for performing administrative tasks. Listing 3.4 shows how to create the `persistent://manning/chapter03/example-topic` topic using the Java API. This API provides an alternative to the CLI tool and is particularly useful inside of unit tests when you want to create and tear down the necessary Pulsar topics programmatically, rather than relying on an external tool.

Listing 3.4   Using the Java admin API

```java
import org.apache.pulsar.client.admin.PulsarAdmin;
import org.apache.pulsar.common.policies.data.TenantInfo;

public class CreateTopic {
    public static void main(String[] args) throws Exception {
        PulsarAdmin admin = PulsarAdmin.builder()
            .serviceHttpUrl("http://localhost:8080")        ⟵  Create an admin client for the Pulsar cluster running inside Docker.
            .build();

        TenantInfo config = new TenantInfo(
            Stream.of("admin").collect(                      Specify the admin roles for the tenant.
            Collectors.toCollection(HashSet::new)),
            Stream.of("standalone").collect(
            Collectors.toCollection(HashSet::new)));        ⟵  Specify the clusters that the tenant can operate on.

        admin.tenants().createTenant("manning", config);      Create the tenant.
        admin.namespaces().createNamespace("manning/chapter03");  ⟵  Create the namespace.
        admin.topics().createNonPartitionedTopic(
            "persistent://manning/chapter03/example-topic");  ⟵  Create the topic.
    }
}
```

3.3   *Pulsar clients*

Pulsar provides a CLI tool called *pulsar-client* that allows you to send and receive messages from a topic in a running Pulsar cluster. This tool also resides inside the bin folder of your Pulsar installation, and thus, we will need to use the `docker exec` command again to interact with this tool.

Since the topic has already been created, we can start by first attaching a consumer to it, which will establish a subscription and ensure that no messages are lost. This can be accomplished by running the command shown in the following listing. The consumer is a *blocking script*, meaning it will keep consuming messages from the topic until the script is stopped by you (with Ctrl+C).

Listing 3.5 Starting a command-line consumer

The number of messages to consume;
0 means consume forever.

The name of
the topic we are
consuming from

```
$ docker exec -it pulsar /pulsar/bin/pulsar-client consume \
persistent://manning/chapter03/example-topic \
--num-messages 0 \
--subscription-name example-sub \
--subscription-type Exclusive
```

The unique name of the subscription

The type of subscription

```
INFO  org.apache.pulsar.client.impl.ConnectionPool - [[id: 0xe410f77d,
     L:/127.0.0.1:39276 - R:localhost/127.0.0.1:6650]] Connected to server
18:08:15.819 [pulsar-client-io-1-1] INFO
     org.apache.pulsar.client.impl.ConsumerStatsRecorderImpl - Starting Pulsar
     consumer perf with config: {
  "topicNames" : [ ],
  "topicsPattern" : null,
  "subscriptionName" : "example-sub",
  "subscriptionType" : "Exclusive",
  "receiverQueueSize" : 1000,
  "acknowledgementsGroupTimeMicros" : 100000,
  "negativeAckRedeliveryDelayMicros" : 60000000,
  "maxTotalReceiverQueueSizeAcrossPartitions" : 50000,
  "consumerName" : "3d7ce",
  "ackTimeoutMillis" : 0,
  "tickDurationMillis" : 1000,
  "priorityLevel" : 0,
  "cryptoFailureAction" : "FAIL",
  "properties" : { },
  "readCompacted" : false,
  "subscriptionInitialPosition" : "Latest",
  "patternAutoDiscoveryPeriod" : 1,
  "regexSubscriptionMode" : "PersistentOnly",
  "deadLetterPolicy" : null,
  "autoUpdatePartitions" : true,
  "replicateSubscriptionState" : false,
  "resetIncludeHead" : false
}
...
```

Consumer configuration details

You can see the subscription name
we specified on the command line.

You can see the
subscription type
we specified on the
command line.

Start consuming from the
latest available message.

```
18:08:15.980 [pulsar-client-io-1-1] INFO
     org.apache.pulsar.client.impl.MultiTopicsConsumerImpl -
     [persistent://manning/chapter02/example] [example-sub] Success
     subscribe new topic persistent://manning/chapter02/example in topics
     consumer, partitions: 2, allTopicPartitionsNumber: 2
18:08:47.644 [pulsar-client-io-1-1] INFO
     com.scurrilous.circe.checksum.Crc32cIntChecksum - SSE4.2 CRC32C
     provider initialized
```

In a different shell, we will start a producer by issuing the command shown in the following listing to send two messages containing the text "Hello Pulsar" to the same topic we just started the consumer on.

Listing 3.6   Sending a message using the Pulsar command-line producer

The number of times to send the message

The name of the topic we are publishing to

```
$ docker exec -it pulsar /pulsar/bin/pulsar-client produce \
persistent://manning/chapter03/example-topic \
--num-produce 2 \
--messages "Hello Pulsar"                    ◁——— The message contents
18:08:47.106 [pulsar-client-io-1-1] INFO
⇒ org.apache.pulsar.client.impl.ConnectionPool - [[id: 0xd47ac4ea,
⇒ L:/127.0.0.1:39342 - R:localhost/127.0.0.1:6650]] Connected to server
18:08:47.367 [pulsar-client-io-1-1] INFO
⇒ org.apache.pulsar.client.impl.ProducerStatsRecorderImpl - Starting
⇒ Pulsar producer perf with config: {              ◁—
  "topicName" : "persistent://manning/chapter02/example",
  "producerName" : null,
  "sendTimeoutMs" : 30000,
  "blockIfQueueFull" : false,
  "maxPendingMessages" : 1000,
  "maxPendingMessagesAcrossPartitions" : 50000,
  "messageRoutingMode" : "RoundRobinPartition",
  "hashingScheme" : "JavaStringHash",
  "cryptoFailureAction" : "FAIL",
  "batchingMaxPublishDelayMicros" : 1000,
  "batchingMaxMessages" : 1000,
  "batchingEnabled" : true,
  "compressionType" : "NONE",
  "initialSequenceId" : null,
  "autoUpdatePartitions" : true,
  "properties" : { }
}
...
18:08:47.689 [main] INFO  org.apache.pulsar.client.cli.PulsarClientTool - 2
⇒ messages successfully produced   ◁—
```

Producer configuration details

The publishing of the messages

After executing the producer command in listing 3.6, you should see something like the code in the following listing inside the shell where you started the consumer. This indicates that the messages were successfully published by the producer and received by the consumer.

Listing 3.7   Receipt of messages in consumer shell

```
----- got message -----
key:[null], properties:[], content:Hello Pulsar
----- got message -----
   key:[null], properties:[], content:Hello Pulsar
```

Congratulations, you have just successfully sent your first messages using Pulsar! Now that we have confirmed that our local Pulsar cluster is working and capable of sending and receiving messages, let's look at some more realistic examples, using various programming languages. Pulsar provides a simple and intuitive client API that encapsulates all the broker–client communication details from the user. Due to the popularity of Pulsar, there are several language-specific implementations of this client, including Java, Go, Python, and C++, just to name a few. This allows each team in your organization to use whatever language they like to implement their services.

While there are significant discrepancies in the features supported by the official Pulsar client libraries based on the programming language you chose (please refer to the official client documentation for details), under the covers they all support transparent reconnection and/or connection failover to brokers, queuing of messages until acknowledged by the broker, and heuristics, such as connection retries with backoff. This allows the developer to focus on the messaging logic, rather than having to handle connection exceptions in their application code.

3.3.1 The Pulsar Java client

In addition to the Java Admin API we looked at earlier in the chapter, Pulsar also provides a Java client that can be used to create producers, consumers, and message readers. The latest version of the Pulsar Java client library is available in the Maven central repository. To use the latest version, simply add the Pulsar client library to your build configuration, as shown in the next listing. Once you have added the Pulsar client library to your project, you can start using it to interact with Pulsar by creating clients, producers, and consumers inside your Java code, as we'll see in the next section.

Listing 3.8 Adding the Pulsar client library to your Maven project

```xml
<!-- Inside your pom.xml -->
<properties>
    <pulsar.version>2.7.2</pulsar.version>
</properties>

<dependency>
  <groupId>org.apache.pulsar</groupId>
  <artifactId>pulsar-client</artifactId>
  <version>${pulsar.version}</version>
</dependency>
```

PULSAR CLIENT CONFIGURATION IN JAVA

When an application wants to create either a producer or a consumer, you first need to instantiate a *PulsarClient* object, using code like that shown in the following listing. In this object, you will provide the URL of the Pulsar broker along with any other connection configuration information that may be required, such as security credentials.

Listing 3.9 Creating a PulsarClient in Java

```java
PulsarClient client = PulsarClient.builder()
        .serviceUrl("pulsar://localhost:6650")   ◁─── The connection URL
        .build();                                      to the Pulsar broker
```

The PulsarClient object handles all the low-level details involved in creating a connection to the Pulsar broker, including automatic retries and connection security if the Pulsar broker has TLS configured. Client instances are thread safe and can be reused for creating and managing multiple producers and consumers.

PULSAR PRODUCERS IN JAVA

In Pulsar, producers are used to write messages to topics. Listing 3.10 shows how you can create a producer in Java by specifying the name of the topic you are going to send messages to. While there are several configuration settings that can be used when creating a producer, all that is required is the topic name itself.

Listing 3.10   Creating a Pulsar producer in Java

```
Producer<byte[]> producer = client.newProducer()
        .topic("persistent://manning/chapter03/example-topic")
        .create();
```

It is also possible to attach metadata to a given message, as shown in listing 3.11, which shows how to specify the message key that is used for routing with a key-shared subscription, along with some message properties. This capability can be used to tag the message with useful information, such as when the message was sent, who sent the message, the device ID if the message is from an embedded sensor, and other information.

Listing 3.11   Specifying metadata in Pulsar messages

```
Producer<byte[]> producer = client.newProducer()
        .topic("persistent://manning/chapter03/example-topic")
        .create();

producer.newMessage()                              You can specify a message key.
        .key("tempurture-readings")  ◁─────────┘
        .value("98.0".getBytes())    ◁─────────┐
  ┌─▷ .property("deviceID", "1234")            Send the message content as a byte array.
        .property("timestamp", "08/03/2021 14:48:24.1")
        .send();
```

You can attach as many properties as you like.

The metadata values you attach to the message will be available to the message consumers who can then use that information when performing their processing logic. For example, a property containing a timestamp value that represents when the message was sent could be used to sort the incoming messages into chronological order of occurrence or to correlate it with messages from another topic.

PULSAR CONSUMERS IN JAVA

In Pulsar, the consumer interface is used to listen on a specific topic and process the incoming messages. After a message has been successfully processed, an acknowledgment should be sent back to the broker to indicate that we are done processing the message within the subscription. This allows the broker to know which message in the topic needs to be delivered to the next consumer on the subscription. In Java, you can create a consumer by specifying a topic and a subscription, as shown in the following listing.

Listing 3.12 Creating a Pulsar consumer in Java

```
Consumer consumer = client.newConsumer()              Specify the topic
    .topic("persistent://manning/chapter03/example-topic")   you want to
    .subscriptionName("my-subscription")                     consume from.
    .subscribe();          You must specify the unique
                           name of your subscription.
```

The subscribe method will attempt to connect the consumer to the topic using the specified subscription, which may fail if the subscription already exists and isn't one of the shared subscription types (e.g., you attempt to connect to an exclusive subscription that already has an active consumer). If you are connecting to the topic for the first time using the specified subscription name, a subscription is created for you automatically. Whenever a new subscription is created, it is initially positioned at the end of the topic by default, and consumers on that subscription will begin reading the first message created after the subscription was created. If you are connecting to a preexisting subscription, it will begin reading from the earliest unacknowledged message within the subscription, as shown in figure 3.2. This ensures that you pick up from where you left off in the event that your consumer is unexpectedly disconnected from the topic.

Figure 3.2 The consumer starts reading messages immediately after the most recently acknowledged message in the subscription. If the subscription is new, then it starts reading the messages that are added to the topic after the subscription was created.

One common consumption pattern is to have the consumer listen on the topic inside a while loop. In listing 3.13, the consumer continuously listens for messages, prints the contents of any message that's received, and then acknowledges that the message has been processed. If the processing logic fails, we use negative acknowledgement to have the message redelivered at a later point in time.

Listing 3.13   Consuming Pulsar messages in Java

```
while (true) {
  // Wait for a message
  Message msg = consumer.receive();    ⟵———  Wait for a message.

  try {
      System.out.println("Message received: " +
                           new String(msg.getData()));
      consumer.acknowledge(msg);       ⟵———
  } catch (Exception e) {
      consumer.negativeAcknowledge(msg);  ⟵——
  }
}
```

Process the message. ⟶

Acknowledge the message so it can be deleted by the broker.

Mark the message for redelivery.

The message consumer shown in listing 3.13 processes the messages in a synchronous manner because the `receive()` method it is using to retrieve messages is a blocking method (i.e., it waits indefinitely for a new message to arrive). While this might be fine for some use cases where the message volume is low, or we are not concerned about the latency between when a message is published and when it is processed, generally synchronous processing is not the best approach. A better approach is to process these messages in an asynchronous manner, which relies on the `MessageListener` interface provided by the Java API, as shown in the following listing.

Listing 3.14   Asynchronous message processing in Java

```
package com.manning.pulsar.chapter3.consumers;

import java.util.stream.IntStream;

import org.apache.pulsar.client.api.ConsumerBuilder;
import org.apache.pulsar.client.api.PulsarClient;
import org.apache.pulsar.client.api.PulsarClientException;
import org.apache.pulsar.client.api.SubscriptionType;

public class MessageListenerExample {

public static void main() throws PulsarClientException {

  PulsarClient client = PulsarClient.builder()     ⟵———
      .serviceUrl(PULSAR_SERVICE_URL)
      .build();

  ConsumerBuilder<byte[]> consumerBuilder =    ⟵———
      client.newConsumer()
        .topic(MY_TOPIC)
        .subscriptionName(SUBSCRIPTION)
        .subscriptionType(SubscriptionType.Shared)
        .messageListener((consumer, msg) -> {    ⟵———
          try {
            System.out.println("Message received: " +
                  new String(msg.getData()));
```

The Pulsar client used to connect to Pulsar

The consumer factory that will be used to create the consumer instances later

The business logic to execute when a message is received

```
            consumer.acknowledge(msg);
        } catch (PulsarClientException e) {


        }
    })
```

> Create five consumers on the topic, each with the same MessageListener implementation.

```
  IntStream.range(0, 4).forEach(i -> {
    String name = String.format("mq-consumer-%d", i);
    try {
        consumerBuilder
         .consumerName(name)
         .subscribe();
    } catch (PulsarClientException e) {
      e.printStackTrace();
    }
  });


  ...
  }
}
```

> Connects the consumer to the topic to start receiving messages

When using the `MessageListener` interface, as shown in listing 3.14, you pass in the code that you want executed whenever a message is received. In this case I used a Java Lambda to provide the code inline, and you can see that I still have access to the consumer that I can use to acknowledge the message. Using the listener pattern allows you to separate the business logic from the management of the threads because the Pulsar consumer automatically creates a thread pool for running the `MessageListeners` instances and handles all the threading logic for you. Putting this all together, we have a Java program in the following listing that instantiates a Pulsar client and uses it to create a producer and a consumer that exchange messages over the `my-topic` topic.

Listing 3.15 Endless Pulsar producer and consumer pair

```
import org.apache.pulsar.client.api.Consumer;
import org.apache.pulsar.client.api.Message;
import org.apache.pulsar.client.api.Producer;
import org.apache.pulsar.client.api.PulsarClient;
import org.apache.pulsar.client.api.PulsarClientException;

public class BackAndForth {

  public static void main(String[] args) throws Exception {
    BackAndForth sl = new BackAndForth();
    sl.startConsumer();
    sl.startProducer();
  }
  private String serviceUrl = "pulsar://localhost:6650";
  String topic = "persistent://manning/chapter03/example-topic";;
  String subscriptionName = "my-sub";

  protected void startProducer() {
      Runnable run = () -> {
```

```
        int counter = 0;
        while (true) {
          try {
           getProducer().newMessage()
              .value(String.format("{id: %d, time: %tc}",
                ++counter, new Date()).getBytes())
              .send();
            Thread.sleep(1000);
          } catch (final Exception ex) { }
        }};
      new Thread(run).start();
 }

 protected void startConsumer() {
   Runnable run = () -> {
     while (true) {
       Message<byte[]> msg = null;
       try {
         msg = getConsumer().receive();
         System.out.printf("Message received: %s \n",
         new String(msg.getData()));
       getConsumer().acknowledge(msg);
     } catch (Exception e) {
       System.err.printf(
         "Unable to consume message: %s \n", e.getMessage());
       consumer.negativeAcknowledge(msg);
     }
   }};
   new Thread(run).start();
 }

 protected Consumer<byte[]> getConsumer() throws PulsarClientException {
   if (consumer == null) {
     consumer = getClient().newConsumer()
         .topic(topic)
         .subscriptionName(subscriptionName)
         .subscriptionType(SubscriptionType.Shared)
         .subscribe();
   }
   return consumer;
 }

 protected Producer<byte[]> getProducer() throws PulsarClientException {
    if (producer == null) {
      producer = getClient().newProducer()
        .topic(topic).create();
    }
    return producer;
 }

 protected PulsarClient getClient() throws PulsarClientException {
    if (client == null) {
      client = PulsarClient.builder()
        .serviceUrl(serviceUrl)
        .build();
```

```
        }
      return client;
    }
}
```

As you can see, this code creates both a producer and consumer on the same topic and runs them simultaneously in separate threads. If you run this code, you should see output like the following listing.

Listing 3.16 Endless Pulsar producer and consumer pair output

```
Message received: {id: 1, time: Sun Sep 06 16:24:04 PDT 2020}
Message received: {id: 2, time: Sun Sep 06 16:24:05 PDT 2020}
Message received: {id: 3, time: Sun Sep 06 16:24:06 PDT 2020}
...
```

Notice how the first two messages we sent earlier are not included in the output, since the subscription was created *after* those messages were published. This is in direct contrast to the Reader interface, which we will examine shortly.

DEAD LETTER POLICY

While there are several configuration options for a Pulsar consumer that are described in the online documentation (https://pulsar.apache.org/docs/en/client-libraries-java/#configure-consumer), I wanted to highlight the dead-letter-policy configuration, which is useful when you encounter messages that cannot be processed successfully, such as when you are parsing unstructured messages from a topic. Under normal processing conditions, these messages would cause an exception to be thrown.

At this point you have a couple of options; the first is to trap any exceptions, and simply acknowledge these messages as successfully processed, which effectively ignores them. Another option is to have them redelivered by negatively acknowledging them. However, this approach might result in an infinite redelivery loop for these messages if the underlying issue with the messages cannot be resolved (e.g., a message that cannot be parsed will always throw an exception no matter how many times you process it). A third option is to route these problematic messages to a separate topic, known as a dead-letter topic. This allows you to avoid the infinite redelivery loop, while retaining the messages for further processing and/or examination at a later point in time.

Listing 3.17 Configure the dead letter topic policy on a consumer

```
Consumer consumer = client.newConsumer()
    .topic("persistent://manning/chapter03/example-topic")
    .subscriptionName("my-subscription")
    .deadLetterPolicy(DeadLetterPolicy.builder()
      .maxRedeliverCount(10)
        .deadLetterTopic("persistent://manning/chapter03/my-dlq"))
    .subscribe();
```

Set the max redelivery count. → `.maxRedeliverCount(10)`

Set the dead-letter topic name. `.deadLetterTopic("persistent://manning/chapter03/my-dlq")`

To configure a dead-letter policy for a particular consumer, Pulsar requires you to specify a few properties, such as the max redelivery count, when you first build it, as shown in listing 3.17. When a message exceeds the user-specified maximum redelivery count, it will be sent to the dead-letter topic and acknowledged automatically. These messages can then be examined at a later point in time.

PULSAR READERS IN JAVA

The reader interface allows applications to manage the positions from which they will consume messages. When you connect to a topic using a reader, you must specify which message the reader will begin consuming messages from when it connects to the topic. In short, the reader interface provides Pulsar clients with a low-level abstraction that allows them to manually position themselves within a topic, as shown in figure 3.3.

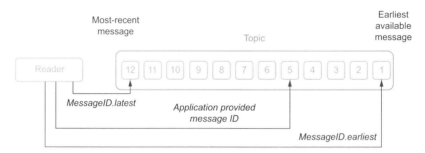

Figure 3.3   When connecting to a topic, the reader interface enables you to begin with the earliest available message, the latest available message, or an application provided message ID.

The reader interface is helpful for use cases like using Pulsar to provide effectively-once processing semantics for a stream processing system. For this use case, it's essential that the stream processing system is able to rewind topics to a specific message and begin reading there. If you choose to explicitly provide a message ID, your application will be responsible for knowing this message ID in advance, perhaps fetching it from a persistent data store or cache. Once you've instantiated a PulsarClient object, you can create a Reader, as shown in the following listing.

Listing 3.18   Creating a Pulsar reader

```
Reader<byte[]> reader = client.newReader()
    .topic("persistent://manning/chapter03/example-topic")      ⬅  Specify the
    .readerName("my-reader")                                        topic you want
    .startMessageId(MessageId.earliest)      ⬅                      to read from.
    .create();                          Specify that we want
                                        to read from the
while (true) {                          earliest message.
  Message msg = reader.readNext();
  System.out.printf("Message received: %s \n", new String(msg.getData()));
}
```

If you run this code, you should see output like the following listing. You would start reading from the very first messages that were published to the topic, which were the two "Hello Pulsar" messages we send from the CLI tool.

Listing 3.19 Earliest message reader output

```
Message read: Hello Pulsar
Message read: Hello Pulsar
Message read: {id: 1, time: Sun Sep 06 18:11:59 PDT 2020}
Message read: {id: 2, time: Sun Sep 06 18:12:00 PDT 2020}
Message read: {id: 3, time: Sun Sep 06 18:12:01 PDT 2020}
Message read: {id: 4, time: Sun Sep 06 18:12:02 PDT 2020}
Message read: {id: 5, time: Sun Sep 06 18:12:04 PDT 2020}
Message read: {id: 6, time: Sun Sep 06 18:12:05 PDT 2020}
Message read: {id: 7, time: Sun Sep 06 18:12:06 PDT 2020}
```

In the example shown in listing 3.18, a reader is created on the specified topic and iterates over each message in the topic, starting with the oldest message in the topic. There are several configuration options for a Pulsar reader that are described in the online documentation (https://pulsar.apache.org/docs/en/client-libraries-java/#reader), but for most cases the default options are sufficient.

3.3.2 The Pulsar Python client

There is also an officially supported Pulsar client for the Python programming language. The latest version of the Pulsar client library can be easily installed using the pip package manager with the commands shown in the following listing.

Listing 3.20 Creating a Pulsar producer in Python

```
pip3 install pulsar-client==2.6.3 –user    ⟵——— Install the Pulsar client.

pip3 list   ⟵——— List all the packages.

Package        Version
-------------- ---------      Confirm that the correct
...                          version of the Pulsar
pulsar-client  2.6.3    ⟵——  client has been installed.
```

Since Python 2.7 has already passed its official end of life, I decided to use Python 3 for all the examples throughout the chapter. Once you have installed the Pulsar client libraries, you can start using them to interact with Pulsar by creating producers and consumers inside your Python code.

PULSAR PRODUCERS IN PYTHON

When a Python application wants to create either a producer or a consumer, you first need to instantiate a client object, using code like that shown in listing 3.21, where you provide the URL of the Pulsar broker. As was the case for Java-based clients, the Python client object handles all the low-level details involved in creating a connection to the Pulsar broker, including automatic retries and connection security if the Pulsar broker has TLS configured. Client instances are thread safe and can be reused for managing multiple producers and consumers.

Listing 3.21   Creating a Pulsar producer in Python

```
import pulsar                                              Create a Pulsar client by
                                                           providing the connection
client = pulsar.Client('pulsar://localhost:6650')   ◁──┘  URL to the Pulsar broker.

producer = client.create_producer(
    'persistent://public/default/my-topic',
    block_if_queue_full=True,
    batching_enabled=True,                      Use the Pulsar client
    batching_max_publish_delay_ms=10)   ◁──┘    to create a producer.

for i in range(10):
    producer.send(('Hello-%d' % i).encode('utf-8'),   ◁───── Send the message contents.
        properties=None)                        ◁──┐
                                                    │  You can attach properties to a message if you want.
client.close()   ◁───── Close the client.
```

As you can see from listing 3.21, the Python library provides several different configuration options when you create your clients, producers, and consumers, so you should view the available online documentation (https://pulsar.apache.org/api/python/2.8.0-SNAPSHOT/) for the Python client to learn more about these options. In our case, we enabled message batching on the client side, which means that, rather than sending/receiving each individual message to and from the broker, messages will be grouped together in batches before being transmitted. This allows us to increase the overall throughput of the messages at the expense of increased latency on each individual message.

PULSAR CONSUMERS IN PYTHON

In Pulsar, the consumer interface is used to listen on a specific topic and process the incoming messages. After a message has been successfully processed, an acknowledgement should be sent back to the broker to indicate that we are done processing the message within the subscription. This allows the broker to know which message in the topic needs to be delivered to the next consumer on the subscription. In Python, you can create a consumer by specifying a topic and a subscription, as shown in the following listing.

Listing 3.22   Creating a Pulsar consumer in Python

```
import pulsar                                              Create a Pulsar client by
                                                           providing the connection
client = pulsar.Client('pulsar://localhost:6650')   ◁──┘  URL to the Pulsar broker.

consumer = client.subscribe(        ◁──┐  Use the Pulsar client to
                                        │  create a consumer.
```

```
            'persistent://public/default/my-topic',        ◁────────┐  You must specify the topic
            'my-subscription',                        ◁─────────┐    │  you want to consume from.
            consumer_type=pulsar.ConsumerType.Exclusive         └────┘
            initial_position=pulsar.InitialPosition.Latest,        You must specify the unique
            message_listener=None,                                 name of your subscription.
            negative_ack_redelivery_delay_ms=60000)
```

```
                                                      Wait for a new
while True:                                           message to arrive.
    msg = consumer.receive()       ◁───┘                                  Once we have
    try:                                                                  successfully
        print("Received message '%s' id='%s'",                           processed
                msg.data().decode('utf-8'), msg.message_id())            the message,
        consumer.acknowledge(msg)                           ◁───────┘    acknowledge it.
    except:
        consumer.negative_acknowledge(msg)   ◁───┐
                                                 │   If we encountered an error, send a
client.close()      ◁────  Close the client.          negative acknowledgment to have
                                                      the message resent.
```

The subscribe method will attempt to connect the consumer to the topic using the specified subscription, which may fail if the subscription already exists and it isn't one of the shared subscription types (e.g., you attempt to connect to an exclusive subscription that already has an active consumer). If you are connecting to the topic for the first time using the specified subscription name, a subscription is created for you automatically. Whenever a new subscription is created, it is initially positioned at the end of the topic by default, and consumers on that subscription will begin reading the first message created after the subscription was created. If you are connecting to a preexisting subscription, it will begin reading from the earliest unacknowledged message within the subscription, as we saw earlier in figure 3.2.

As you can see in listing 3.22, the Python library provides several different configuration options when specifying the subscription, including the subscription type, starting position, and others. I highly recommend that you view the available online documentation (https://pulsar.apache.org/api/python/2.8.0-SNAPSHOT/) for the Python client to see the most up-to-date listing of these options.

The message consumer shown in listing 3.22 processes the messages in a synchronous manner because the receive() method it is using to retrieve messages is a blocking method (e.g., it waits indefinitely for a new message to arrive). A better approach is to process these messages in an asynchronous manner, as shown in listing 3.23. Using the listener pattern allows you to separate the business logic from the management of the threads because the Pulsar consumer automatically creates a thread pool for running the message listener instances and handles all the threading logic for you.

Listing 3.23 Asynchronous message processing in Python

```
import pulsar                          The listener function needs
                                       to accept the consumer and
def my_listener(consumer, msg):    ◁──┘ the message.
    # process message
    print("my_listener read message '%s' id='%s'",
```

```
        msg.data().decode('utf-8'), msg.message_id())   ◁──────┐      We can access the
    consumer.acknowledge(msg)                              ◁────┤      message contents.
                                                                │
client = pulsar.Client('pulsar://localhost:6650')              │      We can use the consumer to
                                                                       acknowledge the message.
consumer = client.subscribe(
    'persistent://public/default/my-topic',
    'my-subscription',
    consumer_type=pulsar.ConsumerType.Exclusive,
    initial_position=pulsar.InitialPosition.Latest,
    message_listener=my_listener,                 ◁───┐   Sets a message listener
    negative_ack_redelivery_delay_ms=60000)            │   for the consumer

    client.close()
```

PULSAR READERS IN PYTHON

The Python client also provides a reader interface that enables consumers to manage the position from which they will consume messages. When you connect to a topic using a reader, you must specify which message the reader will begin consuming messages from when it connects to the topic. If you choose to explicitly provide a message ID, then your application will be responsible for knowing this message ID in advance and should store that information in a persistent data store somewhere such as a database or cache. The code shown in the following listing connects to the topic, starts reading messages from the earliest available messages, and outputs their contents.

Listing 3.24   Creating a Pulsar reader in Python

```
import pulsar                                              Create a Pulsar client by
                                                           providing the connection
client = pulsar.Client('pulsar://localhost:6650')   ◁──── URL to the Pulsar broker.

reader = client.create_reader(                             Use the Pulsar client to create a
    'persistent://public/default/my-topic',   ◁────────── reader on the specified topic.
    pulsar.MessageId.earliest)          ◁────┐
                                              │            Specify that we want to read
while True:                                   │            from the earliest message.
    msg = reader.read_next()
    print("Read message '%s' id='%s'",
        msg.data().decode('utf-8'), msg.message_id())
```

Read the messages.

```
client.close()      ◁────── Close the client.
```

3.3.3   *The Pulsar Go client*

There is also an officially supported Pulsar client for the Golang programming language, and the latest version of the Pulsar client library can be installed using the following command: go get -u "github.com/apache/pulsar-client-go/pulsar". Once you have installed the Pulsar client libraries, you can start using them to interact with Pulsar by creating producers and consumers inside your Go code.

CREATING A PULSAR CLIENT WITH GO

When a Go application wants to create either a producer or a consumer, you first need to instantiate a client object, using code like the following listing. In this code, you will provide the URL of the Pulsar broker along with any other connection configuration information that may be required, such as security credentials.

Listing 3.25 Creating a Pulsar client in Go

```
import (
    "log"
    "time"
    "github.com/apache/pulsar-client-go/pulsar"     ◁──┘   Import the Pulsar
)                                                          client library.

func main() {
    client, err := pulsar.NewClient(          The client options, including the
    pulsar.ClientOptions{          ◁──┘       broker URL, connection timeout, etc.
        URL:                  "pulsar://localhost:6650",
        OperationTimeout:     30 * time.Second,
        ConnectionTimeout:    30 * time.Second,
    })                                          Check to see if the client
                                                was able to connect.
    if err != nil {                 ◁──┘
        log.Fatalf("Could not instantiate Pulsar client: %v", err)
    }

    defer client.Close()
}
```

Create a new client using the specified client options.

The client object handles all the low-level details involved in creating a connection to the Pulsar broker, including automatic retries and connection security if the Pulsar broker has TLS configured. Client instances are thread safe and can be reused for creating and managing multiple producers and consumers. Once you have created a client, you can use it to create producers, consumers, and readers.

PULSAR PRODUCERS IN GO

As you can see from listing 3.26, after you have created a client object, you can use it to create a producer on any topic you choose. While there are several configuration options for a Pulsar producer described in the online documentation (https://pkg.go .dev/github.com/apache/pulsar-client-go/pulsar#ConsumerOptions), I wanted to highlight the delayed message delivery configuration we used in this example, which allows us to defer delivery of the messages to the topic consumers for a specified amount of time.

Listing 3.26 Creating a Pulsar producer in Go

```
import (
    "context"
    "fmt"
```

```go
        "log"
        "time"

        "github.com/apache/pulsar-client-go/pulsar"        Import the Pulsar
)                                                          client library.


func main() {
    ...                Code that creates the Pulsar client
    producer, err := client.CreateProducer(pulsar.ProducerOptions{
       Topic: topicName,
    })                           Create a new producer for the specified topic.


    ctx := context.Background()
    deliveryTime := (time.Minute * time.Duration(1)) +     Calculate the delivery time
          (time.Second * time.Duration(30))                you want for the message.


    for i := 0; i < 3; i++ {
       msg := pulsar.ProducerMessage{        Create the message to send.
            Payload: []byte(fmt.Sprintf("Delayed-messageId-%d", i)),
            Key: "message-key",
            Properties: map[string]string{
              "delayed": "90sec",                The Go client supports providing
            },                                    both key and properties metadata.
            EventTime: time.Now(),
            DeliverAfter: deliveryTime,           Specify the delivery
        }                                         time for the message.

      messageID, err := producer.Send(ctx, &msg)
        ...                                       Send the message.
    }
}
```

Provide the event timestamp metadata.

Delayed message delivery is useful if you do not want the message to be immediately processed but, rather, processed at a future point in time. Consider the scenario where you receive several messages that contain new subscriptions to your company's newsletter, which contains daily specials and promotions. Rather than immediately sending these customers the previous day's flier, you want to wait until the new edition is available. So, if your marketing team has committed to having a fresh version of the newsletter available every morning at 9 a.m., you can delay the message delivery until after 9 a.m. to ensure the customers get the latest version of the newsletter.

PULSAR CONSUMERS

As we have seen, the consumer interface is used to listen on a specific topic and process the incoming messages. After a message has been successfully processed, an acknowledgment should be sent back to the broker to indicate that we are done processing the message within the subscription. This allows the broker to know which message in the topic needs to be delivered to the next consumer on the subscription. In Go, you can create a consumer by specifying a topic and a subscription, as shown in listing 3.27.

The message consumer shown in listing 3.27 processes the messages in a synchronous manner because the `receive()` method that it is using to retrieve messages is a blocking method (e.g., it waits indefinitely for a new message to arrive). Unlike the previous two client libraries I have discussed, the Go client doesn't currently support asynchronous message consumption using the message listener pattern. Therefore, if you want to perform asynchronous processing, you will need to write all the threading logic yourself.

Listing 3.27 Creating a Pulsar consumer in Go

```
import (
    "context"
    "fmt"
    "log"
    "time"

    "github.com/apache/pulsar-client-go/pulsar"        ⊲─── Import the Pulsar
)                                                           client library.

func main() {         ┌── Code that creates
    ...               └── the Pulsar client                      Create a new
                                                                 consumer for the
  consumer, err := client.Subscribe(pulsar.ConsumerOptions{  ⊲── specified topic.
    Topic:            topicName,
    SubscriptionName: subscriptionName,
  })

  if err != nil {
    log.Fatal(err)
  }
                                                             Blocking call to receive
  for {                                                      incoming messages
    msg, err := consumer.Receive(ontext.Background())  ⊲──┘
    if err != nil {
        log.Fatal(err)        ┌── Send a negative acknowledgment
        consumer.Nack(msg)  ⊲─┘  to have the message redelivered.
    } else {
      fmt.Printf("Received message : %v\n", string(msg.Payload()))
    }                   ┌── Acknowledge the message so it
    consumer.Ack(msg)  ⊲┘  can be marked as processed.
  }
}
```

The subscribe method will attempt to connect the consumer to the topic using the specified subscription, which may fail if the subscription already exists, and it isn't one of the shared subscription types (e.g., you attempt to connect to an exclusive subscription that already has an active consumer). If you are connecting to the topic for the first time using the specified subscription name, a subscription is created for you automatically. Whenever a new subscription is created, it is initially positioned at the end of the topic by default, and consumers on that subscription will begin reading the first message created after the subscription was created. If you are connecting to a preexisting subscription, it will begin reading from the earliest unacknowledged message within the subscription, as we saw earlier in figure 3.2.

As you can see from listing 3.27, the Go library provides several different configuration options when specifying the subscription, including the subscription type, starting position, and others. I highly recommend you view the available online documentation (https://pkg.go.dev/github.com/apache/pulsar-client-go/pulsar) for the Go client to view the most up-to-date listing of these options.

PULSAR READERS

The Go client also provides a reader interface that enables consumers to manage the position from which they will consume messages. When you connect to a topic using a reader, you must specify which message the reader will begin consuming messages from when it connects to the topic. If you choose to explicitly provide a message ID, then your application will be responsible for knowing this message ID in advance and should store that information in a persistent data store somewhere, such as in a database or cache. The code shown in the following listing connects to the topic, starts reading messages from the earliest available messages, and outputs their contents.

Listing 3.28   Creating a Pulsar reader in Go

```go
import (
    "context"
    "fmt"
    "log"
    "time"

    "github.com/apache/pulsar-client-go/pulsar"        // Import the Pulsar client library.
)

func main() {                                           // Code that creates the Pulsar client
    ...

  reader, err := client.CreateReader(pulsar.ReaderOptions{    // Create a new reader for the specified topic.
    Topic:          topicName,
    StartMessageID: pulsar.EarliestMessageID(),         // Start at the earliest message available.
  })

  for {
    msg, err := reader.Next(context.Background())       // Read the next message.
    if err != nil {
      log.Fatal(err)
    } else {
      fmt.Printf("Received message : %v\n", string(msg.Payload()))
    }
  }
}
```

3.4 Advanced administration

Pulsar acts as a black box from a producer or consumer perspective (i.e., you simply connect to the cluster to send and receive messages). While it is good to have the implementation details hidden from the end user, this can be problematic when you need to troubleshoot issues with the message delivery itself. For instance, if your consumer isn't receiving any messages, how do you go about diagnosing the issue? Fortunately, the `pulsar-admin` CLI tool provides some tools that give you deeper insights into the inner workings of the Pulsar cluster.

3.4.1 Persistent topic metrics

Internally, Pulsar collects a lot of topic-level metrics that can help you diagnose and troubleshoot issues between your producers and consumers, such as your consumer not receiving any messages, or backpressure when consumers cannot keep pace with your producers, which would be reflected in the unacknowledged message count growing. You can access these topic statistics from the `pulsar-admin` CLI tool we used earlier to create the tenant, namespace, and topic by issuing the command shown in the following listing.

Listing 3.29 Retrieving Pulsar topic statistics from the command-line

The sum of all local and replication consumers' dispatch rates in messages per second

The sum of all local and replication publishers' rates in bytes per second

The sum of all local and replication publishers' rates in messages per second

The name of the topic we want statistics from

```
$docker exec -it pulsar /pulsar/bin/pulsar-admin topics stats
  persistent://manning/chapter03/example-topic
{
  "msgRateIn" : 137.49506548471038,
  "msgThroughputIn" : 13741.401370605108,
  "msgRateOut" : 97.63210798236112,
  "msgThroughputOut" : 9716.05449008063,
  "bytesInCounter" : 1162174,
  "msgInCounter" : 11538,
  "bytesOutCounter" : 150009,
  "msgOutCounter" : 1500,
  "averageMsgSize" : 99.94105113636364,
  "msgChunkPublished" : false,
  "storageSize" : 1161944,
  "backlogSize" : 1161279,
  "publishers" : [ {
    "msgRateIn" : 137.49506548471038,
    "msgThroughputIn" : 13741.401370605108,
    "averageMsgSize" : 99.0,
    "chunkedMessageRate" : 0.0,
    "producerId" : 0,
    "metadata" : { },
    "producerName" : "standalone-12-6",
    "connectedSince" : "2020-09-07T20:44:45.514Z",
```

The sum of all local and replication consumers' dispatch rates in bytes per second

The total number of messages published to the topic

The total number of messages consumed from the topic

The total amount of disk space used to store the topic messages in bytes

Total rate of messages published by the publisher in messages per second

Timestamp of when the publisher first connected to the topic

```
          "clientVersion" : "2.6.1",
          "address" : "/172.17.0.1:40158"          A list of all the subscriptions for the topic
        } ],
        "subscriptions" : {
The IP      "my-sub" : {                            Total rate of messages delivered on
address of    "msgRateOut" : 97.63210798236112,     this subscription in bytes per second
the producer  "msgThroughputOut" : 9716.05449008063,
              "bytesOutCounter" : 150009,           Total number of messages
              "msgOutCounter" : 1500,               delivered on this subscription
              "msgRateRedeliver" : 0.0,
              "chuckedMessageRate" : 0,             Number of messages in the
              "msgBacklog" : 9458,                  subscription backlog that
              "msgBacklogNoDelayed" : 9458,         haven't been delivered yet
              "blockedSubscriptionOnUnackedMsgs" : false,
              "msgDelayed" : 0,
              "unackedMessages" : 923,              Number of messages that have
              "type" : "Shared",                    been delivered but haven't been
              "msgRateExpired" : 0.0,               acknowledged yet
              "lastExpireTimestamp" : 0,
              "lastConsumedFlowTimestamp" : 1599511537220,
              "lastConsumedTimestamp" : 1599511537452,   Timestamp of when the last
              "lastAckedTimestamp" : 1599511545269,      message was consumed on
              "consumers" : [ {                           this subscription
                "msgRateOut" : 97.63210798236112,
                "msgThroughputOut" : 9716.05449008063,   Timestamp of when the last
                "bytesOutCounter" : 150009,              message acknowledgment was
                "msgOutCounter" : 1500,                  received on this subscription
                "msgRateRedeliver" : 0.0,
                "chuckedMessageRate" : 0.0,
                "consumerName" : "5bf2b",
                "availablePermits" : 0,
                "unackedMessages" : 923,
                "avgMessagesPerEntry" : 6,
                "blockedConsumerOnUnackedMsgs" : false,   Whether or not the consumer
                "lastAckedTimestamp" : 1599511545269,     is blocked due to too many
                "lastConsumedTimestamp" : 1599511537452,  unacknowledged messages
                "metadata" : { },
                "connectedSince" : "2020-09-07T20:44:45.512Z",
                "clientVersion" : "2.6.1",
                "address" : "/172.17.0.1:40160"     The IP address of
              } ],                                  the consumer
              "isDurable" : true,
              "isReplicated" : false
            },
            "example-sub" : {
              "msgRateOut" : 0.0,                   Indicative of a subscription
              "msgThroughputOut" : 0.0,             without any active consumers
              "bytesOutCounter" : 0,
              "msgOutCounter" : 0,
              "msgRateRedeliver" : 0.0,
              "chuckedMessageRate" : 0,             Number of messages in
              "msgBacklog" : 11528,                 the subscription backlog
              "msgBacklogNoDelayed" : 11528,
              "blockedSubscriptionOnUnackedMsgs" : false,
              "msgDelayed" : 0,
```

```
      "unackedMessages" : 0,
      "type" : "Exclusive",
      "msgRateExpired" : 0.0,
      "lastExpireTimestamp" : 0,
      "lastConsumedFlowTimestamp" : 1599509925751,
      "lastConsumedTimestamp" : 0,
      "lastAckedTimestamp" : 0,
      "consumers" : [ ],
      "isDurable" : true,
      "isReplicated" : false
    }
  },
  "replication" : { },
  "deduplicationStatus" : "Disabled"
}
```

As you can see, Pulsar collects an extensive set of metrics for each persistent topic, which can be very useful when attempting to diagnose an issue. The metrics returned include the connected producers and consumers along with all the message production and consumption rates, message backlog, and subscriptions. Therefore, if you are trying to determine why a particular consumer isn't receiving messages, you can verify that the consumer is connected and look at the message consumption rate for its corresponding subscription.

All these metrics are published to Prometheus by default and can be easily viewed through a Grafana dashboard that comes bundled with the Pulsar Kubernetes deployment defined in a Helm chart inside the open source project. You can configure any observability tool that works with Prometheus as well.

3.4.2 Message inspection

Sometimes you may want to view the contents of a particular message or group of messages within a Pulsar topic. Consider the scenario where one of the message producers changes the output format of its messages by encrypting the message contents. Consumers that are currently subscribed to the topic would suddenly start encountering exceptions when they attempt to process these encrypted contents, which would result in the messages not getting acknowledged. Eventually, these messages would accumulate on the topic, since they never get acknowledged. If the change to the producer code was not coordinated with you, then you will be unaware of the underlying issue. Fortunately, you can use the `peek-messages` command of the `pulsar-admin` CLI tool to view the raw bytes of the messages inside a given subscription, as shown in the following listing, which shows the syntax for peeking at the last 10 messages for the subscription `example-sub` on the `persistent://manning/chapter03/example-topic`.

> **Listing 3.30 Peeking at messages inside Pulsar**

```
$ docker exec -it pulsar /pulsar/bin/pulsar-admin \
  Topic peek-messages \
  --count 10 \              ⟵——— Request the last 10 messages.
```

```
  --subscription example-sub \
  persistent://manning/chapter03/example-topic


Batch Message ID: 19460:9:0   ◁——— The message ID
Tenants:
{
  "X-Pulsar-num-batch-message" : "1",
  "publish-time" : "2020-09-07T20:20:13.136Z"  ◁—┐  The time the message was
}                                                  published by the producer

          +-------------------------------------------------+
          | 0  1  2  3  4  5  6  7  8  9  a  b  c  d  e  f |
+--------+-------------------------------------------------+----------------+
|00000000| 7b 69 64 3a 20 31 30 2c 20 74 69 6d 65 3a 20 4d |{id: 10, time: M|
|00000010| 6f 6e 20 53 65 70 20 30 37 20 31 33 3a 32 30 3a |on Sep 07 13:20:|
|00000020| 31 33 20 50 44 54 20 32 30 32 30 7d             |13 PDT 2020}    |
+--------+-------------------------------------------------+----------------+
```

The message contents in raw bytes

As you can see, the `peek-messages` command provides many details about the message, including the message ID, publish time, and the message contents as raw bytes (and as a String). This information should make it easier to determine the issue with the message contents.

Summary

- Docker is an open source container framework that allows you to bundle entire applications into a single image and publish them for reuse.
- There is a completely self-contained Docker image of Pulsar that you can use to run Pulsar on your machine for development.
- Pulsar provides command-line tools that can be used to administer tenants, namespaces, and topics, including creating, listing, and deleting them.
- Pulsar provides client libraries for several popular programming languages, including Java, Python, and Go, that allow you to create Pulsar producers, consumers, and readers.
- You can use Pulsar's command-line tools to retrieve topic statistics that are useful for monitoring and troubleshooting.

Part 2

Apache Pulsar development essentials

Part 2 focuses on Pulsar's built-in serverless computing framework, known as Pulsar Functions, and how it can be used to provide stream processing capabilities without requiring an additional computational framework, such as Apache Flink or Kafka Streams. This type of serverless stream processing is also referred to as *stream-native processing* and has a broad range of applications—from real-time ETL and event-driven programming to microservices development and real-time machine learning.

After covering the basics of the Pulsar Functions framework, I spend a good amount of time focusing on how to properly secure your Pulsar cluster to ensure that all your data is kept safely away from prying eyes. Lastly, I wrap up the section with an introduction to Pulsar's schema registry, which helps you retain information about the structure of the messages being held inside your Pulsar topics in a central location.

Chapter 4 introduces Pulsar's stream-native computing framework, called Pulsar Functions, provides some background on its design and configuration, and shows you how to develop, test, and deploy the individual functions. Chapter 5 introduces Pulsar's connector framework, which is designed to move between Apache Pulsar and external storage systems, such as relational databases, key-value stores, or blob storage. It teaches you how to develop a connector in a step-by-step fashion.

In chapter 6, I provide step-by-step instructions on how to secure your Pulsar cluster to ensure that your data is safe while it is in transit and at rest. Finally, chapter 7 covers Pulsar's built-in schema registry, why it is necessary, and how it can help simplify microservice development. We also cover the schema evolution process and how to update the schemas used inside your Pulsar functions.

Pulsar functions

This chapter covers

- An introduction to the Pulsar Functions framework
- The Pulsar Functions programming model and API
- Writing your first Pulsar function in Java
- Configuring, submitting, and monitoring a Pulsar function

In our previous chapter, we looked at how you can work with Pulsar using some of the various client libraries. In this chapter, we will look at a stream-native processing engine known as Pulsar Functions that makes the development of Pulsar-based applications much simpler. This lightweight processing framework automatically handles a lot of the boilerplate coding required to set up Pulsar consumers and producers, allowing you to focus on the processing logic itself, rather than the consumption and processing of the messages.

4.1 Stream processing

While there isn't an official definition, the term *stream processing* generally refers to the processing of unbounded datasets that stream in continuously from some source system. There are several datasets that occur naturally as continuous streams, such as sensor events, user activity on a website, and financial trades, which can be processed in this manner.

Prior to stream processing, these datasets had to first be stored in a database, file system, or other persistent storage before they could be analyzed. Often, there was an additional data processing phase required to extract the information, transform it into the correct format, and load the data into these systems. Only after the ETL process was completed was the data ready to be analyzed using traditional SQL-based or other tools. As you can imagine, there was a significant latency between the time an event occurred and when it was available for analysis. The goal of stream processing is to minimize that latency so critical business decisions can be made against the most recent data. There are three basic approaches to processing these datasets—batch processing, micro-batching, and streaming-native processing—and each take different approaches regarding how and when to process these endless datasets.

4.1.1   Traditional batching

Historically, the vast majority of data processing frameworks have been designed for batch processing. Traditional data warehouses, Hadoop, and Spark are just a few common examples of systems that process large datasets in batches. Data is often fed into these systems via long-running and complex ETL pipelines that cleanse, prepare, and format the incoming data for consumption. Messaging systems often serve as little more than intermediate buffers that store and route the data between the various processing stages of the pipeline.

These long-running data ingestion pipelines were often implemented using stream processing engines, such as Apache Spark or Flink, that were designed to process large datasets efficiently by performing the processing in parallel. Newly arriving data elements were collected and then processed together at some point in the future as a batch. To maximize the throughput of these frameworks, the accumulation would take place over very large time intervals (hours) or until a certain amount of data (10s GBs) had been collected, which introduced an artificial delay in the data processing pipeline.

4.1.2   Micro-batching

One technique that was introduced to address the processing latency that plagued these traditional batch processing engines was to dramatically reduce either the batch size or the processing interval. In micro-batch processing, newly arriving data elements are still collected into batches, as shown in figure 4.1, but the size of the batches is dramatically reduced by adjusting the time interval to a few seconds. Even though the processing may occur more frequently, the data is still processed one batch at a time, so it is often referred to as micro-batching and is used by such processing frameworks as Spark Streaming.

While this approach does decrease the processing latency between when a data element arrives and when it is processed, it still introduces artificial delays into the process

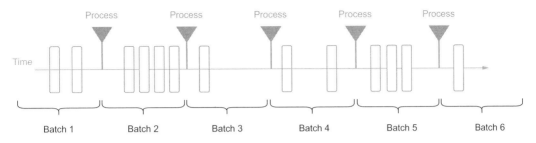

Figure 4.1 With batch processing, the message processing occurs at predetermined intervals and follows a consistent cadence.

that compound as the complexity of the data pipeline increases. Consequently, even micro-batch processing applications cannot rely on consistent response times and need to account for delays between when the data arrives and when it is processed. This makes micro-batch processing more appropriate for use cases that do not require having the most recent data and can tolerate slower response times, whereas stream native processing is better suited for use cases that require near real-time responsiveness, such as fraud detection, real-time pricing, and system monitoring.

4.1.3 Stream native processing

With stream native processing, each new piece of data is processed as soon as it arrives, as illustrated in figure 4.2. Unlike batch processing, there are no arbitrary processing intervals, and each individual data element is processed separately.

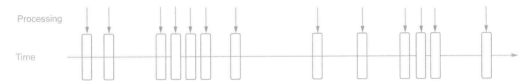

Figure 4.2 With stream processing, the processing is triggered by the arrival of each message, so the processing cadence is irregular and unpredictable.

Although it may seem as though the differences between stream processing and micro-batching are just a matter of timing, there are implications for both the data processing systems and the applications that rely on them. The business value of data decreases rapidly after it is created, particularly in use cases such as fraud prevention or anomaly detection. The high-volume, high-velocity datasets used to feed these use cases often contain valuable, but perishable, insights that must be acted upon immediately. A fraudulent business transaction, such as transferring money or downloading licensed software, must be identified and acted upon before the transaction completes; otherwise it will be too late to prevent the thief from obtaining the funds illegally. To maximize the value of their data for these use cases, developers must fundamentally change their approach to processing real-time data by focusing on reducing the processing latency introduced from traditional batch processing frameworks and utilizing a more reactive approach, such as stream-native processing.

4.2   *What is Pulsar Functions?*

Included with Apache Pulsar is a lightweight computing engine named Pulsar Functions, which allows developers to deploy a simple function implementation in Java, Python, or Golang. This feature allows users to enjoy the benefits of serverless computing similar to those provided by AWS Lambda within an open source messaging platform, rather than being tied to a cloud provider's proprietary API.

Pulsar Functions allows you to apply processing logic to data as it is routed through the messaging system itself. These lightweight compute processes execute natively within the Pulsar messaging system itself as close to the message as they can be and without the need for another processing framework such as Spark, Flink, or Kafka Streams. Unlike other messaging systems, which act as "dumb pipes" for moving data from system to system, Pulsar Functions provides the capability to perform simple computations on messages before they are routed to consumers. Pulsar Functions consumes messages from one or more Pulsar topics, applies a user-supplied function (processing logic) to each incoming message, and publishes the results to one or more Pulsar topics, as shown in figure 4.3.

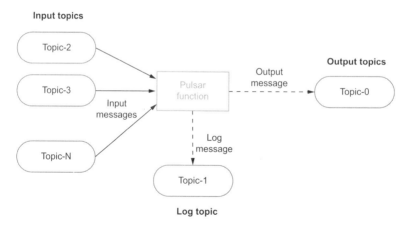

Figure 4.3   Pulsar Functions executes user-defined code on data published to Pulsar topics.

Pulsar functions can be best characterized as Lambda-style functions that are specifically designed to use Pulsar as the underlying message bus. This is because they take several design cues from the popular AWS Lambda framework that allows you to run code without provisioning or managing servers to host the code. Hence, the common term for this programming model is *serverless*.

The Pulsar function framework allows users to develop self-contained pieces of code and then deploy them with a simple REST call. Pulsar takes care of the underlying details required to run your code, including creating the Pulsar consumer and producers for the function's input and output topics. Developers can focus on the business logic itself and not have to worry about the boilerplate code necessary to send messages with Pulsar. In short, the Pulsar Functions framework provides a ready-made computing infrastructure on your existing Pulsar cluster.

4.2.1 Programming model

The programming model behind Pulsar Functions is very straightforward. Pulsar functions receive messages from one or more *input* topics, and every time a message is published to the topic, the function code is executed. Upon being triggered, the function code executes its processing logic upon the incoming message and writes its (optional) output to an *output* topic. Although all functions are required to have an input topic, they are not strictly required to produce any output to an output topic.

It is possible to have the output topic of one Pulsar function be the input topic of another, allowing us to effectively create a *directly acyclic graph* (DAG) of the Pulsar functions, as shown in figure 4.4. In such a graph, each edge represents a flow of data, and each vertex represents a Pulsar function that applies the user-defined logic to process the data. The combinations of Pulsar functions into these DAGs are endless, and it is possible to write an application that is entirely composed of Pulsar functions and structured as a DAG if you so choose.

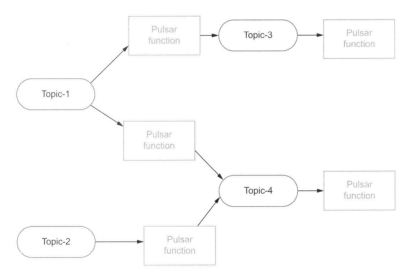

Figure 4.4 Pulsar functions can be logically structured into a processing network.

4.3   *Developing Pulsar functions*

Pulsar functions can currently be written in Java, Python, and Go. Therefore, if you are already familiar with any of these popular languages, you will be able to develop Pulsar functions relatively quickly.

4.3.1   *Language native functions*

Pulsar supports what are commonly referred to as *language-native functions*, which means no Pulsar-specific libraries or special dependencies are required. The benefit of language-native functions is that they don't have any dependencies beyond what's already available in the programming language itself, which makes them extremely lightweight and easy to develop. Currently, language-native functions can only be developed using Java or Python. Golang support for this feature is not yet available.

JAVA LANGUAGE NATIVE FUNCTIONS

In order for a piece of Java code to be used as a language-native function, it must implement the `java.util.Function` interface, which has just a single apply method, as shown in listing 4.1. While this simplistic function merely echoes back any string value it receives, it does demonstrate just how easy it is to develop a function using only features of the Java language itself. Any sort of complex logic can be included inside the apply method to provide more robust stream-processing capabilities.

Listing 4.1   Java-native function

```
import java.util.Function;

public class EchoFunction implements Function    ◁──  Specifies that the input topic
  <String, String> {                                  content will be a string and
                                                      that we will return a string
    public String apply(String input) {    ◁──
      return input;                              The only method defined in the
}                                                function interface, which is executed
}                                                when a message is received
```

PYTHON LANGUAGE-NATIVE FUNCTIONS

For a piece of Python code to be used as a language-native function, it must have a method named `process`, like the functions shown in the following listing, that merely appends an exclamation point to any string value it receives.

Listing 4.2   Python-native function

```
                              The method that gets called
                              when a message arrives
                                                           Returns the provided input
  ⌊▷ def process(input):                                    with an exclamation point
        return "{}!".format(input)    ◁──                   appended to the end
```

As you can see, the language-native approach provides a clean, API-free way of writing Pulsar functions. It is ideal for the development of simple, stateless functions.

4.3.2 *The Pulsar SDK*

Another option is to develop your functions using the Pulsar Functions SDK, which leverages Pulsar-specific libraries that provide a range of functionality not available in the native interfaces, such as state management and user configuration. Additional capabilities and information can be accessed through a `Context` object that is defined inside the SDK, including

- The name, version, and ID of the Pulsar function
- The message ID of each message
- The name of the topic on which the message was sent
- The names of all input topics as well as the output topic associated with the function
- The tenant and namespace associated with the function
- The logger object used by the function, which can be used to write log messages
- Access to arbitrary user config values supplied via the CLI
- An interface for recording metrics

An implementation of the Pulsar SDK is available for Java, Python, and Golang, and each specifies a functional interface that includes the `Context` object as a parameter that is populated and provided by the Pulsar Functions runtime environment.

JAVA SDK FUNCTIONS

To get started developing Pulsar functions using the Java SDK, you'll need to add a dependency on the `pulsar-functions-api` artifact to your project, as shown in the following listing.

> **Listing 4.3 Adding Pulsar SDK dependencies to you pom.xml file**

```
<properties>
    <pulsar.version>2.7.2</pulsar.version>
</properties>

...
<dependency>
    <groupId>org.apache.pulsar</groupId>
    <artifactId>pulsar-functions-api</artifactId>
    <version>${pulsar.version}</version>
</dependency>
```

When you are developing a Pulsar function that is based on the SDK, the function should implement the `org.apache.pulsar.functions.api.Function` interface. As you can see from the following listing, this interface specifies only one method that you need to implement, called `process`.

> **Listing 4.4   The Pulsar SDK function interface definition**

```
@FunctionalInterface
public interface Function<I, O> {
  O process(I input, Context context) throws Exception;
}
```

The process method is called at least once, depending on the processing guarantees you specify for the function for every message that is published to the configured input topic of the function. The incoming input bytes are serialized to the input type I for JSON-based messages as well as simple Java types, such as String, Integer, and Float. If these types do not meet your needs, you can also use your own types as long as you provide your own implementation of the org.apache.pulsar.functions.api.SerDe interface for the type, or you can register the incoming message type in the Pulsar schema registry, which I will cover in greater detail in chapter 7. An implementation of the echo function that demonstrates several different features of the SDK, such as logging and recording metrics, is shown in the following listing.

> **Listing 4.5   Pulsar SDK function in Java**

The class must implement the Pulsar Functions interface.

```
import java.util.stream.Collectors;
import org.apache.pulsar.functions.api.Context;
import org.apache.pulsar.functions.api.Function;
import org.slf4j.Logger;
```

The interface defines a single method with two parameters, including a context object.

```
public class EchoFunction implements Function<String, String> {

    public String process(String input, Context ctx) {
        Logger LOG = ctx.getLogger();
        String inputTopics =
          ctx.getInputTopics().stream()
            .collect(Collectors.joining(", "));

        String functionName = ctx.getFunctionName();

        String logMessage =
            String.format("A message with a value of \"%s\"" +
                "has arrived on one of the following topics: %s\n",
                input, inputTopics);

        LOG.info(logMessage);
        String metricName =
            String.format("function-%s-messages-received", functionName);

        ctx.recordMetric(metricName, 1);
        return input;
    }
}
```

We use the context object to get the list of input topics.

We use the context object to access the LOGGER object.

We use the context object to get the function name.

We generate a log message.

We record a user-defined metric.

The Java SDK's context object enables you to access key/value pairs provided to the Pulsar function via the command line (as JSON). This feature allows you to write generic functions that can be used multiple times but with a slightly different configuration. For instance, let's say you want to write a function that filters events based on a user-defined regular expression. When an event arrives, the contents are compared to the configured regex, and those entries that match the provided pattern are returned, and all others are ignored. Such a function could be useful if you want to verify the format of the incoming data before you begin processing it. An example of such a function that accesses the regular expression from the key/value pairs in the context object is shown in the following listing.

Listing 4.6   User-configured Pulsar function in Java

```java
import java.util.regex.Pattern;
import org.apache.pulsar.functions.api.Context;
import org.apache.pulsar.functions.api.Function;

public class RegexMatcherFunction implements Function<String, String> {

    public static final String REGEX_CONFIG = "regex-pattern";

    @Override
    public String process(String input, Context ctx) throws Exception {
        Optional<Object> config =
            ctx.getUserConfigValue(REGEX_CONFIG);          ◁——— Retrieve the regex
                                                                pattern from the user-
        if (config.isPresent() && config.get().getClass()      provided configs.
            .getName().equals(String.class.getName())) {

            Pattern pattern = Pattern.compile(config.get().toString());
            if (pattern.matcher(input).matches()) {
                String metricName =
                    String.format("%s-regex-matches",ctx.getFunctionName());

                ctx.recordMetric(metricName, 1);
                return input;
            }
        }
        return null;      ◁——— Otherwise, return null.
    }
}
```

If a regex string was provided, then compile the regex.

If the input matches the regex, allow it to pass.

Pulsar Functions can publish results to an output topic, but this isn't required. You can also have functions that don't always return a value, such as the function in listing 4.5 that filters out non-matching inputs. In such a scenario, you can simply return a value of `null` from the function.

PYTHON SDK FUNCTIONS

To get started developing Pulsar functions using the Python SDK, you'll need to add the Pulsar client dependency to your Python installation. The latest version of the Pulsar client library can be easily installed using the pip package manager and the commands shown in the following listing. Once this is installed on your local development environment, you will be able to start developing Pulsar functions in Python that leverage the SDK.

Listing 4.7   Adding Pulsar SDK dependencies to your Python environment

```
pip3 install pulsar-client==2.6.3 –user    ◁——— Install the Pulsar client.

pip3 list     ◁——— List all the packages.

Package       Version
------------- ---------           Confirm that the correct
...                               version of the Pulsar client
pulsar-client 2.6.3    ◁———┘      has been installed.
```

Let's look at a Python-based implementation of the Echo function to demonstrate some of the SDK capabilities in the following listing.

Listing 4.8   Pulsar SDK function in Python

```
from pulsar import Function

class EchoFunction(Function):
    def __init__(self):
        pass

    def process(self, input, context):    ◁——— The function definition required by the Pulsar SDK
        logger = context.get_logger()
        evtTime = context.get_message_eventtime()
        msgKey = context.get_message_key();    ◁——— The Python SDK provides access to message metadata.

        logger.info("""A message with a value of {0}, a key of {1},
          and an event time of {2} was received"""
            .format(input, msgKey, evtTime))

        metricName = """function-%s-
          messages-received""".format(context.get_function_name())
        context.record_metric(metricName, 1)

        return input    ◁——— Echo back the original input value.
```

The Python SDK provides access to the logger.

The Python SDK supports metrics.

The Python SDK's context object provides nearly all the same capabilities as the Java SDK, with two notable exceptions. The first is that, as of version 2.6.0, Python-based Pulsar Functions does not support schemas, which I will discuss in greater detail in chapter 7; essentially this means that the Python function is responsible for the serialization and deserialization of the message bytes into the expected format. The second capability that is not present in Python-based Pulsar Functions is access to the Pulsar Admin API, which, as I discussed in chapter 3, is only available in Java.

GOLANG SDK FUNCTIONS

To get started developing Pulsar functions using the Golang SDK, you'll need to add the Pulsar client dependency to your Golang installation. The latest version of the pulsar client library can be installed using the following command: `go get -u "github.com/apache/pulsar-client-go/pulsar"`. Let's look at a Golang-based implementation of the Echo function that we used earlier to demonstrate some of the SDK capabilities in the following listing.

Listing 4.9 Pulsar SDK function in Go

```go
package main

import (
    "context"
    "fmt"

    "github.com/apache/pulsar/pulsar-function-go/pf"          ← Import the SDK library.

    log "github.com/apache/pulsar/pulsar-function-go/logutil"  ← Import the function logger library.
)

func echoFunc(ctx context.Context, in []byte) []byte {        ← The function code with the correct method signature
    if fc, ok := pf.FromContext(ctx); ok {
        log.Infof("This input has a length of: %d", len(in))   ← The Golang SDK provides access to the logger.

        fmt.Printf("Fully-qualified function name is:%s\\%s\\%s\n",   ← The Golang SDK provides access to function metadata.
            fc.GetFuncTenant(), fc.GetFuncNamespace(), fc. GetFuncName())
    }
    return in                                                 ← Echo back the original input value.
}

func main() {
    pf.Start(echoFunc)                                        ← Register the echofunc with the Pulsar Functions framework.
}
```

When writing Golang-based functions, remember that you need to provide the name of the function you wish to perform the actual logic to the `pf.Start()` method inside the `main()` method call, as shown in listing 4.8. This registers the function with the Pulsar Functions framework and ensures that the specified function is the one that is invoked when a new message arrives. In this case, we named used the `echoFunc` function, but it can be named anything, provided that the method signature matches any of the supported ones shown in the following listing. Any other function signatures will not be accepted, and consequently, no processing logic will be executed inside your Golang function.

Listing 4.10 Supported method signatures in Go

```go
func ()
func () error
func (input) error
```

```
func () (output, error)
func (input) (output, error)
func (context.Context) error
func (context.Context, input) error
func (context.Context) (output, error)
func (context.Context, input) (output, error)
```

There are currently some limitations when it comes to using the SDK to develop Golang-based Pulsar functions, but this is subject to change as the project matures, so I highly recommend checking the most recent version of the online documentation for the latest capabilities. However, as of the writing of this book, Golang functions do not support the recording of function-level metrics (e.g., there isn't a recordMetric method defined inside the context object of the Golang SDK). Furthermore, you cannot implement stateful functions using Golang at this time.

4.3.3   *Stateful functions*

Stateful functions utilize information gathered from previous messages they have processed to generate their output. One such application would be a function that receives temperature reading events from an IoT sensor and calculates the average temperature of the sensor. Providing this value would require us to calculate and store a running average of the previous temperature readings.

When using the Pulsar SDK to develop your functions, regardless of which of the three supported languages you are using, the second parameter in the process method is a Context object that is automatically provided by the Pulsar Functions framework. If you are using Java or Python, then the Context object's API also provides two separate mechanisms for retaining information between successive calls to a Pulsar function. The first mechanism that the Context API provides is a map interface for storing and retrieving key/value pairs via its putState and getState methods. These methods act like any other map interface you are familiar with and allow you to store and retrieve values of any type using string values as the keys.

The other state mechanisms provided by the Context object are counters, which only allow you to retain numeric values using strings as the keys. These counters are a specialized version of the key/value mapping that is functionally designed specifically for storing numerical values. Internally, counters are stored as 64-bit big-endian binary values and can only be changed via the incrCounter and incrCounterAsync methods.

Let's take a function that receives temperature reading events from an IoT sensor and calculates the average temperature of the sensor as an example to show how you would utilize state inside a Pulsar function. The function shown in listing 4.11 receives a sensor reading and compares it to the average temperature reading it has calculated from the previous reading to determine whether it should trigger an alarm of some sort.

Listing 4.11   Average sensor reading function

The function takes in a double and doesn't produce an output message.

```
  public class AvgSensorReadingFunction implements
└─▷  Function<Double, Void> {

      private static final String VALUES_KEY = "VALUES";

      @Override
      public Void process(Double input, Context ctx) throws Exception {
        CircularFifoQueue<Double> values = getValues(ctx);      ◁─────────

        if (Math.abs(input - getAverage(values)) > 10.0) {
          // trigger an alarm.                       ◁─────────
        }
        values.add(input);   ◁─────
        ctx.putState(VALUES_KEY, serialize(values));   ◁────
        return null;
      }

      private Double getAverage(CircularFifoQueue<Double> values) {
        return StreamSupport.stream(values.spliterator(), false)
          .collect(Collectors.summingDouble(Double::doubleValue))
          / values.size();   ◁─────
      }

      private CircularFifoQueue<Double> getValues(Context ctx) {
        if (ctx.getState(VALUES_KEY) == null) {
          return new CircularFifoQueue<Double>(100);   ◁─────
        } else {
          return deserialize(ctx.getState(VALUES_KEY));   ◁────
        }
      }
  }

  . . .
  }
```

We deserialize the Java object used to store the previous sensor readings.

If the current reading is significantly different, then we generate an alert.

We add the current value to the list of observed values.

We store the updated Java object in the state store.

We use the Streams API to calculate the average.

Instantiate the Java object if none exists in the state store.

Convert the bytes in the state store into the Java object we need.

There are a few points I want to highlight from the function in listing 4.11. The first thing you may notice is that the return type of function is defined as Void. This means that the function does not produce an output value. Another point I want to highlight is the fact that the function relies on Java serialization to store and retrieve a list of the last 100 values (sensor readings) it has received. It relies on a third-party library implementation of a FIFO queue to retain the 100 most-recent values to compute the average before comparing it to the most recent sensor reading. If that value significantly deviates from the average, then an alert is raised. Finally, the most recent reading is added to the FIFO queue, which is then serialized and written to the state store.

On subsequent calls, the AvgSensorReadingFunction will retrieve the bytes of the FIFO queue, deserialize them back into the Java object, and use it to calculate the average again. This process repeats indefinitely and only retains the most recent values for comparison against the trend (e.g., the moving average of the sensor readings). This approach is very different from the windowing capability provided by Pulsar Functions that is discussed in chapter 12. In short, the windowing capability provided by the Pulsar Functions framework permits the collection of multiple inputs before executing the function method based on either time or a fixed count. Once the window is filled, the function is provided the entire list of inputs at one time, whereas the function shown in listing 4.6 is provided the values one at a time, and must maintain the previous values inside its state.

So, you might be asking yourself why you wouldn't just use Pulsar's built-in windowing for our use case. In our case, we want to react to every individual reading as it becomes available, rather than waiting to accumulate a sufficient number of readings. This allows us to detect any issue much sooner.

Now, let's wrap up our discussion on stateful functions by looking at the counter interface provided by the `Context` API. A good example of how and when to use this functionality would be a `WordCount` function that stores the number of each individual word, using the counter methods provided by the context object API, as shown in the following listing.

Listing 4.12   WordCount function using stateful counters

```
package com.manning.pulsar.chapter4.functions.sdk;

import java.util.Arrays;
import java.util.List;

import org.apache.pulsar.functions.api.Context;
import org.apache.pulsar.functions.api.Function;

public class WordCountFunction implements Function<String, Integer> {
  @Override
  public Integer process(String input, Context context) throws Exception {
    List<String> words = Arrays.asList(input.split("\\."));
      words.forEach(word -> context.incrCounter(word, 1));
        return Integer.valueOf(words.size());
  }
}
```

The logic of the function is straightforward; it first splits the incoming string object into multiple words, using a regex pattern; then for each word generated from the split it increments the corresponding counter by one. This function is a good candidate for effectively once processing semantics to ensure an accurate result. If you were to use at-least-once processing semantics instead, you could potentially end up processing the same message more than once in a failure scenario, which would result in the double counting of multiple words.

4.4 Testing Pulsar functions

In this section I will walk you through the process of developing and testing your first Pulsar function. Let's use the `KeywordFilterFunction` shown in listing 4.13 to demonstrate the software development lifecycle for a Pulsar function. This function takes in a user-provided keyword and filters out any input string that does not contain that keyword. An example application of this function would be to scan a Twitter feed for tweets related to a particular topic or containing a certain phrase.

Listing 4.13 KeywordFilterFunction

```java
package com.manning.pulsar.chapter4.functions.sdk;

import java.util.Arrays;
import java.util.List;
import java.util.Optional;
import org.apache.pulsar.functions.api.Context;
import org.apache.pulsar.functions.api.Function;

public class KeywordFilterFunction
  implements Function<String, String> {          ◁─── The function takes in a string and returns a string.

public static final String KEYWORD_CONFIG = "keyword";
public static final String IGNORE_CONFIG = "ignore-case";

@Override
public String process(String input, Context ctx) {
  Optional<Object> keyword =
    ctx.getUserConfigValue(KEYWORD_CONFIG);          ◁─── Get the keyword from the context object.
  Optional<Object> ignoreCfg =
    ctx.getUserConfigValue(IGNORE_CONFIG);          ◁─── Get the ignore-case setting from the context object.

  boolean ignoreCase = ignoreCfg.isPresent() ?
        (boolean) ignoreConfig.get(): false;

    List<String> words = Arrays.asList(input.split("\\s"));          ◁─── Split the input string into individual words.

    if (!keyword.isPresent()) {
      return null;
    } else if (ignoreCase && words.stream().anyMatch(
        s -> s.equalsIgnoreCase((String) keyword.get()))) {
      return input;
    } else if (words.contains(keyword.get())) {          ◁─── Check for an exact match.
      return input;
    }
    return null;
  }
}
```

Without a keyword, nothing can match. (annotation pointing to `if (!keyword.isPresent()) {`)

Evaluate each word, ignoring case. (annotation pointing to `} else if (ignoreCase && words.stream().anyMatch(`)

While this code is simplistic, I will walk through the testing process you would typically use when developing a function for production use. Since this is just plain Java code, we can leverage any of the existing unit-testing frameworks, such as JUnit or TestNG, to test the function logic.

4.4.1   *Unit testing*

The first step would be to write a suite of unit tests that test some of the more common scenarios to validate that the logic is correct and produces accurate results for various sentences we send it. Since this code uses the Pulsar SDK API, we will need to use a mocking library, such as Mockito, to mock the Context object, as shown in the following listing.

Listing 4.14   KeywordFilterFunction unit tests

```
package com.manning.pulsar.chapter4.functions.sdk;

import static org.mockito.Mockito.*;
import static org.junit.Assert.*;

public class KeywordFilterFunctionTests {
private KeywordFilterFunction function = new KeywordFilterFunction();

@Mock
private Context mockedCtx;

@Before
public final void setUp() {
  MockitoAnnotations.initMocks(this);
}

  @Test
  public final void containsKeywordTest() throws Exception {
    when(mockedCtx.getUserConfigValue(
        KeywordFilterFunction.KEYWORD_CONFIG))
        .thenReturn(Optional.of("dog"));
```
⟵ **Configure the keyword to be dog.**
```
String sentence = "The brown fox jumped over the lazy dog";
String result = function.process(sentence, mockedCtx);
assertNotNull(result);
assertEquals(sentence, result);
  }
```
We expect the sentence to be returned, since it contained the keyword.
```
  @Test
  public final void doesNotContainKeywordTest() throws Exception {
    when(mockedCtx.getUserConfigValue(
    KeywordFilterFunction.KEYWORD_CONFIG))
    .thenReturn(Optional.of("cat"));
```
⟵ **Configure the keyword to be cat.**
```
    String sentence = "It was the best of times, it was the worst of times";
String result = function.process(sentence, mockedCtx);
assertNull(result);
  }
```
We don't expect the sentence to be returned, since it did not contain the keyword.
```
  @Test
  public final void ignoreCaseTest() {
    when(mockedCtx.getUserConfigValue(
        KeywordFilterFunction.KEYWORD_CONFIG))
```

```
            .thenReturn(Optional.of("RED"));      ⟵──── Configure the keyword to be RED.

    when(mockedCtx.getUserConfigValue(
        KeywordFilterFunction.IGNORE_CONFIG))          Configure the function to ignore
        .thenReturn(Optional.of(Boolean.TRUE));   ⟵┘   case when filtering on the keyword.


    String sentence = "Everyone watched the red sports car drive off.";
    String result = function.process(sentence, mockedCtx);
    assertNotNull(result);          ⟵──────
    assertEquals(sentence, result);          We expect the sentence to be returned,
    }                                        since it contained a lowercase version
}                                            of the keyword.
```

As you can see, these unit tests cover the very basic functionality of the function and rely on the use of a mock object for the Pulsar context object. This type of test suite is just like one you would write to test any Java class that wasn't a Pulsar function.

4.4.2 Integration testing

After we are satisfied with our unit testing results, we will want to see how the Pulsar function will perform on a Pulsar cluster. The easiest way to test a Pulsar function is to start a Pulsar server and run the Pulsar function locally, using the `LocalRunner` helper class. In this mode, the function runs as a standalone process on the machine it is submitted from. This option is best when you are developing and testing your functions, as it allows you to attach a debugger to the function process on the local machine, as shown in figure 4.5.

To use the `LocalRunner`, you must first add a few dependencies to your Maven project, as shown in the following listing. This brings in the `LocalRunner` class that is used to test the function against a running Pulsar cluster.

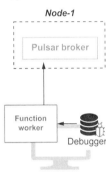

Figure 4.5 When you run a Pulsar function using `LocalRunner`, the function runs on the local machine, allowing you to attach a debugger and step through the code.

Listing 4.15 Including the `LocalRunner` dependencies

```xml
<dependencies>
    . . .
    <dependency>
        <groupId>com.fasterxml.jackson.core</groupId>
        <artifactId>jackson-core</artifactId>
        <version>${jackson.version}</version>
    </dependency>
    <dependency>
        <groupId>org.apache.pulsar</groupId>
        <artifactId>pulsar-functions-local-runner-original</artifactId>
        <version>${pulsar.version}</version>
    </dependency>
</dependencies>
```

Next, we need to write a class to configure and launch the LocalRunner, as shown in the following listing. As you can see, this code must first configure the Pulsar function to execute on the LocalRunner, and it specifies the address of the actual Pulsar cluster instance that will be used for the testing.

Listing 4.16   Testing the `KeywordFilterFunction` with the `LocalRunner`

```
public class KeywordFilterFunctionLocalRunnerTest {
  final static String BROKER_URL = "pulsar://localhost:6650";
  final static String IN = "persistent://public/default/raw-feed";
  final static String OUT = "persistent://public/default/filtered-feed";

  private static ExecutorService executor;
  private static LocalRunner localRunner;
  private static PulsarClient client;
  private static Producer<String> producer;
  private static Consumer<String> consumer;
  private static String keyword = "";

  public static void main(String[] args) throws Exception {
    if (args.length > 0) {
    keyword = args[0];              ◁────  Get the user-
    }                                      provided keyword.
    startLocalRunner();
    init();
    startConsumer();
    sendData();
    shutdown();
  }
                                                         The service URL for
                                                         the Pulsar cluster the
  private static void startLocalRunner() throws Exception {   function will run on
    localRunner = LocalRunner.builder()
            .brokerServiceUrl(BROKER_URL)        ◁─────
            .functionConfig(getFunctionConfig())  ◁──┐
            .build();                                │  Pass in the function
    localRunner.start(false);  ◁──┐                  │  configuration to the
  }                               Start the LocalRunner  LocalRunner.
                                  and function.

  private static FunctionConfig getFunctionConfig() {
    Map<String, ConsumerConfig> inputSpecs =
      new HashMap<String, ConsumerConfig> ();              Specifies that the
                                                           data inside the input
                                                           topic will be strings
    inputSpecs.put(IN, ConsumerConfig.builder()   ◁──────┘
          .schemaType(Schema.STRING.getSchemaInfo().getName())
          .build());
                                                         Initialize
                                                         the user
    Map<String, Object> userConfig = new HashMap<String, Object>();  configuration
    userConfig.put(KeywordFilterFunction.KEYWORD_CONFIG, keyword);   properties
    userConfig.put(KeywordFilterFunction.IGNORE_CONFIG, true);  ◁──  with the user-
                                 Specifies the class name of        provided
    return FunctionConfig.builder()  the function to run locally    keyword.
          .className(KeywordFilterFunction.class.getName())  ◁──┘
          .inputs(Collections.singleton(IN))
```

Specifies the input topic

Specifies the output topic

Pass in the input topic configuration properties.

Pass in the user configuration properties.

Specifies that we want to use a Java Runtime environment for the function

```java
        .inputSpecs(inputSpecs)
        .output(OUT)
        .name("keyword-filter")
        .tenant("public")
        .namespace("default")
        .runtime(FunctionConfig.Runtime.JAVA)
        .subName("keyword-filter-sub")
        .userConfig(userConfig)
        .build();
}

private static void init() throws PulsarClientException {
    executor = Executors.newFixedThreadPool(2);
    client = PulsarClient.builder()
            .serviceUrl(BROKER_URL)
            .build();
    producer = client.newProducer(Schema.STRING).topic(IN).create();
    consumer = client.newConsumer(Schema.STRING).topic(OUT)
            .subscriptionName("validation-sub").subscribe();
}

private static void startConsumer() {
    Runnable runnableTask = () -> {
        while (true) {
            Message<String> msg = null;
            try {
                msg = consumer.receive();
                System.out.printf("Message received: %s \n", msg.getValue());
                consumer.acknowledge(msg);
            } catch (Exception e) {
                consumer.negativeAcknowledge(msg);
            }
        }};
    executor.execute(runnableTask);
}

private static void sendData() throws IOException {
    InputStream inputStream = Thread.currentThread().getContextClassLoader()
        .getResourceAsStream("test-data.txt");

    InputStreamReader streamReader = new InputStreamReader(inputStream,
        StandardCharsets.UTF_8);

    BufferedReader reader = new BufferedReader(streamReader);
    for (String line; (line = reader.readLine()) != null;) {
        producer.send(line);
    }
}

private static void shutdown() throws Exception {
    executor.shutdown();
    localRunner.stop();
    . . .
}
}
```

Initialize a producer and consumer to use for testing.

Launch the consumer in a background thread to read messages from the function output topic.

Send data to the function input topic.

Stop the LocalRunner, consumer, etc.

The easiest way to gain access to a Pulsar cluster is to launch the Pulsar Docker container like we did in chapter 3 by running the following command in a bash window, which will start a Pulsar cluster in standalone mode inside the container. Note that we are also mounting the directory where you cloned the GitHub project associated with this book onto the local machine:

```
$ export GIT_PROJECT=<CLONE_DIR>/pulsar-in-action/chapter4
$ docker run --name pulsar -id \
  -p 6650:6650 -p 8080:8080 \
  -v $GIT_PROJECT:/pulsar/dropbox
  apachepulsar/pulsar:latest bin/pulsar standalone
```

Typically, you would run the `LocalRunner` test from inside your IDE to attach a debugger and step through the function code to identify and resolve any errors you have encountered. However, in this scenario I want to run the `LocalRunner` test using the command line. Therefore, I must first bundle the test class that is located under the `chapter4/src/main/test` folder of the GitHub repo associated with this book into a JAR file along with all the necessary dependencies, including the `LocalRunner` class, by running the Maven assemble command. Once that is complete, we can start the `LocalRunner` commands, as shown in the following listing.

> **Listing 4.17   Starting the `LocalRunner` and entering some data**

**Builds the fat jar containing the LocalRunner
test and all its dependencies**

```
mvn clean compile test-compile assembly:single
...
[INFO] ------------------------------------------------------------
[INFO] BUILD SUCCESS
[INFO] ------------------------------------------------------------
[INFO] Total time:  29.279 s
[INFO] Finished at: 2020-08-15T15:43:58-07:00
java -cp ./target/chapter4-0.0.1-fat-tests.jar
      com.manning.pulsar.chapter4.functions.sdk.KeywordFilter
         FunctionLocalRunnerTest Director

org.apache.pulsar.functions.runtime.thread.ThreadRuntime - ThreadContainer
   starting function with instance config InstanceConfig(instanceId=0,
   functionId=0bc39b7d-fb08-4549-a6cf-ab641d583edd,
   functionVersion=7786da28-
0bb6-4c11-97d9-3d6140cc4261, functionDetails=tenant: "public"
namespace: "default"
name: "keyword-filter"
className: "com.manning.pulsar.chapter4.functions.
   sdk.KeywordFilterFunction"
userConfig: "{\"keyword\":\"Director\",\"ignore-case\":true}"
autoAck: true
parallelism: 1
source {
```

**Run the LocalRunner test, and specify
a keyword of Director to filter on.**

**The output should indicate
that the function was
deployed as expected.**

**The output should display
the function's input topic.**

```
    typeClassName: "java.lang.String"
    subscriptionName: "keyword-filter-sub"
    inputSpecs {
      key: "persistent://public/default/raw-feed"
      value {
        schemaType: "String"
      }
    }
    cleanupSubscription: true
}
sink {
  topic: "persistent://public/default/filtered-feed"
  typeClassName: "java.lang.String"
  forwardSourceMessageProperty: true
}
. . .
```

The output should display the function's output topic.

The output should contain only sentences with the keyword Director in them.

```
Message received: At the end of the room a loud speaker projected from the
➡ wall. The Director walked up to it and pressed a switch.
Message received: The Director pushed back the switch. The voice was
➡ silent. Only its thin ghost continued to mutter from beneath the
➡ eighty pillows.
Message received: Once more the Director touched the switch.
```

Let's review the steps that just occurred. An instance of the `KeywordFilterFunction` was launched locally inside a JVM on my laptop and was connected to the Pulsar instance that was running inside the Docker container we launched earlier. Next, the input and output topics specified in the function configuration were created inside that Pulsar instance automatically. Then all of the data published by the producer running inside the `KeywordFilterFunctionLocalRunnerTest`'s `sendData` method was published to the Pulsar topic inside the Docker container.

The `KeywordFilterFunction` was listening on this same topic, and the processing logic was applied to each line published to that topic. Only those messages that contained the keyword, which in this case was `Director`, were written to the function's configured output topic. The consumer running inside the `KeywordFilterFunction-LocalRunnerTest`'s `startConsumer` method was also reading messages from this output topic and writing them to standard out so that we could verify the results.

4.5 *Deploying Pulsar functions*

After you have compiled and tested your Pulsar functions, you will eventually want to deploy them to a production cluster. The `pulsar-admin functions` command-line tool was designed specifically for this purpose, and it allows you to provide several configuration properties for the functions, including tenant, namespace, input, and output topics. In this section I will walk through the process of configuring and deploying a Pulsar function using this tool.

4.5.1   *Generating a deployment artifact*

When you are deploying a Pulsar function, the first step is to generate a deployment artifact that contains the function code along with all its dependencies. The type of artifact varies depending on the programming language used to develop the function.

JAVA SDK FUNCTIONS

For Java-based functions, the preferred artifact type is a NAR (NiFi archive) file, although JAR files are also acceptable if they include all the necessary dependencies. This holds true whether you want to deploy a simple Java-native language function or one that has been developed using the Pulsar SDK. In either case, an archive file is the deployment artifact. To have your Pulsar function packaged as a NAR file, you need to include a special plugin inside your pom.xml file, as shown in the following listing, which will bundle the function class, along with all its dependencies, for you.

Listing 4.18   Add the NAR Maven plugin to your pom.xml file

```
<build>
  <plugins>
     <plugin>
       <groupId>org.apache.nifi</groupId>
       <artifactId>nifi-nar-maven-plugin</artifactId>
       <version>1.2.0</version>
       <extensions>true</extensions>
       <executions>
           <execution>
               <phase>package</phase>
               <goals>
                   <goal>nar</goal>
               </goals>
           </execution>
       </executions>
     </plugin>
  . . .
  </plugins>
</build>
```

Once this plugin has been added to your project's pom.xml file, all you need to do is run the `mvn clean install` command to generate the NAR file in your project's target folder. This NAR file is the deployment artifact for Java-based Pulsar functions.

PYTHON SDK FUNCTIONS

For Python-based Pulsar functions, there are two deployment options, depending on whether or not you used the Pulsar SDK. If you didn't use the SDK and only want to deploy a Python-native language function, then the Python source file (e.g., my-function.py) is the deployment artifact, and no further packaging is required.

However, if you wish to deploy a Python-based Pulsar function that depends on packages outside of the Python standard libraries, then you must first package all the required dependencies into a single artifact (ZIP file) before you can deploy it. A file named requirements.txt is required inside your Python project folder and is used to maintain a list of all the project dependencies. It is up to the developer to keep this file up to date manually. Note that `pulsar-client` is not needed as a dependency, as it is provided by Pulsar. When you are ready to create your Python deployment artifact, you first need to run the command shown in the following listing to download all the Python dependencies specified in the requirements.txt file into the deps folder of your Python project.

Listing 4.19 Downloading the Python dependencies

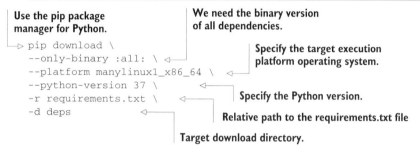

```
pip download \
  --only-binary :all: \
  --platform manylinux1_x86_64 \
  --python-version 37 \
  -r requirements.txt \
  -d deps
```

Use the pip package manager for Python.

We need the binary version of all dependencies.

Specify the target execution platform operating system.

Specify the Python version.

Relative path to the requirements.txt file

Target download directory.

After the download is complete, you need to create a destination folder with the desired package name (e.g., echo-function). Next, you must copy over both the src and deps folders into it and compress the folder into a ZIP archive. The ZIP file generated from the command in the following listing is the deployment artifact for Python-based Pulsar functions.

Listing 4.20 Packaging a Python-based Pulsar function for deployment

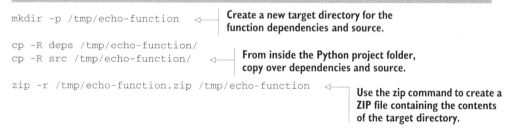

```
mkdir -p /tmp/echo-function

cp -R deps /tmp/echo-function/
cp -R src /tmp/echo-function/

zip -r /tmp/echo-function.zip /tmp/echo-function
```

Create a new target directory for the function dependencies and source.

From inside the Python project folder, copy over dependencies and source.

Use the zip command to create a ZIP file containing the contents of the target directory.

GOLANG SDK FUNCTIONS

For Golang-based Pulsar functions, the preferred artifact type is a single binary-executable file that contains the machine byte code for your function along with all the supporting code needed to execute the code on any computer, regardless of whether that system has the .go source files or even a Go installation. You can use the Go toolchain, as shown in the following listing, to generate this binary executable file.

**Make sure you are in
the project directory.**

```
cd chapter4
```

**Use the Go build command
to generate the binary
executable.**

```
go build echoFunction.go
```

```
go: downloading github.com/apache/pulsar/pulsar-function-go
    v0.0.0-20210723210639-251113330b08
go: downloading github.com/sirupsen/logrus v1.4.2
go: downloading github.com/golang/protobuf v1.4.3
go: downloading github.com/apache/pulsar-client-go v0.5.0
...
```

```
ls -l
```

**Go will automatically download any
packages that you need and include
them in the binary.**

```
-rwxr-xr-x  1 david  staff  23344912 Jul 25 15:23
    echoFunction
-rw-r--r--  1 david  staff       538 Jul 25 15:20
    echoFunction.go
```

**After the build command finishes,
check the directory contents.**

The executable binary that was generated

**The Go source file containing
the Pulsar function**

If you are running macOS or Linux, the binary executable file will be generated inside the directory where you run the command, and it will be named after the source file. This is the artifact that must be deployed to run the Golang-based function inside of Pulsar.

4.5.2 *Function configuration*

Now that we know how to generate a deployment artifact, the next step is to configure and deploy our Pulsar functions. All functions are required to provide some basic configuration details when they are deployed to Pulsar, such as the input and output topics and other details. There are two ways this configuration information can be specified. The first is as command-line arguments passed to the `pulsar-admin` functions CLI tool using the `create` (https://pulsar.apache.org/docs/en/functions-cli/#create) and `update` (https://pulsar.apache.org/docs/en/functions-cli/#update) function commands (e.g., `bin/pulsar-admin functions create`), and the second is via a single configuration file.

Which method you choose is a matter of preference, but I would strongly encourage the use of the latter, as it not only simplifies the deployment process, but also allows you to store the configuration details in source control along with the source code. This allows you to refer to the properties at any time and ensures that you are always running your functions with the correct configuration. If you choose this approach, you will only need to provide two configuration values when you deploy your functions: the name of the function artifact file containing the executable function code and the name of the file containing all the configuration settings. The contents of a configuration file named function-config.yaml are shown in the following listing. We are going to use this file to deploy the `KeywordFilterFunction` to the Pulsar cluster running inside the Docker container we started earlier in the chapter.

Listing 4.22 The function configuration file for the `KeywordFilterFunction`

Every function must have an associated tenant.

```
className: com.manning.pulsar.chapter4.functions.sdk.KeywordFilterFunction
tenant: public                        Every function must have an associated namespace.
namespace: default         ◄─┘
name: keyword-filter        There can be more than one input topic per function.
inputs:            ◄─┘
- persistent://public/default/raw-feed
output: persistent://public/default/filtered-feed
userConfig:           ◄─┐
  keyword : Director      The user configuration key, value map
  ignore-case: false


####################################
# Processing                        Whether or not the function should
####################################  acknowledge the message after it
autoAck: true         ◄─            has processed the message          The delivery
logTopic: persistent://public/default/keyword-filter-log              semantics applied
processingGuarantees: ATLEAST_ONCE                ◄─                to the function
retainOrdering: false     ◄─┐
timeoutMs: 30000            Whether or not the function should
subName: keyword-filter-sub  process the input messages in the
cleanupSubscription: true    order they were published
```

The name of the subscription on the input topic

As you see, this file provides all the properties needed to run the Pulsar function, including the class name, input/output directories, and much more. It also contains the following configuration settings that control how the messages are consumed by the function:

- `auto_ack`—Whether messages consumed from the input topic(s) are automatically acknowledged by the function framework or not. When set to the default value of `true`, each message that doesn't result in an exception is acked automatically when the function is done executing. If set to `false`, the function code is responsible for message acknowledgment.
- `retain-ordering`—Whether messages are consumed in exactly the order they appear on the input topics or not. When set to `true`, negatively acknowledged messages will be redelivered before any unprocessed messages.
- `processing-guarantees`—The processing guarantees (delivery semantics) applied to messages consumed by the function. Possible values are [`ATLEAST_ONCE`, `ATMOST_ONCE`, `EFFECTIVELY_ONCE`].

When executing a stream processing application, you may want to specify the delivery semantics for the data processing within your Pulsar functions. These guarantees are meaningful, since you must always assume there is the possibility of failures in the network or machines that can result in data loss.

In the context of Pulsar Functions, these processing guarantees determine how often a message is processed and how it is handled in the event of failure. Pulsar Functions supports three distinct messaging semantics that you can apply to any function. By default, Pulsar Functions provides at-most-once delivery guarantees, but you can configure your Pulsar function to provide any of the following message processing semantics instead.

AT-MOST-ONCE DELIVERY GUARANTEES

At-most-once processing does not provide any guarantee that data is processed, and no additional attempts will be made to reprocess the data if it was lost before the Pulsar function could process it. Each message that is sent to the function will either be processed one time at the most or not at all.

As you can see in figure 4.6, when a Pulsar function is configured to use at-most-once processing, the message is immediately acknowledged after it is consumed, regardless of whether the message is successfully processed or not. In this scenario, message M2 will be processed next by the function even if message M1 caused a processing exception.

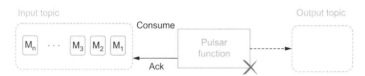

Figure 4.6   With at-most-once processing, the incoming messages are acknowledged, regardless of processing success or failure. This gives each message just one chance at being processed.

You only want to use this processing guarantee if your application can handle periodic data loss without impacting the correctness of the data. One such example would be a function that calculates the average value of a sensor reading, such as a temperature. Over the lifetime of the function, it will process tens of millions of individual temperature readings, and the loss of a handful of these readings will be inconsequential to the accuracy of the computed average.

AT-LEAST-ONCE DELIVERY GUARANTEES

At-least-once processing guarantees that any data published to one of the function's input topics will be successfully processed by the function at least one time. In the event of a processing failure, the message will automatically be redelivered. Therefore, there is the possibility that any given message could be processed more than once.

With this processing semantic, the Pulsar function reads the message from the input topic, executes its logic, and acknowledges the message. If the function fails to acknowledge the message, it is reprocessed. This process is repeated until the function acknowledges the message. Figure 4.7 depicts the scenario in which the function consumes the message but encounters a processing error that causes it to fail to send an acknowledgment. In this scenario, the next message processed by the function would be M1, and would continue to be M1 until the function succeeds.

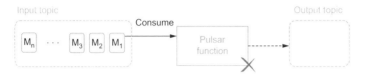

Figure 4.7   With at-least-once processing, if the function encounters an error and fails to acknowledge the message, then the same message will be processed again.

You will only want to use this processing guarantee if your application can handle processing the same data multiple times without impacting the correctness of the data. One such scenario would be if the incoming messages represented records that would be updated in a database. In such a scenario, multiple updates with the same values would have no impact on the underlying database.

EFFECTIVELY-ONCE DELIVERY GUARANTEES

With effectively-once guarantees, a message can be received and processed more than once, which is common in the presence of failures. The crucial thing is that the actual outcome of the function processing on the resulting state will be as if the reprocessed events were observed only once. This is most often what you will want to achieve.

Figure 4.8 depicts the scenario in which an upstream producer to the function's input topic has re-sent the same message, M1. When configured to provide effectively-once processing, the function will check to see if it has previously processed the message (based on user-defined properties), and if so, it will ignore the message and send an acknowledgment so that it will not be reprocessed.

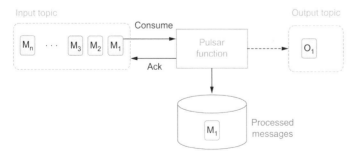

Figure 4.8   With effectively-once processing, duplicate messages will be ignored.

4.5.3   *Function deployment*

Now that we have defined the configuration we want to use for the function, the next step is to deploy the function onto a running Pulsar cluster. As we mentioned earlier, the Pulsar cluster that we started earlier in the chapter that is running inside a Docker container will do just fine. From inside a bash shell, you can execute the command shown in the following listing to deploy the `KeywordFilterFunction` on that Pulsar cluster.

Listing 4.23   Deploy the `KeywordFilterFunction`

Specify the deployment artifact, which must either a locally accessible file or a URL address.

Using the pulsar-admin tool inside the Docker container

```
$ docker exec -it pulsar bin/pulsar-admin functions create \
    --jar /pulsar/dropbox/target/chapter4-0.0.1.nar \
    --function-config-file
    /pulsar/dropbox/src/main/resources/function-config.yaml
```

Specify the function configuration file, which must either a locally accessible file or a URL address.

If everything went as expected, you should see `Created successfully` in the output of the command, which indicates that the function was created and deployed on the Pulsar cluster. Let's take a moment to review what happened and why the command was able to work. First off, we used the `pulsar-admin` CLI tool, which only exists inside the Docker container. Therefore, we needed to use the Docker exec command to run the `pulsar-admin` CLI tool inside the Docker container. In the command, we provided two switches: one to specify the location of the deployment artifact (e.g., the NAR file) and the other to specify the location of the function configuration file. Since we were deploying a Java-based Pulsar function, we used the `--jar` switch to specify the location of the artifact. Had this been a Python-based function, we would have had to use the `--py` switch instead, and similarly, the `--go` switch for a Golang-based function. Using the correct switch is critical because Pulsar uses those switch values to determine which runtime execution environment is needed to run the function (i.e., whether to spin up a JVM, a Python interpreter, or a Go runtime for the function to run in).

Both the configuration file and the function artifact files must either be on the same machine as the `pulsar-admin` CLI tool or downloadable via a URL. Therefore, we mounted the $GIT_PROJECT directory to the /pulsar/dropbox folder inside the Docker container. That made both files locally accessible to the `pulsar-admin` CLI tool. While this is a great trick for local development, bear in mind that in a real production scenario, these files should be physically moved to the Pulsar cluster, preferably as part of the CI/CD release process. We can also check the status of our deployed function using the `function getstatus` command, as shown in listing 4.24, which will give us useful information about the function, including the status of the function, how many messages it has processed, the average processing latency of the function, and any exceptions that the function may have thrown.

Listing 4.24 Checking the status of the `KeywordFilterFunction`

```
# docker exec -it pulsar /pulsar/bin/pulsar-admin functions getstatus -
➥ name keyword-filter
{
   "numInstances" : 1,          ◁—————  The number of requested
   "numRunning" : 1,            ◁        instances of the function
   "instances" : [ {
      "instanceId" : 0,         The actual number of running
      "status" : {              instances of the function
         "running" : true,      If any errors were thrown,
         "error" : "",          ◁————  they would be displayed here.
         "numRestarts" : 0,     ┐  The number of messages received by the function
         "numReceived" : 0,     ◁—┘
         "numSuccessfullyProcessed" : 0, ◁
         "numUserExceptions" : 0,        The number of messages that have been
         "latestUserExceptions" : [ ],   successfully processed by the function
         "numSystemExceptions" : 0,
         "latestSystemExceptions" : [ ],  The last time a message was
         "averageLatency" : 0.0,          processed by the function
         "lastInvocationTime" : 0,       ◁
         "workerId" : "c-standalone-fw-localhost-8080"
      }
   } ]
}
```

Status indicator → `"running" : true,`

The average processing latency per message → `"averageLatency" : 0.0,`

If you ever need to debug a running Pulsar function, the function getstatus command is an excellent place to start. The pulsar-admin functions command provides another command that will show you the configuration settings of a Pulsar function as well. You can check the configuration of a Pulsar function by using the function get command, as shown in the following listing.

Listing 4.25 Checking the configuration of the `KeywordFilterFunction`

```
# docker exec -it pulsar /pulsar/bin/pulsar-admin functions get --name
➥ keyword-filter
{
   "tenant": "public",
   "namespace": "default",
   "name": "keyword-filter",
   "className":
➥ "com.manning.pulsar.chapter4.functions.sdk.KeywordFilterFunction",
   "inputSpecs": {
      "persistent://public/default/raw-feed": {  ◁———— The input topic(s)
         "isRegexPattern": false,
         "schemaProperties": {}
      }
   },
   "output": "persistent://public/default/filtered-feed", ◁——
   "logTopic": "persistent://public/default/keyword-filter-log",
   "processingGuarantees": "ATLEAST_ONCE",
   "retainOrdering": false,                    ◁
   "forwardSourceMessageProperty": true,
```

The processing guarantee for the function → `"processingGuarantees": "ATLEAST_ONCE",`

The output topic

Whether or not the messages are to be processed in the order they were published to the topic

```
"userConfig": {          ⟵─── Any user configuration values
  "keyword": "Director",
  "ignore-case": false       The runtime environment of
},                           functions (e.g., Java, Python, etc.)
"runtime": "JAVA",   ⟵
"autoAck": true,         ⟵
"subName": "keyword-filter-sub",    Whether the function will automatically
"parallelism": 1,    ⟵              acknowledge messages
"resources": {   ⟵
  "cpu": 1.0,                  The number of parallel instances of
  "ram": 1073741824,           the function that were requested
  "disk": 10737418240
},                           The computing resources allocated to the function
"timeoutMs": 30000,
"cleanupSubscription": true
}
```

4.5.4   *The function deployment life cycle*

As we saw in the previous section, there are quite a few configuration parameters available when creating and updating a function. In this section, we will cover how some of those parameters are used within the Pulsar function deployment life cycle. When a function is first created, the associated library bundle is stored in Apache BookKeeper so it can be accessed by any Pulsar broker node in the cluster. The bundle is associated with the fully qualified function name, which is a combination of the tenant, namespace, and function name to ensure that it is globally unique across the Pulsar cluster.

When a Pulsar function is first created, the steps shown in figure 4.9 are performed in sequence. After the function is registered and all its details are persisted to BookKeeper, function workers are created based on the provided configuration parameters and the Pulsar cluster's deployment mode (which we will discuss in the next section). The function workers are the runtime instantiations of the Pulsar function code and can be threads, processes, or Kubernetes pods. Lastly, within each function worker, a Pulsar consumer and subscription is created on the configured input topics. The function workers then await the arrival of incoming messages and perform their processing logic on the incoming messages.

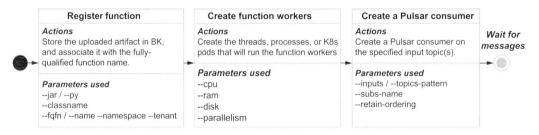

Figure 4.9   The Pulsar function deployment life cycle

4.5.5   Deployment modes

As we have seen, to deploy and manage Pulsar Functions, you need to have a Pulsar cluster running; however, there are a couple of options for where your Pulsar function instances will run. You can have the Pulsar function run on your local development machine (*localrun mode*) in which case it interacts with the broker over the network. This was what we did with the `LocalRunner` test case. For production, you will want to deploy your functions in *cluster mode*.

CLUSTER MODE

In this mode, users submit their functions to a running Pulsar cluster, and Pulsar will take care of distributing them across the function workers for execution. The Pulsar Functions framework supports the following runtime options when running in cluster mode: thread, process, and Kubernetes, as shown in figure 4.10, and these refer to how the function code itself is executed inside a *function worker*, which is the runtime environment used to host Pulsar Functions.

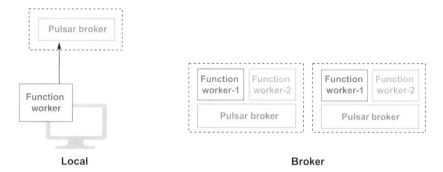

Local

Intended for development and testing, local deployment mode executes the functions on the local machine and interacts with a separate Pulsar broker.

Broker

Intended for modest-scale processing, broker deployment mode executes the functions on a function worker node as worker threads or processes.

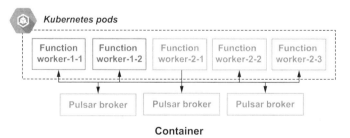

Container

Intended for large-scale processing, in container deployment mode, Pulsar functions run within their own containers that are managed by Kubernetes.

Figure 4.10   A Pulsar function can run as a thread, process, or Kubernetes StatefulSet inside the Pulsar functions workers.

In Pulsar, there are two options for where the function workers can run. One option is to run inside the Pulsar brokers themselves, which simplifies the deployment. The other option is to start the function worker processes on their own separate nodes to provide better resource isolation between them and your brokers.

The benefits of running the function workers on the broker node itself, as either a thread or a separate process, include that it has a smaller hardware footprint, as you won't need as many nodes in your environment, and a reduction in network latency between the function processes and the broker that is serving the messages. However, running the function workers on separate nodes provides better resource isolation and insulates the pulsar broker process from being inadvertently killed by a function worker crashing and bringing the broker down with it.

4.5.6   *Pulsar function data flow*

Before I conclude this chapter, I want to take a moment to document the flow of an individual message through a Pulsar function and tie the various stages back to the configuration parameters supplied when you first create or update a function, so you have a better understanding of how to configure your functions. The data flow inside a Pulsar function is depicted in the state machine shown in figure 4.11, along with the configuration properties that control the function behavior.

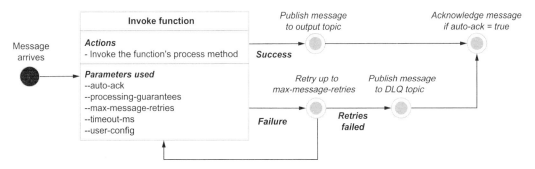

Figure 4.11   The basic message flow for a Pulsar function running inside of a Pulsar worker

When a message arrives on any of the function's configured input topics, the function's process method is called with the message contents as an input parameter. If the function can successfully process the message without encountering any runtime exceptions, the value returned by the method call is published to the configured output topic, unless it is a void function, in which case nothing is published.

However, if the function encounters a runtime exception, the message is retried up to the value configured in the `max-message-retries` parameter. If all these attempts fail, the message is routed to the configured `dead-letter-queue` topic (if any), so it can be retained for future examination. In either case, the message is acknowledged as consumed by the Pulsar function if the `auto-ack` flag was configured to `true`, allowing the next message to be processed.

Summary

- Pulsar Functions is a serverless computing framework that runs on top of Apache Pulsar and allows you to define processing logic that get executed when a new message arrives in a topic.
- Pulsar functions can be written in several popular languages, including Python, Go, and Java, but throughout the remainder of this book we will focus on Java.
- Pulsar functions can be configured, submitted, and monitored from the Pulsar command line interface.
- Pulsar functions can be deployed to run as threads, processes, or Kubernetes pods.

Pulsar IO connectors

This chapter covers

- An introduction to the Pulsar IO framework
- Configuring, deploying, and monitoring Pulsar IO connectors
- Writing your own Pulsar IO connector in Java

Messaging systems are much more useful when you can easily use them to move data into and out of other external systems, such as databases, local and distributed filesystems, or other messaging systems. Consider the scenario where you want to ingest log data from external sources, such as applications, platforms, and cloud-based services, and publish it to a search engine for analysis. This could easily be accomplished with a pair of Pulsar IO connectors; the first would be a Pulsar source that collects the application logs, and the second would be a Pulsar sink that writes the formatted records to Elasticsearch.

Pulsar provides a collection of pre-built connectors that can be used to interact with external systems, such as Apache Cassandra, Elasticsearch, and HDFS, just to name a few. The Pulsar IO framework is also extensible, which allows you to develop your own connectors to support new or legacy systems as needed.

5.1 What are Pulsar IO connectors?

The Pulsar IO connector framework provides developers, data engineers, and operators an easy way to move data into and out of the Pulsar messaging platform without having to write any code or become experts in both Pulsar and the external system. From an implementation perspective, Pulsar IO connectors are just specialized Pulsar functions purpose-built to interface with external systems through an extensible API interface.

Compare this to a scenario in which you had to implement the logic for interacting with an external system, such as MongoDB, inside a Java class that uses the Pulsar Java client. Not only would you have to become familiar with the client interface for MongoDB and Pulsar, but you would also have the operational burden of deploying and monitoring a separate process that is now a critical part of your application stack. Pulsar IO seeks to make the movement of data into and out of Pulsar less cumbersome.

Pulsar IO connectors come in two types: *sources*, which ingest data from an external system into Pulsar, and *sinks*, which feed data from Pulsar into an external system. Figure 5.1 illustrates the relationship between sources, sinks, and Pulsar.

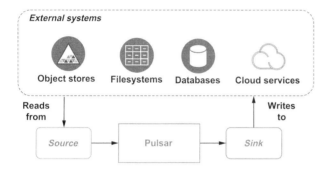

Figure 5.1 Sources consume data from external systems, while sinks write data to external systems.

5.1.1 Sink connectors

While the Pulsar IO framework already provides a collection of built-in connectors for some of the most popular data systems, it was designed with extensibility in mind, allowing users to add new connectors as new systems and APIs are developed. The programming model behind Pulsar IO Connectors is very straightforward, which greatly simplifies the development process. Pulsar IO sink connectors can receive messages from one or more input topics. Every time a message is published to any of the input topics, the Pulsar sink's `write` method is called.

The implementation of the `write` method is responsible for determining how to process the incoming message contents and properties in order to write data to the source system. The Pulsar sink shown in figure 5.2 can use the message contents to determine which database table to insert the record into and then construct and execute the appropriate SQL command to do so.

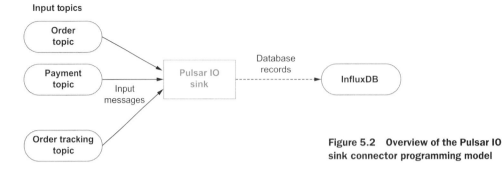

Figure 5.2   Overview of the Pulsar IO sink connector programming model

The easiest way to create a custom sink connector is to write a Java class that implements the `org.apache.pulsar.io.core.Sink` interface shown in listing 5.1. The first method defined in the interface is the `open` method, which is called just once when the sink connector is created and can be used to initialize all the necessary resources (e.g., for a database connector, you can create the JDBC client). The `open` method also provides a single input parameter, named `config`, from which you can retrieve all the connector-specific settings (e.g., the database connection URL, username, and password). In addition to the passed-in config object, the Pulsar runtime also provides a `SinkContext` for the connector that provides access to runtime resources, much like the `Context` object does in the Pulsar Functions API.

Listing 5.1   The Pulsar sink interface

```
package org.apache.pulsar.io.core;

public interface Sink<T> extends AutoCloseable {
    /**
     * Open connector with configuration
     *
     * @param config initialization config
     * @param sinkContext
     * @throws Exception IO type exceptions when opening a connector
     */
    void open(final Map<String, Object> config,
             SinkContext sinkContext) throws Exception;

    /**
     * Write a message to Sink
     * @param record record to write to sink
     * @throws Exception
     */
    void write(Record<T> record) throws Exception;
}
```

The other method defined in the interface is the `write` method, which is responsible for consuming messages from the sink's configured source Pulsar topic and writing the data to the external source system. The `write` method receives an object that implements the `org.apache.pulsar.functions.api.Record` interface, which provides information that can be used when processing the incoming message. It is worth pointing out that the sink interface extends the `AutoCloseable` interface, which includes a `close` method definition that can be used to release any resources, such as database connections or open file writers, before the connector is stopped.

Listing 5.2 The record interface

```
package org.apache.pulsar.functions.api

public interface Record<T> {

    default Optional<String> getTopicName() {        ◁─── If the record originated from a topic, report the topic name.
        return Optional.empty();
    }

    default Optional<String> getKey() {        ◁─── Return a key if the key has one associated.
        return Optional.empty();
    }

    T getValue();        Retrieves the event time of the record from the source

    default Optional<Long> getEventTime() {        ◁───
        return Optional.empty();
    }

    default Optional<String> getPartitionId() {        ◁───
        return Optional.empty();
    }

    default Optional<Long> getRecordSequence() {        ◁───
        return Optional.empty();
    }

    default Map<String, String> getProperties() {        ◁───
        return Collections.emptyMap();
    }

    default void ack() {        ◁───  Acknowledge that the record has been processed.
    }

    default void fail() {        ◁───  Indicate to the source system that this record has failed to be processed.
    }

    default Optional<String> getDestinationTopic() {        ◁───
        return Optional.empty();
    }
}
```

Retrieves the actual data of the record → `T getValue();`

If the record is originated from a partitioned source, return its partition ID. The partition ID will be used as part of the unique identifier by the Pulsar IO runtime to do message deduplication and achieve an exactly-once processing guarantee.

If the record is originated from a sequential source, return its record sequence. The record sequence will be used as part of the unique identifier by Pulsar IO runtime to do message deduplication and achieve an exactly-once processing guarantee.

Retrieves user-defined properties attached to the record

To support message routing on a per message basis

The implementation of the record should also provide two methods: `ack` and `fail`. These two methods will be used by the Pulsar IO connector to acknowledge the records that have been processed and fail the records that have failed. Failure to acknowledge or fail messages within the source connector will result in the messages being retained, which will ultimately cause the connector to stop processing due to backpressure.

5.1.2   Source connectors

Pulsar IO source connectors are responsible for consuming data from external systems and publishing the data to the configured output topic. There are two distinct types of sources supported by the Pulsar IO framework; the first are those that operate on a pull-based model. As you can see in figure 5.3, the Pulsar IO framework repeatedly calls the `Source` connector's `read()` method to pull data from the external source into Pulsar.

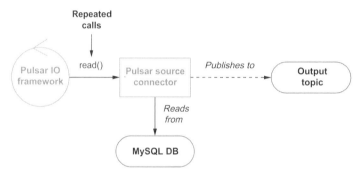

Figure 5.3   The Source connector's `read()` method is repeatedly called, which then pulls the information from the database and publishes it to Pulsar.

In this particular case, the logic inside the connector's `read()` method would be responsible for querying the database, converting the result set into Pulsar messages, and publishing them to the output topic. This type of connector would be particularly useful when you have a legacy order entry application that only writes incoming orders into a MySQL database, and you want to expose these new orders to other systems for real-time processing and analysis.

The easiest way to create a pull-based source connector is to write a Java class that implements the `org.apache.pulsar.io.core.Source` interface, which is shown in listing 5.3. The first method defined in this interface is the `open` method, which is called just once when the source connector is created and should be used to initialize all the necessary resources, such as a database client.

The `open` method specifies an input parameter, named `config` of type `Map`, from which you can retrieve all the connector-specific settings, such as the database connection URL, username, and password. This input parameter contains all of the values specified in the file specified by the `--source-config-file` parameter along with all the default configuration settings and values provided by the various switches used to create or update a function.

Listing 5.3 The Pulsar source interface

```
package org.apache.pulsar.io.core;

public interface Source<T> extends AutoCloseable {
    /**
     * Open source with configuration
     *
     * @param config initialization config
     * @param sourceContext
     * @throws Exception IO type exceptions when opening a connector
     */
    void open(final Map<String, Object> config,
            SourceContext sourceContext) throws Exception;

    /**
     * Reads the next message from source.
     * If source does not have any new messages, this call should block.
     * @return next message from source. The result should never be null
     * @throws Exception
     */
    Record<T> read() throws Exception;

}
```

In addition to the `config` parameter, the Pulsar runtime also provides a `Source-Context` for the connector. Much like the context object defined in the Pulsar Function API, the `SourceContext` object provides access to runtime resources for tasks like collecting metrics, retrieving stateful property values, and more.

The other method defined in the interface is the `read` method, which is responsible for retrieving data from the external source system and publishing it to the target Pulsar topic. The implementation of this method should be blocking on this method if there is no data to return and should never return `null`. The `read()` method returns an object that implements the `org.apache.pulsar.functions.api.Record` interface that we saw earlier in listing 5.2. It is worth pointing out that the source interface also extends the `AutoCloseable` interface that includes a close method definition, which should be used to release any resources, such as database connections, before the connector is stopped

5.1.3 PushSource connectors

The second type of source connectors are those that operate on a push-based model. These connectors continuously gather data and buffer it inside an internal blocking queue for eventual delivery to Pulsar. As you can see from figure 5.4, `PushSource` connectors typically have a background thread running continuously that gathers information from the source system and buffers it inside an internal queue. When the Pulsar IO framework repeatedly calls the `Source` connector's `read()` method, the data inside that internal queue is then published into Pulsar.

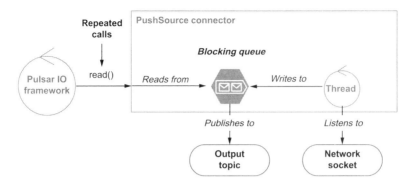

Figure 5.4   The `PushSource` connector's has a background thread running that is listening to a network socket and pushing all the traffic it receives to a blocking queue. When the `read()` method is called, the data is pulled from the blocking queue.

In this particular case, the connector has a background thread that is listening to all incoming traffic on a network socket and publishing it to the internal queue. This type of connector is particularly useful when you are consuming data from an external source that does not retain any information and can be periodically queried at any future point in time. A network socket is just such an example in that if the thread wasn't connected and listening at all times, data sent over that network connection would be lost forever. Contrast this with the previous connector which queries a database. In that scenario, the connector can query the database after an order has been entered into the database and still retrieve the data because the database has retained it.

The easiest way to create a push-based source connector is to write a Java class that extends the abstract `org.apache.pulsar.io.core.PushSource` class shown in the following listing. Since this class implements the Source interface, your class must provide an implementation of all the methods we discussed in the previous section.

Listing 5.4   The `PushSource` class

```
package org.apache.pulsar.io.core;
/**
 * Pulsar's Push Source interface. PushSource read data from
 * external sources (database changes, twitter firehose, etc)
 * and publish to a Pulsar topic. The reason its called Push is
 * because PushSources get passed a consumer that they
 * invoke whenever they have data to be published to Pulsar.
 */
public abstract class PushSource<T> implements Source<T> {

  private LinkedBlockingQueue<Record<T>> queue;
  private static final int DEFAULT_QUEUE_LENGTH = 1000;

  public PushSource() {
    this.queue = new LinkedBlockingQueue<>(this.getQueueLength());   ◁
  }
```

The BatchPushSource uses an internal blocking queue to buffer messages.

```
  @Override
  public Record<T> read() throws Exception {
   return queue.take();
  }
```
Messages are read from the internal queue that blocks if no data is available.

```
  /**
* Attach a consumer function to this Source. This is invoked by the
* implementation to pass messages whenever there is data to be
* pushed to Pulsar.
*
* @param record next message from source which should be sent to
*  a Pulsar topic
*/
  public void consume(Record<T> record) {
    try {
    queue.put(record);
    } catch (InterruptedException e) {
      throw new RuntimeException(e);
    }
  }
```
Incoming messages are stored in the internal queue that blocks if it is full.

```
  /**
* Get length of the queue that records are push onto
* Users can override this method to customize the queue length
* @return queue length
*/
  public int getQueueLength() {
   return DEFAULT_QUEUE_LENGTH;
  }
}
```
You must override this method if you want to increase the size of the internal queue.

The key architectural feature of the PushSource is the LinkedBlockingQueue that is used to buffer messages before they are published to Pulsar. This queue allows you to have a continuously running process that listens for incoming data and publishes it to Pulsar. It is also worth noting that the internal queue can be constrained to the desired size, which allows you to limit the memory consumption of the PushSource connector. When the blocking queue reaches the configured size limit, no more records can be published to the queue. This will result in the background thread getting blocked, which could lead to data loss when the queue is full. Therefore, it is important to size the queue properly.

5.2 Developing Pulsar IO connectors

In the previous section, I introduced the source and sink interfaces provided by the Pulsar IO connector framework and provided a high-level discussion of what each method does. I will build upon that foundation in this section as I walk you through the process of developing new connectors.

5.2.1 Developing a sink connector

I will start with a very basic sink connector that receives an endless stream of string values and writes them to a local temp file, as shown in listing 5.5. While this sink connector does have some limitations, specifically that you cannot write an endless stream of data to a single file, it does serve as a good example that can be used to demonstrate the process of developing a Sink connector.

Listing 5.5   Local file Pulsar IO sink

```
import org.apache.pulsar.io.core.Sink;    ⟵—— Import the source interface.

public class LocalFileSink implements Sink<String> {

    private String prefix, suffix;
    private BufferedWriter bw = null;
    private FileWriter fw = null;

    public void open(Map<String, Object> config,
                     SinkContext sinkContext) throws Exception {

        prefix = (String) config.getOrDefault("filenamePrefix", "test-out");
        suffix = (String) config.getOrDefault
           ("filenameSuffix", ".tmp");      ⟵—
```

Retrieve the target filename prefix and suffix from the provided configuration properties.

```
        File file = File.createTempFile(prefix, suffix);   ⟵—
        fw = new FileWriter(file.getAbsoluteFile(), true);   ⟵—
        bw = new BufferedWriter(fw);
    }
```

Create the new file in the temporary directory.

Initialize the file and buffered writers.

```
    public void write(Record<String> record) throws Exception {
        try {
            bw.write(record.getValue());    ⟵—
            bw.flush();
         ⤷  record.ack();
        } catch (IOException e) {
            record.fail();
            throw new RuntimeException(e);    ⟵—
        }
    }
```

Acknowledge that we processed the message successfully, so it can be purged.

Retrieve the value from the incoming record, and write it to the open file.

Indicate that we weren't able to process the message, so it can be retained and retried at a later time.

```
    public void close() throws Exception {    ⟵—
        try {
            if (bw != null)
               bw.close();
            if (fw != null)
               fw.close();
        } catch (IOException ex) {
            ex.printStackTrace();
        }
    }
}
```

Close both of the open file streams to ensure the data is flushed to disk.

The `open` method of the connector retrieves the configuration properties provided by the user and creates the empty target file inside the temp directory of the host. Next, the instance-level `FileWriter` and `BufferedWriter` variables are initialized to point to the newly created target file, while the close method will attempt to close both of the writers when the connector is stopped.

The sink's `write` method is invoked whenever a new message arrives in any of the sink's configured input topics. The method appends the record value to the target file via the `BufferedWriter`'s `write` method before acknowledging that the message has been successfully processed. In the unlikely event that we cannot write the record's contents to the temp file, an `IOException` will be thrown, and the sink will fail the message before propagating the exception.

5.2.2 *Developing a PushSource connector*

Next, let's write a custom push-based source connector that scans a directory for new files and publishes the contents of these files line by line to Pulsar, as shown in listing 5.6. We want this connector to periodically scan for new files and publish their contents as soon as the file is written to the directory we are scanning. We can do this by extending the `PushSource` class, which is a specialized implementation of the source interface that is designed to use a background process to continuously produce records.

Listing 5.6 A PushSource connector

```
import org.apache.pulsar.io.core.PushSource;
import org.apache.pulsar.io.core.SourceContext;

public class DirectorySource extends PushSource<String> {     An internal thread
  private final ScheduledExecutorService scheduler =          pool for running the
  Executors.newScheduledThreadPool(1);              ◁         background thread

  private DirectoryConsumerThread scanner;            Get the runtime settings from
                                                      the configuration properties
  private Logger log;                                        that are passed in.

@Override
public void open(Map<String, Object> config, SourceContext context)
  throws Exception {
  String in = (String) config.getOrDefault("inputDir", ".");    ◁
  String out = (String) config.getOrDefault("processedDir", ".");
  String freq = (String) config.getOrDefault("frequency", "10");
  scanner = new DirectoryConsumerThread(this, in, out, log);     ◁
  scheduler.scheduleAtFixedRate(scanner, 0, Long.parseLong(freq),
    TimeUnit.MINUTES);
  log.info(String.format("Scheduled to run every %s minutes", freq));
  }

@Override
```

Start the back- ground thread.

Create the background thread, passing in a reference to the source connector and the configs.

```
public void close() throws Exception {
  log.info("Closing connector");
  scheduler.shutdownNow();
}
}
```

The open method of the source connector retrieves the configuration properties provided by the user that specifies the local directory to read the files from, and then launches a background thread of type DirectoryConsumerThread that is responsible for scanning the directory and reading each of the file's contents line by line. The background thread class shown in the following listing takes the source connector instance as a parameter to its constructor method, which it then uses to pass the file contents to an internal blocking queue inside the threads process method.

Listing 5.7   The DirectoryConsumerThread process

```
import org.apache.pulsar.io.core.PushSource;

public class DirectoryConsumerThread extends Thread {
  private final PushSource<String> source;      ◁──────┐   A reference to the
  private final String baseDir;                        │   PushSource connector
  private final String processedDir;

public DirectoryConsumerThread(PushSource<String> source, String base, String
➡ processed, Logger log) {
  this.source = source;
  this.baseDir = base;
  this.processedDir = processed;
  this.log = log;
}

public void run() {
  log.info("Scanning for files.....");
  File[] files = new File(baseDir).listFiles();
  for (int idx = 0; idx < files.length; idx++) {
   consumeFile(files[idx]);      ◁──────┐
  }                                     │   Process all of the files in the
}                                           configured base directory.

private void consumeFile(File file) {
  log.info(String.format("Consuming file %s", file.getName()));
  try (Stream<String> lines = getLines(file)) {            Process each line in
     AtomicInteger counter = new AtomicInteger(0);         the file individually.
     lines.forEach(line ->
        process(line, file.getPath(), counter.incrementAndGet()));      ◁──────┘

     log.info(String.format("Processed %d lines from %s",      When we are finished
        counter.get(), file.getName()));                       with a file, move it to
     Files.move(file.toPath(),Paths.get(processedDir)          the processed directory.
        .resolve(file.toPath().getFileName()), REPLACE_EXISTING);      ◁──────┘
     log.info(String.format("Moved file %s to %s",
        file.toPath().toString(), processedDir));
```

Split each file into individual lines.

```
  } catch (IOException e) {
    e.printStackTrace();
  }
}


private Stream<String> getLines(File file) throws IOException {
  if (file == null) {
    return null;
  } else {
    return Files.lines(Paths.get(file.getAbsolutePath()),
      Charset.defaultCharset());
  }
}


private void process(String line, String src, int lineNum) {
  source.consume(new FileRecord(line, src, lineNum));
}
}
```

Splits the given file into a stream of individual lines

Creates a new Record for each line of text in the file

I also created a new record type, `FileRecord`, as shown in listing 5.8, for this Push-Source connector. This allows me to retain some additional metadata about the file content, including the name of the source file and line number. This type of metadata can be used for downstream processing of these records by other Pulsar functions, as it would allow you to sort the records by file name or type or ensure that you are processing the lines of a given file in sequence (based on the line number).

Listing 5.8 The `FileRecord` class

```
import org.apache.pulsar.functions.api.Record;

public class FileRecord implements Record<String> {

  private static final String SOURCE = "Source";
  private static final String LINE = "Line-no";
  private String content;
  private Map<String, String> props;

  public FileRecord(String content, String src, int lineNumber) {
    this.content = content;
    this.props = new HashMap<String, String>();
    this.props.put(SOURCE, srcFileName);
    this.props.put(LINE, lineNumber + "");
  }

  @Override
  public Optional<String> getKey() {
    return Optional.ofNullable(props.get(SOURCE));
  }

  @Override
  public Map<String, String> getProperties() {
```

The actual contents of the file for this particular line

The message properties

Use the source file as the key for key-based subscriptions, etc.

```
    return props;          ⊲─┐
  }                          │    The message properties
                                  expose the metadata.

  @Override
  public String getValue() {
    return content;      ⊲─┐
  }                        │    The message value is the raw
}                               file contents themselves.
}
```

The thread's `process` method calls the `PushSource`'s `consume()` method, passing in the file contents. As we saw in listing 5.4, the `consume()` method inside the `PushSource` simply writes the incoming data directly to the internal blocking queue. This decouples the reading of the file contents from the Pulsar framework's call to the `PushSource` connector's `read()` method. The use of a background thread is a common design pattern for `PushSource` connectors that retrieve the data from the external system and then invoke the source's consume method to push the data to the output topic.

5.3   *Testing Pulsar IO connectors*

In this section, I will walk you through the process of developing and testing a Pulsar connector. Let's use the `DirectorySource` connector shown in listing 5.6 to demonstrate the software development lifecycle for a Pulsar connector. This connector takes in a user-provided directory and publishes the contents of all the files within the given directory line by line.

While this code is fairly simplistic, I will walk through the testing process you would typically use when developing a connector for production use. Since this is just plain Java code, we can leverage any of the existing unit testing frameworks, such as JUnit or TestNG, to test the function logic.

5.3.1   *Unit testing*

The first step is to write a suite of unit tests that test some of the more common scenarios in order to validate that the logic is correct and produces accurate results for various sentences we send it. Since this code uses the Pulsar SDK API, we will need to use a Mocking library, such as Mockito, to mock the `SourceContext` object, as shown in the following listing.

Listing 5.9   `DirectorySource` unit tests

```
public class DirectorySourceTest {
  final static Path SOURCE_DIR =
    Paths.get(System.getProperty("java.io.tmpdir"), "source");
  final static Path PROCESSED_DIR =
    Paths.get(System.getProperty("java.io.tmpdir"),"processed");  ⊲─┐  Using the
                                                                      tmp folder
                                                                      for testing
  private Path srcPath, processedPath;
  private DirectorySource spySource;   ⊲─┐
                                          │  We will spy on the
                                             DirectorySource connector.
  @Mock
```

```
    private SourceContext mockedContext;

    @Mock
    private Logger mockedLogger;
```

Class that captures all of the records written by the DirectorySource connector

```
    @Captor
    private ArgumentCaptor<FileRecord> captor;

    @Before
    public final void init() throws IOException {
        MockitoAnnotations.initMocks(this);
        when(mockedContext.getLogger()).thenReturn(mockedLogger);
        FileUtils.deleteDirectory(SOURCE_DIR.toFile());
        FileUtils.deleteDirectory(PROCESSED_DIR.toFile());
        srcPath = Files.createDirectory(SOURCE_DIR,
          PosixFilePermissions.asFileAttribute(
            PosixFilePermissions.fromString("rwxrwxrwx")));
        processedPath = Files.createDirectory(PROCESSED_DIR,
          PosixFilePermissions.asFileAttribute(
            PosixFilePermissions.fromString("rwxrwxrwx")));
        spySource = spy(new DirectorySource());
    }
```

Clear out the tmp folder before running each test.

Create the source and processed folder used during the test.

Instantiate the DirectorySource connector.

```
    @Test
    public final void oneLineTest() throws Exception {
      Files.copy(getFile("single-line.txt"),Paths.get(srcPath.toString(),
        "single-line.txt"), COPY_ATTRIBUTES);
      Map<String, Object> configs = new HashMap<String, Object>();
      configs.put("inputDir", srcPath.toFile().getAbsolutePath());
      configs.put("processedDir", processedPath.toFile().getAbsolutePath());

      spySource.open(configs, mockedContext);
      Thread.sleep(3000);

      Mockito.verify(spySource).consume(captor.capture());
      FileRecord captured = captor.getValue();
      assertNotNull(captured);
      assertEquals("It was the best of times",
        captured.getValue());
      assertEquals("1", captured.getProperties().get(FileRecord.LINE));
      assertTrue(captured.getProperties().get(FileRecord.SOURCE)
        .contains("single-line.txt"));
    }
```

Copy the test file into the source directory.

Run the DirectorySource connector.

Verify that a single record was published.

Retrieve the published record for validation.

Validate the record contents.

Validate the record properties.

```
    @Test
    public final void multiLineTest() throws Exception {
      Files.copy(getFile("example-1.txt"),Paths.get(srcPath.toString(),
        "example-1.txt"), COPY_ATTRIBUTES);
      Map<String, Object> configs = new HashMap<String, Object>();
      configs.put("inputDir", srcPath.toFile().getAbsolutePath());
      configs.put("processedDir", processedPath.toFile().getAbsolutePath());

      spySource.open(configs, mockedContext);
      Thread.sleep(3000);
```

Run the DirectorySource connector.

```
    Mockito.verify(spySource, times(113)).consume(captor.capture());    ◁──┐
                                                                   Verify that the expected
    final AtomicInteger counter = new AtomicInteger(0);            number of records were
    captor.getAllValues().forEach(rec -> {                                  published.
      assertNotNull(rec.getValue());
      assertEquals(counter.incrementAndGet() + "",
        rec.getProperties().get(FileRecord.LINE));
      assertTrue(rec.getProperties().get(FileRecord.SOURCE)
        .contains("example-1.txt"));    ◁──┐
                                      Validate each of the records'
    });                               values and properties.
  }

  private static Path getFile(String fileName) throws IOException {
    . . .
  }
}
```

As you can see, these unit tests cover the very basic functionality of Functions and rely on the use of a mock object for the Pulsar context object. This type of test suite is quite similar to one you would write to test any Java class that wasn't a Pulsar function.

5.3.2   Integration testing

After we are satisfied with our unit testing results, we will want to see how the Pulsar function will perform on a Pulsar cluster. The easiest way to test a Pulsar function is to start a Pulsar server and run the Pulsar function locally using the `LocalRunner` helper class. In this mode, the function runs as a standalone process on the machine it is submitted from. This option is best when you are developing and testing your connectors, as it allows you to attach a debugger to the connector process on the local machine. In order to use the `LocalRunner`, you must first add a few dependencies to your maven project, which brings in the `LocalRunner` class that is used to test the function against a running Pulsar cluster, as shown in the following listing.

Listing 5.10   Including the `LocalRunner` dependencies

```
<dependencies>
  . . .
  <dependency>
      <groupId>com.fasterxml.jackson.core</groupId>
      <artifactId>jackson-core</artifactId>
      <version>2.11.1</version>
  </dependency>
  <dependency>
    <groupId>org.apache.pulsar</groupId>
    <artifactId>pulsar-functions-local-runner-original</artifactId>
    <version>2.6.1</version>
  </dependency>
</dependencies>
```

Next, we need to write a class to configure and launch the `LocalRunner`, as shown in listing 5.11. As you can see, this code must first configure the Pulsar connector to execute on the `LocalRunner` and specify the address of the actual Pulsar cluster instance that will be used for the testing. The easiest way to gain access to a Pulsar cluster is to launch the Pulsar Docker container like we have done previously by running the following command in a bash window: `docker run -d -p 6650:6650 -p 8080:8080 --name pulsar apachepulsar/pulsar-standalone`. This will start a Pulsar cluster in standalone mode inside the container. Typically, you would run the `LocalRunner` test from inside your integrated development environment (IDE) in order to attach a debugger and step through the function code to identify and resolve any errors you have encountered.

Listing 5.11 Testing the `DirectorySource` with the `LocalRunner`

```
public class DirectorySourceLocalRunnerTest {
  final static String BROKER_URL = "pulsar://localhost:6650";
  final static String OUT = "persistent://public/default/directory-scan";
  final static Path SOURCE_DIR =
     Paths.get(System.getProperty("java.io.tmpdir"), "source");
  final static Path PROCESSED_DIR =
     Paths.get(System.getProperty("java.io.tmpdir"), "processed");      ◁─┐

                                                        Using the tmp
  private static LocalRunner localRunner;               folder for testing
  private static Path srcPath, processedPath;

  public static void main(String[] args) throws Exception {
    init();
    startLocalRunner();
    shutdown();
  }

  private static void startLocalRunner() throws Exception {
    localRunner = LocalRunner.builder()
           .brokerServiceUrl(BROKER_URL)       ◁────         Connect the LocalRunner
           .sourceConfig(getSourceConfig())    ◁──┐          to the Docker container.
           .build();
    localRunner.start(false);
  }                                              Deploy the
                                                 DirectorySource connector.

  private static void init() throws IOException {
    Files.deleteIfExists(SOURCE_DIR);
    Files.deleteIfExists(PROCESSED_DIR);
    srcPath = Files.createDirectory(SOURCE_DIR,
      PosixFilePermissions.asFileAttribute(
        PosixFilePermissions.fromString("rwxrwxrwx")));
    processedPath = Files.createDirectory(PROCESSED_DIR,     Create the source
      PosixFilePermissions.asFileAttribute(                 and processed folder
        PosixFilePermissions.fromString("rwxrwxrwx")));  ◁── used during the test.

    Files.copy(getFile("example-1.txt"), Paths.get(srcPath.toString(),
      "example-1.txt"), COPY_ATTRIBUTES);
```

Copy the test file into the source directory.

```
        }

        private static void shutdown() throws Exception {     ⊲──┐   Stops the LocalRunner
          Thread.sleep(30000);                                          after 30 seconds
          localRunner.stop();
          System.exit(0);
        }

        private static SourceConfig getSourceConfig() {
          Map<String, Object> configs = new HashMap<String, Object>();
          configs.put("inputDir", srcPath.toFile().getAbsolutePath());
          configs.put("processedDir", processedPath.toFile().getAbsolutePath());

          return SourceConfig.builder()
              .className(DirectorySource.class.getName())    ⊲──┐   Specify the DirectorySource
              .configs(configs)                                         as the connector we want to
              .name("directory-source")                                 run.
              .tenant("public")
              .namespace("default")
              .topicName(OUT)    ⊲──┐   Specifies the output topic
              .build();                  for the source connector
        }

        private static Path getFile(String fileName) throws IOException {
          . . .    ⊲──┐   Reads the file from the
        }                  project resources folder
      }
```

Configure the DirectorySource connector.

5.3.3 *Packaging Pulsar IO connectors*

Since Pulsar IO connectors are specialized Pulsar functions, they are expected to be self-contained software bundles. Thus, you will need to package your connector with all of its dependencies as either a fat JAR or a NAR file. NAR stands for *NiFi archive*. It is a custom packaging mechanism used by Apache NiFi that provides Java ClassLoader isolation. In order to have your Pulsar IO connector packaged as a NAR file, all that is required is to include the `nifi-nar-maven-plugin` in your maven project for your connector, as shown in the following listing.

Listing 5.12 Creating a NAR package

```
<build>
  ...
  <plugin>
    <groupId>org.apache.nifi</groupId>
    <artifactId>nifi-nar-maven-plugin</artifactId>
    <version>1.2.0</version>
    <extensions>true</extensions>
    <executions>
      <execution>
        <phase>package</phase>
        <goals>
          <goal>nar</goal>
```

```
            </goals>
          </execution>
        </executions>
      </plugin>
  </build>
```

The build plugin in listing 5.12 is used to generate a NAR file, which by default includes all of the project dependencies in the generated archive file. This is the preferred method for bundling and deploying Java-based Pulsar IO connectors. With this plugin added to your pom.xml file, all that you need to do is run the `mvn clean install` command to produce a NAR file that can be used to deploy your connector onto a production Pulsar cluster. Once you have packaged up your connector along with all of its dependencies inside a NAR file, the next step is to deploy the connector to a Pulsar cluster.

5.4 *Deploying Pulsar IO connectors*

As specialized Pulsar functions, IO connectors utilize the same runtime environment that provides all the benefits of the Pulsar Functions framework, including fault tolerance, parallelism, elasticity, load balancing, on-demand updates, and much more. With respect to deployment options, you can have the Pulsar IO connector run on your local development machine, in localrun mode, inside the function workers in the Pulsar cluster, or in cluster mode. In the previous section, we were using the Local-Runner to run our connector in localrun mode. In this section, I will walk you through the process of running the `DirectorySource` connector we developed in cluster mode.

Figure 5.5 shows a cluster-mode deployment inside a Kubernetes environment, where each connector runs in its own container alongside other non-connector function instances. In cluster mode, Pulsar IO connectors leverage the fault-tolerance capability offered by the Pulsar Functions runtime scheduler to handle failures. If a connector is running on a machine that fails, Pulsar will automatically attempt to restart the task on one of the remaining running nodes in the cluster.

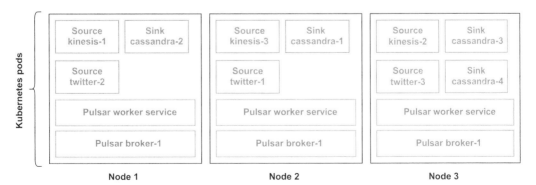

Figure 5.5   Pulsar IO connector deployment on Kubernetes

5.4.1   *Creating and deleting connectors*

If you haven't already done so, run the `mvn clean install` command to create the NAR file for the `DirectorySource` connector. Also, you will want to stop any running Docker Pulsar containers, as you will need to start a new instance with some additional parameters that allow you to access the NAR file from inside the Pulsar Docker container, as shown in the following listing.

Listing 5.13   Starting Pulsar Docker container with mounted volumes

```
$ export GIT_PROJECT=<CLONE_DIR>/pulsar-in-action/chapter5
$ docker run --name pulsar -id \
  -p 6650:6650 -p 8080:8080 \
  -v $GIT_PROJECT:/pulsar/dropbox
apachepulsar/pulsar-standalone
```

Makes the project directory accessible inside the Docker container

Set this to the directory where you cloned the book's associated repo.

As you can see from listing 5.13, we have added a -v switch to the usual command we have been using to launch a Pulsar Docker container. That switch mounts the local directory where you cloned the source code for this chapter onto your machine to a folder named /pulsar/dropbox inside the Docker container itself. This is necessary to deploy the connector, since the NAR file has to be physically accessible by the Pulsar cluster for it to be deployed. We will also use this mounted directory to access the configuration file that must be provided when creating a connector.

As you may have noticed, we have always provided hard-coded values for the configuration property inside the unit and integration tests, but when deploying to production, we want to specify those values in a more dynamic manner. This is where the configuration file comes in, as it allows us to specify connector-specific configurations along with other standard connector properties such as parallelism.

Listing 5.14   Contents of the `DirectorySource` connector config file

```
tenant: public
namespace: default
name: directory-source

className: com.manning.pulsar.chapter5.source.DirectorySource
topicName: "persistent://public/default/directory-scan"
parallelism: 1
processingGuarantees: ATLEAST_ONCE

# Connector specific config
configs:
    inputDir: "/tmp/input"
    processedDir: "/tmp/processed"
    frequency: 10
```

As you can see in listing 5.14, the configuration file we are going to use to deploy the connector contains values for source and processed directories along with several properties used by the Pulsar IO framework to create the Pulsar IO connector. The configuration file is then provided to the `bin/pulsar-admin source create` command when you want to create a new source connector, as shown in the following listing.

Listing 5.15 The output of the `create` command

Create the input and output folders inside the container, and copy over a test file.

```
docker exec -it pulsar mkdir -p /tmp/input
docker exec -it pulsar chmod a+w /tmp/input
docker exec -it pulsar mkdir -p /tmp/processed
docker exec -it pulsar chmod a+w /tmp/processed
docker exec -it pulsar cp /pulsar/dropbox/src/test/resources/example-1.txt
  /tmp/input
```

Using the source, create a command to create the connector.

```
docker exec -it pulsar /pulsar/bin/pulsar-admin source create \
 --archive /pulsar/dropbox/target/chapter5-0.0.1.nar \
 --source-config-file /pulsar/dropbox/src/main/resources/config.yml
```

Specifies the configuration file to use

```
"Created successfully"
```

A response message indicating that the source was created

```
docker exec -it pulsar /pulsar/bin/pulsar-admin source list
[
  "directory-source"
]
```

Specifies the NAR file that contains the source connector class

List the active source connectors to confirm it was created.

When you create the connector, you should receive a reassuring `Created success-fully` message to indicate that the connector was launched successfully. If you did not receive the success message, you will need to debug the error, as described in the next section.

5.4.2 Debugging deployed connectors

If you encounter any errors or unexpected behavior inside a Pulsar IO connector that has been deployed, the best place to start debugging is the log files on the Pulsar worker node where the connector is running. By default, all of the connector's startup information and captured stderr output is written to a log file. The name of the file is based on the connector name and matches the following pattern in a production environment: logs/functions/tenant/namespace/function-name/function-name-instance-id .log. In standalone mode, which is what we are currently using, the base directory is /tmp instead of /logs with the rest of the path staying the same. Let's examine the log file for the `DirectorySource` connector that we created in the previous section, shown in the following listing, and review some of the information that is available to you for debugging.

Listing 5.16   The first section of the `DirectorySource` log file

```
cat /tmp/functions/public/default/directory-source/
   directory-source-0.log     ⊲────┐
                                    Examining the connector's log file
20:53:30.671 [main] INFO
   org.apache.pulsar.functions.runtime.JavaInstanceStarter - JavaInstance
   Server started, listening on 36857
20:53:30.676 [main] INFO
   org.apache.pulsar.functions.runtime.JavaInstanceStarter -
   Starting runtimeSpawner
20:53:30.678 [main] INFO
   org.apache.pulsar.functions.runtime.RuntimeSpawner -
   public/default/directory-source-0 RuntimeSpawner starting function
20:53:30.689 [main] INFO
   org.apache.pulsar.functions.runtime.thread.ThreadRuntime -
   ThreadContainer starting function with instance config
   InstanceConfig(instanceId=0, functionId=c368b93f-34e9-4bcf-801f-
   d097b1c0d173, functionVersion=247cbde2
-b8b4-45bb-a3cb-8926c3b33217, functionDetails=tenant: "public"    ⊲─┐
namespace: "default"                                                │ The connector
name: "directory-source"                                           │ configuration
className: "org.apache.pulsar.functions.api.utils.IdentityFunction" │ details section
autoAck: true
parallelism: 1                                            ┌─ The
source {                                                  │  connector
  className: "com.manning.pulsar.chapter5.source.DirectorySource" ⊲─┤ class name
  configs:                                              ⊲─┐
     "{\"processedDir\":\"/tmp/processed\",\"inputDir\":\"/tmp/input\",
     \"frequency\":\"2\"}"
  typeClassName: "java.lang.String"                    The configuration map │
}
sink {
  topic: "persistent://public/default/directory-scan"  ⊲──── The output topic
  typeClassName: "java.lang.String"
}
resources {
  cpu: 1.0
  ram: 1073741824
  disk: 10737418240
}
componentType: SOURCE
, maxBufferedTuples=1024, functionAuthenticationSpec=null, port=36857,
   clusterName=standalone, maxPendingAsyncRequests=10
00)

...
20:53:31.223 [public/default/directory-source-0] INFO
   org.apache.pulsar.functions.instance.JavaInstanceRunnable - Initialize
   function class loader for function directory-source at function cache
   manager, functionClassLoader:
   org.apache.pulsar.common.nar.NarClassLoader[/tmp/pulsar-nar/chapter5-
   0.0.1.nar-unpacked]     ⊲────┐
                                The NAR file and version we are
                                using to deploy the connector
```

The first section of the log file contains the basic information about the connector, such as the tenant, namespace, name, parallelism, resources, and so on, which can be used to check whether the connector has been configured correctly or not. A little further down in the log file, you should see a message indicating which artifact file the connector was created from, which allows you to confirm that you are using the correct artifact file.

Listing 5.17 The last section of the `DirectorySource` log file

```
org.apache.pulsar.client.impl.ProducerStatsRecorderImpl - Starting
 Pulsar producer perf with config: {                           ◁──────┐
  "topicName" : "persistent://public/default/directory-scan",   The Pulsar
  "producerName" : null,                                         producer for the
  "sendTimeoutMs" : 0,                                           source connector
  ...
  "multiSchema" : true,         ◁───  Additional source
  "properties" : {                    connector properties
    "application" : "pulsar-source",
    "id" : "public/default/directory-source",
    "instance_id" : "0"
  }
}
20:53:33.704 [public/default/directory-source-0] INFO
    org.apache.pulsar.client.impl.ProducerStatsRecorderImpl
    - Pulsar client config: {                  ◁────
  "serviceUrl" : "pulsar://localhost:6650",   The Pulsar client configuration,
  "authPluginClassName" : null,                including security settings
  "authParams" : null,
  ...
  "proxyProtocol" : null         ◁───  Additional Pulsar client
}                                    configuration properties
20:53:33.726 [public/default/directory-source-0] INFO
    org.apache.pulsar.client.impl.ProducerImpl - [persistent://public/
default/directory-scan] [null] Creating producer on cnx [id: 0xbcd9978b,
    L:/127.0.0.1:44010 - R:localhost/127.0.0.1:6650]
20:53:33.886 [pulsar-client-io-1-1] INFO           Log messages from the
    org.apache.pulsar.client.impl.ProducerImpl -   DirectorySource connector
    [persistent://public/default/direc
tory-scan] [standalone-0-0] Created producer on cnx [id: 0xbcd9978b,
    L:/127.0.0.1:44010 - R:localhost/127.0.0.1:6650]
20:53:33.983 [public/default/directory-source-0] INFO  function-directory-
    source - Scheduled to run every 2 minutes          ◁──────────┘
20:53:33.985 [pool-6-thread-1] INFO  function-directory-source - Scanning
    for files.....
20:53:33.987 [pool-6-thread-1] INFO  function-directory-source - Processing
    file example-1.txt
20:53:33.987 [pool-6-thread-1] INFO  function-directory-source - Consuming
    file example-1.txt
20:53:34.385 [pool-6-thread-1] INFO  function-directory-source - Processed
    113 lines from example-1.txt
20:53:34.385 [pool-6-thread-1] INFO  function-directory-source - Moved file
    /tmp/input/example-2.txt to /tmp/processed
```

The next section of the log file, shown in listing 5.18, contains some information about the Pulsar producers and consumers that are created on behalf of the connector and will be used to publish and consume data from the configured input and output topics. Any connectivity issues with either of these will result in errors at this point. All the log statements added to your code will follow this section and allow you to monitor the progress of your connector or see any of the exceptions that were raised.

When you are finished with the connector and don't want it to run any more, you can use the `bin/pulsar-admin source delete` command to stop all the running instances of the connector. The only parameters you need to provide are the connector's tenant, namespace, and name to uniquely identify the connector that you wish to delete (e.g., in order to delete the source we just created you would simply execute the following command: `bin/pulsar-admin source delete --tenant public --namespace default --name directory-source`).

5.5   *Pulsar's built-in connectors*

Pulsar provides a wide variety of existing sources and sinks, collectively referred to as *built-in connectors*, that you can use to get started using the Pulsar IO connector framework without having to write any code. Pulsar releases all the built-in connectors as individual archives. All that is required to use these connectors is a copy of the built-in connector's archive (NAR) file on your Pulsar cluster and a simple YAML or JSON configuration file that specifies the runtime parameters used to connect to the external system. If you are running Pulsar in standalone mode, as we are by using the Pulsar standalone Docker image, then these built-in connectors' individual archives are already included as part of the distribution.

Let's walk through a simple scenario that uses these built-in connectors to move data from Pulsar into MongoDB. While this example is a bit simplistic in nature, it will demonstrate how easy it is to use the connector's framework and help demonstrate some of the high-level steps required to deploy and use Pulsar IO connectors. The first step in this process will be to create an instance of MongoDB that we can interact with.

5.5.1   *Launching the MongoDB cluster*

The following command will run the latest MongoDB container in detached mode for us. We are also mapping the container ports with host ports, so we can access the database from our local machine if we want to. Once the container has launched, we will have a functional MongoDB deployment available for us to work with:

```
$ docker run -d \
  -p 27017-27019:27017-27019 \
  --name mongodb \
  mongo
```

At this point we will have a MongoDB Docker container currently running in detached mode. Next, you will need to execute the mongo command to launch the MongoDB shell client. Once inside the shell we will need to create a new database and collection to store the data. Next, we will need to create a new database named `pulsar_in_action` and define a collection inside the database that we will use for storing the data, using the commands shown in following listing.

Listing 5.18 Creating a Mongo database table

Start the MongoDB interactive shell.

```
docker exec -it mongodb mongo
MongoDB shell version v4.4.1          Among the output, you should
...                                   see the MongoDB shell version.
>


>use pulsar_in_action;                Creates a database with
switched to db pulsar_in_action       the name pulsar_in_action
                                                                    Creates a collection
                                                                    named example inside
                                                                    the database and
> db.example.save({ firstname: "John", lastname: "Smith"})          defines the schema
WriteResult({ "nInserted" : 1 })
                                             Query the database to confirm the
                                             record was added successfully.
> db.example.find({firstname: "John"})
{ "_id" : ObjectId("5f7a53aedccb229a78960d2c"), "firstname" : "John",
   "lastname" : "Smith" }
```

Now that we have a MongoDB cluster running locally and a database created, we can proceed with configuring a MongoDB sink connector. It will then read messages from a Pulsar topic and write the messages into a MongoDB table we created.

5.5.2 Link the Pulsar and MongoDB containers

Since we are going to run the MongoDB Pulsar connector inside the Pulsar Docker container, there must be network connectivity between the two containers. The easiest way to accomplish this in Docker is by using the `--link` command line argument when launching the Pulsar container. However, since we already started the Pulsar container, we will first need to stop it and remove it before restarting it with the `--link` switch. Therefore, you will need to execute all of the commands shown in the following listing before proceeding.

Listing 5.19 Commands to link Pulsar and MongoDB containers

```
$ docker stop pulsar          Stops the currently running Pulsar container

$ docker rm pulsar
                              Deletes the old Pulsar container, so we can
                              create a new one with the same name
$ docker run -d \
  -p 6650:6650 -p 8080:8080 \
  -v $PWD/data:/pulsar/data \
  --name pulsar \                          Links the MongoDB container
  --link mongodb \                         to the Pulsar container
  apachepulsar/pulsar-standalone
```

```
$ docker exec -it pulsar bash      ◁――― Exec into the new
                                          Pulsar container

apt-get update && apt-get install vim --fix-missing -y ◁―――
―▷ vim /pulsar/examples/mongodb-sink.yml
```

> **We need to install the vim text editor in the Pulsar container so we can edit the config file.**

> **Launch the text editor inside the Pulsar container to create the configuration file.**

By providing the name of the container running the MongoDB instance we wish to interact with in the `--link` switch, Docker creates a secure network channel between the two containers that allows the Pulsar container to talk to the MongoDB container via the link name. We will see this when we configure the MongoDB sink connector.

5.5.3   Configure and create the MongoDB sink

Configuring Pulsar IO connectors is straightforward. All you need to do is to provide a YAML configuration file when you create the connectors. In order to run a MongoDB sink connector, you will need to prepare a YAML config file containing all the information that the Pulsar IO runtime needs to know to connect to the local MongoDB instance. First, you need to create a local file in the examples subdirectory named mongodb-sink.yml and edit it to have the content shown in the following listing.

> **Listing 5.20   The MongoDB sink connector configuration file**

```
tenant: "public"
namespace: "default"
name: "mongo-test-sink"
configs:
    mongoUri: "mongodb://mongodb:27017/admin"   ◁―――
    database: "pulsar_in_action"   ◁―――
    collection: "example"   ◁―――
    batchSize: 1
    batchTimeMs: 1000
```

> **We can use the name specified with the –link switch here instead of a hostname or IP address.**

> **We must specify the Mongo database we are writing to.**

> **We must specify the Mongo collection we are writing to.**

For more information on the MongoDB sink connector configuration, please refer to the documentation (http://pulsar.apache.org/docs/en/io-mongo/#sink). The Pulsar command line interface provides commands for running and managing Pulsar IO connectors, so you can run the command shown in the following listing from the Pulsar container command line to start the MongoDB sink connector.

> **Listing 5.21   Starting the MongoDB sink connector**

> **Using the sink, create the command.**

```
―▷ /pulsar/bin/pulsar-admin sink create \
       --sink-type mongo \
       --sink-config-file /pulsar/examples/mongodb-sink.yml \
―▷ --inputs test-mongo
"Created successfully"   ◁―――
```

> **Indicates we want to use the built-in sink connector for MongoDB**

> **Use the configuration file we created earlier.**

> **Specifies the input topic**

> **A response message indicating that the sink was created**

Once the command is executed, Pulsar will create a sink connector named `mongo-test-sink`, and the sink connector will begin writing the messages in the `test-mongo` topic to the MongoDB collection `examples` in the `pulsar_in_action` database. Now, let's send some messages to the `test-mongo` topic to confirm that the connector is functioning as expected by executing the commands in the following listing from inside the Docker container.

Listing 5.22 Sending messages to the connector's input topic

We are producing messages.

```
/pulsar/bin/pulsar-client produce \
-m "{firstname: \"Mary\", lastname: \"Smith\"}" \
-s % \
-n 10 \
test-mongo
```

The message contents, including escaped quotes

Specifies we want to send the same message 10 times

Defines a non-comma record separator character; otherwise the message contents would be split

The destination topic

You can now query the MongoDB instance to confirm that the MongoDB connector worked as expected. Return to the MongoDB shell we opened earlier to create the database and run some different queries to confirm that the records were added to the MongoDB table as expected, as shown in the next listing.

Listing 5.23 Querying the MongoDB table after the messages are sent

Query by lastname field.

10 instances of the new record created from the messages we just sent

```
> db.example.find({lastname: "Smith"})
{ "_id" : ObjectId("5f7a53aedccb229a78960d2c"), "firstname" : "John",
  "lastname" : "Smith" }         <——— The original record we published
{ "_id" : ObjectId("5f7a68bbb94aa03489fa5ca9"), "firstname" : "Mary",
  "lastname" : "Smith" }
{ "_id" : ObjectId("5f7a68bbb94aa03489fa5caa"), "firstname" : "Mary",
  "lastname" : "Smith" }
{ "_id" : ObjectId("5f7a68bbb94aa03489fa5cab"), "firstname" : "Mary",
  "lastname" : "Smith" }
{ "_id" : ObjectId("5f7a68bbb94aa03489fa5cac"), "firstname" : "Mary",
  "lastname" : "Smith" }
{ "_id" : ObjectId("5f7a68bbb94aa03489fa5cad"), "firstname" : "Mary",
  "lastname" : "Smith" }
{ "_id" : ObjectId("5f7a68bbb94aa03489fa5cae"), "firstname" : "Mary",
  "lastname" : "Smith" }
{ "_id" : ObjectId("5f7a68bbb94aa03489fa5caf"), "firstname" : "Mary",
  "lastname" : "Smith" }
{ "_id" : ObjectId("5f7a68bbb94aa03489fa5cb0"), "firstname" : "Mary",
  "lastname" : "Smith" }
{ "_id" : ObjectId("5f7a68bbb94aa03489fa5cb1"), "firstname" : "Mary",
  "lastname" : "Smith" }
{ "_id" : ObjectId("5f7a68bbb94aa03489fa5cb2"), "firstname" : "Mary",
  "lastname" : "Smith" }
```

This concludes our quick introduction to the built-in Pulsar IO connectors. Now, you should have a better understanding of how to configure and deploy Pulsar connectors and how the overall IO connectors framework works.

5.6   *Administering Pulsar IO connectors*

The `pulsar-admin` CLI tool provides a collection of commands that enables you to manage, monitor, and update Pulsar IO connectors. We will discuss some of these commands that were designed specifically for Pulsar IO connectors, including how and when they should be used and what information they provide. It is worth noting that both the sink and source commands have the exact same subcommands, so we will only focus on the sink command, but the information is applicable to source connectors as well.

5.6.1   *Listing connectors*

The first command we will look at is the `pulsar-admin sink list` command, which will return a list of all the sinks currently running on the Pulsar cluster, which is useful when you want to make sure the connector you just created was accepted and is running. If you were to run this command after you deployed the `mongo-test-sink` connector, the expected output would be similar to what is shown in the following listing.

> **Listing 5.24   Output of the `list` command inside the Docker container**

```
docker exec -it pulsar /pulsar/bin/pulsar-admin sink list
[
  "mongo-test-sink"
]
```

This shows that the `mongo-test-sink` was indeed created and is the only sink connector currently running in the Pulsar cluster. The `list` command is not to be confused with the `available-sources` or `available-sinks` commands, which will return a list of all the built-in connectors that are supported by the Pulsar cluster. By default, the built-in connectors are included in the Pulsar standalone Docker container, so the output of the command should be as shown in the following listing. The `available-sinks` command can also help you confirm that you have successfully installed a custom connector manually.

> **Listing 5.25   Output of the `available-sinks` command inside the Pulsar Docker container**

```
docker exec -it pulsar /pulsar/bin/pulsar-admin sink available-sinks
aerospike
Aerospike database sink
----------------------------------------
cassandra
Writes data into Cassandra
----------------------------------------
data-generator
```

```
Test data generator source
----------------------------------------
elastic_search
Writes data into Elastic Search
----------------------------------------
flume
flume source and sink connector
----------------------------------------
hbase
Writes data into hbase table
----------------------------------------
hdfs2
Writes data into HDFS 2.x
----------------------------------------
hdfs3
Writes data into HDFS 3.x
----------------------------------------
influxdb
Writes data into InfluxDB database
----------------------------------------
jdbc-clickhouse
JDBC sink for ClickHouse
----------------------------------------
jdbc-mariadb
JDBC sink for MariaDB
----------------------------------------
jdbc-postgres
JDBC sink for PostgreSQL
----------------------------------------
jdbc-sqlite
JDBC sink for SQLite
----------------------------------------
kafka
Kafka source and sink connector
----------------------------------------
kinesis
Kinesis connectors
----------------------------------------
mongo
MongoDB source and sink connector
----------------------------------------
rabbitmq
RabbitMQ source and sink connector
----------------------------------------
redis
Writes data into Redis
----------------------------------------
solr
Writes data into solr collection
----------------------------------------
```

5.6.2 *Monitoring connectors*

Another useful command for monitoring Pulsar IO connectors is the `pulsar-admin sink status` command. This command will return runtime information about the specified connector, such as how many instances are running and if any of the instances have encountered errors.

Listing 5.26   Output of the `Sink status` command

The total number of instances of the connector that were requested

```
docker exec -it pulsar /pulsar/bin/pulsar-admin sink status \
  --name mongo-test-sink
  {
    "numInstances" : 1,
    "numRunning" : 1,
    "instances" : [ {
      "instanceId" : 0,
      "status" : {
        "running" : true,
        "error" : "",
        "numRestarts" : 0,
        "numReadFromPulsar" : 0,
        "numSystemExceptions" : 0,
        "latestSystemExceptions" : [ ],
        "numSinkExceptions" : 0,
        "latestSinkExceptions" : [ ],
        "numWrittenToSink" : 0,
        "lastReceivedTime" : 0,
        "workerId" : "c-standalone-fw-d513daf5b94e-8080"
      }
    } ]
  }
```

The total number of instances of the connector that are running

An array of information for each instance

The current status of the connector

Any applicable error messages

The number of times the connector attempted to restart. This number increases whenever the connector failed to start, and it is relaunched.

The number of messages consumed from the Pulsar input topic by this instance

The last time an incoming message was consumed by this instance

As you can see from listing 5.26, the `pulsar-admin sink status` command would be particularly useful for checking on the status of a connector immediately after you have deployed it to make sure it started properly. The `pulsar-admin sink get` command can be used to return the configuration information about a Pulsar IO connector, which is useful when you want to inspect the configuration settings of your connector to ensure it is properly configured, as shown in the next listing.

Listing 5.27   Output of the `sink get` command

```
docker exec -it pulsar /pulsar/bin/pulsar-admin sink get \
--name mongo-test-sink
{
  "tenant": "public",
  "namespace": "default",
  "name": "mongo-test-sink",
  "className": "org.apache.pulsar.io.mongodb.MongoSink",
  "inputSpecs": {
    "test-mongo": {
      "isRegexPattern": false
    }
  },
```

The tenant, namespace, and name of the connector

The classname of the connector implementation

The input topics for the sink connector

Whether or not the sink is configured to consume from multiple topics based on some regular expression

```
  "configs": {                              ◁───┐    All of the user-defined
    "mongoUri": "mongodb://mongodb:27017/admin",  │    configuration properties we
    "database": "pulsar_in_action",                    provided in the sink-config-file
    "collection": "example",
    "batchSize": "1.0",
    "batchTimeMs": "1000.0"          All of the default property values
  },                                 for properties we did not specify
  "parallelism": 1,          ◁───────┘
  "processingGuarantees": "ATLEAST_ONCE",
  "retainOrdering": false,
  "autoAck": true,
  "archive": "builtin://mongo"
}
```

What makes this command even more useful is the fact that the output of the command is a properly formatted JSON connector configuration that can be saved as a file, modified, and used to update the configuration of the running connector with the update command. This frees you from having to retain a copy of the configuration you deployed a specific connector with, as the data can easily be retrieved from the running connector with this command.

Listing 5.28   Updating the Mongo DB connector

```
/pulsar/bin/pulsar-admin sink update \
    --sink-type mongo \
    --sink-config-file /pulsar/examples/mongodb-sink.yml \
    --inputs prod-mongo \
    --processing-guarantees EFFECTIVELY_ONCE
```

The pulsar-admin sink update command allows you to dynamically change the configuration parameters of an already-submitted sink connector without having to delete and re-create it. The update command takes in a variety of command-line options, which are described in greater detail in the Apache documentation (pulsar .apache.org/docs/en/pulsar-admin/), that allow you to change almost any of the connector's configurations, including the archive file if you wanted to deploy a new version of the connector. This makes modifying, testing, and deploying a much more streamlined process. Listing 5.28 shows how to update the Mongo sink connector we deployed earlier to use a different Pulsar topic as the input source and change the processing guarantees.

That wraps up our quick introduction to some of the commands available for monitoring and administering Pulsar IO connectors. My goal was to provide enough of a high-level overview of the capabilities provided by the framework itself to enable you to get started. I strongly recommend referring to the online documentation for details on the various switches and parameters for each of these commands.

Summary

- Pulsar IO connectors are an extension of the Pulsar Functions framework specifically designed to interface with external systems such as databases.
- Pulsar IO connectors come in two basic types: *sources*, which pull data out of external systems into Pulsar, and *sinks*, which publish data from Pulsar into external systems.
- Pulsar provides a set of built-in connectors you can use to interact with several popular systems without having to write a single line of code.
- The Pulsar CLI tool allows you to administer Pulsar IO connectors, including creating, deleting, and updating connectors.

Pulsar security

This chapter covers

- Encrypting data transmitted into and out of a Pulsar cluster
- Enabling client authentication using JSON Web Tokens (JWTs)
- Encrypting data stored inside Apache Pulsar

This chapter covers how to secure your cluster in order to prevent unauthorized access to the data sent through Apache Pulsar. While the tasks I am going to cover are not important in a development environment, they are critically important for a production deployment to reduce the risk of unauthorized access to sensitive information, ensure data loss prevention, and protect your organization's public reputation. Modern systems and organizations utilize a combination of security controls and safeguards to provide multiple layers of defense that prevent access to data within the system. This is particularly true for those that must maintain regulatory compliance with security regulations, such as HIPPA, PCI-DSS, or GDPR, just to name a few.

Pulsar integrates well with several existing security frameworks that allow you to leverage these tools to secure your Pulsar cluster at multiple levels in order to mitigate the risk of a lapse in one of the security mechanisms, resulting in a total security failure. For instance, even if an unauthorized user were able to access your system with a compromised password, they would still need a valid encryption key to read the encrypted message data.

6.1   *Transport encryption*

By default, the data transmitted between a Pulsar broker and a Pulsar client is sent in plain text. This means any sensitive data contained within a message, such as passwords, credit card numbers, and social security numbers, is susceptible to being intercepted by eavesdroppers as it is transmitted over the network. Therefore, the first layer of defense is ensuring that the data transmitted between a Pulsar broker and a Pulsar client is encrypted *before* it is transmitted.

Pulsar allows you to configure all communication to use transport layer security (TLS), which is a common cryptographic protocol that provides data encryption *only* as it is transported across the network. This is why it is often referred to as encryption for "data in motion"—the data is decrypted on the receiving end and therefore no longer encrypted once it reaches its destination.

ENABLING TLS ON PULSAR

Now that I have covered the basics of TLS wire encryption at a fairly high level, let's focus on how we can use this technology to secure our communications between our Pulsar brokers and our clients. Since the Pulsar documentation does a fair job of outlining the steps required to enable TLS on Pulsar, I have decided that, rather than republish those same steps here, I will capture all of those steps in a single script that can be used to automate the process inside a Docker-based image.

I will then discuss the commands contained within the scripts in greater detail, as they relate to the discussion we had in the previous section, so you have a better understanding of why these steps are important and how you might modify them to suit your needs in a true production environment. If you look inside the GitHub repo (https://github.com/david-streamlio/pulsar-in-action) associated with this book, you will find a Dockerfile similar to the one shown in listing 6.1 under the docker-image/pulsar-standalone folder.

For those of you unfamiliar with Docker, a Dockerfile is a simple text file that contains a series of instructions that are executed sequentially by the Docker client when creating an image. They can be thought of as recipes or blueprints for building Docker images and provide a simple way to automate the image-creation process. Now that we have a better understanding of Docker images, it is time to create our own. Our goal is to create an image that extends the capability of the `pulsar-standalone` image we used previously to include all of the security features I will be discussing throughout this chapter.

Listing 6.1 Dockerfile contents

Use the existing pulsar-standalone image as a
starting point to effectively extend its capabilities.

Overwrite the broker
configuration with
one that contains
our updated security
settings.

Overwrite
the client
configuration
with one that
contains our
updated client
credentials.

```
FROM apachepulsar/pulsar-standalone:latest
ENV PULSAR_HOME=/pulsar

COPY conf/standalone.conf $PULSAR_HOME/conf/standalone.conf
COPY conf/client.conf $PULSAR_HOME/conf/client.conf

ADD manning $PULSAR_HOME/manning

RUN chmod a+x $PULSAR_HOME/manning/security/*.sh \
        $PULSAR_HOME/manning/security/*/*.sh \
            $PULSAR_HOME/manning/security/authentication/*/*.sh

####################################################################
# Transport Encryption using TLS
####################################################################
RUN ["/bin/bash", "-c",
      "/pulsar/manning/security/TLS-encryption/enable-tls.sh"]
```

Copy the contents of the manning folder
into the image at /pulsar/manning.

Give execute
permission to all
of the scripts we
need to execute.

Execute the specified script to generate
the certificates required for TLS.

I will start by specifying that I wish to use the non-secured `apachxpulsar/pulsar-standalone:latest` image as the base image by using the `FROM` keyword. For those of you familiar with object-oriented languages, this is effectively the same as inheriting from a base class. All of the base image's services, features, and configurations are automatically included in our image, which ensures that our Docker images will also provide a complete Pulsar environment for testing purposes without having to replicate those commands in our Dockerfile.

After setting the `PULSAR_HOME` environment variable, I use the `COPY` keyword to replace both the Pulsar broker and client configuration files with ones that are properly configured to secure the Pulsar instance. This is an important step, as once a container based on this image is launched, it is impossible to change these settings and have them take effect. Next, we add the contents of the `manning` directory to the Docker image and run a command to enable execute permission on all of the bash scripts that were added in the previous command, so we can execute them.

At the end of the Dockerfile are a series of bash scripts that get executed in order to generate the necessary security credentials, certificates, and keys required to secure a Pulsar cluster. Let's examine the first script, named `enable-tls.sh`, which performs all the steps necessary to enable TLS wire encryption on the Pulsar cluster.

The `pulsar-standalone` Docker image includes OpenSSL, which is an open source library that provides several command-line tools for issuing and signing digital certificates. Since we are running in a development environment, we will use these tools to act as our own certificate authority to produce self-signed certificates rather than use an internationally trusted third-party certificate authority (CA) (e.g., VeriSign,

DigiCert) to sign our certificates. In a production environment you should *always* rely on a third-party CA.

Acting as a CA means dealing with cryptographic pairs of private keys and public certificates. The very first cryptographic pair we'll create is the root pair. This consists of the root key (ca.key.pem) and root certificate (ca.cert.pem). This pair forms the identity of your CA. Let's examine the first part of the `enable-tls.sh` script, which generate these. As we can see from the following listing, the first command in the script generates the root key, while the second command creates the public X.509 certificate using the root key that was generated in the previous step.

Listing 6.2 Portion of enable-tls.sh that creates CA

```
#!/bin/bash

export CA_HOME=$(pwd)
export CA_PASSWORD=secret-password          ◁──  We use an environment variable
                                                 to set the password for the CA
                                                 root key.

mkdir certs crl newcerts private
chmod 700 private/
touch index.txt index.txt.attr
echo 1000 > serial

# Generate the certificate authority private key
openssl genrsa -aes256 \                  ◁──
    -passout pass:${CA_PASSWORD} \              ◁──
    -out /pulsar/manning/security/cert-authority/private/ca.key.pem \
    4096                        ◁──
```

Encrypt the root key with AES 256-bit encryption.

Generates the private key that is secured with a strong password

Use 4096 bits for the root key.

```
# Restrict Access to the certificate authority private key
chmod 400 /pulsar/manning/security/cert-authority/private/ca.key.pem   ◁──
```

Anyone in possession of the root key and password can issue trusted certificates.

```
# Create the X.509 certificate.
openssl req -config openssl.cnf \
  -key /pulsar/manning/security/cert-authority/private/ca.key.pem \   ◁──
  -new -x509 \                    ◁──
  -days 7300 \                  ◁──
  -sha256 \
  -extensions v3_ca \
  -out /pulsar/manning/security/cert-authority/certs/ca.cert.pem \
  -subj '/C=US/ST=CA/L=Palo Alto/CN=gottaeat.com' \  ◁──
  -passin pass:${CA_PASSWORD}
```

Requests a new X.509 certificate

Give the root certificate a long expiry date.

Generates the root certificate using the root key

Specify the organization for which the certificate is valid.

Allows us to provide the password for the root key from the command line without a prompt

At this point the script has generated a password-protected private key (ca.key.pem) and root certificate (ca.cert.pem) for our internal CA. The script purposely generates the root certificate to a known location, so we can refer to it from inside the broker's configuration file, `/pulsar/conf/standalone.conf`. Specifically, we have preconfigured the `tlsTrustCertsFilePath` property to point to the location where the root certificate was generated. In a production environment where you are using a third-party

CA, you will be provided with a certificate that can be used to authenticate the X.509 certificates and update the property to point to that certificate instead.

Now that we have created a CA certificate, the next step is to generate a certificate for the Pulsar broker and sign it with our internal CA. When using a third-party CA, you would issue this request to them and wait for them to send you a certificate; however, since we are acting as our own certificate authority, we can issue the certificate ourselves, as shown in the following listing.

Listing 6.3 Portion of enable-tls.sh that generates the Pulsar broker certificate

We use an environment variable to set the password for the server certificate's private key.

```
export BROKER_PASSWORD=my-secret

# Generate the Server Certificate private key
openssl genrsa -passout pass:${BROKER_PASSWORD} \
        -out /pulsar/manning/security/cert-authority/broker.key.pem \
        2048

# Convert the key to PEM format
openssl pkcs8 -topk8 -inform PEM -outform PEM \
        -in /pulsar/manning/security/cert-authority/broker.key.pem \
        -out /pulsar/manning/security/cert-authority/broker.key-pk8.pem \
        -nocrypt

# Generate the server certificate request
openssl req -config /pulsar/manning/security/cert-authority/openssl.cnf \
        -new -sha256 \
        -key /pulsar/manning/security/cert-authority/broker.key.pem \
        -out /pulsar/manning/security/cert-authority/broker.csr.pem \
        -subj '/C=US/ST=CA/L=Palo Alto/O=IT/CN=pulsar.gottaeat.com' \
        -passin pass:${BROKER_PASSWORD}

# Sign the server certificate with the CA
openssl ca -config /pulsar/manning/security/cert-authority/openssl.cnf \
        -extensions server_cert \
        -days 1000 -notext -md sha256 -batch \
        -in /pulsar/manning/security/cert-authority/broker.csr.pem \
        -out /pulsar/manning/security/cert-authority/broker.cert.pem \
        -passin pass:${CA_PASSWORD}
```

Generates the private key that is secured with a strong password

Use 2048 bits for the private key.

The broker expects the key to be in PKCS 8 format.

Specify the organization and hostname for which the certificate is valid.

Specify that this certificate is intended to be used by a server.

Allows us to provide the password for the key from the command line without a prompt

We need to provide the password for the CA's private key, since we are acting as the CA.

Give the server certificate a long expiry date.

At this point you have a broker certificate (broker.cert.pem) and its associated private key (broker.key-pk8.pem) that you can use along with ca.cert.pem to configure TLS transport encryption for your broker and proxy nodes. Again, the script purposely generates the broker certificate to a known location, so we can refer to it from inside the broker's configuration file, /pulsar/conf/standalone.conf. Let's take a look at all the properties that were changed to enable TLS for Pulsar.

Listing 6.4   TLS property changes to the standalone.conf file

```
#### To Enable TLS wire encryption #####
tlsEnabled=true
brokerServicePortTls=6651
webServicePortTls=8443

# The Broker certificate and associated private key
tlsCertificateFilePath=/pulsar/manning/security/cert-authority/broker
   .cert.pem
tlsKeyFilePath=//pulsar/manning/security/cert-authority/broker.key-pk8.pem

# The CA certificate
tlsTrustCertsFilePath=/pulsar/manning/security/cert-authority/certs/ca.cert
   .pem

# Used for TLS negotiation to specify which ciphers we consider safe.
tlsProtocols=TLSv1.2,TLSv1.1
tlsCiphers=TLS_DH_RSA_WITH_AES_256_GCM_SHA384,TLS_DH_RSA_WITH_AES_256_CBC_SHA
```

Since I have enabled TLS transport encryption, I also need to configure the command-line tools, such as `pulsar-admin` and `pulsar-perf`, to communicate with the secure Pulsar broker by changing the following properties in the `$PULSAR_HOME/conf/client.conf` file, as shown in the following listing.

Listing 6.5   TLS property changes to the client.conf file

```
#### To Enable TLS wire encryption #####
# Use the TLS protocols and ports
webServiceUrl=https://pulsar.gottaeat.com:8443/
brokerServiceUrl=pulsar+ssl://pulsar.gottaeat.com:6651/

useTls=true
tlsAllowInsecureConnection=false
tlsEnableHostnameVerification=false
tlsTrustCertsFilePath=pulsar/manning/security/cert-authority/certs/ca.cert.pem
```

If you haven't already done so, change to the directory that contains the Dockerfile, and run the following command, `docker build . -t pia/pulsar-standalone-secure:latest`, to create the Docker image, and tag it as shown in the following listing.

Listing 6.6   Building the Docker image from the Dockerfile

Change to the directory that contains the Dockerfile.

Command to build the Docker image from the Dockerfile, and tag it.

```
$ cd $REPO_HOME/pulsar-in-action/docker-images/pulsar-standalone
$ docker build . -t pia/pulsar-standalone-secure:latest
Sending build context to Docker daemon   3.345MB
Step 1/7 : FROM apachepulsar/pulsar-standalone:latest
 ---> 3ed9bffff717
Step 2/7 : ENV PULSAR_HOME=/pulsar
```

Pulls down the apachepulsar/pulsar-standalone:latest image from the public repository

```
 ---> Running in cf81f78f5754
Removing intermediate container cf81f78f5754
 ---> 48ea643513ff
Step 3/7 : COPY conf/standalone.conf $PULSAR_HOME/conf/standalone.conf
 ---> 6dcf0068eb40
Step 4/7 : COPY conf/client.conf $PULSAR_HOME/conf/client.conf
 ---> e0f6c81a10c4
Step 5/7 : ADD manning $PULSAR_HOME/manning                    ◁─────
 ---> e253e7c6ed8e
Step 6/7 : RUN chmod a+x $PULSAR_HOME/manning/security/*.sh
⟹ $PULSAR_HOME/manning/security/*/*.sh
⟹ $PULSAR_HOME/manning/security/authentication/*/*.sh
 ---> Running in 42d33f3e738b
Removing intermediate container 42d33f3e738b
 ---> ddccc85c75f4
Step 7/7 : RUN ["/bin/bash", "-c",
⟹ "/pulsar/manning/security/TLS-encryption/enable-tls.sh"]  ◁─────
 ---> Running in 5f26f9626a25
Generating RSA private key, 4096 bit long modulus
.....................++++
...............................................................................
        ......................................................................
        ......................................................................
        ......................++++
e is 65537 (0x010001)
Generating RSA private key, 2048 bit long modulus
.....................+++++
...........................................+++++
e is 65537 (0x010001)
Using configuration from /pulsar/manning/security/cert-authority/openssl.cnf
Check that the request matches the signature
Signature ok
Certificate Details:                         ◁─────
        Serial Number: 4096 (0x1000)
        Validity
            Not Before: Jan 13 00:55:03 2020 GMT
            Not After : Oct  9 00:55:03 2022 GMT    ◁─────
        Subject:
            countryName               = US
            stateOrProvinceName       = CA
            organizationName          = gottaeat.com
            commonName                = pulsar.gottaeat.com
        X509v3 extensions:
            X509v3 Basic Constraints:
                CA:FALSE
            Netscape Cert Type:
                SSL Server              ◁─────
            Netscape Comment:
                OpenSSL Generated Server Certificate
            X509v3 Subject Key Identifier:
                DF:75:74:9D:34:C6:0D:F0:9B:E7:CA:07:0A:37:B8:6F:D7:DF:52:0A
            X509v3 Authority Key Identifier:

    keyid:92:F0:6D:0F:18:D4:3C:1E:88:B1:33:3A:9D:04:29:C0:FC:81:29:02
```

Copies the entire contents of the manning directory into the Docker image

Executes the enable-tls.sh script

The details of the server certificate that is generated by the enable-tls.sh script

The expiration date of the certificate

Indicates that the certificate generated can be used as a server certificate

```
              DirName:/C=US/ST=CA/L=Palo Alto/O=gottaeat.com
              serial:93:FD:42:06:D8:E9:C3:89

          X509v3 Key Usage: critical
              Digital Signature, Key Encipherment
          X509v3 Extended Key Usage:
              TLS Web Server Authentication
Certificate is to be certified until Oct  9 00:55:03 2022 GMT (1000 days)

Write out database with 1 new entries
Data Base Updated
Removing intermediate container 5f26f9626a25
 ---> 0e7995c14208
Successfully built 0e7995c14208
Successfully tagged pia/pulsar-standalone-secure:latest
```
◁──┐ **Success message, including the tag used to reference the image**

Once the `enable-tls.sh` script has been executed and the properties have all been configured to point to the correct values, the `pulsar-standalone` image will only accept connections over a secure TLS channel. You can verify this by using the sequence of commands shown in listing 6.7 to launch a container with the new Docker image. Notice that I am using the `–volume` switch to create a logical mount point between my laptop's $HOME directory and a directory inside the Docker container itself. This allows me to publish the TLS client credentials that only exist inside the container to a location on our machine where I can access them. Next, I need to secure shell (ssh) into the container and run the `publish-credentials.sh` script inside the newly launched bash session to make these credentials available to me in the ${HOME}/exchange folder on our local machine.

Listing 6.7   Publishing the TLS credentials

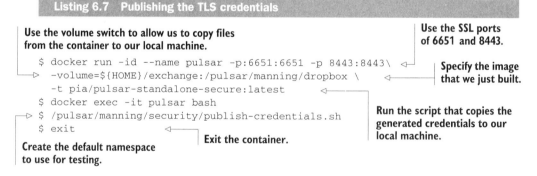

Use the volume switch to allow us to copy files from the container to our local machine.

Use the SSL ports of 6651 and 8443.

```
$ docker run -id --name pulsar -p:6651:6651 -p 8443:8443\
  –volume=${HOME}/exchange:/pulsar/manning/dropbox \
  -t pia/pulsar-standalone-secure:latest
$ docker exec -it pulsar bash
$ /pulsar/manning/security/publish-credentials.sh
$ exit
```

Specify the image that we just built.

Run the script that copies the generated credentials to our local machine.

Exit the container.

Create the default namespace to use for testing.

Next, I will attempt to connect to it over the TLS secured port (6651), using the following Java program, which is available in the GitHub repo associated with this book.

Listing 6.8   Using the TLS credentials to connect to Pulsar

```
import org.apache.pulsar.client.api.*;
public class TlsClient {
    public static void main(String[] args) throws PulsarClientException {
        final String HOME = "/Users/david/exchange";
```

```
                  final String TOPIC = "persistent://public/default/test-topic";

                  PulsarClient client = PulsarClient.builder()
                    .serviceUrl("pulsar://localhost:6651/")    ◁──── Specify the pulsar+ssl
  The location  ┌──▷ .tlsTrustCertsFilePath(HOME + "/ca.cert.pem")      protocol. Failure to do
  of the file   │    .build();                                          so will result in a
containing the  │                                                       connection failure.
  trusted TLS   │  Producer<byte[]> producer =
  certificates  └    client.newProducer().topic(TOPIC).create();

                  for (int idx = 0; idx < 100; idx++) {
                    producer.send("Hello TLS".getBytes());
                  }
                    System.exit(0);
                }
              }
```

That concludes the configuration of TLS wire encryption on the Pulsar broker. From
this point forward, all communication with the broker will be over SSL, and all traffic
will be encrypted to prevent unauthorized access to the data contained inside the messages that are published to and consumed from the Pulsar broker. You can experi-
ment some more with this container, but once you are finished, you should be sure to
run `docker stop pulsar && docker rm pulsar` to stop the container and remove it.
Both of these steps are necessary to rebuild the Docker image in the next section to
enable support for authentication in the `pulsar-standalone` image.

6.2 Authentication

An authentication service provides a way for a user to confirm their identity by providing some credentials, such as a username and password, to validate who you claim to
be. Pulsar supports a pluggable authentication mechanism, which clients can use to
authenticate themselves. Currently, Pulsar supports different authentication providers. In this section, we will walk through the steps required to configure both TLS
authentication and JWT authentication.

6.2.1 TLS authentication

In TLS client authentication, the client uses a certificate to authenticate itself. Obtaining
a certificate requires interaction with a CA that will issue a certificate that can be trusted
by the Pulsar broker. For a client certificate to pass a server's validation process, the digital
signature found on it should have been signed by a CA recognized by the server. Therefore, I have used the same CA that issued the server certificate in the previous section to
generate the client certificates to ensure that the client certificates are trusted.

With TLS client authentication, the client generates a key pair for authentication
purpose and retains the private key of the key pair in a secure location. The client then
issues a certificate request to a trusted CA and receives back an X.509 digital certificate.

These client certificates typically contain pertinent information like a digital signature, expiration date, name of client, name of CA, revocation status, SSL/TLS version
number, serial number, common name, and possibly more, all structured using the

X.509 standard. Pulsar uses the common name field of the certificate to map the client to a specific role, which is used to determine what actions the client is authorized to perform.

When a client attempts to connect to a Pulsar broker that has TLS authentication enabled, it can submit a client certificate for authentication as part of the TLS handshake. Upon receiving the certificate, the Pulsar broker uses it to identify the certificate's source and determine whether the client should be granted access.

Don't confuse client certificates with the server certificate we used to enable TLS wire encryption. Both are X.509 digital certificates, but they are two different things. A server certificate is sent from the Pulsar broker to the client at the start of a session and is used by the client to authenticate the server. A client certificate, on the other hand, is sent from the client to the broker at the start of a session and is used by the server to authenticate the client. In order to enable TLS-based authentication, we append a command to the Dockerfile from the previous section that executes another script named `gen-client-certs.sh`. This script generates TLS client certificates that can be used for authentication, as shown in the following listing.

Listing 6.9   Updated Dockerfile contents

```
FROM apachepulsar/pulsar-standalone:latest
ENV PULSAR_HOME=/pulsar

...

RUN ["/bin/bash", "-c",
     "/pulsar/manning/security/TLS-encryption/enable-tls.sh"]

RUN ["/bin/bash", "-c",
     "/pulsar/manning/security/authentication/tls/gen-client-certs.sh"]  ◁
#A Same content as shown in figure 6.1
```

> **Execute the specified script to generate TLS client certs for role-based authentication.**

Let's take a look at the `gen-client-certs.sh` script in the following listing to see exactly what steps are required to generate TLS client certificates that can be used to authenticate with the Pulsar broker.

Listing 6.10   Contents of the gen-client-certs.sh file

Sets the local variable CLIENT_ID to the first parameter passed to the function call

```
#!/bin/bash

cd /pulsar/manning/security/cert-authority
export CA_HOME=$(pwd)
export CA_PASSWORD=secret-password

function generate_client_cert() {

   ⊳ local CLIENT_ID=$1
     local CLIENT_ROLE=$2        ◁
     local CLIENT_PASSWORD=$3    ◁
```

Sets the local variable CLIENT_ROLE to the second parameter passed to the function call

Sets the local variable CLIENT_PASSWORD to the third parameter passed to the function call

```
# Generate the Client Certificate private key
openssl genrsa -passout pass:${CLIENT_PASSWORD} \    ◁──
  -out /pulsar/manning/security/authentication/tls/${CLIENT_ID}.key.pem \
  2048

# Convert the key to PEM format
openssl pkcs8 -topk8 -inform PEM -outform PEM -nocrypt \
  -in /pulsar/manning/security/authentication/tls/${CLIENT_ID}.key.pem \
  -out /pulsar/manning/security/authentication/tls/${CLIENT_ID}-pk8.pem

# Generate the client certificate request
openssl req -config /pulsar/manning/security/cert-authority/openssl.cnf \
  -key /pulsar/manning/security/authentication/tls/${CLIENT_ID}.key.pem \
  -out /pulsar/manning/security/authentication/tls/${CLIENT_ID}.csr.pem \
  -subj "/C=US/ST=CA/L=Palo Alto/O=gottaeat.com/
  ⇒ CN=${CLIENT_ROLE}" \                              ◁──
  -new -sha256 \
  -passin pass:${CLIENT_PASSWORD}     ◁──

# Sign the server certificate with the CA
openssl ca -config /pulsar/manning/security/cert-authority/openssl.cnf \
  -extensions usr_cert \               ◁──
  -days 100 -notext -md sha256 -batch \
  -in /pulsar/manning/security/authentication/tls/${CLIENT_ID}.csr.pem \
  -out /pulsar/manning/security/authentication/tls/${CLIENT_ID}.cert.pem \
  -passin pass:${CA_PASSWORD}                         ◁──

# Remove the client key and certifcate request once we are finished
rm -f /pulsar/manning/security/authentication/tls/${CLIENT_ID}.csr.pem
rm -f /pulsar/manning/security/authentication/tls/${CLIENT_ID}.key.pem
}

# Create a certificate for Adam with admin role-level access
generate_client_cert admin admin admin-secret

# Create a certificate for the web app with webapp role-level access
generate_client_cert webapp-service webapp webapp-secret

# Create a certificate for Peggy who with payment-role level access
generate_client_cert peggy payments payment-secret

# Create a certificate for David who needs driver-role level access
generate_client_cert david driver davids-secret
```

Use the CLIENT_PASSWORD to secure the private key.

Pulsar uses the value associated with the common name (CN) to determine the client's role.

We need to pass in the password associated with the client key used to generate the CSR.

Specify that we want a client certificate.

We need to provide the CA password to approve and sign the client's certificate request.

In a production environment, the clients would use their own private keys to generate the certificate requests and only send over the CSR files. Since I am automating the process, I have taken the liberty of generating these as part of the script for a small set of users, each with a different role.

At this point, there are now several pairs of private keys and client certificates that have been generated and signed by our CA that can be used to authenticate to the pulsar-standalone instance. The properties shown in the following listing have also been added to the standalone.conf file in order to enable TLS-based authentication on the broker.

Listing 6.11   TLS authentication property changes to the standalone.conf file

```
#### To enable TLS authentication          Turn on authentication.
authenticationEnabled=true          ◁──────┘
authenticationProviders=org.apache.pulsar.broker.                    Specifies the TLS
                                                                     authentication
   authentication.AuthenticationProviderTls          ◁──────────────  provider
```

Changes are also required to the client.conf file, as shown in the following listing, which grants all of the Pulsar command-line tools admin-level permissions, including the ability to define authorization rules at the Pulsar-namespace level.

Listing 6.12   TLS authentication property changes to the client.conf file

Tells the client to use **TLS authentication**
when connecting to Pulsar

```
## TLS Authentication ##
authPlugin=org.apache.pulsar.client.impl.auth.AuthenticationTls
authParams=tlsCertFile:/pulsar/manning/security/authentication/tls/
   admin.cert.pem,tlsKeyFile:/pulsar/manning/security/authentication/tls/
   admin-pk8.pem     ◁──────┐
                            Specifies the client certificate and
                            associated private key to use
```

Let's rebuild the image to include the changes necessary to generate the TLS client certificates and enable TLS-based authentication that was discussed in this section by executing the commands shown in the following listing.

Listing 6.13   Building the Docker image from the Dockerfile

Change to the directory that   Command to build the Docker image
contains the Dockerfile.   from the Dockerfile and tag it

```
$ cd $REPO_HOME/pulsar-in-action/docker-images/pulsar-standalone
$ docker build . -t pia/pulsar-standalone-secure:latest          ◁─────
Sending build context to Docker daemon  3.345MB
Step 1/8 : FROM apachepulsar/pulsar-standalone:latest  ◁──   Notice there are now eight
 ---> 3ed9bffff717   Execution of steps 2 through 7           steps instead of seven.
...                  ◁─────
Step 8/8 : RUN ["/bin/bash", "-c",                     Executes the gen-client-certs.sh script
    "/pulsar/manning/security/authentication/tls/gen-client-certs.sh"]  ◁───┘
 ---> Running in 5beaabba5865
Generating RSA private key, 2048 bit long modulus  ◁───┐
........+++++                                            The following stanza will be
..................+++++                                  repeated five times—once for
e is 65537 (0x010001)                                   each client cert generated.
Using configuration from /pulsar/manning/security/cert-authority/openssl.cnf
Check that the request matches the signature
Signature ok
Certificate Details:
```

-

```
        Serial Number: 4097 (0x1001)          ◁──┐  The certificate serial number
        Validity                                   │  will be different for each client.
            Not Before: Jan 13 02:47:54 2020 GMT
            Not After : Apr 22 02:47:54 2020 GMT
        Subject:
            countryName              = US            The common name will be
            stateOrProvinceName      = CA            different for each client and
            organizationName         = gottaeat.com  is used to associate it to a
            commonName               = admin   ◁──┘  particular role.
        ....


    Write out database with 1 new entries
    Data Base Updated
    Generating RSA private key, 2048 bit long modulus
                                                     Success message,
                                                     including the tag
    ...                                              used to reference
    Successfully built 6ef6eddd675e                  the image
    Successfully tagged pia/pulsar-standalone-secure:latest  ◁──┘
```

Left margin annotations:
Four more occurrences of the stanza should appear—one for each client certificate generated.

Next, I need to follow the steps shown in listing 6.7 again to launch a new container based on the updated Docker image, ssh into the container, and run the `publish-credentials.sh` script inside the newly launched bash session to make these client certificates available to us in the ${HOME}/exchange folder on our local machine. For instance, the certificate file admin.cert.pem and the associated private key file admin-pk8.pem can now be used together to authenticate to the `pulsar-standalone` instance. Next, I will attempt to use TLS authentication by using the Java program shown in the following listing, which is available in the GitHub repo associated with this book.

Listing 6.14 Authenticating with TLS client certificates

Use the Pulsar+ssl protocol. Failure to do so will result in a connection failure.

```java
import org.apache.pulsar.client.api.*;

public class TlsAuthClient {
  public static void main(String[] args) throws PulsarClientException {
    final String AUTH =
     "org.apache.pulsar.client.impl.auth.AuthenticationTls";
    final String HOME = "/Users/david/exchange";
    final String TOPIC = "persistent://public/default/test-topic";

    PulsarClient client = PulsarClient.builder()
        .serviceUrl("pulsar+ssl://localhost:6651/")
        .tlsTrustCertsFilePath(HOME + "/ca.cert.pem")
        .authentication(AUTH,
            "tlsCertFile:" + HOME + "/admin.cert.pem," +
            "tlsKeyFile:" + HOME + "/admin-pk8.pem")
        .build();

    Producer<byte[]> producer =
      client.newProducer().topic(TOPIC).create();
```

Annotations: **Use TLS authentication.** · **The location of the file containing the trusted TLS certificates** · **The client certificate location** · **The private key associated with the client certificate**

```
    for (int idx = 0; idx < 100; idx++) {
      producer.send("Hello TLS Auth".getBytes());
    }
    System.exit(0);
  }
}
```

TLS client authentication is useful in cases where a server is keeping track of hundreds of thousands or millions of clients, as in IoT, or in a mobile app with millions of installs exchanging secure information. For example, a manufacturing company with hundreds of thousands of IoT devices can issue a unique client certificate to each device, then limit connections to only their devices by having Pulsar only accept connections where the client presents a valid client certificate signed by the company's certificate authority.

In the case of a mobile application, where you want to prevent your customers' sensitive data, such as credit card information, from getting stolen by someone spoofing your mobile app, you can issue a unique certificate to every app installation and use them to validate that the request is coming from an approved version of your mobile application, not a spoofed version.

6.2.2 *JSON Web Token authentication*

Pulsar supports authenticating clients using security tokens that are based on JWT, which is a standardized format used to create JSON-based access tokens that assert one or more claims. Claims are factual statements or assertions. The two claims that can be found in all JWT are `iss` (issuer), which identifies the party that issued the JWT, and `sub`, which identifies the subject or party the JWT carries information about.

In Pulsar, JWTs are used to authenticate a Pulsar client and associate it with some role, which will then be used to determine what actions it is authorized to perform, such as publish or consume from a given topic. Typically, the administrator of the Pulsar cluster would generate a JWT that has a `sub` claim associated with a specific role (e.g., admin that identifies the owner of the token). The admin would then provide the JWT to a client over a secure communication channel, and the client could then use that token to authenticate with Pulsar and be assigned to the admin role.

The JWT standard defines the structure of a JWT as consisting of the following three parts: the header, which contains basic information; the payload, which contains the claims; and the signature, which can be used to validate the token. Data from each of these parts is encoded separately and concatenated together, using periods to delineate the fields. The resulting strings look something like figure 6.1, which can be transmitted easily over HTTP.

Since JWTs are based on an open standard, the contents of a JWT are readable to anyone in possession of it. This means that anyone can attempt to gain access to your system with a JWT they generate themselves or by altering an intercepted JWT and modifying one or more of the claims to impersonate a validated user. This is where

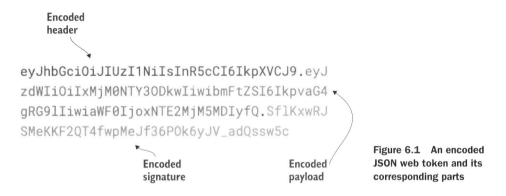

Figure 6.1 An encoded JSON web token and its corresponding parts

the signature comes into play, as it provides a means to establish the authenticity of the entire JWT.

The signature is calculated by encoding the header and payload, using Base64 URL encoding and concatenating the two together along with a secret. That string is then passed through the cryptographic hashing algorithm specified in the header. With JWTs, there are two cryptographic schemes you can use; the first is referred to as a shared secret scheme in which both the party that generates the signature and the party that verifies it must know the secret. Since both parties are in possession of the secret, each party can verify the authenticity of a JWT by calculating the signature for themselves and validate that the value they computed matches the value in the JWT's signature section. Any discrepancy indicates that the token has been tampered with. This scheme is useful when you want or need both parties to be able to exchange information back and forth in a secure manner. The second scheme uses an asymmetric public/private key pair in which the party with the public key can validate the authenticity of any JWT it receives, and the party with the private key can generate valid JWTs.

There are several online tools available that allow you to encode and decode JWTs, and figure 6.2 shows the side-by-side output from one such tool that was used to decode two different JWTs. The output on the left is from a token that is using the shared secret scheme. As you can see, the contents of the token can be easily read by the tool without any additional credentials. However, the secret key is required in order to validate the token's signature to confirm it hasn't been tampered with.

The output on the right side of the figure is from a JWT using the asymmetric scheme, whose contents can also be easily read without any additional credentials. However, the public key is required to verify the token's signature. The tool also requires a private key only if you wish to use it to generate a new JWT. Hopefully, this helps clarify the differences between the two and why both the JWT token and an associated key are required to configure Pulsar brokers and clients to use JWT for authentication.

Lastly, it is worth mentioning that anyone in possession of a valid JWT can use it to authenticate with Pulsar. Therefore, adequate precautions should be taken to prevent an issued JWT from falling into unwanted hands. This includes only sending JWT

Figure 6.2 Verification methods for shared secret vs. public/private key pair signed JWTs

tokens over a TLS-encrypted connection and storing the contents of a JWT in a safe location on the client machine. To enable JWT authentication, we append a command to the Dockerfile from the previous section, which executes another script named gen-tokens.sh that generates JWTs that can be used for authentication, as shown in the following listing.

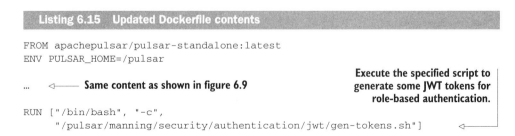

Listing 6.15 Updated Dockerfile contents

```
FROM apachepulsar/pulsar-standalone:latest
ENV PULSAR_HOME=/pulsar

...     <────  Same content as shown in figure 6.9

RUN ["/bin/bash", "-c",
     "/pulsar/manning/security/authentication/jwt/gen-tokens.sh"]   <────
```

Execute the specified script to generate some JWT tokens for role-based authentication.

Let's take a look at the gen-token.sh script in the following listing to see exactly what steps are required to generate the JWTs that can be used to authenticate with the Pulsar broker.

Listing 6.16 Contents of the gen-token.sh file

```
#!/bin/bash

# Create a public/private keypair.
/pulsar/bin/pulsar tokens create-key-pair \
    --output-private-key \
      /pulsar/manning/security/authentication/jwt/my-private.key \
    --output-public-key \
      /pulsar/manning/security/authentication/jwt/my-public.key

# Create the token for the admin role
/pulsar/bin/pulsar tokens create --expiry-time 1y \
    --private-key \
      file:///pulsar/manning/security/authentication/jwt/my-private.key \
    --subject admin > /pulsar/manning/security/authentication/jwt/admin-
    token.txt
...
```

We are going to use asymmetric encryption, so we need to create a key pair.

Create a token and give it the subject of admin.

Repeats token creation process for additional roles

After this script is executed, there will be several JWT tokens that have been generated and stored as text files on the Pulsar broker. These tokens, along with the public key, will need to be distributed to the Pulsar clients so they can be used to authenticate to the pulsar-standalone instance. The properties shown in the following listing have also been modified inside the standalone.conf file to enable JWT-based authentication.

Listing 6.17 JWT authentication property changes to the standalone.conf file

```
#### JWT Authentication #####
authenticationEnabled=true
authorizationEnabled=true
authenticationProviders=org.apache.pulsar.broker.authentication.
    AuthenticationProviderTls,org.apache.pulsar.broker.authentication.
    AuthenticationProviderToken
tokenPublicKey=file:///pulsar/manning/security/
    authentication/jwt/my-public.key
```

This is required for any authentication mechanism in Pulsar.

Enable authorization.

Append the JWT token provider to the list of authentication providers.

The location of the public key of the JWT key pair which is used for signature validation

If you want to use JWT authentication, you will need to make the changes shown in the following listing to the client.conf file. Since we have previously enabled TLS authentication for the client, we will need to comment out those properties for now, since the client can only use one authentication method at a time.

```
#### JWT Authentication #####
authPlugin=org.apache.pulsar.client.impl.auth.AuthenticationToken
authParams=file:///pulsar/manning/security/authentication/jwt/admin-token.txt

#### TLS Authentication ####
#authPlugin=org.apache.pulsar.client.impl.auth.AuthenticationTls
#authParams=tlsCertFile:/pulsar/manning/security/authentication/tls/admin.cert
    .pem,tlsKeyFile:/pulsar/manning/security/authentication/tls/admin-pk8.pem
```

Comment out both of the TLS authentication properties.

Now, let's rebuild the image to include the changes necessary to generate the JWTs and enable JWT-based authentication by executing the commands shown in the following listing. Be sure to have stopped and removed any previous running instances of the Pulsar image before doing so.

Listing 6.19   Building the Docker image from the Dockerfile

Change to the directory that contains the Dockerfile.

Command to build the Docker image from the Dockerfile and tag it

```
$ cd $REPO_HOME/pulsar-in-action/docker-images/pulsar-standalone
$ docker build . -t pia/pulsar-standalone-secure:latest
Sending build context to Docker daemon  3.345MB
Step 1/9 : FROM apachepulsar/pulsar-standalone:latest
 ---> 3ed9bffff717
....
Step 8/9 : RUN ["/bin/bash", "-c", "/pulsar/manning/security/authentication/jwt/
    gen-tokens.sh"]
Step 9/9 : CMD ["/pulsar/bin/pulsar", "standalone"]
 ---> Using cache
 ---> a229c8eed874
Successfully built a229c8eed874
Successfully tagged pia/pulsar-standalone-secure:latest
```

Notice that there are now nine steps instead of eight.

Executes the gen-token.sh script

Success message, including the tag used to reference the image

Next, we need to follow the steps shown in listing 6.7 again to launch a new container based on the updated Docker image, ssh into the container, and run the `publish-credentials.sh` script inside the newly launched bash session to make these JWTs available to us in the ${HOME}/exchange folder on our local machine. Next, we will attempt to use JWT authentication by using the Java program shown in the following listing, which is available in the GitHub repo associated with this book.

Listing 6.20   Authenticating with JWT

```
import org.apache.pulsar.client.api.*;

public class JwtAuthClient {
public static void main(String[] args) throws PulsarClientException {
    final String HOME = "/Users/david/exchange";
    final String TOPIC = "persistent://public/default/test-topic";

    PulsarClient client = PulsarClient.builder()
```

```
      .serviceUrl("pulsar+ssl://localhost:6651/")
      .tlsTrustCertsFilePath(HOME + "/ca.cert.pem")
      .authentication(
          AuthenticationFactory.token(() -> {
        try {
          return new String(Files.readAllBytes(
            Paths.get(HOME+"/admin-token.txt")));
        } catch (IOException e) {
          return "";
        }
        })).build();

    Producer<byte[]> producer =
      client.newProducer().topic(TOPIC).create();

    for (int idx = 0; idx < 100; idx++) {
      producer.send("Hello JWT Auth".getBytes());
    }
      System.exit(0);
  }
}
```

That concludes the configuration of authentication on the Pulsar broker. From this point forward, all Pulsar clients will be required to present valid credentials to be authenticated. Thus far, we have only implemented two of the four authentication mechanisms supported by Pulsar, TLS, and JWT. Additional authentication methods can be enabled by following the steps outlined in Pulsar's online documentation.

6.3 Authorization

Authorization occurs only after a client has been successfully authenticated by Pulsar's configured authentication provider, which determines whether or not you have sufficient permission to access a given topic. If you only enable authentication, any authenticated user has the ability to perform *any* action on *any* namespace or topic within the cluster.

6.3.1 Roles

In Pulsar, roles are used to define a collection of privileges, such as permission to access a particular set of topics that are assigned to groups of users. Apache Pulsar uses the configured authentication providers to establish the identity of a client and then assign a *role token* to that client. These role tokens are then used by the authorization mechanism to determine what actions the clients are allowed to make.

Role tokens are analogous to physical keys that are used to open a lock. Many people may have a copy of the key, and the lock doesn't care who you are, only that you have the right key. Within Pulsar, the hierarchy of roles falls into three categories, each with their own capabilities and intended uses. As you can see from figure 6.3, the role hierarchy closely mirrors Pulsar's cluster/tenant/namespace hierarchy when it comes to structuring data. Let us examine each of these roles in greater detail.

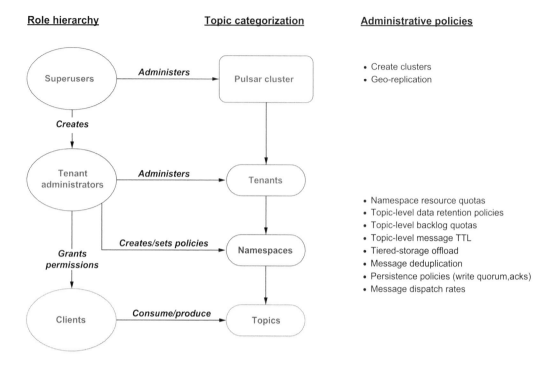

Figure 6.3   The Pulsar role hierarchy and its corresponding administrative tasks

SUPERUSERS

Just as the name implies, superusers can perform any action at any level of the Pulsar cluster; however, it is considered a best practice to delegate the administration of a tenant and its underlying namespaces to another person who will be responsible for the administration of that particular tenant's policies. Therefore, superusers' primary activity is the creation of tenant admins, which can be accomplished from the `pulsar-admin` CLI by executing a command similar to the one shown in the following listing.

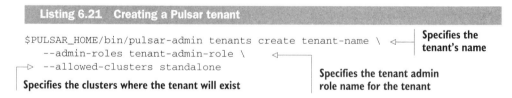

This allows the superuser to focus on cluster-wide administrative tasks, such as cluster creation, broker management, and configuring tenant-level resource quotas to ensure all the tenants receive their fair share of the cluster's resources. Typically, the administration of a tenant is given to a user that is responsible for designing the layout of the topics required for the tenant, such as a department head, project manager, or application team leader.

TENANT ADMINISTRATORS

The primary focus of the tenant administrator is the design and implementation of namespaces within their tenant. As I discussed earlier, namespaces are nothing more than a logical collection of topics that have the same policy requirements. Namespace-level policies apply to each topic within a given namespace and allow you to configure things such as data retention policies, backlog quotas, and tiered-storage offload.

CLIENTS

Last are the client roles, which can be any application or service that has been granted permission to consume from or produce to topics with the Pulsar cluster. These permissions are granted by the tenant admins at either the namespace level, meaning they apply to all the topics in a particular namespace, or on a per-topic basis. Listing 6.22 shows an example of both scenarios.

6.3.2 *An example scenario*

Let's imagine you are working for a food delivery company named GottaEat that allows customers to order food from a variety of participating restaurants and have it delivered directly to you. Rather than employ their own fleet of drivers, your company has decided to enlist private individuals to deliver the food to keep costs down. The company will use three separate mobile applications to conduct business: a publicly available one for customers, a restricted one for all participating restaurateurs, and a restricted one for all authorized delivery drivers.

ORDER PLACEMENT USE CASE

Next, let's walk through a very basic use case for your company, the placement of an order by a customer, all the way through to when it is assigned to a driver for delivery using a microservices-based application that uses Apache Pulsar for communicating via messages. We will focus on how you might structure your namespaces under the `restaurateurs` and `driver` tenants, along with what permissions you would want to grant. The `microservices` tenant will be used by multiple tenants, so it is created and managed by the application team. Figure 6.4 shows the overall message flow in the order entry use case.

In this use case, a customer uses the company's mobile application to select some food items, enter the desired delivery address, provide their payment information, and submit the request. The order information is published to the `persistent://microservices/orders/new` topic by the mobile application.

The payment verification microservice consumes the inbound order and communicates with the credit card payment system to secure payment for the items before placing the order in the `persistent://microservices/orders/paid` topic to indicate that payment has been captured for the items. The service also replaces the raw credit card information with an internal tracking ID that be used at a later time to access the payment.

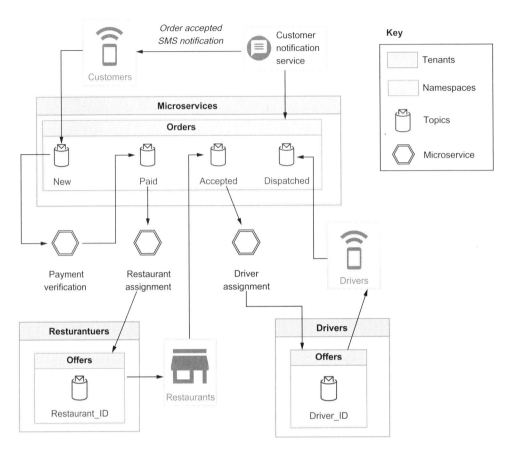

Figure 6.4 Message flow during the order placement use case

The restaurant assignment microservice is responsible for finding a restaurant that can fulfill the order by consuming from the `persistent://microservices/orders/paid` topic and determining a subset of candidate restaurants based on the food items and delivery location. It then sends out an offer to each of these restaurants by publishing the order details to a specific restaurant's topic that only they can access (e.g., `persistent://restaurateurs/offers/restaurant_4827`) to ensure the order is only fulfilled by one restaurant. If the offer is rejected, or after a certain amount of time elapses, the offer is rescinded and sent to the next restaurant in the list until it is fulfilled. Once a restaurant accepts the order via their mobile application, a message containing the restaurant details, including location, is published to the `persistent://microservices/orders/accepted` topic.

Once the order has been accepted, the driver assignment microservice will consume the message from the `accepted` topic and will attempt to locate a driver who can deliver the order to the customer. It selects a list of potential drivers based on their location, planned routes, etc., and publishes a message to a topic that only the driver can access (e.g., `persistent://drivers/offers/driver_5063`) to ensure the order is only dispatched to a single driver. If the offer is rejected, or after a certain amount of time elapses, the offer is rescinded and sent to the next driver in the list until it is accepted. If a driver accepts the delivery, a message containing the driver details is published to the `persistent://microservices/orders/dispatched` topic to indicate that the order is scheduled for delivery.

All of the messages stored inside the topics of the `persistent://microservices/orders` namespace contain both a `customer_id` and `order_id` data element. A customer notification service is subscribed to all of the topics shown, and when it receives a new record in any of these topics, it parses out those fields and uses the information to send out a notification to the corresponding customer's mobile app, so they can track the progress of their order.

TENANT CREATION

As the Pulsar superuser your first task would be to create all three of the tenants and their associated tenant admin roles. So, let's review the steps required to create the necessary tenants for this use case, as shown in the following listing.

Listing 6.22 Creating the Pulsar tenants

```
$PULSAR_HOME/bin/pulsar-admin tenants create microservices \
  --admin-roles microservices-admin-role

$PULSAR_HOME/bin/pulsar-admin tenants create drivers \
  --admin-roles drivers-admin-role

$PULSAR_HOME/bin/pulsar-admin tenants create restaurateurs \
  --admin-roles restaurateurs -admin-role
```

Since we are delegating the administration of these tenants to someone else within our organization, I will take a moment to outline the characteristics of the individuals who should serve in this capacity on a tenant-by-tenant basis:

- Since the microservices tenant is used to share information across multiple services and applications, a good candidate for the corresponding tenant admin should be an IT professional responsible for architectural decisions across departments, such as an enterprise architect.
- For the restaurateurs' tenant, a good candidate would be the person(s) in charge of the acquisition of new restaurateurs, as they will be the ones responsible for soliciting, vetting, and managing these partners. They can include the creation of restaurateurs' private topics as part of the onboarding process, etc.
- Similarly, a good candidate for administering the driver's topic would be the person(s) in charge of the acquisition of new drivers.

AUTHORIZATION POLICIES

Based on the requirements for this use case, we would devise an overall security design similar to the one shown in figure 6.5, which defines the following security requirements:

- The application that requires access
- The authentication method it will use
- The topics and namespaces it will access, and how
- The roleID we will assign to these permissions

Application	Authentication	RoleID	Authorization policies
Driver assignment microservice	JWT	DA_service	microservices/orders/accepted (consume) drivers/offers/driver_* (publish)
Resturant assignment microservice	JWT	RA_service	microservices/orders/paid (consume) restaurants/offers/restaurant_* (publish)
Payment verificaton microservice	JWT	PV_service	microservices/orders/new (consume) microservices/orders/paid (produce)
Customer notificaton microservice	JWT	CN_service	microservices/orders/* (consume)
Customer mobile application	TLS Cert	Customer	microservices/orders/new (publish)
Driver mobile application	TLS Cert	Driver_<id>	drivers/offers/driver_ID (consume) microservices/orders/dispatched (produce)
Restaurant mobile application	TLS Cert	Restaurant_<id>	microservices/orders/accepted (produce) restaurants/offers/restaurant_ID (consume)

Figure 6.5 Application-level security requirements for the order placement use case

For example, we know that the driver assignment microservice will use a JWT to authenticate with Pulsar and be assigned the DA_service role token, which will grant consume permission on the persistent://microservices/orders/accepted topic and produce permission on all the topics in the persistent://drivers/offers namespace. Therefore, the commands shown in listing 6.23 would need to be executed to enable the security policies for the DA_service role, and similar commands would be required for the other services as well. It is worth mentioning that, even though there may be multiple instances of the driver assignment service running, they can all use the same RoleID. This is *not* the case for some of the mobile applications,

since we will need to know exactly which user is accessing the system to enforce our
security policies.

Listing 6.23 Enabling security for the driver assignment microservice

**Create the microservices/order namespace;
this only needs to be done once.**

```
$PULSAR_HOME/bin/pulsar-admin namespaces create microservice/orders

$PULSAR_HOME/bin/pulsar tokens create \     ◁─── Create a JWT for the DA_service role.
    --private-key file:///path/to/private-secret.key \
    --subject DA_service > DA_service-token.txt     ◁───  Save the token in a text
                                                          file to share with the
                                                          service deployment team.
$PULSAR_HOME/bin/pulsar-admin namespaces grant-permission \
    drivers/offers --actions produce --role DA_service ◁─┐  Grant the DA_service
                                                          role permission to
$PULSAR_HOME/bin/pulsar-admin topics grant-permission \  publish to any topic
    persistent://microservices/orders/accepted \         in the drivers/offers
    --actions produce \          Grant the DA_service role  namespace.
    --role DA_service ◁────       permission to consume
                                  from a single topic.
```

The JWT should be saved to a file and shared with the team that will be deploying the
driver assignment service, so they can make it available to the service at runtime by
either bundling it with the service or placing it in a secure location, such as a Kubernetes secret. The mobile applications, in contrast, will use custom client certificates
that are generated after the driver or restaurateur has been successfully onboarded
and issued a unique ID, as the client certificate that is generated will be associated
with that specific ID in order to uniquely identify to the user when they connect (e.g.,
driver_4950 would be issued a client certificate associated with a common name of
driver_4950 and would be granted a role token for that role). We can see this in the
following listing, which shows the steps that would be taken by the driver-admin-role
to add a new driver to the Pulsar cluster.

Listing 6.24 Onboarding a new driver

**Use the driver-provided private key
to generate a certificate request.**

                                          **Use the CN field to specify the
                                          new roleID for this driver.**

```
openssl req -config file:///path/to/openssl.cnf \
     -key file:///path/to/driver-4950.key.pem -new -sha256 \
     -out file:///path/to/driver-4950.csr.pem \
     -subj "/C=US/ST=CA/L=Palo Alto/O=gottaeat.com/CN=driver_4950" \   ◁───
     -passin pass:${CLIENT_PASSWORD}
                                          Use the CSR to generate a TLS client
                                          certificate for the new driver.
openssl ca -config file:///path/to/openssl.cnf \
     -extensions usr_cert \
     -days 100 -notext -md sha256 -batch \     The name of the client certificate
     -in file:///path/to/driver-4950.csr.pem \ ◁─  file, which will be bundled with
     -out file:///path/to/driver-4950.cert.pem \ ◁─ the mobile app download
```

```
      -passin pass:${CA_PASSWORD}

$PULSAR_HOME/bin/pulsar-admin topics grant-permission \
   persistent://drivers/offers/driver_4950 \
   --actions consume \
   --role driver_4950

$PULSAR_HOME/bin/pulsar-admin topics grant-permission \
   persistent://microservices/orders/dispatched \
   --actions produce \
   --role driver_4950
```

Grant the driver_4950 role permission to consume from a dedicated topic.

Grant the driver role permission to produce to the general dispatched topic.

In listing 6.24, we see that a TLS client certificate is generated specifically for the new driver, based on their ID. This certificate is then bundled together with the driver mobile application code to ensure it is always used to authenticate with Pulsar when connecting to the cluster. The driver will then be sent a link they can use to download and install it on their smartphone.

6.4   *Message encryption*

The new orders topic will contain sensitive credit card information that must not be accessible to any consumer other than the payment verification service. Even though we have configured TLS wire encryption to secure the information during transit into the Pulsar cluster, we also need to ensure that the data is stored in an encrypted format. Fortunately, Pulsar provides methods that allow you to encrypt messages' contents on the producer side before sending them to the broker. These message contents will remain encrypted until a consumer with the correct private key consumes them.

In order to send and receive encrypted messages, you will first need to create an asymmetric key pair. A script named gen-rsa-key.sh is included in the Docker image we have been using, which can be used to generate a public/private key pair. The following listing shows the contents of the script, which is located in the /pulsar/manning/security/message-encryption folder.

Listing 6.25   Contents of `gen-rsa-keys.sh`

```
# Generate the private key
openssl ecparam -name secp521r1 \
   -genkey \
   -param_enc explicit \
   -out /pulsar/manning/security/encryption/ecdsa_privkey.pem

# Generate the public key
openssl ec -pubout \
   -outform pem \
   -in /pulsar/manning/security/encryption/ecdsa_privkey.pem \
   -out /pulsar/manning/security/encryption/ecdsa_pubkey.pem
```

You should give the public key to the producer application, which, in this particular case, is the client mobile application. The private key should only be shared with the payment verification service, since it will need to consume the encrypted messages that are published to the `persistent://microservices/orders/new` topic. The following listing shows sample code of how to use the public key with a message producer to encrypt the data before it is sent.

Listing 6.26   Encrypted producer configuration

The client must have access to the public key.

Initialize the crypto reader to use the public key.

```
String pubKeyFile = "path to ecdsa_pubkey.pem";
CryptoKeyReader cryptoReader
    = new RawFileKeyReader(pubKeyFile, null);

Producer<String> producer = client
  .newProducer(Schema.STRING)
  .cryptoKeyReader(cryptoReader)
  .cryptoFailureAction(ProducerCryptoFailureAction.FAIL)
  .addEncryptionKey("new-order-key")
  .topic("persistent://microservices/orders/new")
  .create();
```

Configure the producer to use the public key to encrypt the messages via the CryptoReader.

Tells the producer to throw an exception if the message cannot be encrypted

Provides a name for the encryption key

The following listing shows sample code of how to configure the consumer inside the payment verification service to use the private key to decrypt the messages it consumes from the `persistent://microservices/orders/new` topic.

Listing 6.27   Configuring a Pulsar client to read from an encrypted topic

```
String privKeyFile = "path to ecdsa_privkey.pem";
CryptoKeyReader cryptoReader
    = new RawFileKeyReader(null, privKeyFile);

ConsumerBuilder<String> builder = client
  .newConsumer(Schema.STRING)
  .consumerName("payment-verification-service")
  .cryptoKeyReader(cryptoReader)
  .cryptoFailureAction(ConsumerCryptoFailureAction.DISCARD)
  .topic("persistent://microservices/orders/new")
  .subscriptionName("my-sub");
```

The client must have access to the public key.

Initialize the crypto reader to use the public key.

Configure the consumer to use the private key to decrypt the messages via the CryptoReader.

Tells the consumer to discard the message if it cannot be decrypted

Now that I've covered the steps required to configure the message producers and consumers to support message encryption, I want to drill down into the details of how it is implemented internally within Pulsar and some of the key design decisions you should be aware of to better understand how to leverage it in your applications. Figure 6.6 shows the steps taken on the producer side when message encryption is enabled. When the producers' `send` method is called with the raw message bytes, the producer first makes an internal call to the Pulsar client library to get the current symmetric

AES encryption key. The encryption key is considered current because these keys are automatically rotated every four hours to limit the impact of someone gaining unauthorized access to the key, limiting the data exposed to a four-hour window in the event of a compromised key, rather than the entire history of the topic.

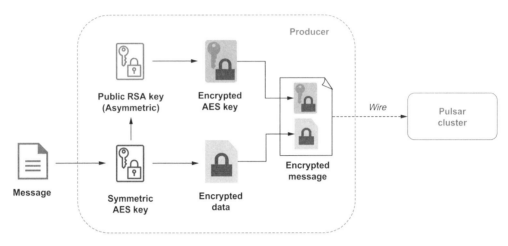

Figure 6.6   Message encryption on the Pulsar producer

The current AES key is then used to encrypt the raw message bytes of the message, which are then placed in the outbound message's payload. Next, the public key of the RSA asymmetric key pair we generated earlier is used to encrypt the AES key itself, and the resulting encrypted AES key is placed in the outbound message's header properties.

By encrypting the AES Key with the public key of an asymmetric key pair, we can rest assured that only a consumer with the corresponding private key of the key pair can decrypt (and thus read) the AES key that was used to encrypt the message payload. At this point, all of the data within the outbound message is encrypted: the message payload with the AES key and the message header that contains the AES key, which itself has been encrypted with a public RSA key. The message is then sent over the wire to the Pulsar cluster for delivery to its intended consumers.

Upon receipt of an encrypted message, a consumer performs the steps shown in figure 6.7 to decrypt the message and access the raw data. First, the consumer reads the message headers and looks for the `encryption key` property, which contains the encrypted AES key. It then uses the private RSA key from the asymmetric key pair to decrypt the contents of the `encryption key` property to produce the AES key. Now that the consumer is in possession of the AES key, it can decrypt the message contents with it due to the fact that it is a symmetrical key, meaning it is used to both encrypt and decrypt data.

Choosing to store the AES key used to encrypt the message with the encrypted message contents themselves alleviates Pulsar from the responsibility of having to

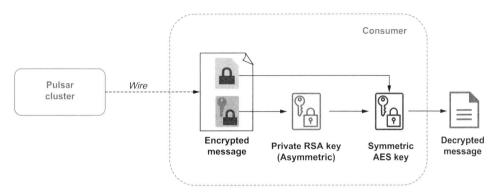

Figure 6.7 Message decryption on the Pulsar consumer

store and manage these encryption keys internally. However, if you lose or delete the
RSA private key used to decrypt the RSA key, your message is irretrievably lost and can-
not be decrypted by Pulsar. Therefore, it is a best practice to store and manage the
RSA key pairs in a third-party key management service, such as AWS KMS.

Now that I have brought up the possibility of a lost RSA key, you might be wonder-
ing what exactly happens in such a scenario. Obviously, you never want this to occur,
but it can happen, so you need to consider how you want your application to respond
and what options you have on both the producer and consumer side.

First, let's consider the producer side. There are really only two options here. First,
you can choose to continue sending the messages without encrypting them. This
might be a good option if the value of the data exceeds the risk of having it stored in
an unencrypted format for a limited amount of time. For instance, in the order placement scenario we discussed earlier, it would be better to allow the customer orders to
be sent rather than to shut down the entire business due to a missing RSA key. Since
the data is being sent over a secure TLS connection, the risk is minimal.

The other option is for the producer to fail the messages and throw an exception,
which is a good option when risk of the exposing the data outweighs the potential
business value of having it delivered in a timely manner. This would typically be some
sort of non-customer-facing application, such as a backend payment processing system, that does not have a strict business SLA. You can specify which action you want
your producer to take by using the `setCryptoFailureAction()` method in the producer configuration, as was shown in listing 6.26.

If consumption fails due to decryption failure on the consumer side, then you have
three options; first, you can elect to deliver the encrypted contents to the consuming
application. However, it will then be the consuming application's responsibility to
decrypt the message. This option is useful when your consumer's logic is *not* based on
the message contents, such as routing of the message to downstream consumers based
on the information in the message headers.

The second option is to fail the message, which will make the Pulsar broker redeliver it. This option is useful if you are a shared subscription type, so there are multiple consumers on the same subscription. When you fail the message, you are hoping the decryption issue is isolated to just the current consumer, such as a missing private key on that consumer's host machine, and if the message is redelivered to another consumer, it will be able to decrypt the message and consume it successfully. Do *not* use this option with an exclusive subscription type, as this will result in the message being redelivered indefinitely to the same consumer, who cannot process it.

The last option is to have the consumer discard the message, which is useful for an exclusive subscription consumer that needs access to the message contents in order to perform its logic. As we discussed earlier, failing the message will result in an infinite number of message redelivers, and the consumer will be stuck reprocessing the message. Such a scenario would halt message consumption on the subscription and steadily increase in the message backlog for the entire topic. Therefore, discarding the message is the only way to prevent this from occurring, but at the cost of message loss.

Summary

- Pulsar supports TLS wire encryption, which ensures that all data transferred between clients and the Pulsar broker is encrypted.
- Pulsar supports TLS authentication with client certificates, which allows you to distribute these credentials only to trusted users and limit cluster access to only those in possession of a valid client certificate.
- Pulsar allows you to use JSON web tokens to authenticate users and map them to a specific role.
- Once authenticated, a user is granted a role token that is used to determine which resources within the Pulsar cluster the user is authorized to read from and write to.
- Pulsar supports message-level encryption to provide security for data stored on the local disk in the bookies. This prevents unauthorized access to any sensitive data that may be inside those messages.

Schema registry

7

This chapter covers

- Using the Pulsar schema to simplify your microservice development
- Understanding the different schema compatibility types
- Using the `LocalRunner` class to run and debug your functions inside your IDE
- Evolving a schema without impacting existing consumers

Traditional databases employ a process referred to as *schema-on-write*, where the table's columns, rows, and types are all defined before any data can be written into the table. This ensures that the data conforms to a predetermined specification and the consuming clients can access the schema information directly from the database itself, which enables them to determine the basic structure of the records they are processing.

Apache Pulsar messages are stored as unstructured byte arrays, and the structure is applied to this data only when it's read. This approach is referred to as *schema-on-read* and was first popularized by Hadoop and NoSQL databases. While the schema-on-read approach makes it easier to ingest and process new and dynamic data sources on the fly, it does have some drawbacks, including the lack of

191

a metastore that clients can access to determine the schema for the Pulsar topic they are consuming from.

Pulsar clients just see a stream of individual records that can be of any type and need an efficient way to determine how to interpret each arriving record. This is where the Pulsar schema registry comes into play. It is a critical component of the Pulsar technology stack that tracks the schema of all the topics inside of Pulsar.

As we saw in the last chapter, the development team for the food delivery service company GottaEat has decided to embrace the microservice architectural style in which applications are comprised of a collection of loosely coupled, independently developed services. In such an architecture, different microservices will need to collaborate on the same data, and in order to do that, they will need to know the basic structure of the event, including the fields and their associated types. Otherwise, the event consumers will not be able to perform any meaningful calculations on the event data. In this chapter, I will demonstrate how Pulsar's schema registry can be used to greatly simplify the sharing of this information across the application teams at GottaEat.

7.1   *Microservice communication*

When you build microservice architectures, one of the concerns you need to address is that of interservice communication. There are different options for interservice communication, each with their own respective strengths and weaknesses. Typically, these various types of communication can be classified across two different decision factors. The first factor is whether the communication between the services is synchronous or asynchronous, and the second factor is whether the communication is intended for a single receiver or multiple receivers, as shown in figure 7.1

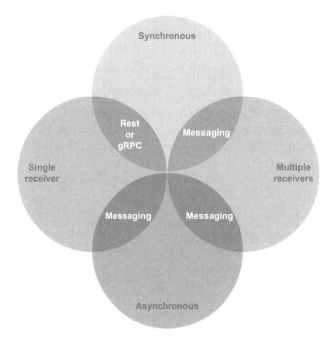

Figure 7.1   Microservice communication factors and appropriate communication protocols

Protocols such as HTTP/REST or gRPC are most commonly used as synchronous request/response-based interservice communication mechanisms. With synchronous communication, one service sends a request and waits for a response from another service. The calling service's execution is blocked and cannot continue its task until it receives a response. This communication pattern is similar to procedure calls in traditional application programming in which a specific method is made to an external service with a specific set of parameters.

With asynchronous communication, one service sends a message and does not need to wait for a response. If you want an asynchronous publish/subscribe-based communication mechanism, messaging systems such as Pulsar are a perfect fit. A messaging system is also required to support publish/subscribe interservice communication between a single service that has multiple message receivers. It is not practical to have a service block until all of the intended recipients have acknowledged the message, as some of them may be offline. A much better approach is to have the messaging system retain the messages.

These factors and communication mechanisms are good to know so you have clarity on the possible communication mechanisms you can use, but they're not the most important concerns when building microservices. What is most important is being able to integrate your microservices, while maintaining the independence of microservices, and doing so requires the establishment of a contract between the collaborating services, regardless of the communication mechanism you chose.

7.1.1 *Microservice APIs*

As with any software development project, clear requirements help development teams create the right software, and having well-defined service contracts up front allows microservice developers to write code without having to make assumptions about the data that will be provided to them or the expected output for any particular method within their service. In this section, I will cover how each of the communication styles supports service contracts.

REST AND GRPC PROTOCOLS

When evaluating the synchronous request/response-based interservice communication mechanisms, one of the biggest differences between REST and gRPC is the format of the payload. The conceptual model used by gRPC is to have services with clear interface definitions and structured messages for requests and responses. This model translates directly to programming language concepts like interfaces, functions, methods, and data structures. It also allows gRPC to automatically generate client libraries for you. These libraries can then be shared between the microservice development teams and act as a formal contract between them.

While the REST paradigm doesn't mandate any structure, message payloads typically use a loosely-typed data serialization system, such as JSON. Consequently, REST APIs don't have a formal mechanism for specifying the format of the messages passed between services. The data is passed back and forth as raw bytes, which must be deserialized by the receiving service(s). However, these message payloads have an implied structure that the payload must adhere to. Therefore, any changes to the message payloads must be coordinated between the teams that are developing the services to ensure any changes made by one team do not impact the others. One such example would be the removal of a field that is required by other services. Making such a change would violate the informal contract between the services and cause issues for the consuming services that depend on that particular field to perform their processing logic.

This problem isn't just limited to the REST protocol either, but rather it is a side effect of the loosely-typed data communication protocol being used. Consequently, this issue also exists with message-based interservice communication that uses a loosely-typed data serialization system.

MESSAGING PROTOCOL

As we saw in figure 7.1, most of the interservice communication patterns can only be supported by a message-based communication protocol. Within Pulsar each message consists of two distinct parts: the message payload, which is stored as raw bytes, and a collection of user defined properties that are stored as key/value pairs. Storing the message payload as raw bytes provides maximum flexibility, but the trade-off is that each message consumer is required to transform these bytes into a format the consuming applications are expecting, as shown in figure 7.2.

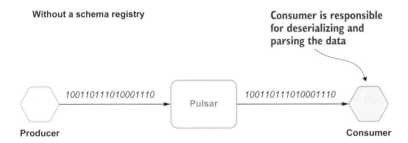

Figure 7.2   Pulsar takes raw bytes as input and delivers raw bytes as output.

Different microservices will need to communicate via messages, and in order to do so, both the producer and consumer will need to agree on the basic structure of the messages they are exchanging, including the fields and their associated types. The metadata that defines the structure of these messages is commonly referred to as message schemas. They provide a formal definition of how the raw message bytes should be translated into a more formal type structure (e.g., how the 0s and 1s stored inside the message payload map to a programming-language object type).

Message schemas are the closest we come to a formal contract between the services that generate the messages and the services that consume them. It is useful to think about message schemas as APIs. Applications depend on APIs and expect that any changes made to APIs are still compatible and that applications can still run.

7.1.2 The need for a schema registry

A schema registry provides a central location for storing information about the schemas used within your organization, which in turn greatly simplifies the sharing of this information across application teams. It serves as a single source of truth for the message schemas used across all your services and development teams, which makes it easier for them to collaborate. Having an external repository of message schemas helps answer the following questions for any given topic:

- If I am consuming messages, how do I parse and interpret the data?
- If I am producing messages, what is the expected format?
- Do all of the messages have the same format, or has the schema changed?
- If the schema has changed, what are the different message formats inside the topic?

Having a central schema registry along with the consistent use of schemas across the organization makes data consumption and discovery much easier. If you define a standard schema for a common business entity that almost all applications will use, such as a customer, product, or order, then all message-producing applications will be able to generate messages in the latest format. Similarly, consuming applications won't need to perform any transformations on the data in order to make it conform to a different format. From a data discovery perspective, having the structure of the messages clearly defined in the schema registry allows data scientists to understand the structure of the data better without having to ask the development teams.

7.2 The Pulsar schema registry

The Pulsar schema registry enables message producers and consumers on Pulsar topics to coordinate on the structure of the topic's data through the Pulsar broker itself without needing an additional serving layer for the metadata. Other messaging systems, such as Kafka, require a separate standalone schema registry component.

7.2.1 Architecture

By default, Pulsar uses the Apache BookKeeper table service for schema storage, since it provides durable, replicated storage that ensures the schema data is not lost. It also provides the added benefit of a convenient key/value API. Since Pulsar schemas are applied and enforced at the topic level, the topic name is used as the key, and the values are represented by a data structure known as `SchemaInfo` that consists of the fields shown in the following listing.

Listing 7.1   A Pulsar `SchemaInfo` example

A unique name, which should match the topic name that the schema is associated with

Will either be one of the predefined schema types, such as STRING or struct, if you are using a generic serialization library, such as Apache Avro or JSON

```
{
    "name": "my-namespace/my-topic",
    "type": "STRING",
```

```
    "schema": "",
    "properties": {}
}
```

A collection of user-defined properties

If you are using a supported
serialization type, such as Avro, then
this will contain the raw schema data.

As you can see in figure 7.3, a Pulsar client relies on the schema registry to get the schema associated with the topic it is connected to and invoke the associated serializer/deserializer to transform the bytes into the appropriate type. This alleviates the consumer code from the responsibility of having to do the transformation and allows it to focus on the business logic.

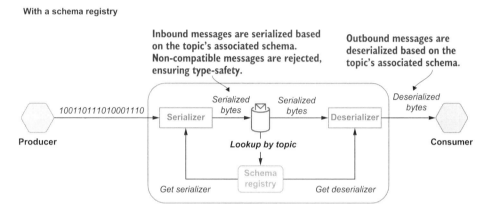

With a schema registry

Inbound messages are serialized based on the topic's associated schema. Non-compatible messages are rejected, ensuring type-safety.

Outbound messages are deserialized based on the topic's associated schema.

Figure 7.3   The Pulsar schema registry is used to serialize the bytes before they are published to a topic and to deserialize them before they are delivered to the consumers.

The schema registry uses the values of the type and schema fields to determine how to serialize and de-serialize the bytes contained inside the message body. The Pulsar schema registry supports a variety of schema types, which can be categorized as either *primitive* types or *complex* types. The type field is used to specify which of these categories the topic schema falls into.

PRIMITIVE TYPES

Currently, Pulsar provides several primitive schema types, such as BOOLEAN, BYTES, FLOAT, STRING, and TIMESTAMP, just to name a few. If the type field contains the name of one of these predefined schema types, then the message bytes will be automatically serialized/deserialized into the corresponding programming language-specific type, as shown in table 7.1.

Table 7.1   Pulsar primitive types

BOOLEAN	A single binary value: 0 = false, 1 = true
INT8	An 8-bit signed integer
INT16	A 16-bit signed integer
INT32	A 32-bit signed integer

Table 7.1 Pulsar primitive types *(continued)*

INT64	A 64-bit signed integer
FLOAT	A 32-bit, single precision floating point number (IEEE 754)
DOUBLE	A 64-bit, double precision floating point number (IEEE 754)
BYTES	A sequence of 8-bit unsigned bytes
STRING	A Unicode character sequence
TIMESTAMP	The number of milliseconds since Jan 1, 1970 stored as an INT64 value

For primitive types, Pulsar does not require or use any data in the `schema` field because the schema is already implied and, thus, is not necessary.

COMPLEX TYPES

When your messages require a more complex type, you should use one of generic serialization libraries supported by Pulsar, such as Avro, JSON, or protobuf. This would be denoted with an empty string in the `type` field of the `SchemaInfo` object associated with the topic, and the `schema` field will contain a UTF-8 encoded JSON string of the schema definition. Let's consider how this is applied to an Apache Avro schema definition to better illustrate how the Schema registry simplifies the process.

Apache Avro is a data serialization format that supports the definition of complex data types via language-independent schema definitions in JSON. Avro data is serialized into a compact binary data format that can only be read using the schema that was used when writing it. Since Avro requires that readers have access to the original writer schema in order to deserialize the binary data, the associated schema is typically stored with it at the beginning of the file. Avro was originally intended to be used for storing files with a large number of records of the same type, which allowed you to store the schema once and reuse it as you iterated through the records.

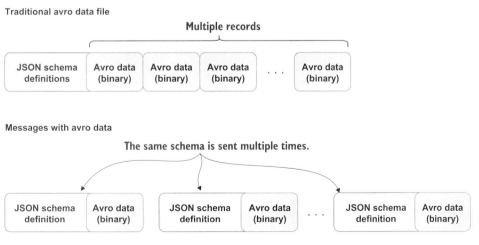

Figure 7.4   Avro messages would require the associated schema to be included with every message to ensure you could parse the binary message contents.

However, in a messaging use case, the schema would have to be sent with every single message, as shown in figure 7.4. Including the schema inside every Pulsar message would be inefficient in terms of memory, network bandwidth, and disk space. This is where Pulsar's schema registry comes in. When you register a typed producer or consumer that uses an Avro schema, the JSON representation of the Avro schema is stored inside the `schema` field of the associated `SchemaInfo` object. The raw bytes of the messages are then serialized or deserialized based upon the Avro schema definition stored inside the Schema registry, as shown in figure 7.3. This eliminates the need to include it with every single message. Furthermore, the corresponding serializer or deserializer is cached inside the producers/consumers, so it can be used on all subsequent messages until a different schema version is encountered.

7.2.2   Schema versioning

Every `SchemaInfo` object stored with a topic has a version associated with it. When a producer publishes a message using a given `SchemaInfo`, the message is tagged with the associated schema version, as shown in figure 7.5. Storing the schema version with the message allows the consumer to use the version to look up the schema in the schema registry and use it to deserialize the message.

Messages with Avro data and schema version

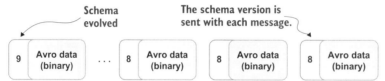

Figure 7.5   When using the Schema Registry, Avro messages would contain a schema version rather than the entire schema description. Consumers will use the schema version to retrieve the proper deserializer based on the version.

This is a simple and efficient way to associate the Avro schema with each Avro message without having to attach the schema's JSON description. The schemas are versioned in increasing order (e.g., v1, v2, …, etc.), and when the first typed consumer or producer with a schema connects to a topic, that schema is tagged as version 1. Once the initial schema is loaded, the brokers are provided the schema info for the topics they are serving and retain a copy of it locally for schema enforcement.

Within a messaging system such as Pulsar, messages may be retained for an indefinite period of time. Consequently, some consumers will need to process these messages with older versions of the schema. Therefore, the schema registry retains a versioned history of all the schemas used in Pulsar to serve these consumers of historical messages.

7.2.3   Schema compatibility

As you may recall, I started this chapter with a discussion of the importance of maintaining compatibility of messages used by microservices, even as requirements and applications evolve. In Pulsar, every producer and consumer is free to use their own schema, so it is quite possible that a topic could contain messages that conform to different schema versions, as shown in figure 7.5, where the topic contains messages with schema version 8 and messages with schema version 9.

It is important to point out that the schema registry does *not* ensure that every producer and consumer is using the exact same schema but, rather, that the schemas they are using are compatible with one another. Consider the scenario where a development team changes the schema of the messages it is producing by adding or removing a field or changing one of the existing field types from string to timestamp. In order to maintain the implicit producer–consumer contract and avoid accidently breaking consumer microservices, we need to ensure that the producers are publishing messages that contain all the information the consumers require. Otherwise, we run the risk of introducing messages that will break existing applications because you have removed a field that is required by these applications.

When you configure the schema registry to validate schema compatibility, the Pulsar schema registry will perform a compatibility check when the producer connects to the topic. If the change will not break the consumers and cause exceptions, the change is considered compatible, and the producer is allowed to connect to the topic and produce messages with the new schema type. This approach helps prevent disparate development teams from introducing changes that break existing applications that are already consuming from Pulsar topics.

PRODUCER SCHEMA COMPATIBILITY VERIFICATION

Every time a typed producer connects to a topic, as shown in figure 7.6, it will transmit a copy of the schema it is using to the broker. A `SchemaInfo` object is created based on the passed-in schema and is passed to the schema registry. If the schema is already associated with the topic, the producer is allowed to connect and can then proceed to publish messages using the specified schema.

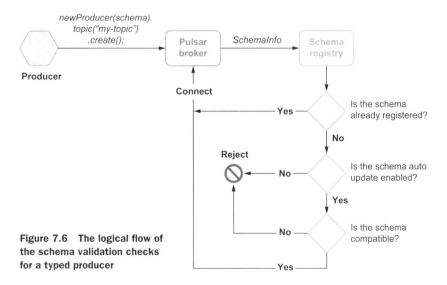

Figure 7.6 The logical flow of the schema validation checks for a typed producer

If the schema is not already registered with the topic, the schema registry checks the `AutoUpdate` strategy setting for the associated namespace to determine whether or not the producer is permitted to register a new schema version on the topic. At this point, the producer will be rejected if the policy prohibits the registration of new schema versions. If schema updates are permitted, then the compatibility strategy check is performed, and if it passes, the schema is registered with the schema registry, and the producer is allowed to connect with the new schema version. If the schema is determined to be incompatible, then the producer is rejected.

CONSUMER SCHEMA COMPATIBILITY VERIFICATION

Every time a typed consumer connects to a topic, as shown in figure 7.7, it will transmit a copy of the schema it is using to the broker. A `SchemaInfo` object is created based on the passed-in schema and is passed to the schema registry.

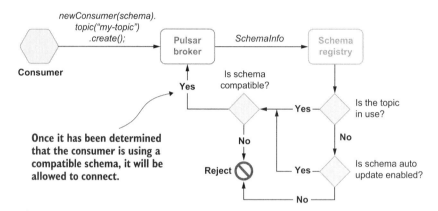

Figure 7.7   The logical flow of the schema validation checks for a typed consumer

If the topic doesn't have any active producers or consumers, any registered schemas, or any existing data, then it is considered *not in use.* In the absence of all of the aforementioned items, the schema registry checks the `AutoUpdate` strategy setting for the associated namespace to determine whether or not the consumer is permitted to register a new schema version on the topic. The consumer will be rejected if it is prohibited from registering its schema; otherwise, the compatibility strategy check is performed, and if it passes, the schema is registered with the schema registry, and the consumer is allowed to connect with the new schema version. If the schema is determined to be incompatible, then the consumer is rejected. The compatibility check is also performed if the topic is *in use.*

7.2.4   *Schema compatibility check strategies*

The Pulsar schema registry supports six different compatibility strategies, which can be configured on a per-topic basis. It is important to point out that all of the compatibility checks are from the consumer's perspective, even when it comes to the compatibility checks for producers, as the goal is to prevent the introduction of messages that the existing consumers cannot process. The Schema registry will use the underlying serialization library's (e.g., Avro's) compatibility rules to determine whether or not the new schema is compatible with the current schema. The Pulsar schema registry's default compatibility type is BACKWARD, which is described in greater detail, along with the others, in the following sections.

BACKWARD COMPATIBILITY

Backward compatibility means that the consumer can use a newer version of the schema and still be able to read messages from a producer that is using the previous version. Consider the scenario where both the producer and consumer start out using the same version of the Avro schema: v1. One of the teams responsible for developing one of the consumers decides to add a new field called status to the schema to support a new customer loyalty program that has various status tiers, such as silver, gold, and platinum, as shown in figure 7.8. In this case, the new schema version, v2, would be considered backward compatible, since it specifies a default value for the newly added field.

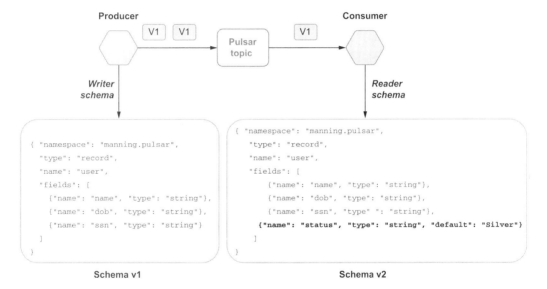

Figure 7.8 **Backward compatible changes are those that allow a consumer that is using a newer version of the schema to still be able to process messages that are written using the previous version of the schema.**

This allows data written with v1 of the schema to be read by the consumer, since the default value specified in the newer schema will be used for the missing field when deserializing the messages serialized with v1, thereby treating all members as having silver status in the consuming application.

To support this type of use case, you can use the BACKWARD schema compatibility strategy. However, that only supports the case where you have consumers that are one schema version ahead of your producers. If you want to support producers that are more than one schema version behind your consumers, you can use the BACKWARD_ TRANSITIVE compatibility strategy instead.

Let's expand upon the use case from the previous example. Now we have a new microservice added to the application that is responsible for determining a customer's loyalty status and is producing messages that contain the status field.

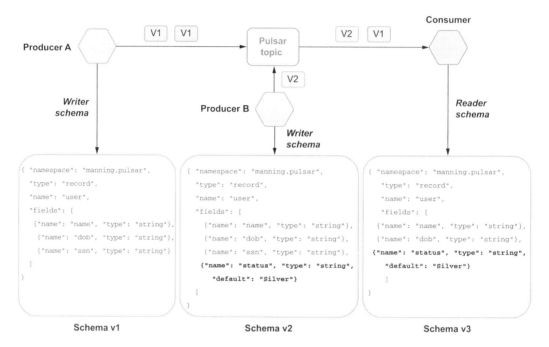

Figure 7.9   **Backward transitive compatible changes are those that allow a consumer that is using a newer version of the schema to still be able to process messages that are written using any of the previous versions of the schema.**

Also, the microservice that originally introduced the need for the status field has undergone a security review, and it has been determined that having the customer's social security number poses too big of a security risk, so it has been removed. As you can see from figure 7.9, we still have the original producer that is using schema v1, the new microservice that is using v2 of the schema that includes the status field, and a consumer that is using a third schema version that has removed the ssn field.

In order to be considered backward transitive compatible, the new consumer schema version, v3, would have to be able to process messages from both active producers (e.g., schema versions v1 and v2). Since v3 specifies a default value for the status field, data written with v1 of the schema can be read by the consumer, since the default value specified in v3 of the schema will be used for the missing field when deserializing the messages serialized with v1. Similarly, since the messages serialized with v2 of the schema contain all of the fields required in v3, the consumer can simply ignore the extra `ssn` field in these messages.

FORWARD COMPATIBILITY

Forward compatibility means that the consumer can use an older version of the schema and still be able to read messages from a producer that is using a new version. Consider the scenario where both the producer and consumer start out using the same version of the protobuf schema: v1. One of the teams responsible for developing one of the producers decides to add a new field called `age` to the schema to support a new marketing program based on different age groups, as shown in figure 7.10.

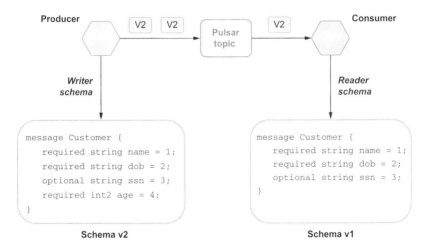

Figure 7.10 Forward compatible changes are those that allow a consumer that is using an older version of the schema to still be able to process messages that are written using a newer version of the schema.

In this case, the new schema version, v2, would be considered forward compatible, since it simply added a new field that wasn't in the previous version. This allows data written with v2 of the schema to be read by the consumer, since the newly added field will be ignored when deserializing the messages serialized with v2. The consumer can continue processing the messages, since it does not have any dependency on the newly added `age` field.

To support this type of use case, you can use the `FORWARD` schema compatibility strategy. However, that only supports the case where you have consumers that are one schema version behind the message producers. If you want to support producers that are more than one schema version ahead of your consumers, then you can use the `FORWARD_TRANSITIVE` compatibility strategy instead.

Let's expand upon the use case from the previous example. Now we have a new microservice added to the application that is responsible for determining a customer's demographic based on the `age` field, and that returns a message containing a brand-new field, `demo`, and eliminates the optional `ssn` field, as shown in figure 7.11

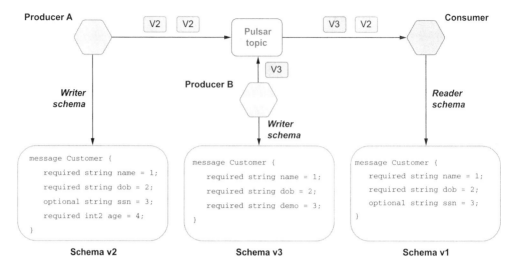

Figure 7.11   Forward transitive compatible changes are those that allow a consumer using an older version of the schema to still be able to process messages that are written using any of the newer versions of the schema.

In order to be considered forward transitive compatible, the consumer schema version, v1, would have to be able to process messages from both active producers (e.g., schema versions v2 and v3). Since v1 specifies that the ssn field is optional, data written with v3 of the schema can be read by the consumer, because this field is not required, and the consumer must be prepared to handle null values for this field. Also, since the messages serialized with v2 and v3 both contain additional fields that are not specified in v1, the consumer can simply ignore these extra fields in the messages, as they are not required by the consumer.

FULL COMPATIBILITY

Full compatibility means the schema is both backward and forward compatible. Data serialized using an older version of the schema can be deserialized with the new schema, and data serialized using a newer version of the schema can also be deserialized with the previous version of the schema.

In some data formats, such as JSON, there are no full-compatible changes. Every modification is either only forward or backward compatible. But in other data formats, like Avro or protobuf, where you can define fields with default values, adding or removing a field with a default value is considered a fully compatible change. To support this type of use case, you can use either the FULL or FULL_TRANSITIVE schema compatibility strategies.

7.3 *Using the schema registry*

Let's consider a scenario from the GottaEat food delivery company that allows customers to find and order food from any participating restaurant in the company's network and have it delivered to any location they choose. Orders can be placed via the company website or mobile application. Delivery of the food order is handled via a network of independent drivers who are required to download a specialized mobile application onto their smartphones. The drivers will receive notifications of food orders that are available for delivery within their area and have the option of accepting or declining the orders.

Once an order has been accepted by the driver, it is added to their itinerary for the evening, and the driver will receive directions to the restaurant for pickup and the customer location for delivery inside the driver's mobile application. Participating restaurateurs are notified of incoming orders and are responsible for reviewing the incoming orders and providing a time window for pickup. This information allows the system to better schedule the drivers and prevent them from arriving too early (and wasting their time) or too late (and the food being cold or late).

As the lead architect on this project, you have decided that a microservices architecture is best suited to meet the needs of the business. It also allows you to model the problem as an event-driven problem, which lends itself nicely to message-based communication between independent microservices. To this end, you have sketched out the high-level design for the order entry use case shown in figure 7.12 and need to determine how to implement this design using Pulsar. The overall flow of the use case is as follows:

1 Customers submit their orders using the company website or mobile application, and they are published to the `customer order` topic.

2 An order validation service subscribes to the `customer order` topic and validates the order, including taking the provided payment information, such as the credit card number or gift card, and obtaining confirmation of payment.

3 Orders that are validated get published to the `validated order` topic and are consumed by both the customer notification service (e.g., sending an SMS message to the customer confirming the order was placed on the mobile app) and the restaurant notification service that publishes the order into the individual `restaurant order` topic associated with the order (e.g., `persistent://resturants/orders/<resturant-id>`).

4 The restaurants review the incoming orders from their topic, update the status of the order from `new` to `accepted`, and provide a pickup time window of when they feel the food will be ready.

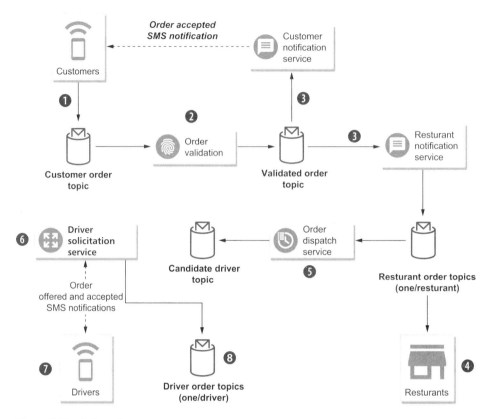

Figure 7.12   Order entry use case

5   The order dispatcher service is responsible for assigning the accepted orders to drivers and uses Pulsar's regex subscription capability to consume from *all* of the individual `restaurant order` topics (e.g., `persistent://resturants/orders/*`) and filters on a status of `accepted`. It uses that information, along with the driver's existing list of deliveries, to select a handful of candidate drivers to offer the order to and then publishes this list to a candidate driver's topic.

6   The driver solicitation service consumes from the candidate driver's topic and pushes a notification to each of the drivers in the list, offering them the order. When one of the drivers accepts the order, a notification is sent back to the solicitation service, which in turn publishes the order to the driver's individual order topic (i.e., `persistent://drivers/orders/<drivers-id>`).

Additional use cases are required to handle the routing of the driver, the notification of the customer regarding the order status, etc. But for now, I will focus on the order entry use case and how Pulsar's schema registry will simplify the development of these microservices. Let's examine the structure of the GitHub project associated with this chapter of the book. For this section, please refer to the code in the 0.0.1 branch. As you can see, it is a multi-module maven project that contains three submodules that I will discuss in the upcoming sections.

7.3.1 Modelling the food order event in Avro

The first module, `domain-schema`, contains all of the Avro schema definitions for the GottaEat order entry use case. Avro schemas can be defined in either plain JSON or Avro IDL text files, but the schema files need to live somewhere, and this module serves that purpose.

As you can see from the contents of the `domain-schema` module, I have created an Avro IDL schema definition file named src/main/resources/avro/order/food-order.avdl, which contains the schema definition shown in listing 7.2. This file represents the initial data model for the food order object that will be used across multiple services, and it will be used to generate the Java classes that will be used by all of the consuming Java-based microservices.

Listing 7.2   food-order.avdl

The namespace for these types, which corresponds with the Java package name

```
⌐‒> @namespace("com.gottaeat.domain.order")
    protocol OrderProtocol {
      import idl "../common/common.avdl";          ◁──── We import Avro type definitions
      import idl "../payment/payment-commons.avdl";        from other files, which enables
      import idl "../resturant/resturant.avdl";            compositional schemas.

      record FoodOrder {  ◁──── The FoodOrder record definition
        long order_id;
        long customer_id;
        long resturant_id;
        string time_placed;
        OrderStatus order_status;                   Each FoodOrder can contain
        array<OrderDetail> details;        ◁──────  one or more food items in it.
        com.gottaeat.domain.common.Address delivery_location;   ◁──
        com.gottaeat.domain.payment.CreditCard payment_method;    Using a type defined
        float total = 0.0;                                        inside one of the
      }                                                           included schema
                                                                  definitions
      record OrderDetail {
        int quantity;
        float total;
        com.gottaeat.domain.resturant.MenuItem food_item;
      }

      enum OrderStatus {
        NEW, ACCEPTED, READY, DISPATCHED, DELIVERED
      }
    }
```

We will use the Avro plugin to automatically generate Java classes based on the schema definitions in our project by adding the configuration shown in the following listing to the plugins section of the Maven pom.xml file.

Listing 7.3   Configuring the Avro Maven plugin

```
<plugin>
  <groupId>org.apache.avro</groupId>
  <artifactId>avro-maven-plugin</artifactId>
  <version>1.9.1</version>
  <executions>
     <execution>
        <phase>generate-sources</phase>          We want to generate
        <goals>                                   Java source files.
           <goal>idl-protocol</goal>
        </goals>                                  The definitions are
        <configuration>                           in the IDL format.
          <sourceDirectory>
             ${project.basedir}/src/main/resources/avro/order
          </sourceDirectory>
          <outputDirectory>                       Use the directory containing
             ${project.basedir}/src/main/java     the food-order.avdl as the
          </outputDirectory>                      source directory.
        </configuration>
     </execution>
  </executions>
</plugin>
```

Where to output the generated source files

With the Avro schemas defined and the Maven plugin configured, we can execute the command shown in listing 7.4 to generate the Java classes into the project's source folder, as specified in listing 7.3. This command will generate the Java classes source files, compile them, and jar them into the domain-schema-0.0.1.jar JAR file before finally publishing that JAR file to your local Maven repository.

Listing 7.4   Generating the Java classes from the Avro schema

```
$ cd ./domain-schema
$ mvn install
[INFO] Scanning for projects...
[INFO] --------------------< com.gottaeat:domain-schema >--------------------
[INFO] Building domain-schema 0.0.1
[INFO] -------------------------------[ jar ]-------------------------------
[INFO]
[INFO] --- avro-maven-plugin:1.9.1:idl-protocol (default) @ domain-schema ---
[INFO]
[INFO] --- maven-compiler-plugin:3.8.1:compile (default-compile)
[INFO] Compiling 8 source files to domain-schema/target/classes
[INFO]
[INFO] --- maven-jar-plugin:2.4:jar (default-jar) @ domain-schema ---
[INFO] Building jar: /domain-schema/target/domain-schema-0.0.1.jar
[INFO]
```

```
[INFO] --- maven-install-plugin:2.4:install (default-install)
[INFO] Installing /domain-schema/target/domain-schema-0.0.1.jar to ..
[INFO] ------------------------------------------------------------------------
[INFO] BUILD SUCCESS
[INFO] ------------------------------------------------------------------------
```

You will find the generated classes inside their respective subfolders, under the project's source folder, as shown in listing 7.5. These files are too lengthy to reproduce here, but if you open them with a text editor, you will see that the files contain POJOs that have been auto-generated by Avro and contain all the field definitions in the schema definitions, along with methods to serialize and deserialize the object to and from Avro's binary format.

> **Listing 7.5   Listing all of the generated Java classes**

```
ls -R src/main/java/*
gottaeat

src/main/java/com/gottaeat:
domain

src/main/java/com/gottaeat/domain:
common        order        payment        resturant

src/main/java/com/gottaeat/domain/common:
Address.java

src/main/java/com/gottaeat/domain/order:
FoodOrder.java  OrderDetail.java  OrderProtocol.java  OrderStatus.java

src/main/java/com/gottaeat/domain/payment:
CardType.java  CreditCard.java

src/main/java/com/gottaeat/domain/resturant:
MenuItem.java
```

At this point, we have a domain model in Java for our food order event that can be used by the other microservices in the project.

7.3.2   *Producing food order events*

Rather than create a dependency on the customer mobile application that is being developed by a different team, we have decided to use this tool to generate load for testing purposes. The `customer-mobile-app-simulator` module contains an IO Connector intended to simulate the mobile application that customers will use to place food orders. The connector is defined inside the `CustomerSimulatorSource` class, as shown in the following listing.

Listing 7.6   The `CustomerSimulatorSource` IO connector

**Implements the source interface, which
defines the three overridden methods**

**The class that produces
random food orders**

```
import org.apache.pulsar.io.core.Source;
import org.apache.pulsar.io.core.SourceContext;
public class CustomerSimulatorSource implements Source<FoodOrder> {

    private DataGenerator<FoodOrder> generator = new FoodOrderGenerator();

    @Override
    public void close() throws Exception {
    }

    @Override
    public void open(Map<String, Object> map, SourceContext ctx)
        throws Exception {

    }

    @Override
    public Record<FoodOrder> read() throws Exception {
        Thread.sleep(500);
        return new CustomerRecord<FoodOrder>(generator.generate());
    }

    static private class CustomerRecord<V> implements Record<FoodOrder> {
        ...
    }
    ...
}
```

**Pause
a half
second
between
orders.**

**Publishes
a newly
generated food
order to the
output topic**

**A wrapper class for sending
the FoodOrder objects**

**Where the
LocalRunner code lives**

As you may recall from chapter 5, the source connector's read method is invoked by
Pulsar's internal function framework repeatedly, and the return value gets published to
the configured output topic. In this case, the return value is a random food order based
on the Avro schemas in the domain-schema module generated by another class inside
the project, named FoodOrderGenerator. I have decided to use the LocalRunner for
debugging the CustomerSimulatorSource class, as shown in the following listing.

Listing 7.7   Using `LocalRunner` to debug the `CustomerSimulatorSource` IO connector

```
...
public static void main(String[] args) throws Exception {
    SourceConfig sourceConfig = SourceConfig.builder()
        .className(CustomerSimulatorSource.class.getName())
        .name("mobile-app-simulator")
        .topicName("persistent://orders/inbound/food-orders")
        .schemaType("avro")
        .build();

    // Assumes you started docker container with --volume=${HOME}/exchange
```

**Specify the
connector class
we want to run.**

**The topic the connector will
publish messages to**

```
String credentials_path = System.getProperty("user.home") +
                File.separator + "exchange" + File.separator;

LocalRunner localRunner = LocalRunner.builder()
  .brokerServiceUrl("pulsar+ssl://localhost:6651")
  .clientAuthPlugin("org.apache.pulsar.client.impl.auth.AuthenticationTls")
  .clientAuthParams("tlsCertFile:" + credentials_path +
        "admin.cert.pem,tlsKeyFile:" + credentials_path + "admin-pk8.pem")
  .tlsTrustCertFilePath(credentials_path + "ca.cert.pem")
  .sourceConfig(sourceConfig)
  .build();

localRunner.start(false);
Thread.sleep(30 * 1000);
localRunner.stop();

}
```

Specify the URL of the Pulsar broker we are going to interact with.

Specify the TLS authentication credentials needed to connect to Pulsar.

Starts the LocalRunner

Stops the LocalRunner

As you can see from listing 7.7, I have configured the `LocalRunner` to connect to a locally running instance of the `pulsar-standalone-secure` Docker image that I created in chapter 6. This is why there are several security-related configuration settings in the source code that rely on the security credentials generated for that container, such as the TLS client certificate and trust store.

7.3.3 Consuming the food order events

Lastly, let's look at the `order-validation-service` module, which contains a single Pulsar function, named `OrderValidationService`, which, for the purposes of this chapter, will be just a skeletal implementation of the microservice shown in figure 7.12 and will accept the incoming food orders and validate them for correctness and confirmation of payment, etc. Over time, additional logic will be added, but for now, the function will simply write all of the food orders it receives to standard output (stdout) before forwarding to the configured output topic.

Listing 7.8 The `OrderValidationService` function

```
import org.apache.pulsar.functions.api.Context;
import org.apache.pulsar.functions.api.Function;
import com.gottaeat.domain.order.FoodOrder;

public class OrderValidationService implements Function<FoodOrder, FoodOrder> {

@Override
public FoodOrder process(FoodOrder order, Context ctx) throws Exception {
    System.out.println(order.toString());
    return order;
}
  ...
}
```

This class also includes a main method that contains a `LocalRunner` configuration, so we can debug this class locally, as shown in the following listing.

Listing 7.9   The `OrderValidationService LocalRunner` code

```
public static void main(String[] args) throws Exception {

    Map<String, ConsumerConfig> inputSpecs =                    We will be consuming
        new HashMap<String, ConsumerConfig> ();                  Avro messages.
    inputSpecs.put("persistent://orders/inbound/food-orders",
                    ConsumerConfig.builder().schemaType("avro").build());

    FunctionConfig functionConfig =
        FunctionConfig.builder()                                The function class
        .className(OrderValidationService.class.getName())      we want to run
        .inputs(Collections.singleton(
            "persistent://orders/inbound/food-orders"))
        .inputSpecs(inputSpecs)                                 The topic the function will
        .name("order-validation")                               consume messages from
        .output("persistent://orders/inbound/valid-food-orders")
        .outputSchemaType("avro")
        .runtime(FunctionConfig.Runtime.JAVA)                   Specify the URL of the Pulsar broker
        .build();                                               we are going to interact with.

    // Assumes you started docker container with --volume=${HOME}/exchange
    String credentials_path = System.getProperty("user.home") +
                        File.separator + "exchange" + File.separator;

    LocalRunner localRunner = LocalRunner.builder()
    .brokerServiceUrl("pulsar+ssl://localhost:6651")
    .clientAuthPlugin("org.apache.pulsar.client.impl.auth.AuthenticationTls")
    .clientAuthParams("tlsCertFile:" + credentials_path +
        "admin.cert.pem,tlsKeyFile:" + credentials_path + "admin-pk8.pem")
    .tlsTrustCertFilePath(credentials_path + "ca.cert.pem")
    .functionConfig(functionConfig)                             Specify the TLS
    .build();                                                   authentication
                                                                credentials needed
    localRunner.start(false);   ◁—— Starts the local runner    to connect to Pulsar.
    Thread.sleep(30 * 1000);
    localRunner.stop();         ◁—— Stops the local runner
}
```

The topic the function will publish messages to

As you can see from listing 7.8, we have configured the `LocalRunner` to connect to the same Pulsar instance. This is why there are several security-related configuration settings in the source code that rely on the security credentials generated inside that container, such as the TLS client certificate and trust store.

7.3.4 *Complete example*

Now that we have walked through the code inside each of the Maven modules, it is time to walk through an end-to-end demonstration of the interaction between the `CustomerSimulatorSource` and the `OrderValidationService`. It is important to note that, for this first demonstration, both of these classes will be using the exact same version of the schema (e.g., the domain-schema-0.0.1.jar). Consequently, both the producer's and consumer's schemas will be compatible with one another.

First, we need to have a running instance of the `pia/pulsar-standalone-secure` Docker image to serve as the Pulsar cluster we will use for testing. Therefore, you will need to execute the commands shown in the following listing to start an instance (if you don't already have one running), publish the security credentials needed by both of the `LocalRunner` instances, and create the topics that will be used.

Listing 7.10 Preparing the Pulsar cluster

Launches the Pulsar standalone image, and maps a volume for sharing the security credentials

Publish all of the security credentials to the ${HOME}/exchange directory on your local machine.

```
$ docker run -id --name pulsar --hostname pulsar.gottaeat.com -p:6651:6651
    -p 8443:8443 -p 80:80 --volume=${HOME}/exchange:/pulsar/manning/dropbox
    -t pia/pulsar-standalone-secure:latest

$ docker exec -it pulsar bash          ◁───  SSH into the Docker container
                                             you just launched.

root@pulsar:/# /pulsar/manning/security/publish-credentials.sh    ◁──
root@pulsar:/# /pulsar/bin/pulsar-admin tenants create orders    ◁──
root@pulsar:/# /pulsar/bin/pulsar-admin namespaces create orders/inbound
root@pulsar:/# /pulsar/bin/pulsar-client consume -n 0 -s my-sub
    persistent://orders/inbound/food-orders      Create the tenant and namespace
                                                 we are going to use.
```
Start a consumer on the specified topic.

The last line in listing 7.10 starts a consumer on the topic containing the `FoodOrder` events generated by the `CustomerSimulatorSource`. This will automatically create the topic and allow us to confirm that the messages are getting published. Leave this command shell open so we can monitor the messages as they come in, and switch to your local IDE that you are using to review the code from the GitHub project associated with this chapter of the book. Navigate to the `customer-mobile-app-simulator` module, and run the `CustomerSimulatorSource` as a Java application, which will execute the `LocalRunner` code shown in listing 7.7.

If everything goes as expected, you should start seeing Avro messages appear in the command shell window as the messages are getting delivered to the consumer. When you look at the example of the expected output that follows, you will see that payloads contain a mix of readable text and binary data:

```
----- got message -----
????????20200310?AFrench Fries
Large@?@Fountain Drink
Small??709 W 18th StChicagoIL
66012&5555 6666 7777 8888
66011123?A
```

This is because the consumer we launched from the command line does not have a schema associated with it. Consequently, the raw bytes of the message, which in this case are encoded in Avro's binary format, are not deserialized before being delivered to the consumer and are treated as raw bytes instead. This should give insight into the actual content of the messages that are being transmitted from producer to consumer.

Next, let's switch back to your IDE, navigate to the `order-validation-service` module and run the `OrderValidationService` as a Java application, which will execute the `LocalRunner` code shown in listing 7.9 to start the consumer. You should see messages printed to stdout that contain food order data, but in JSON format now instead of the Avro binary data we were seeing in the schema-less consumer window. This is because the function has a schema associated with it, which means the Pulsar framework is automatically serializing the raw message bytes into the appropriate Java class based on the Avro schema definition:

```
{"order_id": 4, "customer_id": 471, "resturant_id": 0, "time_placed": "2020-
    03-14T09:16:13.821", "order_status": "NEW", "details": [{"quantity": 10,
    "total": 69.899994, "food_item": {"item_id": 3, "item_name": "Fajita",
    "item_description": "Chicken", "price": 6.99}}], "delivery_location":
    {"street": "3422 Central Park Ave", "city": "Chicago", "state": "IL",
    "zip": "66013"}, "payment_method": {"card_type": "VISA",
    "account_number": "9999 0000 1111 2222", "billing_zip": "66013", "ccv":
    "555"}, "total": 69.899994}

{"order_id": 5, "customer_id": 152, "resturant_id": 1, "time_placed": "2020-
    03-14T09:16:14.327", "order_status": "NEW", "details": [{"quantity": 6,
    "total": 12.299999, "food_item": {"item_id": 1, "item_name":
    "Cheeseburger", "item_description": "Single", "price": 2.05}},
    {"quantity": 8, "total": 31.6, "food_item": {"item_id": 2, "item_name":
    "Cheeseburger", "item_description": "Double", "price": 3.95}}],
    "delivery_location": {"street": "123 Main St", "city": "Chicago",
    "state": "IL", "zip": "66011"}, "payment_method": {"card_type": "VISA",
    "account_number": "9999 0000 1111 2222", "billing_zip": "66013", "ccv":
    "555"}, "total": 43.9}
```

One of the best features of Avro that makes it a great solution for message-based microservice communication is its support for schema evolution. When a service that is writing messages updates its schema, the services consuming the messages can continue processing them without requiring any coding changes, provided that the producer's new schema is compatible with the older version being used by the consumers.

Currently, both our producer and consumer are using the same version of the domain-schema JAR file (i.e. 0.0.1), and thus are also using the exact same schema version. While this is the expected behavior, it does not effectively demonstrate Pulsar's schema evolution capabilities. I will demonstrate this capability in the next section by walking through the project code on the 0.0.2 branch of the associated GitHub project. Therefore, you will need to switch to the 0.0.2 branch before walking through the examples and, most importantly, leave your Docker container running as is.

7.4 Evolving the schema

During our weekly meeting with the customer mobile application team, we are informed that their initial testing has revealed a gap in their requirements. Specifically, the current food order schema does not support the ability for customers to customize their food orders to their particular tastes. Currently, a customer cannot specify that they want no onions on their hamburgers or extra guacamole on their burritos. Consequently, the schema will have to be revised, and an additional field named `customizations` will be added to the original `menu item` type, as shown in the following listing.

Listing 7.11 Evolving the schema

```
@namespace("com.gottaeat.domain.resturant")

protocol ResturantsProtocol {

  record MenuItem {
    long item_id;
    string item_name;
    string item_description;
    array<string> customizations = [""];     ◁─── The newly added field to support
    float price;                                   customizations of individual food
  }                                                items with a default value
}
```

After making this change to the schema inside the `domain-schema` module, you should also update the artifact version in the pom.xml file to 0.0.2 so we can differentiate between the two versions. Once these changes have been made to the source code, you should execute the command shown in the following listing to generate the Java classes' source files, compile them, and jar them into the domain-schema-0.0.2.jar JAR file.

Listing 7.12 Generating the Java classes from the updated Avro schema

```
$ cd ./domain-schema
$ mvn install
```

Make sure that the version being built is 0.0.2. If you fail to update the version number in the pom.xml file and leave it as 0.0.1, you will overwrite the existing jar that has the old schema version in it, and your results will differ from the ones shown. If you happen to inadvertently overwrite the domain-schema-0.0.1.jar, you can remove the newly added field and rebuild the jar file. Then, add the field back, change the version number to 0.0.2, and rebuild it again. You can easily verify that the Java classes you generated were based on the new schema version by looking for the `customizations` field in the `src/main/java/com/gottaeat/domain/restaurant/MenuItem.java` class.

Next, I will update the version number of the `domain-schema` dependency in the `customer-mobile-app-simulator` module to use the updated schema, as shown in the following listing.

Listing 7.13   Update the version of the domain-schema dependency

```
<dependency>
  <groupId>com.gottaeat</groupId>
  <artifactId>domain-schema</artifactId>
  <version>0.0.2</version>
</dependency>
```

The `FoodGenerator` was updated in the 0.0.2 branch to include customizations to the food orders, so it will require the newer version of the jar that was built in listing 7.11. If you experienced any compile errors, you most likely were still referencing the older version. You can now refresh the Maven dependencies to ensure you are using the 0.0.2 version of the `domain-schema` jar and run the `CustomerSimulatorSource`'s `LocalRunner` again. The updated logic inside the `FoodGenerator` always adds a customization to every fountain drink to specify which type it is (e.g., Coca-Cola, Sprite, etc.). It also randomly adds some customizations to the other food items:

```
----- got message -----
n?.2020-03-14T15:10:16.773?@Fountain Drink        Fountain drink
SmallCoca-Cola??123 Main StChicagoIL     ◁------  customization of Coca-Cola
66011&1234 5678 9012 3456
66011000?@
----- got message -----
p?.2020-03-14T15:10:17.273?@Fountain Drink         Food item customization
Large                                              of Sour Cream
     Sprite@??@BurritBeefSour Cream??@?_A  ◁------
                  FajitaChickenExtra Cheese??@ 844 W Cermark RdChicagoIL
66014&1234 5678 9012 3456
66011000???A
```

If you observe the schema-less consumer console window again, you will see an occasional record with some customizations, as shown in the preceding code. This indicates that we are producing messages based on the updated schema version 0.0.2, which is what we expected. Lastly, I will now run the `OrderValidationService LocalRunner` inside the `order-validation-service` module, which is still configured to use the 0.0.1 version of the `domain-schema` jar that contains the older version of the schema.

Since the 0.0.2 version of the schema is backward compatible with the 0.0.1 version used by the `OrderValidationService`, it will be able to consume the messages based on the newer schema version. As you can see from the deserialized Avro messages shown next, since these newer messages are being deserialized with the older schema, the newly added `customizations` field is ignored. This is as expected and does not impact the functionality of the consumer whatsoever, since it was never aware of these fields to begin with:

```
{"order_id": 55, "customer_id": 73, "resturant_id": 0, "time_placed": "2020-
    03-14T15:10:16.773", "order_status": "NEW", "details": [{"quantity": 7,
    "total": 7.0, "food_item": {"item_id": 10, "item_name": "Fountain
    Drink", "item_description": "Small", "price": 1.0}}],
    "delivery_location": {"street": "123 Main St", "city": "Chicago",
    "state": "IL", "zip": "66011"}, "payment_method": {"card_type": "AMEX",
    "account_number": "1234 5678 9012 3456", "billing_zip": "66011", "ccv":
    "000"}, "total": 7.0}

{"order_id": 56, "customer_id": 168, "resturant_id": 0, "time_placed": "2020-
    03-14T15:10:17.273", "order_status": "NEW", "details": [{"quantity": 2,
    "total": 4.0, "food_item": {"item_id": 11, "item_name": "Fountain
    Drink", "item_description": "Large", "price": 2.0}}, {"quantity": 1,
    "total": 7.99, "food_item": {"item_id": 1, "item_name": "Burrito",
    "item_description": "Beef", "price": 7.99}}, {"quantity": 2, "total":
    13.98, "food_item": {"item_id": 3, "item_name": "Fajita",
    "item_description": "Chicken", "price": 6.99}}], "delivery_location":
    {"street": "844 W Cermark Rd", "city": "Chicago", "state": "IL", "zip":
    "66014"}, "payment_method": {"card_type": "AMEX", "account_number":
    "1234 5678 9012 3456", "billing_zip": "66011", "ccv": "000"}, "total":
    25.97}
```

It is also worth pointing out that no code changes were required to the OrderValidationService. Therefore, had this been a production environment, the currently running instance of the service could remain running without disruption even though
the mobile application had made changes to its code base, making them completely
decoupled from one another even when an API change (message format) is made.

Summary

- We discussed the different microservice communication styles and why Pulsar is a
  perfect fit for asynchronous publish/subscribe-based interservice communication.
- The Pulsar schema registry enables message producers and consumers to coordinate on the structure of the data at the topic level and enforces schema compatibility for message producers.
- The Pulsar schema registry supports eight different compatibility strategies,
  including forward, backward, and full, and each of the compatibility checks are
  from the consumer's perspective.
- The Avro's interface definition language (IDL) is a great way to model events
  consumed within Pulsar because it allows you to modularize your types and
  share them across services easily.
- The Pulsar schema registry can be configured to enforce forward and/or backward schema compatibility for a Pulsar topic by ensuring that the connecting
  producer or consumer are using a schema that is compatible with all existing
  clients.

Part 3

Hands-on application development with Apache Pulsar

In this part, we move beyond the theory and simplistic examples and dive into the use of Pulsar Functions as a development framework for microservices applications by walking through a much more realistic use case based on a fictional food delivery service called GottaEat. This section demonstrates how to implement common design patterns from both the enterprise integration world and the microservices world, highlighting the usage of various patterns, such as content-based routing and filtering, resiliency, and data access within a real-world scenario.

Chapter 8 demonstrates how to implement common messaging routing patterns, such as message splitting, content-based routing, and filtering. It also shows how to implement various message transformation patterns, such as value extraction and message translation.

Chapter 9 stresses the importance of having resiliency built into your microservices and demonstrates how to implement this inside your Java-based Pulsar functions with the help of the resiliency4j library. It covers various scenarios that can occur in an event-based program and the patterns you can use to insulate your microservices from these failure scenarios to maximize your application uptime.

Chapter 10 focuses on how you can access data from a variety of external systems from inside your Pulsar functions. It demonstrates different methods of acquiring information within your microservices and considerations you should take in terms of latency.

Chapter 11 walks you through the process of deploying different machine learning model types inside of a Pulsar function, using various ML frameworks. It also covers the very important aspect of how to feed the necessary information into the model to get an accurate prediction

Finally, chapter 12 covers the use of Pulsar Functions within an edge computing environment to perform real-time analytics on IoT data. It starts with a detailed description of what an edge computing environment looks like and describes the various layers of the architecture before showing how to leverage Pulsar Functions to process the information on the edge and only forward summaries, rather than the entire dataset.

Pulsar
Functions patterns

This chapter covers

- Designing an application based on Pulsar Functions
- Implementing well-established messaging patterns using Pulsar Functions

In the previous chapter, I introduced a hypothetical food delivery service named GottaEat and outlined the basic order entry use case in which customers place orders with the company's mobile application. As you may recall, the first microservice in that process was the `OrderValidationService`, which is responsible for ensuring that the order is valid before forwarding the order to the drivers for delivery if it is valid or notifying the customer of any errors with the order.

However, the term *validate* is a bit more complicated than merely ensuring all of the fields are of the proper type and format. In this particular scenario, an order is only considered valid if the method of payment provided by the customer is approved, the funds from the bank are authorized, there is at least one restaurant open and willing to provide all of the requested food items, and, most importantly, the delivery address provided by the customer can be resolved to both a latitude–longitude pair and a street address. If we are unable to confirm all of these, then the order is considered invalid, and the customer must be notified accordingly. Consequently, the `OrderValidationService` is not a simple microservice that can make all of these decisions on its own, but instead, it must coordinate with other systems. It is, therefore, a good example of how a Pulsar application can be composed of several smaller functions and services.

The `OrderValidationService` must integrate with several other microservices and external systems to perform the payment processing, geo-encoding, and food order placement required to fully validate an order. Therefore, it is best to look for existing solutions to these types of challenges rather than reinvent the wheel, and the catalog of patterns contained within the book *Enterprise Integration Patterns*, by Gregor Hohpe and Bobby Woolf (Addison-Wesley Professional, 2003), serves as a great reference in this regard. It contains several technology-agnostic, time-tested patterns to solve common integration challenges. These patterns are categorized according to the type of problem they address and are applicable to most message-based integration platforms. In the next sections, I will demonstrate how these patterns can be implemented using Pulsar Functions.

8.1   Data pipelines

In order to effectively design your Pulsar Functions-based applications, you will want to familiarize yourself with the concepts of Dataflow programming and data pipelines. I will describe these programming models at a high level and point out how Pulsar Functions is a natural fit for this programming style.

8.1.1   Procedural programming

Traditionally, computer programs were modeled as a series of sequential operations where each operation depended upon the output of the previous operation. These programs could not be executed in parallel because they operated on the same data and, therefore, had to wait for the previous operation to complete before executing the next. Consider the logic for a basic order entry application in this programming model. You would write a simple function called `processOrder` that would perform the following sequence of steps (either directly or indirectly via a call to another function) to complete the process and return an order number to indicate success:

1   Check the inventory for the given item to make sure it is in stock.
2   Retrieve customer information (shipping address, payment method, coupons, loyalty, etc.).
3   Calculate the price, including sales tax, shipping, coupons, loyalty discounts, etc.
4   Collect the payment from the customer.
5   Decrease the item count in the inventory.
6   Notify the fulfillment center of the order so it can be processed and shipped.
7   Return the order number to the customer.

Each of these steps acts upon the same order and depends upon the output from the previous step; for example, you cannot collect payment from the customer before you have calculated the price. Thus, each step has to wait for the previous step to complete before proceeding, making it is impossible to perform any of these steps in parallel.

8.1.2 DataFlow programming

In contrast, dataflow programming focuses on the movement of data through a series of independent data processing functions that are connected via explicitly defined inputs and outputs. These predefined sequences of operations are commonly referred to as *data pipelines* and are what your Pulsar Functions applications should be modelled as. Here the focus is on moving the data through a series of stages, each of which processes the data and produces a new output. Each processing stage in a data pipeline should be able perform its processing based solely on the content of the incoming message. This eliminates any processing dependencies and allows each function to execute as soon as data is available.

A common analogy for a data pipeline is an assembly line in an automobile factory. Rather than assembling a car in one location piece by piece, each car passes through a series of stages during construction. A different piece of the car is added at each stage, but this can be done in parallel rather than sequentially. Consequently, multiple cars can be assembled in parallel, effectively increasing the throughput of the factory.

Pulsar Functions-based applications should be designed as topologies consisting of several individual Pulsar functions that perform the data processing operations and are connected together via Pulsar input and output topics. These topologies can be thought of as directed acyclic graphs (DAGs) with the functions/microservices acting as the processing units and the edges representing the input/out topic pairings used to direct data from one function to another, as shown in figure 8.1.

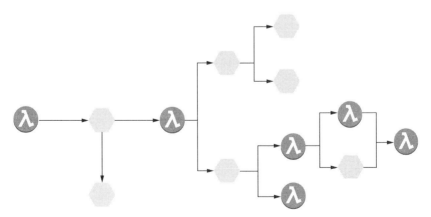

Figure 8.1 A Pulsar application is best represented as a data pipeline through which data flows from left to right through the functions and microservices to implement the business logic in a series of steps.

The data pipeline acts as a distributed processing framework where each function inside the data pipeline is an independent processing unit that can execute as soon as the next input arrives. Additionally, these loosely coupled components communicate asynchronously with one another, which allows them to operate at their own rates and not be blocked waiting for a response from another component. This, in turn, allows you to have multiple instances of any component running in parallel to provide the necessary throughput you require. Therefore, when you design your application, keep this in mind, as you will want to keep your functions and services as independent as possible to exploit this parallelism if needed. Let's revisit the order entry use case to demonstrate how you would implement it as a data pipeline similar to the one shown in figure 8.2. As the term *dataflow* implies, it is best to focus on the flow of data shown along the bottom of the figure.

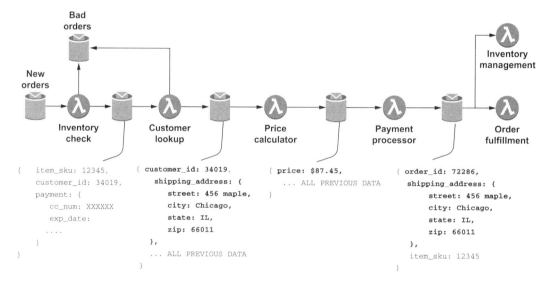

Figure 8.2   The data flow for the order entry use case. As the data flows through the various steps in the process, the original order data is augmented with additional information that will be used in the next step of the process.

As you can see, each step in the process passes the original order through along with an additional piece of information that is required in the subsequent step (e.g., the customer ID and shipping address have been added to the message by the customer lookup service). Since all of the data required for the processing at that stage is in the message, each function can execute as soon as the next piece of data arrives.

The payment processor removes the payment information from the message and publishes messages containing the newly generated order ID, the shipping address, and the item SKU. Multiple functions are consuming these messages; the inventory management function uses the SKU to decrease the item count from the available inventory, while the order fulfillment function needs the SKU and the shipping address to send the item to the customer. Hopefully, this gives you a better idea of how Pulsar Functions-based applications should be designed and modelled before we jump into some of the more advanced design patterns in the next section.

8.2 Message routing patterns

A message router is an architectural pattern that is used to control the flow of data through the topology of a Pulsar application by directing messages to different topics based on specific conditions. Each of the patterns covered in this section provide proven guidelines for dynamically routing messages, and I will cover how you can implement them using Pulsar Functions.

8.2.1 Splitter pattern

The `OrderValidationService` receives a message that contains three related pieces of information that must be validated in different ways: the delivery address, the payment information, and the food order itself. Validating each of these pieces of information requires interacting with an external service that may have a slow response time. A naïve approach to this problem would be to perform these steps in a serial fashion, one after another. However, this approach will result in very high latency time for each incoming order. This is due to the fact that when performing these three subtasks sequentially, the overall latency will be equal to the sum of the individual latencies.

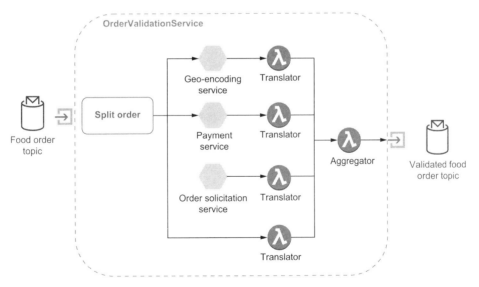

Figure 8.3 **The topology of the `OrderValidationService` is comprised of several other microservices and functions and utilizes the splitter pattern.**

Since there are no dependencies between the results of these intermediate validation services (e.g., the payment validation isn't dependent on the result of geo-encoding), a better approach would be to have each of these tasks performed in parallel. With parallel execution, the overall latency would be reduced to the latency of the longest-running subtask. In order to achieve this parallel subtask execution, the Order-ValidationService will implement the *splitter* pattern to break out the individual elements of the message so they may be processed with different services. As you can see in figure 8.3, the OrderValidationService is composed of several smaller functions that implement the entire validation process.

Our solution should also be efficient in terms of its use of network resources and avoid sending the entire food order item to each microservice, since they only need a portion of the message to perform their processing. As you can see from the code in the next listing, we only send a portion of the message along with the order ID to each of these intermediate services. The order ID will be used to combine the results from these intermediate service calls into a final result, using the aggregator function.

Listing 8.1   The OrderValidationService's implementation of the splitter pattern

Initialize all of the topic names so we
know where to publish the messages.

```
public class OrderValidationService implements Function<FoodOrder, Void> {

  private boolean initalized;
  private String geoEncoderTopic, paymentTopic,
  private String resturantTopic, orderTopic;

  @Override
  public Void process(FoodOrder order, Context ctx) throws Exception {
    if (!initalized) {
      init(ctx);
    }

    ctx.newOutputMessage(geoEncoderTopic, AvroSchema.of(Address.class))
      .property("order-id", order.getMeta().getOrderId() + "")
      .value(order.getDeliveryLocation()).sendAsync();

    ctx.newOutputMessage(paymentTopic, AvroSchema.of(Payment.class))
      .property("order-id", order.getMeta().getOrderId() + "")
      .value(order.getPayment()).sendAsync();

    ctx.newOutputMessage(orderTopic, AvroSchema.of(FoodOrderMeta.class))
      .property("order-id", order.getMeta().getOrderId() + "")
      .value(order.getMeta()).sendAsync();

    ctx.newOutputMessage(resturantTopic, AvroSchema.of(FoodOrder.class))
      .property("order-id", order.getMeta().getOrderId() + "")
      .value(order).sendAsync();

    return null;
  }
  private void init(Context ctx) {
    geoEncoderTopic = ctx.getUserConfigValue("geo-topic").toString();
```

Add the order-ID to the message properties
so we can use it to correlate the results.

Send just
the Payment
element of
the message
to the Pay-
ment Service.

Send just the address element of the
message to the GeoEncoder Service.

Send just the
FoodOrder
element of the
message to
the Order-
Solicititation
Service.

Send the food order metadata to the
aggregator topic directly, since we
don't need to process it.

```
    paymentTopic = ctx.getUserConfigValue("payment-topic").toString();
    resturantTopic = ctx.getUserConfigValue("restaurant-topic").toString();
    orderTopic = ctx.getUserConfigValue("aggregator-topic").toString();
    initalized = true;
}
```

The asynchronous nature of the processing of these individual message elements makes collecting the results challenging. Each of these elements is processed by different services with different response times (e.g., the geo-encoder will invoke a web service, the payment service needs to communicate with a bank to secure the funds, and each restaurant will need to respond manually to either accept or reject the order). These types of issues make the process of combing multiple, but related, messages complicated, which is where the *aggregator* pattern comes into play.

An aggregator is a stateful component that receives all of the response messages from the invoked services (e.g., `GeoEncoder`, `Payment`, etc.) and correlates the responses back together using the order ID. Once a complete set of responses has been collected, a single aggregated message is published to the output topic. When you choose to implement the aggregator pattern, you must consider the following three key factors:

- *Correlation*—How are messages correlated together?
- *Completeness*—When are we ready to publish the resulting message?
- *Aggregation*—How are the incoming messages combined into a single result?

For our particular use case, we have decided that the order ID will serve as the correlation ID, which will help us identify which response messages belong together. The result will be considered complete only after we have received all three messages for the order. This is also referred to as the "wait for all" strategy. Lastly, the resulting responses will be combined into a single object of type `ValidatedFoodOrder`.

Let's take a look at the aggregator code shown in listing 8.2 for the implementation details. Given the strongly typed nature of Pulsar Functions, I cannot define the interface to accept multiple response object types (e.g., an `AuthorizedPayment` object from the `Payment` service, an `Address` type from the `GeoEncoder` service, etc.). Therefore, I use a translator function between these services and the `OrderValidation-Aggregator`. Each of these translator functions converts the intermediate services natural return type into a `ValidatedFoodOrder` object, which allows me to accept messages from each of these services within a single Pulsar function.

Listing 8.2 The `OrderValidationService`'s aggregator function

```
public class OrderValidationAggregator implements
    Function<ValidatedFoodOrder, Void> {

  @Override
  public Void process(ValidatedFoodOrder in, Context ctx) throws Exception {
```

```
Map<String, String> props = ctx.getCurrentRecord().getProperties();
String correlationId = props.get("order-id");

ValidatedFoodOrder order;
if (ctx.getState(correlationId.toString()) == null) {
  order = new ValidatedFoodOrder();
} else {
  order = deserialize(ctx.getState(correlationId.toString()));
}

updateOrder(order, in);

if (isComplete(order)) {
  ctx.newOutputMessage(ctx.getOutputTopic(),
                       AvroSchema.of(ValidatedFoodOrder.class))
    .properties(props)
    .value(order).sendAsync();
  ctx.putState(correlationId.toString(), null);
} else {
  ctx.putState(correlationId.toString(), serialize(order));
}

return null;
}

private boolean isComplete(ValidatedFoodOrder order) {
  return (order != null && order.getDeliveryLocation() != null
    && order.getFood() != null && order.getPayment() != null
    && order.getMeta() != null);
}

private void updateOrder(ValidatedFoodOrder val,
                         ValidatedFoodOrder res) {
  if (res.getDeliveryLocation() != null
    && val.getDeliveryLocation() == null) {
    val.setDeliveryLocation(response.getDeliveryLocation());
  }

  if (resp.getFood() != null && val.getFood() == null) {
    val.setFood(response.getFood());
  }

  if (resp.getMeta() != null && val.getMeta() == null) {
    val.setMeta(response.getMeta());
  }

  if (resp.getPayment() != null && val.getPayment() == null) {
    val.setPayment(response.getPayment());
  }

}

private ByteBuffer serialize(ValidatedFoodOrder order) throws IOException {
    ...
```

Check to see if we have already received some responses for this order.

If we have, then deserialize the bytes into a ValidatedFood-Order object.

Every message will be of type ValidatedFoodOrder but will only contain one of the four fields.

Check to see if we have received all four messages, which indicates that we are done.

Once the order is aggregated, we can purge it.

If not, serialize the object, and store it in the context until the next message arrives.

An object is only considered complete if we have received all four messages.

Copies over whatever fields are in the received object

Helper method to convert a ValidatedFoodOrder object into a ByteBuffer

```
}

private ValidatedFoodOrder deserialize(ByteBuffer buffer) throws IOException,
    ClassNotFoundException {
    ...                          ◁─────────────
  }                                            Helper method to read a ValidatedFoodOrder
}                                              object from a ByteBuffer
```

It is important to point out that due to the parallel nature of streaming architectures in general, the aggregator may receive messages from multiple orders at any time and in no particular order. Therefore, the aggregator maintains an internal list of active orders it has already received messages for. If no list exists for a given order ID, then it is assumed to be the first message in the collection, and an entry is added to the internal list. This list needs to be purged periodically to ensure it doesn't grow indefinitely, which is why the aggregator makes sure to purge the list once an aggregation is complete.

8.2.2 *Dynamic router pattern*

The *splitter* pattern is useful when you want to process different pieces of the message in parallel, and you already know in advance exactly how many elements you will have and that the number will remain static. However, there are situations where you cannot determine where the message will be routed ahead of time, and you must make that determination based on the content of the message itself and other external conditions. One such example is the OrderSolicitationService, which is one of the three microservices invoked by the OrderValidationService.

This service notifies a subset of participating restaurants of incoming food orders they can fulfill and awaits a response from each of the restaurateurs as to whether or not they will accept the order, and if so, when it will be ready for pick up. Obviously, the list of restaurants is dependent on several factors. We want to route the orders based on the restaurants' ability to provide the food (i.e., orders for Big Macs go to McDonalds, etc.). At the same time, we don't want to indiscriminately broadcast the order to every single McDonald's restaurant, so we narrow the list down based on their proximity to the delivery location. Since this list is constructed in response to each message, the *recipient list* pattern is the best choice.

The overall flow of the OrderSolicitationService is depicted in figure 8.4, which consists of three distinct phases. The first phase computes the intended list of recipients based on the factors we've already discussed. During the second phase, the recipient list is iterated over, and the FoodOrder is forwarded to each recipient. The third and final phase is when the service awaits the responses from each of the recipients and selects a "winner" to fulfill the order. Once a winner is selected, all the other recipients are notified that they have "lost" and that the food order is no longer available.

The actual implementation of this logic is shown in listing 8.3 and relies on the message properties to convey metadata that is critical for the aggregator. First of all, the order ID is included within the message to identify which FoodOrder the response is associated with. The all-restaurants property is used to encode all of the candidates

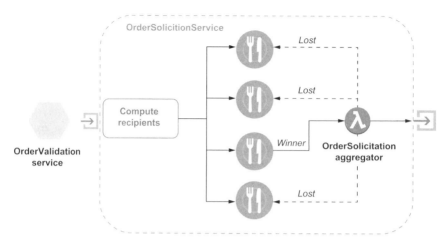

Figure 8.4   The topology of the OrderSolicitationService, which implements the dynamic router pattern

that have been solicited for this order. Having this information in the message enables the aggregator to know all of the restaurants it needs to send the "you didn't win" message to. The last piece of metadata contained within the message properties is the `return-addr` property, which contains the name of the topic the aggregator is subscribed to. This allows us to avoid having to hard-code this information into each message recipient's logic, and instead, we can provide this information dynamically. This is an implementation of the return address pattern defined in *Enterprise Integration Patterns*.

Listing 8.3   The `OverSolicitationService`'s implementation of the recipient list pattern

```
public class OrderSolicitationService implements Function<FoodOrder, Void> {

    private String rendevous = "persistent://resturants/inbound/accepted";

    @Override
    public Void process(FoodOrder order, Context ctx) throws Exception {

        List<String> cand = getCandidates(order,                          ⊲─┐ Build the recipient
                            order.getDeliveryLocation());                   │ list based on the
                                                                            │ order and delivery
                                                                            │ address.
        if (CollectionUtils.isNotEmpty(cand)) {
            String all = StringUtils.join(cand, ",");
            int delay = 0;
            for (String topic: cand) {  ⊲─┤ Send the FoodOrder to
                try {                       every recipient in the list.
                    ctx.newOutputMessage(topic, AvroSchema.of(FoodOrder.class))
                    .property("order-id", order.getMeta().getOrderId() + "")  ⊲─┘
                    .property("all-restaurants", all)
                    .property("return-addr", rendevous)   ⊲─┤ Tell each recipient where to
                                                              send their response message.
```

Include all the restaurants so we can notify the losers.

Use the order ID for correlation.

```
                .value(order).deliverAfter( (delay++ * 10), TimeUnit.SECONDS);
        } catch (PulsarClientException e) {
            e.printStackTrace();
        }
    }
}

return null;
}

private List<String> getCandidates(FoodOrder order, Address deliveryAddr) {
    ...
}
}
```

Stagger the delivery of the messages to minimize the number of rejected responses.

The logic to build the recipient list

The recipient list is returned in order of preference (e.g., the restaurant closest to the delivery location, the one that has received the least amount of business from us tonight, etc.), and we use Pulsar's delayed message delivery capabilities to space out the solicitation requests. The goal of this is to minimize the number of times we need to reject a FoodOrder that was accepted by a restaurant. We don't want to aggravate our participating restauranteurs by bombarding them with orders that they accept but are ultimately rejected. Therefore, we scale up the number of restaurants we notify slowly to prevent having too many outstanding solicitations at the same time.

Since the OrderSolicitationService can send the FoodOrder to multiple recipients, it will need to reconcile the responses and award the order to only one of the respondents. While there are many strategies available, for now it will just accept the first response. This reconciliation logic will be implemented using an aggregator similar to the one we used for the OverValidationService. As you can see in listing 8.3, I am using the message properties to pass along the name of the topic that each of the recipients should respond to. The corresponding aggregator should be configured to listen to this topic, so it receives the response messages and can notify the non-winning restaurants that the order has been awarded to a different restaurant. This restauranteur's mobile application can then react to the non-winning notification by removing the order from view.

Listing 8.4   The OverSolicitationService's implementation of the aggregator pattern

```
public class OrderSolicitationAggregator implements
    Function<SolicitationResponse, Void> {

@Override
public Void process(SolicitationResponse response, Context context)
    throws Exception {

  Map<String, String> props = context.getCurrentRecord().getProperties();
  String correlationId = props.get("order-id");
  List<String> bids = Arrays.asList(
    StringUtils.split(props.get("all-restaurants")));

  if (context.getState(correlationId) == null) {
```

Decode all the IDs of all the solicited restaurants.

First response back wins

Remove the winner from the list of all restaurants.

Get the restaurant ID of the winner from the response message.

```
  // First response wins
  String winner = props.get("restaurant-id");
  bids.remove(winner);
  notifyWinner(winner, context);
  notifyLosers(bids, context);

  // Record the time we received the winning bid.
  ByteBuffer bb = ByteBuffer.allocate(32);
  bb.asLongBuffer().put(System.currentTimeMillis());
  context.putState(correlationId, bb);
  }

  return null;
}

private void notifyLosers(List<String> bids, Context context) {
  ...
  }

private void notifyWinner(String s, Context context) {
  ...
  }
}
```

Send a message to the winning restaurant letting them know they won.

Send a message to all the non-winning restaurants.

As you can see in listing 8.4, the correlation will still be done by the order ID, but the completeness criteria will be "first one wins" instead of waiting for a response from all the message recipients as we did for the splitter pattern. Even though we do our best to prevent sending multiple outstanding solicitation messages, the aggregator still needs to accommodate this scenario. It does so by retaining the time that the winning bid was received for each order. This allows the aggregator to ignore all subsequent responses for the same order, since we know that another restaurant has already been awarded the order. In order to prevent this data structure from growing too large and causing an out-of-memory condition, I have incorporated a background process that periodically wakes up and purges all records in the list that are older than a certain period of time, which can be determined by the timestamp of the winning bid.

8.2.3 *Content-based router pattern*

A content-based router uses the message contents to determine which topic to route it to. The basic concept is that the content of each message is inspected and then routed to a specific destination based on values found or not found in the content. For the order validation use case, the PaymentService receives a message that will vary, depending on the payment type being used by the customer.

Currently, the system supports credit card payments, PayPal, Apple Pay, and electronic checks. Each of these payment methods must be validated by different external systems. Therefore, the goal of the PaymentService is to direct the message to the proper system based on the content of the message. Figure 8.5 depicts the scenario in which the method of payment on the order was a credit card, and the payment details are forwarded to the CreditCardService.

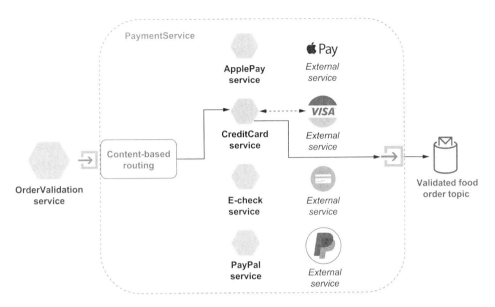

Figure 8.5 The `PaymentService` topology implements the content-based router pattern and routes the payment information to the appropriate service based on the method of payment provided with the order.

Each of the supported payment types has an associated intermediate microservice (e.g., `ApplePayService`, `CreditCardService`, etc.) that is configured with the proper credentials, endpoint, etc. These intermediate microservices then make a call to the proper external service to get payment authorization, and upon receipt of the authorization, forward the response on to the `OrderValidationService`'s aggregator, where it is combined with the other responses associated with the order. The next listing shows the implementation of the *content-based routing* pattern inside the `PaymentService`.

Listing 8.5 The `PaymentService`'s implementation of the content-based router pattern

```
public class PaymentService implements Function<Payment, Void> {
private boolean initalized = false;
private String applePayTopic, creditCardTopic, echeckTopic, paypalTopic;

public Void process(Payment pay, Context ctx) throws Exception {
  if (!initalized) {
    init(ctx);
  }

  Class paymentType = pay.getMethodOfPayment().getType().getClass();
  Object payment = pay.getMethodOfPayment().getType();

  if (paymentType == ApplePay.class) {
    ctx.newOutputMessage(applePayTopic, AvroSchema.of(ApplePay.class))
        .properties(ctx.getCurrentRecord().getProperties())
      .value((ApplePay) payment).sendAsync();
```

> Send AplePay objects to the ApplePayService.

```
    } else if (paymentType == CreditCard.class) {
      ctx.newOutputMessage(creditCardTopic, AvroSchema.of(CreditCard.class))
        .properties(ctx.getCurrentRecord().getProperties())
        .value((CreditCard) payment).sendAsync();
    } else if (paymentType == ElectronicCheck.class) {
      ctx.newOutputMessage(echeckTopic, AvroSchema.of(ElectronicCheck.class))
        .properties(ctx.getCurrentRecord().getProperties())
        .value((ElectronicCheck) payment).sendAsync();
    } else if (paymentType == PayPal.class) {
      ctx.newOutputMessage(paypalTopic, AvroSchema.of(PayPal.class))
        .properties(ctx.getCurrentRecord().getProperties())
        .value((PayPal) payment).sendAsync();
    } else {
      ctx.getCurrentRecord().fail();
    }

    return null;
  }

  private void init(Context ctx) {
    applePayTopic = (String)ctx.getUserConfigValue("apple-pay-topic").get();
    creditCardTopic = (String)ctx.getUserConfigValue("credit-topic").get();
    echeckTopic = (String)ctx.getUserConfigValue("e-check-topic").get();
    paypalTopic = (String)ctx.getUserConfigValue("paypal-topic").get();
    initalized = true;
  }
}
```

Send CreditCard objects to the CreditCardService.

Send ElectronicCheck objects to the ElectronicCheckService.

Send PayPal objects to the PayPalService.

Reject any other payment method.

The output topics for the intermediate services are configurable.

After the `CreditCardService` receives an authorization number for the transaction, it is then sent to the `validatedFoodOrder` topic, since we will need that authorization number to collect the funds.

8.3   *Message transformation patterns*

Common examples of streaming data include IoT sensors, server and security logs, real-time advertising, and click-stream data from mobile apps and websites. In each of these scenarios, we have data sources that are continuously generating thousands or millions of unstructured or semi-structured data elements—most commonly, plain text, JSON, or XML. Each of these data elements must be transformed into a format that is suitable for processing and analysis.

This category of processing is common among all streaming platforms, and these data transformation tasks are similar to traditional ETL processing, since the primary concern is to ensure that the ingested data is normalized, enriched, and transformed into a format more suitable for processing. Message transformation patterns are used to manipulate the content of the messages as they flow through the DAG's topology to address these types of issues within your streaming architecture. Each of the patterns covered in this section provides proven guidelines for dynamically transforming messages.

8.3.1 Message translator pattern

As we saw earlier, the `OrderValidationService` makes several asynchronous calls to different services, each of which produces messages with different schema types. All of these messages must be combined by the `OrderValidationAggregator` into a single response. However, a Pulsar function can only be defined to accept incoming messages of a single type, so we cannot publish these messages directly to the service's input topic, as shown in figure 8.6, as the schemas would not be compatible.

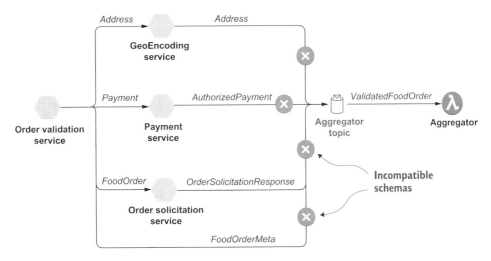

Figure 8.6 **Each of the intermediate microservices produce messages with different schema types. Therefore, they cannot publish them directly to the** `OrderValidationAggregator`'s **input topic.**

To accommodate the consumption of messages with different schemas, the results from each of these intermediate microservices must be routed through a message translator function, which converts these response messages into the same type as the `OrderValidationAggregator`'s input topic, which, in this case, is the schema shown in listing 8.6. I have chosen to use an object type that is a composite of each of these message types. This approach allows me to simply copy the response from each of the intermediate services directly into the corresponding placeholder inside the `ValidatedFoodOrder` object.

Listing 8.6 The `ValidatedFoodOrder` definition

The FoodOrderMeta data forwarded from the OrderValidationService

```
record ValidatedFoodOrder {
    FoodOrderMeta meta;
    com.gottaeat.domain.resturant.SolicitationResponse food;
    com.gottaeat.domain.common.Address delivery_location;
    com.gottaeat.domain.payment.AuthorizedPayment payment;
}
```

The response type from the OrderSolicitationService

The response type from the GeoEncoding-Service

The response type from the PaymentService

While the logic for consuming each response message type is slightly different, the concept is essentially the same. As you can see in listing 8.7, the logic for handling the AuthorizedPayment messages produced by the PaymentService is straightforward. Simply create an object of the appropriate type, and copy over the AuthorizedPayment object published by the PaymentService into the corresponding field in the wrapper object before sending it to the aggregator for consumption.

Listing 8.7   The `PaymentAdaptor` implementation

```
public class PaymentAdapter implements Function<AuthorizedPayment, Void> {

    @Override
    public Void process(AuthorizedPayment payment, Context ctx)
            throws Exception {
        ValidatedFoodOrder result = new ValidatedFoodOrder();   ⟵  Create the new wrapper object.
        result.setPayment(payment);   ⟵  Update the payment field with the AuthorizedPayment.

        ctx.newOutputMessage(ctx.getOutputTopic(),
                AvroSchema.of(ValidatedFoodOrder.class))   ⟵  Publish a message of type ValidatedFoodOrder to the aggregator's input topic.
            .properties(ctx.getCurrentRecord().getProperties())   ⟵  Copy over the order ID so we can correlate it with the other response messages.
            .value(result).send();

        return null;
    }
}
```

There are similar adaptors for each of the other microservices as well. Once all of the object values have been populated, the order is considered validated and can be published to the validatedFoodOrder topic for further processing.

It is worth noting that each of these adaptor functions must consume from a topic that stores the microservice's respective response messages before publishing the wrapper objects to the OrderValidationAggregator's input topic. Therefore, you will need to create these response topics and configure the microservices to publish to them, as shown in figure 8.7. In addition to being useful in situations where you need to combine the results of several different Pulsar functions, this pattern can also be used to accommodate the ingestion of data from external systems, such as databases, and translate them into the required schema format for processing.

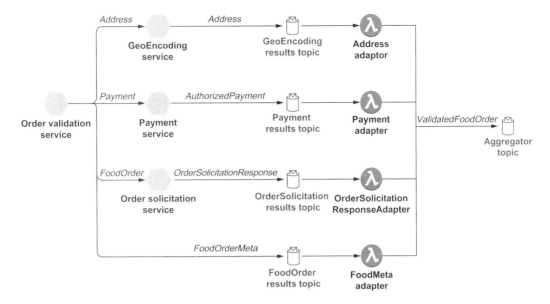

Figure 8.7 Each of the intermediate microservices publish their response messages to topics with the appropriate schema type. The associated adapter functions then consume those messages and convert them to the `ValidatedFoodOrder` schema type expected in the aggregator topic.

8.3.2   Content enricher pattern

When processing streaming events, it is often useful to augment the incoming message with additional information that the downstream system requires. In our example, the incoming customer order event to the `OrderValidationService` will contain a raw, unvalidated street address, but the consuming microservices also require a geo-encoded location with a latitude and longitude pair to provide navigation to the delivery drivers.

This type of problem is typically addressed with the *content enricher* pattern, which is the term for a process that uses information inside an incoming message to augment the original message contents with the new information. In our particular use case, we will retrieve data from an external source and add it to the outgoing message, as shown in figure 8.8. Our `GeoEncodingService` will take the delivery address details provided by the customer and pass them to the Google Maps API web service. The resulting latitude and longitude that corresponds to the address will then be included in the outbound message.

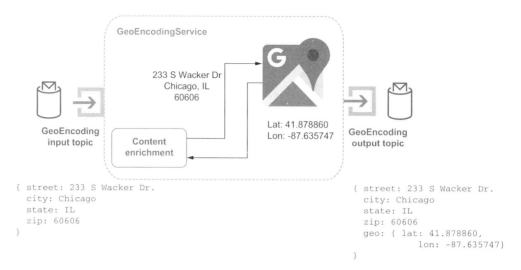

```
{ street: 233 S Wacker Dr.          { street: 233 S Wacker Dr.
  city: Chicago                       city: Chicago
  state: IL                           state: IL
  zip: 60606                          zip: 60606
}                                     geo: { lat: 41.878860,
                                             lon: -87.635747}
                                    }
```

Figure 8.8 The `GeoEncoderService` implements the content enrichment pattern by using the provided street address to look up the corresponding latitude and longitude and add it to the address object.

The following listing shows the implementation of the `GeoEncodingService` that invokes the Google Maps service and augments the incoming `Address` object with the associated latitude and longitude value.

Listing 8.8   The `GeoEncoderService`'s implementation of the content enricher pattern

```java
public class GeoEncoderService implements Function<Address, Address> {
  boolean initalized = false;
  String apiKey;
  GeoApiContext geoContext;

  public Void process(Address addr, Context context) throws Exception {
    if (!initalized) {
      init(context);
    }

    Address result = new Address();
    result.setCity(addr.getCity());
    result.setState(addr.getState());
    result.setStreet(addr.getStreet());
    result.setZip(addr.getZip());

    try {
      GeocodingResult[] results =
        GeocodingApi.geocode(geoContext, formatAddress(addr)).await();

      if (results != null && results[0].geometry != null) {
        Geometry geo = results[0].geometry;
        LatLon ll = new LatLon();
        ll.setLatitude(geo.location.lat);
```

```
            ll.setLongitude(geo.location.lng);
            result.setGeo(ll);
        }

        } catch (InterruptedException | IOException | ApiException ex) {
            context.getCurrentRecord().fail();
            context.getLogger().error(ex.getMessage());
        } finally {
            return result;
        }
    }

    private void init(Context context) {
        apiKey = context.getUserConfigValue("apiKey").toString();
        geoContext = new GeoApiContext.Builder()
                    .apiKey(apiKey).maxRetries(3)
                    .retryTimeout(3000, TimeUnit.MILLISECONDS).build();
        initalized = true;
    }
}
```

The service uses an API key provided by the configuration properties to invoke the Google Maps web service and uses the first response it gets as the source of the latitude and longitude values. If the call to the web service isn't successful, we fail the message so it can be retried at a later time.

While using an external service is one of the most common uses for the content enrichment pattern, there are implementations that merely perform internal calculations based on the message contents, such as computing the message size or MD5 hash of the message contents and adding that to the message properties. This allows the message consumer to validate that the message contents have not been altered.

Another common use case is to retrieve the current time from the operating system and append that timestamp to the message to indicate when it was received or processed. This information is useful for maintaining the message order if you wish to process the messages in the order they were received, or for identifying bottlenecks in the DAG if you appended a received timestamp at each step of the process.

8.3.3 *Content filter pattern*

Often, it can be useful to remove or mask one or more data elements from an incoming message due to security or other concerns. The content filter pattern is essentially the inverse of the content enricher pattern because it is designed to perform this type of transformation.

The OrderValidationService we discussed earlier is an example of a content filter that breaks up the incoming FoodOrder message into smaller pieces before routing them to the appropriate microservice for processing. Not only does this minimize the amount of data sent to each service, but it also hides the sensitive payment information from all the other services that do not require access to that information.

Consider another scenario where an event contains a sensitive data element, such as a credit card number. The content filter can detect such patterns in the messages and remove the data element entirely; mask it with a one-way hashing function, such as SHA-256; or encrypt the data field.

Summary

- The Pulsar Functions framework is a distributed processing framework that is well suited for Dataflow programming, where the data is processed in stages that can be executed in parallel like an assembly line.
- Applications based on Pulsar Functions can be modelled as data pipelines, where the functions perform the computations and direct data, using the input/out topics.
- When designing your message-passing microservice application, it is often to use existing design patterns, such as those found in Gregor Hohpe and Bobby Woolf's book *Enterprise Integration Patterns* and other sources.
- Well-established messaging patterns can be implemented using Pulsar Functions, which allows you to use time-tested solutions inside your applications.

Resiliency patterns

This chapter covers

- Making your Pulsar Functions-based applications resilient to adverse events
- Implementing well-established resiliency patterns using Pulsar Functions

As the architect of the GottaEat order entry microservice, your primary goal is to develop a system that can accept incoming food orders from customers 24 hours a day, 7 days a week, and within a response time acceptable to the customer. Your system must be available at all times; otherwise, your company will not only lose revenue and customers, but its reputation will suffer as well. Therefore, you must design your system to be both highly available and resilient to provide continuity of service. Everyone wants their systems to be resilient, but what does that actually mean? Resilience is the ability of a system to withstand disruptions caused by adverse events and conditions, while maintaining an acceptable level of performance relative to any number of quantitative metrics, such as availability, capacity, performance, reliability, robustness, and usability.

Being resilient is important because no matter how well your Pulsar application is designed, an unanticipated incident, such as the loss of electrical power or network communications, will eventually emerge and disrupt the topology. Implicit in

241

this statement is the idea that adverse events and conditions *will* occur. It really isn't a matter of if but when. Resiliency is about what your software does when these disruptive events occur. Does the Pulsar function detect these events and conditions? Does it properly respond to them once they are detected? Does the function properly recover afterward?

A highly resilient system will utilize several reactive resiliency techniques to actively detect these adversities and respond to them to return the system back to its normal operating state automatically, as shown in figure 9.1. This is particularly useful in a streaming environment, where any disruption of service can result in the data not being captured from the source and being lost forever.

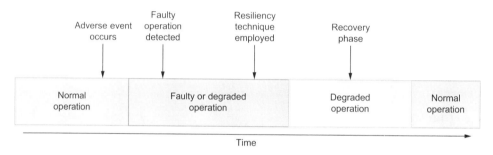

Figure 9.1   A resilient system will automatically detect adverse events or conditions and take proactive measures to return itself to a normal operating state.

Obviously, the key to employing any reactive technique is the ability to detect the adverse conditions. In this chapter we will cover how to detect faulty conditions with a Pulsar Functions application and some of the resiliency techniques you can use within your Pulsar functions to make them more resilient.

9.1   *Pulsar Functions resiliency*

As we saw in chapter 8, all Pulsar Functions-based applications are essentially topologies consisting of several individual Pulsar functions interconnected via input and output topics. These topologies can be thought of as DAGs with data flowing through different paths based on the values of the messages. From a resiliency perspective, it makes sense to consider this entire DAG as the system that must be insulated from the impact of adverse conditions.

9.1.1   *Adverse events*

In order to implement an overall resiliency strategy, we must first identify all of the adverse events that could potentially impact a running Pulsar application topology. Rather than attempting to list out every single possible condition that can occur with a Pulsar function, we will classify the adverse events into the following categories: function death, lagging function, and non-progressing function.

FUNCTION DEATH

Let's start with the most drastic event first, *function death*, which is when a Pulsar function within the application topology terminates abruptly. This condition can be caused by any number of physical factors, such as a server crash or power outage, or non-physical factors, such as an out-of-memory condition within the function itself. Regardless of the underlying reason, the impact on the system will be severe, as data flowing through the DAG will come to an abrupt halt.

If the function shown in figure 9.2 dies, all of the downstream consumers will stop receiving messages, and the DAG will be essentially blocked at this point in the flow. From an end-user perspective, the application will have stopped producing output, which in our situation, means that the entire food order entry process will come to a screeching halt.

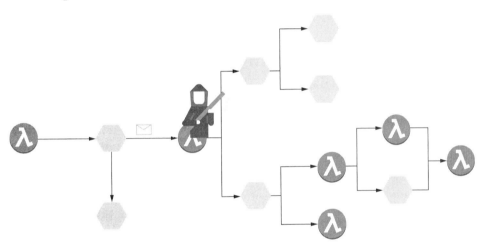

Figure 9.2   When a function dies and stops consuming messages, the entire application is essentially blocked at that point in the DAG, and all downstream processing will stop.

Fortunately, the `functions` input topic will act as a buffer and retain the incoming messages up to the limit imposed by the message retention policy for the topic. I only mention this caveat to impress upon you the importance of resolving this issue sooner rather than later because eventually messages could get dropped if the function is not restarted.

If you are using the recommend Kubernetes runtime to host your Pulsar functions, then the Pulsar Functions framework will automatically detect the failure of the associated K8s pod and restart it for you as long as you have sufficient computing resources in your Kubernetes environment. You should also have proper monitoring and alerting in place to detect the loss of a physical host and respond accordingly as an additional layer of resiliency.

LAGGING FUNCTION

Another condition that will have a negative impact on the performance of a Pulsar application is the *lagging function,* which occurs when there is a *sustained* arrival rate of messages into a function's input topic that is greater than the function is capable of processing. Under these circumstances, the function will fall further and further behind in the processing of the incoming messages, which will lead to a growing lag between the time a message is ready to be processed and when it eventually is processed.

Let's consider a scenario where function A is publishing 150 events per second to another function's input topic, as shown in figure 9.3. Unfortunately, function B can only process 75 events per second, which leaves a 75-event-per-second deficit that is getting buffered inside the topic. If this processing imbalance remains in place, the volume of messages within the input topic will continue to grow.

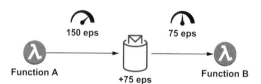

Figure 9.3   Function B is only able to process 75 events per second, while function A is producing events at a rate of 150 per second. This leads to a backlog of 75 events per second, which introduces one second of latency per second.

Initially, this lag will start to impact the business SLA, and in our use case, the order entry process will be slow for our customers, as they have to wait for their orders to get processed and confirmed. Eventually, the lag will be too great for customers to bear, and they will abandon their orders due to the lack of responsiveness of the mobile application. This could lead to situations where the customer's order is placed into the queue and processed *after* the customer has decided, due to lack of a response, that their order was never placed, which would be a nightmare from a business perspective, as we would have to refund the charged amount and notify the restaurant that the order had been cancelled.

To put some numbers behind this statement, let's imagine the scenario where such a condition was to start inside our order validation DAG during a peak business time, such as a Friday night around 7 p.m. Orders that were placed 10 minutes later would be placed behind the 45,000 (75 eps × 60 sec × 10 minutes) other orders that have built up inside function B's input topic. At a processing rate of 75 per second, it would take 10 minutes to process those existing messages before finally processing the order. Thus, an order placed at 7:10 wouldn't get processed until after 7:20 pm! Therefore, in order to meet your business SLAs and avoid abandoned orders due to a lagging function, we will need to conduct performance testing to determine the average processing rate of each function in the order validation service and continuously monitor it for any processing imbalance in the future.

Fortunately, if you are using the recommended Kubernetes runtime to host your Pulsar functions, then the Pulsar Functions framework allows you to scale up the parallelism of any function using the command shown in listing 9.1, which should help alleviate the imbalance. Therefore, the remedy for this adverse event is to update the function's parallelism count to an acceptable level. Since the message input-versus-consumed ratio is 2:1 in our hypothetical example, you would want the ratio of function A versus function B instances to be at least the same, if not more.

Listing 9.1 Increasing the function parallelism

```
$ bin/pulsar-admin functions update \
  --name FunctionA \
  --parallelism 5 \
  ...
```

While adjusting the ratio of instances to be exactly 2:1 would theoretically alleviate the problem, I recommend having one or two additional instances beyond that ratio on the consumer side. Not only will this provide excess processing capacity that will allow your application to handle any additional surge in messages, but it will also make your function resilient to the loss of one or more instances before any lag is experienced.

NON-PROGRESSING FUNCTION

A *non-progressing function* is different from a lagging function in two aspects; the first is their ability to successfully process messages. With a lagging function, all of the messages are processed successfully, albeit at too slow of a pace to keep up, whereas with a non-progressing function, some or all of the messages cannot be processed successfully.

The second aspect is the way in which the problem can be resolved. With a lagging function, the most common remedy is to increase the parallelism of the function instances to accommodate the incoming message volume. Unfortunately, there is no easy fix for a non-progressing function, and the only resolution is to add processing logic inside the Pulsar function itself to detect and react to these processing exceptions. So, let's take a step back and review the limited number of options we have when dealing with processing exceptions within a Pulsar function.

You can effectively ignore the error entirely and explicitly acknowledge the message, which tells the broker that you are done processing it. Obviously, this is not a viable option for some use cases, such as our payment service where we need an authorized payment to continue processing the order. Another option is to negatively acknowledge (i.e., negative ack) the message within a catch block of your Pulsar function code, which tells the broker to redeliver the message Lastly, there is the possibility that no acknowledgment is sent from your function at all due to an uncaught exception or a network timeout when calling a remote service. As you can see from figure 9.4, in either case these messages will be marked for redelivery.

As more and more of these negatively acknowledged messages build up in the topic, the system will gradually slow, as they are repeatedly tried, fail, and tried again. This wastes processing cycles on non-productive work, and what's worse is that these messages will never get cleared from the topic, which will only compound their impact over time—hence, the term *non-progressing function*, as it is failing to make progress on the new messages.

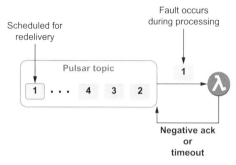

Figure 9.4   When a Pulsar function sends a negative acknowledgement or fails to acknowledge a message within the configured time, the message is scheduled for redelivery after a one-minute delay.

Let's revisit the scenario in which a function can successfully process 75 events per second, and that function is making a call to a remote service, such as a credit card authorization service. Furthermore, the endpoint that the function is calling is actually a load balancer, which distributes the calls across three different instances of the service, and one of them goes down. Every third message will immediately throw an exception, and the message will be negatively acked, resulting in approximately 25 events per second not succeeding. This would drop the effective processing rate of the function from 75 eps to 50 eps. This decrease in the processing rate is the first telltale sign of a non-progressing function.

   Scaling up the instances will not solve the problem either because that will also scale up the number of faults at a commensurate rate. If we were to double the parallelism of the functions to achieve a 150 eps consumption rate, we would end up with 50 eps that are failing and getting reprocessed. In fact, no matter how many instances we add, a third of all messages will still need reprocessing. It is also worth noting that each of these reprocessed messages will experience a one-minute latency penalty as well, which will have a negative impact on your application's perceived responsiveness.

   Now let's consider the impact of a network outage on this same function. Every time a message is processed, a call is made to the load balancer, but since the network is down, we cannot reach it. Not only do 100% of the messages fail, but each message takes 30 seconds to process, since it has to wait for a network timeout exception to be thrown. The impact to the DAG will be the same as if the function had died, but unfortunately it hasn't. Instead, this function is effectively in a zombie state, and even restarting the function won't help, since the underlying issue is external to the function itself.

   While the underlying issues preventing the messages from being processed can be vastly different, they can be classified into two broad categories based on their likelihood of self-correcting: *transient faults* and *non-transient faults*. Transient faults include the temporary loss of network connectivity to components and services, the momentary unavailability of a service, or timeouts that can occur when your Pulsar function calls a remote service that is busy. These types of faults are often self-correcting, and if the message is reprocessed after a suitable delay, it is likely to succeed. One such scenario would be if the payment service is making a call to an external credit card authorization service during a period when the service is overloaded with requests.

There is a high probability of a subsequent call succeeding once the service has had a chance to recover.

Non-transient faults, in contrast, require external intervention in order to be resolved and include things like catastrophic hardware failures, expired security credentials, or bad message data. Consider the scenario where the order validation service publishes a message to the payment service's input topic that contains invalid payment information, such as a bad credit card number. No matter how many times we attempt to get authorization to use the card as a method of payment, it will always be declined. Another potential scenario would be where our credentials for the payment service have expired, and consequently, all of our attempts to authorize *any* customer's credit card will fail.

Oftentimes, it will be difficult to distinguish one scenario from the other, and we need to be able to detect non-transient faults, such as the invalid credit card number, from transient faults, such as an overloaded remote service, so we can respond to them differently. Fortunately, we can use the corresponding exception types and other data to make intelligent guesses as to the transient nature of a given fault and determine the proper course of action accordingly.

9.1.2 Fault detection

When it comes to the detection of faulty conditions within a Pulsar Functions topology, one only needs to examine the degree to which data is flowing through the entire topology. Simply put, is the application keeping up with the data volume being fed to it from the input topic, or is it falling behind? Data should flow through the DAG just like blood flowing through your body: uninterrupted and at a steady pace. There shouldn't be any blockages that are cutting off the flow to certain areas.

All of the adverse events we have discussed thus far have a similar impact on the flow of data: a steady increase in unprocessed messages. Within Pulsar, the key metric that indicates such a blockage is message backlog. The presence of an ever-increasing message backlog at the Pulsar application's input topic is an indication of degraded or faulty operation. To be clear, I am not talking about the absolute number of messages in the backlog but rather the *trend* of that number itself over a period of time, such as your peak business hours.

When a Pulsar application or function cannot keep up with the growing data volume in its input topic, as shown in figure 9.5, this condition is known as *backpressure* and is indicative of a lack of processing capacity and degraded performance within

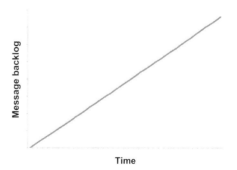

Figure 9.5 The condition where the message backlog for a particular subscription increases steadily over time is referred to as backpressure and is indicative of degraded performance within a Pulsar function or application.

the application, which must be remedied to meet the business SLAs. The term back-pressure is borrowed from fluid dynamics and used to indicate some resistance or opposing force restricting the desired flow of data through the topology just like a clog in your kitchen sink creates an opposing force to the water draining. Similarly, this condition is not isolated to the Pulsar function that is consuming the messages, but also has an impact throughout the entire topology.

All of the adverse events we have discussed thus far—function death, function lag, and non-progressing functions—can be detected by the presence of backpressure on the function's input topic(s). You should monitor the following topic-level metrics to detect backpressure within a Pulsar function:

- *pulsar_rate_in*, which measures the rate at which messages are coming into the topic in messages per second
- *pulsar_rate_out*, which measures the rate at which messages are being consumed from the topic in messages per second
- *pulsar_storage_backlog_size*, which measures the total backlog size of the topic in bytes

All of these metrics are periodically published to Prometheus and can be monitored by any observability framework that integrates with that platform. Any increase in message backlog within any of the function's input topics is indicative of one or more of these events and should trigger an alert.

9.2 *Resiliency design patterns*

In the previous section, we discussed some of the options for providing resiliency to your Pulsar applications using features provided by the Pulsar Functions framework itself, such as automatic restarts for functions that die. However, it is not uncommon for your Pulsar functions to have to interact with an external system to perform their processing. Doing so indirectly introduces the resiliency issues of these external systems into your Pulsar application. If these remote systems are unresponsive, the result will be lagging or non-progressing functions inside your application.

As we saw in chapter 8, the GottaEat order validation process depends on several third-party services to accept any incoming food orders, and if we are unable to communicate with these external systems for any reason, our entire business will come to a complete halt. Given that our all of our interaction with these services is over a network connection, there is the distinct possibility of intermittent network failures, periods of high latency, and unreachable services, and other interruptions. Therefore, it is critical that our application is resilient to these types of failures and is able to recover from them automatically. While you could attempt to implement these patterns yourself, this is one of those scenarios where it is best to use a third-party library that was developed by experts to solve these types of problems.

Issues arising from interacting with remote services are so common that Netflix developed its own fault tolerance library named Hystrix and open sourced it in 2013;

it contained several resiliency patterns that deal with exactly these types of issues. While this library is no longer being actively developed, several of its concepts have been implemented in a new open source project called resilience4j. As we shall see, this makes it easy to utilize these patterns inside your Java-based Pulsar functions because the majority of the logic has already been implemented inside the resilience4j library itself, allowing you to focus on which patterns to use. Therefore, we will need to add the configuration shown in listing 9.1 to the dependencies section of the Maven pom.xml file to add the library to our project.

> **Listing 9.2   Adding the resilience4j library to the project**

```
<dependencies>
    <dependency>
        <groupId>io.github.resilience4j</groupId>
        <artifactId>resilience4j-all</artifactId>
        <version>1.7.1</version>
    </dependency>

    ...
</dependencies>
```

In the following sections, I will introduce these patterns and how they can be used to make your Pulsar Functions-based microservices that interact with external systems resilient to these failure scenarios. In addition to providing the context and problem that the pattern solves, I will also cover the issues and considerations to take when implementing the pattern and examples of when the pattern would be applicable to your use case. Lastly, it is worth noting that these patterns were designed such that they can be used in combination with one another. This is particularly useful when you need to utilize more than one of these patterns within your Pulsar function (e.g., you may want to use both the retry and circuit breaker patterns when interacting with an external web service).

9.2.1   *Retry pattern*

When communicating with a remote service, any number of transient faults may occur, including a loss of network connectivity, the temporary unavailability of a service, and service timeouts that can occur when the remote service is extremely busy. These types of faults are generally self-correcting, and subsequent calls to the service are likely to succeed. If you encounter such a failure inside your Pulsar function, then the *retry* pattern allows you to handle the failure in one of three ways, depending on the error; if the error indicates that the failure isn't transient in nature, such as an authentication failure due to bad credentials, then you should not retry the call, since the same failure is likely to occur.

   If the exception indicates that the connection either timed out or otherwise indicates that the request was rejected due to the system being busy, then it is best to wait for a period of time before retrying the call to allow the remote service time to recover. Otherwise, you may want to retry the call immediately, since you have no reason to believe the subsequent call will fail. In order to implement this type of logic inside your function, you will need to wrap the remote service call inside a decorator, as shown in the following listing.

Listing 9.3   Utilizing the retry pattern inside a Pulsar function

We rely on several classes within
the resilience4j library.

```
  import io.github.resilience4j.retry.Retry;
  import io.github.resilience4j.retry.RetryConfig;
▷ import io.github.resilience4j.retry.RetryRegistry;
  import io.vavr.CheckedFunction0;
  import io.vavr.control.Try;


  public class RetryFunction implements Function<String, String> {

    public String apply(String s) {

      RetryConfig config =
        RetryConfig.custom()
          .maxAttempts(2)
          .waitDuration(Duration.ofMillis(1000))
          .retryOnResult(response -> (response == null))
          .retryExceptions(TimeoutException.class)
          .ignoreExceptions(RuntimeException.class)
          .build();

      CheckedFunction0<String> retryableFunction =
        Retry.decorateCheckedSupplier(
          RetryRegistry.of(config).retry("name"),
          () -> {
            HttpGet request =
              new HttpGet("http://www.google.com/search?q=" + s);

            try (CloseableHttpResponse response =
                   HttpClients.createDefault().execute(request)) {
              HttpEntity entity = response.getEntity();
              return (entity == null) ? null : EntityUtils.toString(entity);
            }
          });

      Try<String> result = Try.of(retryableFunction);
      return result.getOrNull();
    }
  }
```

This is the method defined in the function interface that will be invoked for each message.

Specifies a maximum of two retry attempts

Create our own custom retry configuration.

Specifies a pause of one second between retries

Perform a retry if the returned result is null.

Specifies the list of exceptions that are treated as transient faults and retried

Specifies the list of exceptions that are treated as non-transient and not retried

Decorate the function with our custom retry configuration.

Provide the lambda expression that will be executed and retried if necessary.

Execute the decorated function until a result is received or the retry limit is reached.

Return the result or null if no response was received.

The code shown in listing 9.2 simply takes as input a string, calls the Google search API with the given input string, and returns the result. Most importantly, it will make multiple attempts to call the HTTP endpoint without having to negatively acknowledge the message and have it redelivered to the function. Instead, the message is delivered from the Pulsar topic just once, and the retries are all made within the same call to the Pulsar function's apply method, as shown in figure 9.6. This allows us to avoid the wasteful cycle of having the same message delivered multiple times before deciding to give up on the external system.

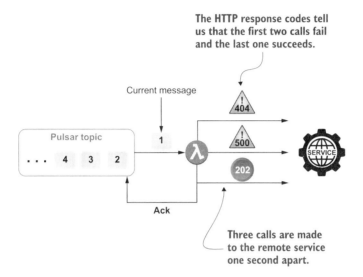

The HTTP response codes tell us that the first two calls fail and the last one succeeds.

Current message

Pulsar topic

. . . 4 3 2

Ack

Three calls are made to the remote service one second apart.

Figure 9.6   When using the retry pattern, the remote service is called repeatedly with the same message. In this particular case, the first two calls fail, but the third one succeeds, so the message is acknowledged. This allows us to avoid having to negatively ack the message and delay the processing by one minute each time.

The first parameter passed into the `Retry.decorateCheckedSupplier` method is the retry object we configured earlier in the code, which defines the number of retry attempts to make, how long to pause between them, and which exceptions indicate that we should retry the function call and which ones indicate we should not.

For those of you not familiar with the use of lambda expressions inside Java, the actual logic that will be called is encapsulated inside the second parameter, which takes in a function definition, as indicated by the `()->` syntax, and includes all the code inside the following brackets. The resulting object is a decorated function that is then passed into the `Try.of` method, which handles all of the retry logic automatically for you. The term *decorated* comes from the decorator pattern, which is a well-known design pattern that allows behavior to be dynamically added to an object runtime.

While you could have implemented similar logic using a combination of try/catch statements and a counter for the number of attempts, one can easily argue that the decorated function approach provided by the resilience4j library is a much more elegant solution which also allows you to dynamically configure the retry properties via user configuration properties provided when the Pulsar function is deployed.

ISSUES AND CONSIDERATIONS

While this is a very useful pattern to use when interacting with an external system, such as a web service or a database, be sure to consider the following factors when implementing it inside your Pulsar function:

- Adjust the retry interval to match the business requirements of your application. An overly aggressive retry policy with very short intervals between retries could generate additional load on a service that is already overloaded, making matters even worse. One might want to consider using an exponential backoff policy that increases the time between the retries in an exponential manner (e.g., 1 sec, 2 sec, 4 sec, 8 sec, etc.).

- Consider the criticality of the operation when choosing the number of retries to attempt. In some scenarios it may be best to fail fast rather than impact the processing latency with multiple retry attempts. For a customer-facing application, for example, it is better to fail after a small number of retries with a short delay between them than to introduce a lengthy delay to the end user.

- Be careful when using this pattern on operations that are idempotent; otherwise you might experience unintended side effects (e.g., a call made to an external credit card authorization service that is received and processed successfully but fails to send a response). Under these circumstances, if the retry logic sends the request again, the customer's credit card would be charged twice.

- It is important to log all retry attempts so the underlying connectivity issues can be identified and corrected as soon as possible. In addition to regular log files, Pulsar metrics can be used to communicate the number of retry attempts to the Pulsar administrator.

9.2.2   *Circuit breaker pattern*

The retry pattern was designed to handle transient faults because it enables an application to retry an operation in the expectation that it will succeed. The *circuit breaker* pattern, on the other hand, prevents an application from performing an operation that is likely to fail due to a non-transient fault.

The circuit breaker pattern, which was popularized by Michael Nygard in his book *Release It!* (Pragmatic Bookshelf, 2nd ed., 2018), is designed to prevent overwhelming a remote service with additional calls when we already know that it is has been unresponsive. Therefore, after a certain number of failed attempts, we will consider that the service is either unavailable or overloaded and reject all subsequent calls to the service. The intent is to prevent the remote service from becoming further overloaded by bombarding it with requests that we already know are unlikely to succeed.

The pattern gets its name from the fact that its operation is modelled after the physical electric circuit breakers found inside houses. When the number of faults within a given period of time exceeds a configurable threshold, the circuit breaker *trips*, and all invocations of the function that is decorated with the circuit breaker will fail immediately. The circuit breaker acts as a state machine that starts in the *closed* state, which indicates that the data can flow through the circuit breaker.

As we can see in figure 9.7, all incoming messages result in a call to the remote service. However, the circuit breaker keeps track of how many calls to the service produce an exception. When the number of exceptions exceeds a configured threshold, it is

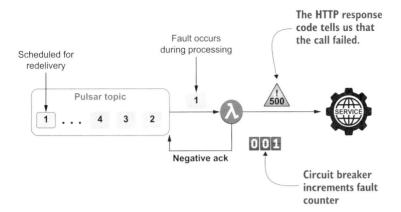

Figure 9.7   A circuit breaker starts in the *closed* state, which means that the service will be called for every message that is processed. The service call made when processing message 1 throws an exception, so the fault counter is incremented, and the message is negatively acked. If the counter exceeds the configured threshold, the circuit breaker will trip and transition to an open state.

an indication that the remote service is either unresponsive or too busy to process additional requests. Therefore, in order to prevent additional load on an already over-loaded service, the circuit breaker transitions to the *open* state, as shown in figure 9.8. This is analogous to what an electrical circuit breaker does when it experiences an electrical surge and trips (opens) the circuit to prevent the flow of electricity into an already overloaded power outlet.

Once the circuit breaker has been tripped, it will remain so for a preconfigured amount of time. No calls will be made to the service until that time period has expired. This gives the service time to fix the underlying issue before allowing the

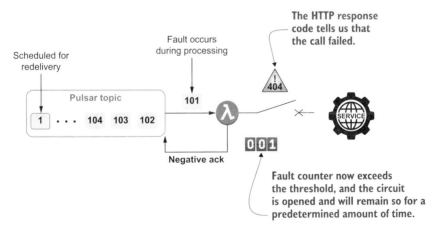

Figure 9.8   Once the circuit breaker's fault counter exceeds the configured threshold, the circuit transitions to the open state, and all subsequent messages are immediately negatively acked. This prevents making additional calls to a service that are likely to fail and gives the service some time to recover.

application to resume making calls to it. After the time period has elapsed, the circuit transitions to the *half-open* state in which a limited number of requests are permitted to invoke the remote service.

The half-open state is intended to prevent a recovering service from being flooded with requests from all the backlogged messages. As the service recovers, its capacity to handle requests might be limited at first. Only sending a limited number of requests prevents the recovering system from being overwhelmed after it has recovered. The circuit breaker maintains a success counter that is incremented for every message that is allowed to invoke the service and completes successfully, as shown in figure 9.9.

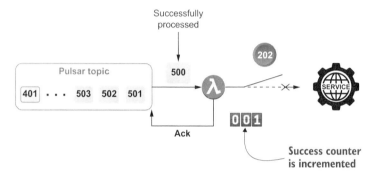

Figure 9.9   **When the circuit breaker is in the half-open state, a limited number of messages are permitted to invoke the service. Once a sufficient number of these calls complete successfully, the circuit transitions back to the closed state. However, if *any* of the messages fail, the circuit breaker immediately transitions back to the open state.**

If all of these requests are successful, as indicated by the success counter, it is assumed that the fault that was causing the previous issue has been resolved and that the service is ready to accept requests again. Thus, the circuit breaker will then switch back to the closed state and resume normal operations. However, if any of the messages sent during the half-open state fail, the circuit breaker will immediately switch back to the open state (no failure count threshold applies) and restart the timer to give the service additional time to recover from the fault.

This pattern provides stability to the application while the remote service recovers from a non-transient fault by quickly rejecting a request that is likely to fail and might lead to cascading failures throughout the entire application. Oftentimes, this pattern is combined with the retry pattern to handle both transient and non-transient faults within the remote service. To utilize the circuit breaker pattern inside your Pulsar function, you need to wrap the remote service call inside a decorator, as shown in listing 9.4 which shows the implementation of the `CreditCardAuthorizationService` that is called from the GottaEat payment service when the customer uses a credit card for payment.

Listing 9.4   Utilizing the circuit breaker pattern inside a Pulsar function

```
...
import io.github.resilience4j.circuitbreaker.*;      ⟵——— We are using classes from
import io.vavr.CheckedFunction0;                                the circuitbreaker package.
import io.vavr.control.Try;

public class CreditCardAuthorizationService
    implements Function<CreditCard, AuthorizedPayment> {

  public AuthorizedPayment process(CreditCard card, Context ctx)
      throws Exception {

    CircuitBreakerConfig config = CircuitBreakerConfig.custom()
        .failureRateThreshold(20)
        .slowCallRateThreshold(50)
        .waitDurationInOpenState(Duration.ofMillis(30000))      ⟵
        .slowCallDurationThreshold(Duration.ofSeconds(10))
        .permittedNumberOfCallsInHalfOpenState(5)               ⟵
        .minimumNumberOfCalls(10)
        .slidingWindowType(SlidingWindowType.TIME_BASED)        ⟵
            .slidingWindowSize(5)             ⟵
            .ignoreException(e -> e instanceof
                UnsuccessfulCallException &&
        ((UnsuccessfulCallException)e).getCode() == 499 )       ⟵
        .recordExceptions(IOException.class,
                        UnsuccessfulCallException.class)⟵
        .build();

    CheckedFunction0<String> cbFunction =
      CircuitBreaker.decorateCheckedSupplier(
          CircuitBreakerRegistry.of(config).circuitBreaker("name"),   ⟵
          () -> {
        OkHttpClient client = new OkHttpClient();
        StringBuilder sb = new StringBuilder()
            .append("number=").append(card.getAccountNumber())
            .append("&cvc=").append(card.getCcv())
            .append("&exp_month=").append(card.getExpMonth())
            .append("&exp_year=").append(card.getExpYear());

        MediaType mediaType =
                MediaType.parse("application/x-www-form-urlencoded");
        RequestBody body =
                RequestBody.create(sb.toString(), mediaType);

        Request request = new Request.Builder()
            .url("https://noodlio-pay.p.rapidapi.com/tokens/create")
            .post(body)
            .addHeader("x-rapidapi-key", "SIGN-UP-FOR-KEY")
            .addHeader("x-rapidapi-host", "noodlio-pay.p.rapidapi.com")
            .addHeader("content-type",
                        "application/x-www-form-urlencoded")
            .build();
        try (Response response = client.newCall(request).execute()) {
          if (!response.isSuccessful()) {
```

The number of failures before transitioning to the open state

Any call that takes more than 10 seconds is considered slow and added to the count.

The minimum number of calls before the failure count is applicable

The number of slow calls before transitioning to the open state

How long to remain in the open state before transitioning to the half-open state

The number of calls that can be made in the half-open state

Use a time window of five minutes before restarting failure count.

Using a time-based window for the failure count

List of exceptions that are not added to the failure count

List of exceptions that are added to the failure count

Use our own custom circuit breaker configuration.

Provide the lambda expression that will be executed if permitted by the circuit breaker.

```
            throw new UnsuccessfulCallException(response.code());
        }
        return getToken(response.body().string());
    }
      }
    );

    Try<String> result = Try.of(cbFunction);
    return authorize(card, result.getOrNull());
  }

private String getToken(String json) {
  ...
  }


private AuthorizedPayment authorize(CreditCard card, String token) {
  ...
  }
}
```

Executes the decorated function until a result is received or the retry limit is reached

Return the authorized payment or null if no response was received.

The first parameter passed into the `CircuitBreaker.decorateCheckedSupplier` method is a `CircuitBreaker` object based on the configuration defined earlier in the code, which specifies the failure count threshold, how long to remain in the open state, and which exceptions indicate a failed method call and which ones do not. Additional details on these parameters and others can be found in the resilience4j documentation (https://resilience4j.readme.io/docs/circuitbreaker).

The actual logic that will be called if the circuit breaker is closed is defined inside a lambda expression which was passed in as the second parameter. As you can see, the logic inside the function definition sends an HTTP request to a third-party credit card authorization service named Noodlio Pay, which returns an authorization token that can later be used to collect payment from the credit card provided. The resulting object is a decorated function that is then passed into the `Try.of` method, which handles all of the circuit breaker logic automatically for you. If the call is successful, the authorization token is extracted from the Noodlio Pay response object and returned inside the AuthorizedPayment object.

ISSUES AND CONSIDERATIONS

While this is a very useful pattern to use when interacting with an external system, such as a web service or a database, be sure to consider the following factors when implementing it inside your Pulsar function:

- Consider adjusting the circuit breaker's strategy based on the severity of the exception itself, as a request might fail for multiple reasons, and some of the errors might be transient and others non-transient. In the presence of a non-transient error, it might make sense to open the circuit breaker immediately rather than waiting for a specific number of occurrences.

- Avoid using a single circuit breaker within a Pulsar function that utilizes multiple independent providers. For example, the GottaEat payment service uses four different remote services based on the method of payment provided by the customer. If the call to the payment service went through a single circuit breaker, then error responses from one faulty service could trip the circuit breaker and prevent calls to the other three services that are likely to succeed.

- A circuit breaker should log all failed requests so the underlying connectivity issues can be identified and corrected as quickly as possible. In addition to regular log files, Pulsar metrics can be used to communicate the number of retry attempts to the Pulsar administrator.
- The circuit breaker pattern can be used in combination with the retry pattern.

9.2.3 *Rate limiter pattern*

While the circuit breaker pattern was designed to prohibit service calls only after a preconfigured number of faults had been detected over a period of time, the *rate limiter* pattern, on the other hand, prohibits service calls after a preconfigured number of calls have been made within a given period, regardless of whether or not they were successful. As the name implies, the rate limiter pattern is used to limit the frequency at which a remote service can be called and is useful for situations where you want to restrict the number of calls made over a given period of time. One such example would be if we called a web service, such as the Google API, that restricts the number of calls you can make with a free API key to only 60 per minute.

When using this pattern, all incoming messages result in a call to the remote service up to a preconfigured number. The rate limiter keeps track of how many calls have been made to the service, and once the limit is reached, prohibits any additional calls for the remainder of the preconfigured time window, as shown in figure 9.10. In order to utilize the rate limiter pattern inside your Pulsar function, you need to wrap the remote service call inside a decorator, as shown in listing 9.4.

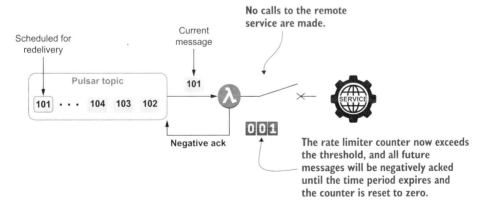

Figure 9.10 If the rate limiter is configured to permit 100 calls per minute, then the first 100 messages would be permitted to invoke the service. The 101st message and all subsequent messages will not be permitted to call the service and, instead, will be negatively acknowledged. After one minute elapses, another 100 messages can be processed.

Listing 9.5   Utilizing the rate limiter pattern inside a Pulsar function

```
import io.github.resilience4j.decorators.Decorators;
import io.github.resilience4j.ratelimiter.*;

...
public class GoogleGeoEncodingService implements Function<Address, Void> {

  public Void process(Address addr, Context ctx) throws Exception {

    if (!initalized) {
      init(ctx);
    }

    CheckedFunction0<String> decoratedFunction =
        Decorators.ofCheckedSupplier(getFunction(addr))
        .withRateLimiter(rateLimiter)
        .decorate();

    LatLon geo = getLocation(
        Try.of(decoratedFunction)
          .onFailure(
            (Throwable t) -> ctx.getLogger().error(t.getMessage())
        ).getOrNull());

    if (geo != null) {
      addr.setGeo(geo);
      ctx.newOutputMessage(ctx.getOutputTopic(),
                           AvroSchema.of(Address.class))
         .properties(ctx.getCurrentRecord().getProperties())
        .value(addr)
        .send();
    } else {
      // We made a valid call, but didn't get a valid geo back
    }
    return null;
  }

  private void init(Context ctx) {
    config = RateLimiterConfig.custom()
        .limitRefreshPeriod(Duration.ofMinutes(1))
        .limitForPeriod(60)
        .timeoutDuration(Duration.ofSeconds(1))
        .build();

    rateLimiterRegistry = RateLimiterRegistry.of(config);
    rateLimiter = rateLimiterRegistry.rateLimiter("name");
    initalized = true;
  }

  private CheckedFunction0<String> getFunction(Address addr) {
    CheckedFunction0<String> fn = () -> {
      OkHttpClient client = new OkHttpClient();
      StringBuilder sb = new StringBuilder()
      .append("https://maps.googleapis.com/maps/api/geocode")
```

Initializes the rate limiter

Decorates the REST call to the Google Maps API

Parses the response from the REST call

Assigns the rate limiter

Invokes the decorated function

The rate interval is one minute.

Sets a limit of 60 calls per rate interval

Wait one second between subsequent calls.

Returns a function containing the REST API call logic

```
          .append("/json?address=")
          .append(URLEncoder.encode(addr.getStreet().toString(),
          StandardCharsets.UTF_8.toString())).append(",")
          .append(URLEncoder.encode(addr.getCity().toString(),
              StandardCharsets.UTF_8.toString())).append(",")
          .append(URLEncoder.encode(addr.getState().toString(),
              StandardCharsets.UTF_8.toString()))
          .append("&key=").append("SIGN-UP-FOR-KEY");

      Request request = new Request.Builder()         If we got a valid response,
        .url(sb.toString())                           return the JSON string with
        .build();                                       the latitude/longitude.

    try (Response response = client.newCall(request).execute()) {
       if (response.isSuccessful()) {
       return response.body().string();            ◁────────────────┐
        } else {
       String reason = getErrorStatus(response.body().string());
         if (NON_TRANSIENT_ERRORS.stream().anyMatch(   ◁──┐
              s -> reason.contains(s))) {                   Determine the error
          throw new NonTransientException();               type based on the
         } else if (TRANSIENT_ERRORS.stream().anyMatch(    error message.
              s -> reason.contains(s))) {
          throw new TransientException();
         }
       return null;
        }
     }
    };
    return fn;
   }
                                              Parses the JSON response
   private LatLon getLocation(String json) {  ◁──┐ from the Google Maps
   ...                                              REST API call
   }
}
```

This function calls the Google Maps API and limits the number of attempts to 60 per minute to stay in compliance with Google's terms of use for a free account. If the number of calls exceeds this amount, then Google will block access to the API for our account as a preventative measure for a brief period of time. Therefore, we have taken proactive steps to prevent that condition from occurring.

ISSUES AND CONSIDERATIONS

While this is a very useful pattern to use when interacting with an external system, such as a web service or a database, be sure to consider the following factors when implementing it inside your Pulsar function:

- This pattern will almost certainly decrease the throughput for the function, so be sure to account for this throughout the entire data flow to make sure the upstream functions don't overwhelm the rate-limited function.

- This pattern should be used to protect a remote service from getting over-whelmed with calls or to restrict the number of calls to avoid exceeding a quota which would result in you getting locked out by the third-party vendor.

9.2.4 *Time limiter pattern*

The *time limiter* pattern is used to limit the amount of time spent calling a remote service before terminating the connection from the client side. This effectively short circuits the timeout mechanism on the remote service and allows us to determine when to give up on the remote call and terminate the connection from the client side.

This behavior is useful when you have a tight SLA on the entire data pipeline and have allocated a small amount of time for interacting with the remote service. This allows the Pulsar function to continue processing without a response from the web service rather than waiting 30 or more seconds for the connection to timeout. Doing so boosts the throughput of the function, since it no longer has to waste 30 seconds waiting on a response from a faulty service.

Consider the scenario where you first make a call to an internal caching service, such as Apache Ignite, to see if you have the data you need prior to making a call to an external service to retrieve the value. The purpose of doing so is to speed up the processing inside your function by eliminating the need for a lengthy call to a remote service. However, you run the risk of your caching service itself being unresponsive, which would result in a lengthy pause while making that call. This would defeat the entire purpose of the cache. Therefore, you decide to allocate a time budget to the cache call of 500 milliseconds to limit the impact an unresponsive cache can have on your function.

Listing 9.6   Utilizing the time limiter pattern inside a Pulsar function

```
import io.github.resilience4j.timelimiter.TimeLimiter;
import io.github.resilience4j.timelimiter.TimeLimiterConfig;
import io.github.resilience4j.timelimiter.TimeLimiterRegistry;

public class LookupService implements Function<Address, Address> {
private TimeLimiter timeLimiter;
private IgniteCache<Address, Address> cache;
private String bypassTopic;
private boolean initalized = false;

    public Address process(Address addr, Context ctx) throws Exception {
        if (!initalized) {
            init(ctx);                     ◁───┐ Initializes the time limiter
        }                                       │ and the ignite cache

        Address geoEncodedAddr = timeLimiter.executeFutureSupplier(
            () -> CompletableFuture.supplyAsync(() ->
            { return cache.get(addr); }));

        if (geoEncodedAddr != null) {     ◁───┐
```

The cache lookup that is executed asynchronously

Invokes the cache lookup and limits the duration of the call via the time limiter

If we have a cache hit, then publish the value to the different output topic.

```
          ctx.newOutputMessage(bypassTopic, AvroSchema.of(Address.class))
              .properties(ctx.getCurrentRecord().getProperties())
              .value(geoEncodedAddr)
              .send();
          }

          return null;
        }
```

The bypass topic is configurable.

```
        private void init(Context ctx) {
          bypassTopic = ctx.getUserConfigValue("bypassTopicName")
               .get().toString();
          TimeLimiterConfig config = TimeLimiterConfig.custom()
               .cancelRunningFuture(true)
```

Cancel running calls that exceed the time limit.

Sets a time limit of 500 milliseconds

```
               .timeoutDuration(Duration.ofMillis(500))
               .build();

          TimeLimiterRegistry registry = TimeLimiterRegistry.of(config);
          timeLimiter = registry.timeLimiter("my-time-limiter");
```

Creates the time limiter based on the configuration

Configures the Apache Ignite client

```
          IgniteConfiguration cfg = new IgniteConfiguration();
            cfg.setClientMode(true);
            cfg.setPeerClassLoadingEnabled(true);

          TcpDiscoveryMulticastIpFinder ipFinder =
           new TcpDiscoveryMulticastIpFinder();

           ipFinder.setAddresses(Collections.singletonList(
              "127.0.0.1:47500..47509"));
```

Connects to the Apache Ignite service

```
          cfg.setDiscoverySpi(new TcpDiscoverySpi().setIpFinder(ipFinder));
          Ignite ignite = Ignition.start(cfg);
          cache = ignite.getOrCreateCache("geo-encoded-addresses");
        }
      }
```

Retrieves the local cache that stores geo-encoded addresses

In order to utilize the time limiter pattern inside your Pulsar function, you need to wrap the remote service call inside a `CompletableFuture` and execute it via the `TimeLimter`'s `executeFutureSupplier` method, as shown in listing 9.6. This lookup function assumes that the cache is populated inside the function that calls the Google Maps API. This allows us to restructure the geo-encoding process slightly to have the lookup occur before the call to the `GeoEncodingService`, as shown in figure 9.11.

Again, this type of design is intended to speed up the geo-encoding process, and thus, we need to limit the amount of time we are willing to wait to get a response back from Apache Ignite before abandoning the call. If the cache lookup succeeds, then the `LookupService` will publish a message directly to the same `GeoEncoding` output topic as the `GeoEncodingService` does. The downstream consumer doesn't care who published the message as long as it has the correct contents.

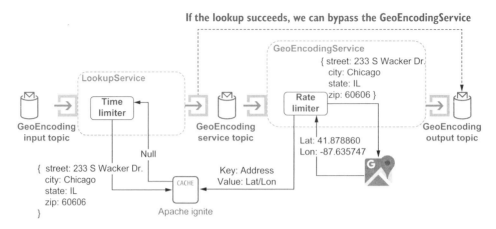

Figure 9.11 The lookup service can be used to prevent unnecessary calls to the `GeoEncodingService` if we already have the latitude/longitude pair for a given address. The cache is populated with the results from the Google Maps API calls.

ISSUES AND CONSIDERATIONS

While this is a very useful pattern to use when interacting with an external system such as a web service or a database, be sure to consider the following factors when implementing it inside your Pulsar function:

- Adjust the time limit to match the business SLA requirements of your application. An overly aggressive time limit will cause successful calls to be abandoned too soon, resulting in unnecessary work on the remote service and missing data inside your Pulsar function.
- Do not use this pattern on operations that are idempotent; otherwise you might experience unintended side effects. It is best to only use this pattern on lookup calls and other non-state changing functions or services.

9.2.5   *Cache pattern*

If you would prefer *not* to write a separate function just to perform lookups, the resiliency4j library also provides a way to decorate a function call with a cache as well. Listing 9.7 shows how to decorate a Java lambda expression with a cache abstraction. The cache abstraction stores the result of every invocation of the function in a cache instance and tries to retrieve a previous cached result from the cache before it invokes the lambda expression.

Listing 9.7   Utilizing the resiliency cache inside a Pulsar function

```
import javax.cache.CacheManager;
import javax.cache.Caching;
import javax.cache.configuration.MutableConfiguration;
import io.github.resilience4j.cache.Cache;
import io.github.resilience4j.decorators.Decorators;
```

```
...
public class GeoEncodingServiceWithCache implements Function<Address, Void> {

    public Void process(Address addr, Context ctx) throws Exception {

      if (!initalized) {
         init(ctx);      ⟵——— Initializes the cache
      }
                                                                        Decorates the
                                                                        REST call to the
      CheckedFunction1<String, String> cachedFunction = Decorators   Google Maps API
         .ofCheckedSupplier(getFunction(addr))            ⟵
         .withCache(cacheContext)        ⟵——— Assigns the cache
         .decorate();
                                                                       Checks the cache
                                                                       before invoking
      LatLon geo = getLocation(                                        the function
      Try.of(() -> cachedFunction.apply(addr.toString())).get());  ⟵

         if (geo != null) {          If we have the latitude/longitude,
            addr.setGeo(geo);        then send it.
            ctx.newOutputMessage(ctx.getOutputTopic(),AvroSchema.of(Address.class))
               .properties(ctx.getCurrentRecord().getProperties())
               .value(addr)
               .send();
         }
         return null;
      }

    private void init(Context ctx) {
      CacheManager cacheManager =              Uses the configured
         Caching.getCachingProvider().getCacheManager();  ⟵  cache implementation

      cacheContext = Cache.of(cacheManager.createCache(  ⟵——— Creates the address cache
         "addressCache", new MutableConfiguration<>()));
         initalized = true;
      }
                                                     Returns a function containing
                                                        the REST API call logic
      private CheckedFunction0<String> getFunction(Address addr) {    ⟵
         // Same as before
      }
                                               If we got a valid response,
                                               return the JSON string with
      private LatLon getLocation(String json) {  ⟵┘ the latitude/longitude.
         // Same as before
      }
    }
```

Arrows in left margin:

Parses the response from the cache or REST call — points to `LatLon geo = getLocation(` / `ctx.newOutputMessage(...)`

You should configure the function to use a distributed cache implementation, such as Ehcache, Caffeine, or Apache Ignite. If the cache retrieval from the distributed cache fails, the exception will be ignored, and the lambda expression will be called to retrieve the value instead. Please refer to your preferred vendor's documentation for more details on how to configure and use a vendor-specific implementation of the JCache functional specification.

The trade-off when using this approach versus the separate lookup service approach is that you lose the ability to limit the amount of time you are willing to wait for the cache call to complete. Therefore, in the unlikely event that the distributed cache service is down, each call could take up to 30 seconds while waiting for a network timeout.

ISSUES AND CONSIDERATIONS

While this is a very useful pattern to use when interacting with an external system, such as a web service or a database, be sure to consider the following factors when implementing it inside your Pulsar function:

- This is only useful on datasets that are relatively static in nature, such as geo-encoded addresses. Don't try caching data that is likely to change frequently; otherwise you run the risk of using incorrect data inside your application.
- Limit the size of the cache to avoid causing out-of-memory conditions within your Pulsar function. If you need a larger cache, you should consider using a distributed cache, such as Apache Ignite.
- Prevent data in your cache from becoming stale by implementing an aging policy on the data so it is automatically purged once it reaches a certain age.

9.2.6 *Fallback pattern*

The *fallback* pattern is used to provide your function with an alternative resource in the event that the primary resource is unavailable. Consider the case where you are calling an internal database through a load balancer endpoint, and the load balancer fails. Rather than allowing the failure of that single piece of hardware to cause your entire application to fail, you could bypass the load balancer entirely and connect directly to the database instead. The following listing shows how to implement such a function.

Listing 9.8 Utilizing the fallback pattern inside a Pulsar function

The primary connection goes through the load balancer.

The backup connection goes directly to the database server.

```
import io.github.resilience4j.decorators.Decorators;
import io.vavr.CheckedFunction0;
import io.vavr.control.Try;

public class DatabaseLookup implements Function<String, FoodOrder> {
  private String primary = "jdbc:mysql://load-balancer:3306/food";
  private String backup = "jdbc:mysql://backup:3306/food";
  private String sql = "select * from food_orders where id=?";
  private String user = "";
  private String pass = "";
  private boolean initalized = false;

  public FoodOrder process(String id, Context ctx) throws Exception {
    if (!initalized) {
```

The DB credentials set inside the init method from user properties

```
            init(ctx);
        }


    CheckedFunction0<ResultSet> decoratedFunction =
        Decorators.ofCheckedSupplier( () -> {
         try (Connection con =
              DriverManager.getConnection(primary, user, pass)) {
            PreparedStatement stmt = con.prepareStatement(sql);
            stmt.setLong(1, Long.parseLong(id));
            return stmt.executeQuery();
          }
         })
        .withFallback(SQLException.class, ex -> {
          try (Connection con =
              DriverManager.getConnection(backup, user, pass)) {
            PreparedStatement stmt = con.prepareStatement(sql);
            stmt.setLong(1, Long.parseLong(id));
            return stmt.executeQuery();
          }
          })
        .decorate();

        ResultSet rs = Try.of(decoratedFunction).get();
        return ORMapping(rs);
    }
  private void init(Context ctx) {
    Driver myDriver;
     try {
       myDriver = (Driver) Class.forName("com.mysql.jdbc.Driver")
        .newInstance();
       DriverManager.registerDriver(myDriver);
       // Set local variables from user properties
        ...
       initalized = true;
     } catch (Throwable t) {
       t.printStackTrace();
     }

  }


  private FoodOrder ORMapping(ResultSet rs) {
    // Performs the Relational-to-Object mapping
  }
}
```

The first call is via the load balancer.

If an SQLException was thrown, retry the query via the backup URL.

Get the successful ResultSet.

Perform the ORM to return the FoodOrder object.

Loads the database driver class and registers it

Another scenario in which this pattern could come into play would be if we had multiple third-party credit card authorization services to choose from, and we wanted to try an alternative service in the event that we could not connect to the primary service for some reason. Note that the first parameter to the withFallback method takes the exception types that trigger the fallback code, so it would be important to only contact the second credit card authorization service if the error indicated that the primary service was unavailable, and *not* if the card was declined.

ISSUES AND CONSIDERATIONS

While this is a very useful pattern to use when interacting with an external system such as a web service or a database, be sure to consider the following factors when implementing it inside your Pulsar function:

- This is only useful in situations where you have either an alternative route to the service that is reachable from the Pulsar function or an alternative (backup) copy of the service that provides the same function.

9.2.7   Credential refresh pattern

The *credentials refresh* pattern is used to automatically detect when your session credentials have expired and need to be refreshed. Consider the case in which you are interacting with an AWS service from inside your Pulsar function that requires session tokens for authentication. Typically, these tokens are intended to be used for short periods of time, and thus have an expiration time associated with them (e.g., 60 minutes). Therefore, if you are interacting with a service that requires such a token, you need a strategy for automatically generating a new token when the current one expires to keep your Pulsar function processing messages. The next listing shows how to automatically detect an expired session token and refresh it using the `Vavr` functional library for Java.

Listing 9.9   Automatic credential refresh

Static credentials used
to get an access token

```
public class PaypalAuthorizationService implements Function<PayPal, String> {
  private String clientId;
  private String secret;                      Local copy of the        First attempt
  private String accessToken;      <—         access token             to authorize
  private String PAYPAL_URL = "https://api.sandbox.paypal.com";        the payment
                                                                       using the
                                                                       current
  public String process(PayPal pay, Context ctx) throws Exception {    access token
    return Try.of(getAuthorizationFunction(pay))        <—
      .onFailure(UnauthorizedException.class, refreshToken())   <—
      .recover(UnauthorizedException.class,
        (exc) -> Try.of(getAuthorizationFunction(pay)).get())  <—
      .getOrNull();
  }
                            Attempt to recover from the unauthorized
                            exception by calling the authorize method again.
  private CheckedFunction0<String> getAuthorizationFunction(PayPal pay) {
    CheckedFunction0<String> fn = () -> {
      OkHttpClient client = new OkHttpClient();         If an unauthorized exception is raised,
      MediaType mediaType =                             invoke the refreshToken function.
        MediaType.parse("application/json; charset=utf-8");
      RequestBody body =
    RequestBody.create(buildRequestBody(pay), mediaType);   <—
                                                             Build the JSON
                                                             request body.
      Request request =
        new Request.Builder()
```

Return the final result.

```
          .url("https://api.sandbox.paypal.com/v1/payments/payment")
          .addHeader("Authorization", accessToken)      <──┐    Provide the current access
          .post(body)                                        token value for authorization.
          .build();

      try (Response response = client.newCall(request).execute()) {   <──┐
        if (response.isSuccessful()) {                           Authorize the
          return response.body().string();                       payment.
        } else if (response.code() == 500) {
          throw new UnauthorizedException();      <──┐   Raise the unauthorized exception
        }                                               based on the response code.
          return null;
    }};

    return fn;
}

private Consumer<UnauthorizedException> refreshToken() {
    Consumer<UnauthorizedException> refresher = (ex) -> {
      OkHttpClient client = new OkHttpClient();
      MediaType mediaType =
        MediaType.parse("application/json; charset=utf-8");
      RequestBody body = RequestBody.create("", mediaType);

      Request request = new Request.Builder().url(PAYPAL_URL +        Requesting new
          "/v1/oauth2/token"?grant_type=client_credentials")   <──┐  access token
      .addHeader("Accept-Language", "en_US")
      .addHeader("Authorization",
          Credentials.basic(clientId, secret))   <──┐   Provide the static credentials
      .post(body)                                       when requesting a new access
      .build();                                         token.

      try (Response response = client.newCall(request).execute()) {
        if (response.isSuccessful()) {
          parseToken(response.body().string());   <──┐  Parse the new access token
        }                                               from the JSON response.
      } catch (IOException e) {
        e.printStackTrace();
        }};
      return refresher;
  }

  private void parseToken(String json) {
  // Parses the new access token from the response object
  }

  private String buildRequestBody(PayPal pay) {
  // Build the payment authorization request JSON
  }
}
```

The key to this pattern is wrapping the first call to the PayPal payment authorization REST API inside of a try container type, which represents a computation that may either result in an exception or return a successfully computed value. It also allows us to chain computations together, which means we can handle exceptions in a more readable manner. In the example shown in listing 9.9, the entire try/fail/refresh token/retry logic is handled in just five lines of code. While you could easily implement the same logic using the more traditional try/catch logic constructs, it would be much harder to follow.

The first call wrapped in the try construct invokes the PayPal payment authorization REST API and, if it is successful, returns the JSON response from that successful call. The more interesting scenario is when that first call fails, because then the function inside the `onFailure` method is called if and only if the exception type is `Unauthorized-Exception`. That only occurs when the first call returns a status code of 500.

The function inside the `onFailure` method attempts to remedy the situation by refreshing the access token. Finally, the recover method is used to make another call to the PayPal payment authorization REST API now that the access token has been refreshed. Thus, if the initial failure was due to an expired session token, this code block will attempt to resolve it automatically without manual intervention or any downtime. The message won't even have to be failed and retried at a later point, which is critical, since our function is interacting directly with a client application where response time is important.

ISSUES AND CONSIDERATIONS

While this is a very useful pattern to use when interacting with an external system, such as a web service that uses expiring authorization tokens, be sure to consider the following factors when implementing it inside your Pulsar function:

- This pattern is only applicable to token-based authentication mechanisms that provide a token refresh API that is exposed to the Pulsar function.
- The tokens returned from the token refresh API should be stored in a secure location to prevent unauthorized access to the service.

9.3   *Multiple layers of resiliency*

As you may have noticed, in the previous section I only used one of these patterns at a time. But what if you want to use more than one of the previous patterns inside your Pulsar function? There are situations where it would be quite useful to have your function utilize the retry, cache, and circuit breaker patterns.

Fortunately, as I mentioned at the beginning of the chapter, you can easily decorate your remote service call with any number of these patterns from the resilience4j library to provide multiple layers of resiliency inside your functions. The following listing demonstrates just how easy this is to accomplish for the `GeoEncoding` function.

Listing 9.10   Multiple resiliency patterns inside a Pulsar function

```
public class GeoEncodingService implements Function<Address, Void> {
  private boolean initalized = false;
    private Cache<String, String> cacheContext;
    private CircuitBreakerConfig config;
```

```
      private CircuitBreakerRegistry registry;
      private CircuitBreaker circuitBreaker;
      private RetryRegistry rertyRegistry;
      private Retry retry;

      public Void process(Address addr, Context ctx) throws Exception {
      if (!initalized) {
        init(ctx);
      }

      CheckedFunction1<String, String> resilientFunction = Decorators
          .ofCheckedSupplier(getFunction(addr))     <──── The Google Maps REST API call
          .withCache(cacheContext)
          .withCircuitBreaker(circuitBreaker)     <──── Decorated with a circuit breaker
          .withRetry(retry)
          .decorate();

      LatLon geo = getLocation(Try.of(() ->
            resilientFunction.apply(addr.toString())).get());   <──── Calls the decorated function to get the actual latitude/longitude

      if (geo != null) {
        addr.setGeo(geo);
        ctx.newOutputMessage(ctx.getOutputTopic(),AvroSchema.of(Address.class))
          .properties(ctx.getCurrentRecord().getProperties())
          .value(addr)
          .send();
      } else {
        // We made a valid call, but didn't get a valid geo back
      }

      return null;
    }
    private void init(Context ctx) {     <──── Initialize the resiliency configurations as before.
      // Configure a cache (once)
      CacheManager cacheManager = Caching.getCachingProvider()
  .getCacheManager();

      cacheContext = Cache.of(cacheManager
        .createCache("addressCache", new MutableConfiguration<>()));

      config = CircuitBreakerConfig.custom()
      ...
      cbRegistry = CircuitBreakerRegistry.of(config);
      circuitBreaker = cbRegistry.circuitBreaker(ctx.getFunctionName());

      RetryConfig retryConfig = RetryConfig.custom()
      ...
      retryRegistry = RetryRegistry.of(retryConfig);
      retry = retryRegistry.retry(ctx.getFunctionName());
      initalized = true;
    }
  }
```

Decorated with a cache

Decorated with a retry policy

In this particular configuration, the cache will be checked before the function is invoked. Any calls that fail will be retried based on the defined configuration, and if a sufficient number of calls fail, the circuit breaker will be tripped to prevent subsequent calls from being made to the remote service until sufficient time has passed to allow the service to recover.

Remember that these code-based resiliency patterns are also used in conjunction with the resiliency capabilities provided by the Pulsar Functions framework, such as auto-restarting K8s pods. Together, these can help minimize your downtime and keep your Pulsar Functions applications running smoothly.

Summary

- There are several different adverse events that can impact a Pulsar function, and message backpressure is a good metric to use for fault detection.
- You can use the resiliency4j library to implement various common resiliency patterns within your Pulsar functions, particularly those that interact with external systems.
- You can utilize multiple patterns inside the same Pulsar function to increase its resiliency to failures.

Data access

Thus far all of the information used by our Pulsar Functions has been provided inside the incoming messages. While this is an effective way to exchange information, it is not the most efficient or desirable way for Pulsar Functions to exchange information with one another. The biggest drawback to this approach is that it creates a dependency on the message source to provide your Pulsar function with the information it needs to do its job. This violates the encapsulation principle of object-oriented design, which dictates that the internal logic of a function should not be exposed to the outside world. Currently, any changes to the logic inside one function might require changes to the upstream function that provides the incoming messages.

Consider a use case where you are writing a function that requires a customer's contact information, including their cell phone number. Rather than passing a message containing all of that information, wouldn't it be easier to just pass the customer ID, which can then be used by our function to query the database and retrieve the information we need instead? In fact, this is a common access pattern if the information required by the function exists in an external data source, such as a database. This approach enforces encapsulation and prevents changes in one function from directly impacting other functions by relying on each function to gather the information it needs instead of providing it inside the incoming message.

In this chapter, I will walk through several uses cases that need to store and/or retrieve data from an external system and demonstrate how to do so using Pulsar Functions. In doing so, I will cover a variety of different data stores and describe the various criteria used to select one technology over another.

10.1   Data sources

The GottaEat application that we have been developing thus far is hosted within the context of a much larger enterprise architecture that consists of multiple technologies and data storage platforms, as shown in figure 10.1. These data storage platforms are used by multiple applications and computing engines within the GottaEat organization and act as a single source of truth for the entire enterprise.

As you can see, Pulsar Functions can access data from a variety of data sources, from low-latency in-memory data grids and disk-backed caches to high-latency data lakes and blob storage. These data stores allow us to access information supplied by other applications and computing engines. For instance, the GottaEat application we have been developing has a dedicated MySQL database it uses to store customer and driver information, such as their login credentials, contact information, and home address. This information is collected by some of the non-Pulsar microservices shown in figure 10.1 that provide non-streaming services, such as user login, account update, etc.

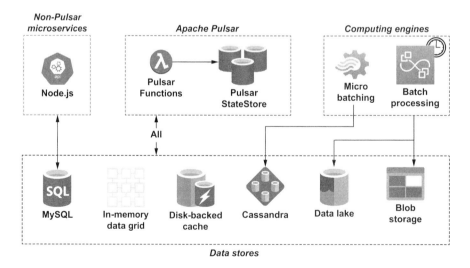

Figure 10.1   The enterprise architecture of the GottaEat organization will be comprised of various computing engines and data storage technologies. Therefore, it is critically important that we can access these various data repositories from our Pulsar functions.

Within the GottaEat enterprise architecture there are distributed computing engines, such as Apache Spark and Apache Hive, which perform batch processing of extremely large datasets stored inside the data lake. One such dataset is the driver location data, which contains the latitude and longitude coordinates of every driver that is logged into our application. The GottaEat mobile application automatically records the driver's location every 30 seconds and forwards it to Pulsar for storage in the data lake. This dataset is then used in the development and training of the company's machine learning models. Given sufficient information, these models can accurately predict various key business metrics, such as estimated delivery times of placed orders or the areas within a city most likely to have the most food orders in the next hour, so we can position drivers accordingly. These computing engines are scheduled to run periodically to calculate various data points that are required by the machine learning models and store them inside the Cassandra database so they can be accessed by the Pulsar functions that are hosting the ML models to provide real-time predictions.

10.2 Data access use cases

In this section, I will demonstrate how to access data from various data stores using Pulsar Functions. Before I jump right into the use cases, I wanted to discuss how to go about deciding which data store is best for a given use case. From a Pulsar Functions perspective, which data store to use will depend on a number of factors, including the availability of the data and the maximum processing time allocated to a particular Pulsar function. Some of our functions, such as delivery time estimation, will be directly interacting with the customer and driver and need to provide a response in near real time. For these types of functions, all the data access should be limited to low-latency data sources to ensure predictable response times.

There are four data stores within the GottaEat architecture that can be classified as low-latency due to their ability to provide subsecond data access time. These include the Pulsar state store backed by Apache BookKeeper, an in-memory data grid (IMDG) provided by Apache Ignite, a disk-backed cache, and the distributed column store provided by Apache Cassandra. The in-memory data retains all of the data in memory, and thus provides the fastest access times. However, its storage capacity is limited by the amount of RAM available on the machines hosting the Pulsar functions. It is used to pass information between Pulsar functions that are not directly connected via topic, such as two-factor authentication within the device validation use case.

10.2.1 Device validation

When a customer first downloads the GottaEat mobile application from the App Store and installs it on their phone, the customer needs to create an account. The customer chooses an email/password to use for their login credentials and submits them along with the mobile number and device ID used to uniquely identify the device. As you can see from figure 10.2, this information is then stored in the MySQL database to be used to authenticate the user whenever they log in in the future.

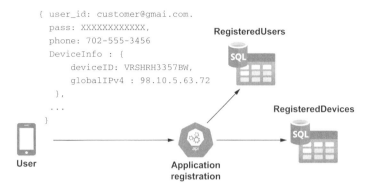

```
{ user_id: customer@gmai.com.
  pass: XXXXXXXXXXXX,
  phone: 702-555-3456
  DeviceInfo : {
      deviceID: VRSHRH3357BW,
      globalIPv4 : 98.10.5.63.72
   },
   ...
  }
```

Figure 10.2   A non-Pulsar microservice handles the application registration use case and stores the provided user credentials and device information in the MySQL database.

When a user logs into the GottaEat application, we will use the information stored in the database to validate the provided credentials and authenticate the device they are using to connect with. Since we recorded the device ID when the user first registered, we can compare the device ID provided when the user logged in with the one on record. This acts like a cookie does for a web browser and allows us to confirm that the user is using a trusted device. As you can see in figure 10.3, after we validate the user's credentials against the values stored in the RegisteredUsers table, we place the user record in the LoggedInUsers topic for further processing by the DeviceValidation function to ensure that the user is using a trusted device.

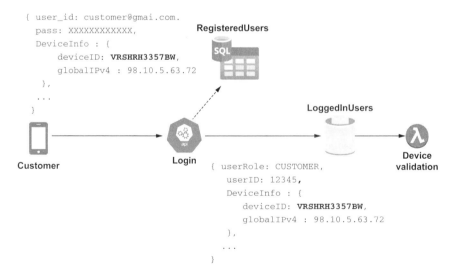

```
{ user_id: customer@gmai.com.
  pass: XXXXXXXXXXXX,
  DeviceInfo : {
      deviceID: VRSHRH3357BW,
      globalIPv4 : 98.10.5.63.72
   },
   ...
  }
```

```
{ userRole: CUSTOMER,
    userID: 12345,
    DeviceInfo : {
      deviceID: VRSHRH3357BW,
      globalIPv4 : 98.10.5.63.72
    },
    ...
  }
```

Figure 10.3   The device ID is provided when the customer logs into the mobile application; we then cross-reference it against known devices that we have previously associated with the user.

This provides an additional level of security and prevents identity thieves from placing fraudulent orders using stolen customer credentials because it also requires the would-be fraudsters to provide the correct device ID in order to place an order. You might be asking yourself: What happens if the customer is simply using a new or different device? This is a perfectly valid scenario that we need to handle for situations where they buy a new cell phone or log into their account from a different device. In such a scenario, we will use SMS-based two-factor authentication in which we send a randomly-generated 5-digit PIN code to the mobile number that the customer provided when they registered and wait for them to respond back with that code. This is a very common technique used to authenticate users of mobile applications.

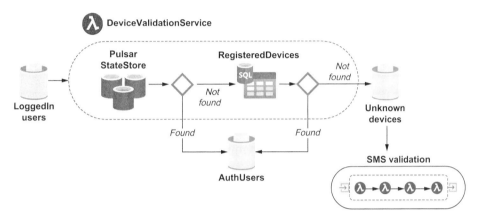

Figure 10.4 Inside the `DeviceValidationService`, we compare the given device ID with the device most recently used by the customer, and if it is the same, we authorize the user. Otherwise, we check to see if it is on the list of known devices for the user and initiate two-factor authentication if necessary.

As you can see in figure 10.4, the device validation process first attempts to retrieve the customer's most recently used device ID from Pulsar's internal state store, which, as you may recall from chapter 4, is a key-value store that can be used by stateful Pulsar functions to retain stateful information. The Pulsar state store uses Apache Book-Keeper for storage to ensure that any information written to it will be persisted to disk and replicated. This ensures that the data will outlive any associated Pulsar function instance that is reading the data.

However, this reliance on BookKeeper for storage comes at a performance cost, since the data has to be written to disk. Therefore, even though the state store provides the same key-value semantics as other data stores, such as the IMDG, it does so at a much higher latency rate. Consequently, it is *not* recommended to use the state store for data that will be read and written frequently. It is better suited for infrequent read/write use cases, such as the device ID, which is only called once per user session.

Listing 10.1 shows the logical flow of the `DeviceValidationService` as it attempts to locate the device ID from two different data sources. The base class contains all of the source code related to connecting to the MySQL database and is also used by the DeviceRegistrationService to update the database if the SMS authentication is successful.

Listing 10.1   The `DeviceValidationService`

```
public class DeviceValidationService extends DeviceServiceBase implements
⇨ Function<ActiveUser, ActiveUser> {

  ...

  @Override
  public ActiveUser process(ActiveUser u, Context ctx) throws Exception {
    boolean mustRegister = false;

    if (StringUtils.isBlank(u.getDevice().getDeviceId())) {            If the user
      mustRegister = true;                                            didn't provide a
    }                                                                  device ID at all

    String prev = getPreviousDeviceId(                                Get the previous
        u.getUser().getRegisteredUserId(), ctx);                     device ID for this user
                                                                      from the state store.

    if (StringUtils.equals(prev, EMPTY_STRING)) {                     The provided device ID matches
      mustRegister = true;                                            the value in the state store.
    } else if (StringUtils.equals(prev, u.getDevice().getDeviceId())) {
      return u;
    } else if (isRegisteredDevice(u.getUser().getRegisteredUserId(),
          u.getDevice().getDeviceId().toString())) {                 See if the device id is in the list
      ByteBuffer value = ByteBuffer.allocate(                         of known devices for the user.
          u.getDevice().getDeviceId().length());
      value.put(u.getDevice().getDeviceId().toString().getBytes());
      ctx.putState("UserDevice-" + u.getDevice().getDeviceId(), value);
    }
                                                                      This is a known device, so update the
                                                                      state store with the provided device ID.
    if (mustRegister) {
      ctx.newOutputMessage(registrationTopic, Schema.AVRO(ActiveUser.class))
        .value(u)
        .sendAsync();              This is an unknown device,
      return null;                 so publish a message in
    } else {                       order to perform SMS
      return u;                    validation.
    }
  }

  private String getPreviousDeviceId(long registeredUserId, Context ctx) {
    ByteBuffer buf = ctx.getState("UserDevice-" + registeredUserId);
    return (buf == null) ? EMPTY_STRING :                            Look up the device ID
        new String(buf.asReadOnlyBuffer().array());                 in the state store using
  }                                                                   the user ID.

  private boolean isRegisteredDevice(long userId, String deviceId) {
    try (Connection con = getDbConnection();
        PreparedStatement ps = con.prepareStatement( "select count(*) "
        + "from RegisteredDevice where user_id = ? "
        + " AND device_id = ?")) {
      ps.setLong(1, userId);
```

There is no previous device ID for this user.

```
      ps.setNString(2, deviceId);
      ResultSet rs = ps.executeQuery();       Return true if the
      if (rs != null && rs.next()) {          provided device ID is
        return (rs.getInt(1) > 0);   <──      associated with the user.
      }
    } catch (ClassNotFoundException | SQLException e) {
      // Ignore these
    }
    return false;
  }
...
}
```

If the device cannot be associated with the current user, a message will be published to the UnknownDevices topic that is used to feed the SMS validation process. As you may have noticed in figure 10.4, the SMS validation process is comprised of a sequence of Pulsar functions that must coordinate with one another to perform the two-factor authentication.

The first Pulsar function within the SMS validation process reads messages off the UnknownDevices topic and uses the registered user ID to retrieve the mobile number we will be sending the SMS validation code to. This is a very straightforward data access pattern in which we use the primary key to retrieve information from a relational database and forward it to another function. While this approach is typically considered an anti-pattern because it violates the encapsulation principle I mentioned earlier, I decided to break it out into its own function for the two reasons. The first is reusability of the code itself, as there are multiple use cases in which we will need to retrieve all of

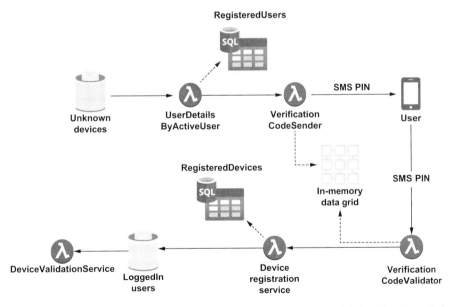

Figure 10.5   The SMS validation process is performed by a collection of Pulsar Functions that send a 5-digit code to the user's registered mobile number and validate the code sent back from the user.

the information about a particular user, and I want to have that logic contained within a single class, rather than spread across multiple functions, so it is easy to maintain. The second reason is that we will need some of this information later on within the Device-Registration service, so I decided to pass all of the information along rather than perform the same database query twice to reduce processing latency.

As you can see from the next listing, the UserDetailsByActiveUser function provides the registered user ID to the UserDetailsLookup class, which performs the database query to retrieve the data and return a UserDetails object.

Listing 10.2   The `UserDetailsByActiveUser` function

```
public class UserDetailsByActiveUser implements       Create an instance of the
   Function<ActiveUser, UserDetails> {               class that performs the
                                                      database lookup.
  private UserDetailsLookup lookupService = new UserDetailsLookup();   ◁

  @Override
  public UserDetails process(ActiveUser input, Context ctx) throws Exception{
    return lookupService.process(
      input.getUser().getRegisteredUserId(),   ◁        Pass in the primary key
      ctx);   ◁                                          field used in the lookup.
  }                     Pass in the context object so that lookup class
}                       can access the database credentials, etc.
```

This pattern of extracting just the primary key from the incoming message and passing it to a different class that performs the lookup can be reused for any use case, and in the case of the GottaEat application, it is used by a different Pulsar function flow to retrieve the user information for a given food order, as shown in the following listing.

Listing 10.3   The `UserDetailsByFoodOrder` function

```
public class UserDetailsByFoodOrder implements       Create an instance of the
   Function<FoodOrder, UserDetails> {               class that performs the
                                                     database lookup.
  private UserDetailsLookup lookupService = new UserDetailsLookup();   ◁

  @Override
  public UserDetails process(FoodOrder order, Context ctx) throws Exception {
    return lookupService.process(
      order.getMeta().getCustomerId(),   ◁        Pass in the primary key
      ctx);   ◁                                   field used in the lookup.
  }                Pass in the context object so that lookup class
}                  can access the database credentials, etc.
```

The underlying lookup class used to provide the information is shown in listing 10.4 and encapsulates the logic required to query the database tables to retrieve all of the information. This data access pattern can be used to retrieve data from any relational database table that you need to access from your Pulsar functions.

Listing 10.4 The `UserDetailsLookup` function

```
public class UserDetailsLookup implements Function<Long, UserDetails> {

  . . .
  private Connection con;
  private PreparedStatement stmt;
  private String dbUrl, dbUser, dbPass, dbDriverClass;

  @Override
  public UserDetails process(Long customerId, Context ctx) throws Exception {

    if (!isInitalized()) {                                    ◁——
      dbUrl = (String) ctx.getUserConfigValue(DB_URL_KEY);
      dbDriverClass = (String) ctx.getUserConfigValue(DB_DRIVER_KEY);
      dbUser = (String) ctx.getSecret(DB_USER_KEY);           Ensure we have all the
      dbPass = (String) ctx.getSecret(DB_PASS_KEY);           required properties from
    }                                                         the user context object.

    return getUserDetails(customerId);
  }

  private UserDetails getUserDetails(Long customerId) {
    UserDetails details = null;

    try (Connection con = getDbConnection();
         PreparedStatement ps = con.prepareStatement("select ru.user_id,
           + " ru.first_name, ru.last_name, ru.email, "
           + "a.address, a.postal_code, a.phone, a.district,"
           + "c.city, c2.country from GottaEat.RegisteredUser ru "
           + "join GottaEat.Address a on a.address_id = c.address_id "
           + "join GottaEat.City c on a.city_id = c.city_id "
           + "join GottaEat.Country c2 on c.country_id = c2.country_id "
           + "where ru.user_id = ?");) {

      ps.setLong(1, customerId);                   ◁——    Use the user ID in the first
                                                          parameter in the prepared
      try (ResultSet rs = ps.executeQuery()) {            statement.
        if (rs != null && rs.next()) {
          details = UserDetails.newBuilder()
        .setEmail(rs.getString("ru.email"))
        .setFirstName(rs.getString("ru.first_name"))
        .setLastName(rs.getString("ru.last_name"))
        .setPhoneNumber(rs.getString("a.phone"))
        .setUserId(rs.getInt("ru.user_id"))
        .build();                ◁——
        }                                          Map the relational data to
      } catch (Exception ex) {                     the UserDetails object.
        // Ignore
      }
    } catch (Exception ex) {
      // Ignore
    }

    return details;
```

Perform the lookup for the given user ID.

```
    }

        . . .

}
```

The UserDetailsByActiveUser function passes the UserDetails to the Verification-CodeSender function, which in turn sends the validation code to the customer and records the associated transaction ID in the IMDG. This transaction ID is required by the VerificationCodeValidator function to validate the PIN sent back by the user; however, as you can see from figure 10.5, there isn't an intermediate Pulsar topic between the VerificationCodeSender function and the VerificationCodeValidator, so we cannot pass this information inside a message. Instead we have to rely on this external data store to pass along this information.

The IMDG is perfect for this task since the information is short lived and does not need to be retained for longer than the time the code is valid. If the PIN sent back by the user is valid, the next function will add the newly authenticated device to the RegisterdDevices table for future reference. Finally, the user will be sent back to the LoggedInUser topic so that the device ID can by updated in the state store.

Since the VerificationCodeSender and VerificationCodeValidator functions use the IMDG to communicate with one another, I decided to have them share a common base class, which provides connectivity to the shared cache, as shown in the following listing.

Listing 10.5   The VerificationCodeBase

```
public class VerificationCodeBase {                    The hostname of the third-party service
                                                       used to perform the SMS verification
  protected static final String API_HOST = "sms-verify-api.com";    ◁──────────┘

  protected IgniteClient client;              ◁──────┤ Apache Ignite thin client
  protected ClientCache<Long, String> cache;  ◁──┐
  protected String apiKey;                        │  Apache Ignite cache
  protected String datagridUrl;                   │  used to store the data
  protected String cacheName;     ◁───────┐
                                          │  The name of the Cache both
  protected boolean isInitalized() {      │  services will be accessing
    return StringUtils.isNotBlank(apiKey);
  }

  protected ClientCache<Long, String> getCache() {
    if (cache == null) {
     cache = getClient().getOrCreateCache(cacheName);
   }
    return cache;
  }

  protected IgniteClient getClient() {
    if (client == null) {
     ClientConfiguration cfg =
```

```
        new ClientConfiguration().setAddresses(datagridUrl);
        client = Ignition.startClient(cfg);                    ⟵——————  Connect the thin client to
    }                                                                    the in-memory data grid.
    return client;
  }
}
```

The VerificationCodeSender uses the mobile phone number from the UserDetails object provided by the UserDetailsByActiveUser function to call the third-party SMS validation service, as shown in the following listing.

Listing 10.6 The `VerificationCodeSender` function

**URL of the third-party service used
to send the SMS verification code**

```
public class VerificationCodeSender extends VerificationCodeBase
  implements Function<ActiveUser, Void> {

private static final String BASE_URL = "https://" + RAPID_API_HOST +
 ⤳  ➡ "/send-verification-code";
    private static final String REQUEST_ID_HEADER = "x-amzn-requestid";

    @Override
    public Void process(ActiveUser input, Context ctx) throws Exception {
      if (!isInitalized()) {                                    ⟵
       apiKey = (String) ctx.getUserConfigValue(API_KEY);
       datagridUrl = ctx.getUserConfigValue(DATAGRID_KEY).toString();
       cacheName = ctx.getUserConfigValue(CACHENAME_KEY).toString();
      }                                                 Ensure we have all the
                                                        required properties from
      OkHttpClient client = new OkHttpClient();         the user context object.
      Request request = new Request.Builder()
        .url(BASE_URL + "?phoneNumber=" + toE164FormattedNumber(
            input.getDetails().getPhoneNumber().toString())
            + "&brand=GottaEat")
      .post(EMPTY_BODY)                                          Send the request
      .addHeader("x-rapidapi-key", apiKey)                       object to the third-
      .addHeader("x-rapidapi-host", RAPID_API_HOST)              party service.
      .build();

      Response response = client.newCall(request).execute();  ⟵——  Retrieve the
      if (response.isSuccessful()) {                                request ID from
        String msg = response.message();                           the response
        String requestID = response.header(REQUEST_ID_HEADER);  ⟵  object.
        if (StringUtils.isNotBlank(requestID)) {                 ⟵
          getCache().put(input.getUser().getRegisteredUserId(), requestID);
        }                                                 If we have a request ID,
      }                                                   store it in the IMDG.
      return null;
    }
}
```

Build the HTTP request object for the third-party service.

Whether the request was successful

If the HTTP call is successful, the third-party service provides a unique request ID value in its response message that can be used by the VerificationCodeValidator function to validate the response sent back by the user. As you can see in listing 10.6, we store this request ID in the IMDG using the user ID as the key. Later, when the user responds with a PIN value, we can then use this value to authenticate the user, as shown in the following listing.

Listing 10.7   The `VerificationCodeValidator` function

Takes in an SMS verification
response object

```
public class VerificationCodeValidator extends VerificationCodeBase
   implements Function<SMSVerificationResponse, Void> {

  public static final String VALIDATED_TOPIC_KEY = "";
  private static final String BASE_URL = "https://" + RAPID_API_HOST
     + "/check-verification-code";
  private String valDeviceTopic;

  @Override
  public Void process(SMSVerificationResponse input, Context ctx)
    throws Exception {

    if (!isInitalized()) {
     apiKey = (String) ctx.getUserConfigValue(API_KEY).orElse(null);
     valDeviceTopic = ctx.getUserConfigValue(VALIDATED_TOPIC_KEY).toString();
    }

    String requestID = getCache().get(input.getRegisteredUserId());

    if (requestID == null) {
      return null;
    }

  OkHttpClient client = new OkHttpClient();
  Request request = new Request.Builder()
      .url(BASE_URL + "?request_id=" + requestID + "&code="
          + input.getResponseCode())
      .post(EMPTY_BODY)
      .addHeader("x-rapidapi-key", apiKey)
      .addHeader("x-rapidapi-host", RAPID_API_HOST)
      .build();

    Response response = client.newCall(request).execute();
    if (response.isSuccessful()) {
      ctx.newOutputMessage(valDeviceTopic,
          Schema.AVRO(SMSVerificationResponse.class))
       .value(input)
       .sendAsync();
    }
  return null;
  }
}
```

Annotations:
- URL of the third-party service used to perform the SMS verification
- Pulsar topic to publish validated device info to
- Get the request ID from the IMDG.
- If there was no request ID found for the user, then we are done.
- Construct the HTTP request to the third-party service.
- If the user responded with the correct PIN, then the device was validated.
- Publish a new message to the validated device topic.

This flow between the two Functions involved in the SMS validation process demonstrates how to exchange information between Pulsar functions that are not connected by an intermediate topic. However, the biggest limitation to this approach is the amount of data that can be retained inside the memory of the data grid itself. For larger datasets that need to be shared across Pulsar functions, a disk-backed cache is a better solution.

10.2.2 Driver location data

Every 30 seconds, a location message is sent from the driver's mobile application to a Pulsar topic. This driver location data is one of the most versatile and critical datasets for GottaEat. Not only does this information need to be stored in the data lake for training the machine learning models, but it is also useful for several real-time use cases, such as in-route travel time estimation to a pickup or drop-off location, providing driving directions, or allowing the customer to track the location of their order when it is in route to them, just to name a few.

The GottaEat mobile application uses the location services provided by the phone's operating system to determine the latitude and longitude of the driver's current location. This information is enriched with the current timestamp and the driver's ID before it is published to the `DriverLocation` topic. The driver location information will be consumed in a variety of ways, which in turn dictates how the data should be stored, enriched, and sorted. One of the ways in which the location data will be accessed is directly by driver ID when we want to find the most recent location of a given driver.

As you can see in figure 10.6, the `LocationTrackingService` consumes these messages and uses them to update the driver location cache, which is a global cache that stores all of the location updates as key/value pairs, where the key is the driver ID and

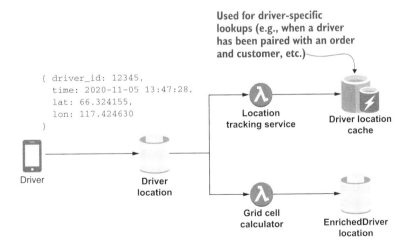

Figure 10.6 Each driver periodically sends their location information to the `DriverLocation` topic. This information is then processed by multiple Pulsar functions before being persisted to a data store.

the value is the location data. I have decided to store this information in a disk-backed cache so it is accessible to any Pulsar Function that needs it. Unlike an IMDG, a disk-backed cache will spill any data that it cannot hold in memory to local disk for storage, whereas an IMDG will silently drop the data. Given the anticipated volume of driver location data we are expecting to have once the company is up and running, a disk-backed cache is the best choice for storing this time-critical information, while ensuring that none of it is lost.

For simplicity's sake, we have decided to use the same underlying technology (Apache Ignite) to provide both the IMDG and the disk-backed cache for GottaEat. Not only does this decision reduce the number of APIs that our developers need to learn and use, but it also simplifies life for the DevOps team as well because they only need to deploy and monitor two different clusters running the same software, as shown in figure 10.7. The only difference between the two clusters is the value of a single Boolean configuration setting called `persistenceEnabled` that enables the storage of cache data to disk, which allows it to store more data.

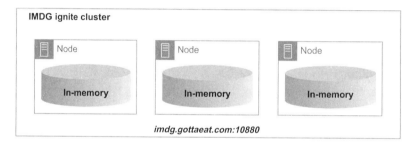

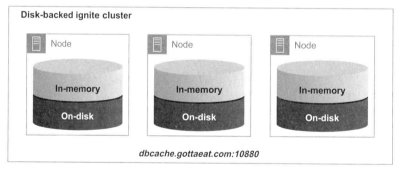

Figure 10.7   Inside the GottaEat enterprise architecture there are two different clusters running Apache Ignite—one that is configured to persist cache data to disk and one that isn't.

As you can see in the code in listing 10.8, the data access for both the IMDG and disk-backed cache use the same API (i.e., you read and write values using a single key). The difference is in the expected data lookup time when retrieving the data. For an IMDG, all of the data is guaranteed to be in memory, and thus will provide a consistently fast lookup time. However, the trade-off is that the data is not guaranteed to be available when you attempt to read it.

In contrast, a disk-backed cache will retain only the most recent data in memory and will store a majority of its data on disk as the data volume grows. Given that a significant amount of the data resides on disk, the overall lookup time for a disk-backed cache will be orders of magnitude slower. Therefore, it is best to use this type of data store when data availability is more important than lookup times.

Listing 10.8 The `LocationTrackingService`

```java
public class LocationTrackingService implements
    Function<ActiveUser, ActiveUser> {

  private IgniteClient client;
  private ClientCache<Long, LatLon> cache;

  private String datagridUrl;
  private String locationCacheName;

  @Override
  public ActiveUser process(ActiveUser input, Context ctx) throws Exception {

    if (!initalized()) {
      datagridUrl = ctx.getUserConfigValue(DATAGRID_KEY).toString();
      locationCacheName = ctx.getUserConfigValue(CACHENAME_KEY).toString();
    }

    getCache().put(
      input.getUser().getRegisteredUserId(),      ⟵—— Use the userID as the key.
      input.getLocation());        ⟵┐
                                      │ Add the location to the disk-backed cache.
    return input;
  }

  private ClientCache<Long, LatLon> getCache() {
    if (cache == null) {                                             Creates the
      cache = getClient().getOrCreateCache(locationCacheName);  ⟵┘  location cache
    }
    return cache;
  }

  private IgniteClient getClient() {   ⟵—— Using an Apache Ignite client
    if (client == null) {
      ClientConfiguration cfg =
          new ClientConfiguration().setAddresses(datagridUrl);
      client = Ignition.startClient(cfg);
    }
    return client;
  }
}
```

The location information stored in the disk-backed cache can then be used to determine the current location of the specific driver assigned to the customer's order, and is then sent to the mapping software on the customer's phone so they can track the status of their order visually, as shown in figure 10.8. Another use of the driver location data is determining which drivers are best suited to be assigned an order. One of the factors in making this determination is the driver's proximity to the customer and/or restaurant that is fulfilling the order. While it is theoretically possible, it would be too time-consuming to calculate the distance between every driver and the delivery location each time an order is placed.

Therefore, we need a way to immediately identify drivers who are close to an order in near-real-time. One way to do this is to divide the map into smaller logical hexagonal areas, known as *cells*, as shown in figure 10.9, and then group the drivers together based on which of these cells they are currently located in. This way, when an order comes in, all we need to do is determine which cell the order is in, and then look first for drivers that are currently in that cell. If no drivers are found, we can expand our search to adjacent cells. By presorting the drivers in this manner, we are able to perform a much more efficient search.

Figure 10.8 The driver location data is used to update the map display on the customer's mobile phone so they can see the driver's current location along with an estimated delivery time.

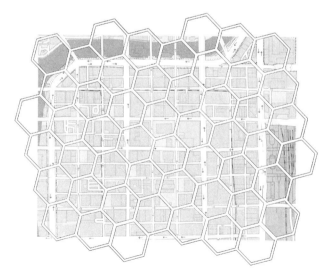

Figure 10.9 We use a global grid system of hexagonal areas that is overlaid onto a two-dimensional map. Each latitude/longitude pair maps to exactly one cell on the grid. Drivers are then bucketed together based on the hexagons they are currently located in.

The other Pulsar function in figure 10.6 is the `GridCellCalculator`, which uses the H3 open source project (https://github.com/uber/h3-java) developed by Uber to determine which cell the driver is currently located in and appends the corresponding cell ID to the location data before publishing it to the `EnrichedDriverLocation` topic for further processing. I left the code for that function out of this chapter, but you can find it in the GitHub repo associated with this book if you want more details.

As you can see from figure 10.10, there is a global collection of disk-backed caches (one for each cell ID) used to retain the location data for drivers within a given cell ID. Pre-sorting the drivers in this manner allows us to narrow our search to only the few cells we are interested in and ignore all the rest. In addition to speeding up driver assignment decisions, bucketing the drivers together by cell ID enables us to analyze geographic information to set dynamic prices and make other decisions on a city-wide level, such as surge pricing and incentivizing our drivers to move into cells without sufficient drivers to accommodate the order volume, etc.

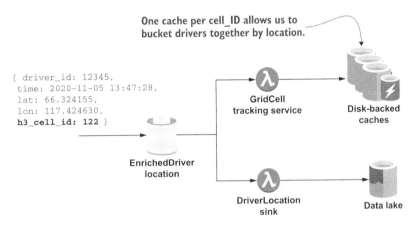

Figure 10.10 Messages inside the `EnrichedDriverLocation` topic have been enriched with the H3 cell ID, which is then used to group drivers together.

As you can see from the code in listing 10.9, the `GridCellTrackingService` uses the cell ID from each incoming message to determine which cache to publish the location data into. The disk-backed caches use the following naming convention: "drivers-cell-XXX," where the XXX is the H3 cell ID. Therefore, when we receive a message with a cell ID of 122, we place it inside the `drivers-cell-122` cache.

Listing 10.9 The `GridCellTrackingService`

```
import com.gottaeat.domain.driver.DriverGridLocation;
import com.gottaeat.domain.geography.LatLon;

public class GridTrackingService
    implements Function<DriverGridLocation, Void> {
```

```
    static final String DATAGRID_KEY = "datagridUrl";

    private IgniteClient client;
    private String datagridUrl;

    @Override
    public Void process(DriverGridLocation in, Context ctx) throws Exception {
      if (!initalized()) {
        datagridUrl = ctx.getUserConfigValue(DATAGRID_KEY).toString();
      }
```

Get the cache for the given cell ID we calculated.

```
      getCache(input.getCellId())
        .put(input.getDriverLocation().getDriverId(),
          input.getDriverLocation().getLocation());
        return null;
    }
```

Use the userID as the key.

Add the location to the disk-backed cache.

```
    private ClientCache<Long, LatLon> getCache(int cellID) {
      return getClient().getOrCreateCache("drivers-cell-" + cellID);
    }
```

Return or create the cache for the specified cell ID.

```
    private IgniteClient getClient() {
      if (client == null) {
        ClientConfiguration cfg =
          new ClientConfiguration().setAddresses(datagridUrl);
        client = Ignition.startClient(cfg);
      }
      return client;
    }

    private boolean initalized() {
      return StringUtils.isNotBlank(datagridUrl);
    }
}
```

The other consumer of the enriched location messages is a Pulsar IO connector named DriverLocationSink that batches up the messages and writes them into the data lake. In this particular case, the final destination of the sink is the HDFS filesystem, which allows other teams within the organization to perform analyses on the data using various computing engines, such as Hive, Storm, or Spark.

Since the incoming data is of higher value to our delivery time estimation data models, the sink can be configured to write the data to a special directory inside HDFS. This allows us to pre-filter the most-recent data and group it together for faster processing by the process that uses this data to precompute data for the delivery time feature vector in the Cassandra database.

Summary

- Pulsar's internal state store provides a convenient location for storing infrequently accessed data without having to rely on an external system.
- You can access a variety of external data sources from inside Pulsar functions, including in-memory data grids, disk-backed caches, relational databases, and many others.
- Consider the latency and data storage capabilities when determining the data storage system you want use. Lower-latency systems are typically better for stream processing systems.

11
Machine learning in Pulsar

This chapter covers

- Exploring how Pulsar Functions can be used to provide near real-time machine learning
- Developing and maintaining the collection of inputs required by the machine learning model to provide a prediction
- Executing any PMML-supported model inside a Pulsar function
- Executing non-PMML models inside a Pulsar function

One of the primary goals of machine learning is the extraction of actionable insights from raw data. Having insights that are actionable means you can use them to make strategic, data-driven decisions that result in a positive outcome for your business and customers. For instance, every time a customer places an order on the GottaEat application, we want to be able to provide the customer with an accurate estimated delivery time. To accomplish this, we would need to develop a machine learning model that predicts the delivery time of any given order based on a number of factors that allow us to make a more accurate decision.

Typically, these actionable insights are generated by machine learning (ML) models that have been developed and trained to take in a predefined set of inputs, known as a *feature vector*, and use that information to make predictions, such as when an order will arrive at the customer's location. It is the responsibility of the data science team to develop and train these models, including the feature vector definitions. Since this is a book about Apache Pulsar and not data science, I will focus primarily on the deployment of these ML models inside the Pulsar Functions framework rather than the development and training of the models themselves.

11.1 Deploying ML models

ML models are developed in a variety of languages and toolkits, each with their own respective strengths and weaknesses. Regardless of how these ML models are developed and trained, they must eventually be deployed to a production environment to provide real business value. At a high level, there are two execution modes for ML models that are deployed to production: a *batch-processing mode* and a near *real-time processing mode*.

11.1.1 Batch processing

As the name suggests, executing a model in batch processing mode refers to the process where you feed a large batch of data into your model to produce multiple predictions at the same time rather than on a case-by-case basis. These batches of predictions can then be cached and reused as needed.

One such example is marketing emails from an e-commerce site that provides a list of product recommendations based on your purchase history with the retailer and what similar customers have purchased. Since these recommendations are based on a historical and slow-changing dataset (i.e., your purchase history) they can be generated at any time. Typically, these marketing emails are generated once per day and delivered to customers based on the customers' local time zones. Since these recommendations are generated for all customers who haven't opted out, this is a great candidate for batch processing with the ML model. However, if your recommendations need to factor in the users' most recent activities, such as the current contents of their shopping cart, then you cannot execute the ML model in batch mode because that data won't be available. In such a scenario, you will want to deploy your ML model in the near real-time processing mode.

11.1.2 Near real-time

Utilizing a ML model to generate predictions on a case-by-case basis using data that is only available in the incoming payload is commonly referred to as near real-time processing. This type of processing is considerably more complex than batch processing, primarily due to the latency constraints placed on systems that need to serve the predictions.

A perfect candidate for near real-time deployment is the estimated time-to-delivery component of the GottaEat food delivery service that provides an estimate of when the food will be delivered for every newly placed food order. Not only does the feature vector of this ML model depend on data provided as part of the order (i.e., the delivery address), but it also needs to generate the estimate within a few hundred milliseconds. In short, when deciding which of these execution modes to use for your ML models you should consider the following factors:

- The availability of all the data required in the model's feature vector and where that data is stored. Whether all the data you need to execute the model is readily available in the system or if some of it is provided in the request itself.

- How quickly the accuracy of the recommendations degrades over time. Can you precompute the recommendation and reuse it for a specific period?

- How quickly you can retrieve all the data used in the feature vector. Is it stored in memory or on non-real-time systems, such as HDFS, traditional databases, and so on.

As you might have guessed, Pulsar functions are great candidates for deploying your ML models in near real-time mode for a multitude of reasons. First and foremost, they get executed immediately when a request comes in and have direct access to the data provided as part of the request, which eliminates any processing and data lookup latency. Secondly, as we saw in the previous chapter, you can retrieve data from a variety of external data sources to populate the feature vector with any necessary data that exists outside of the request itself. Finally, and most importantly, is the flexibility Pulsar Functions provides when it comes to deployment options. The ability to write your functions in Java, Python, or Go allows your data science team to develop a model in the language/framework of their choice and still deploy it inside a Pulsar function using third-party libraries that are bundled with the function to execute the model at runtime.

11.2 *Near real-time model deployment*

Because there are so many ML frameworks, and everything is evolving so quickly, I have decided to present a generic solution that provides all the essential elements required to deploy an ML model within a Pulsar Function. Pulsar Function's broad programming language support enables you to deploy ML models from a variety of frameworks, provided there is a third-party library that supports the execution of those models. For instance, the existence of a Java library for TensorFlow allows you to deploy and execute any ML models that were developed using the TensorFlow toolkit. Similarly, if your ML model relies on the pandas library written in Python, you can easily write a Python-based Pulsar function that includes the pandas library. Regardless of the language of choice, the deployment of a near real-time model within a Pulsar function follows the same high-level pattern.

As you can see from figure 11.1, there is a sequence of one or more Pulsar functions that are responsible for the collection of data required by the feature vector of the model from external data sources based on the original message. This acts as a sort of data enrichment pipeline that augments the incoming data from the message with additional data elements that are needed by the ML model. In the delivery time estimation example, we might only be given the ID of the restaurant that is preparing the order. This pipeline would then be responsible for retrieving the geographical location of that restaurant so it can be given to the model.

Once this data is collected, it is fed into the Pulsar function that will invoke the ML model using a third-party library to execute the model with the proper framework (e.g., TensorFlow, etc.). It is worth noting that the ML model itself is retrieved from

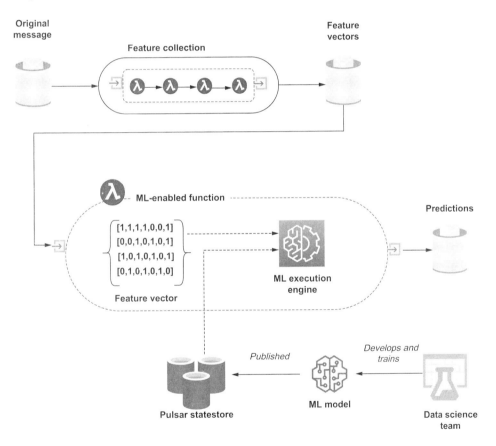

Figure 11.1 The original message that necessitates the need for a prediction is enriched with a sequence of ancillary Pulsar functions to produce a feature vector suited for the ML model. The ML-enabled function can then further populate the feature vector with data from other low-latency data sources before sending it along with the ML model it retrieves from Pulsar's internal state store to the ML execution engine for processing.

the Pulsar function context object, which allows us to deploy the model independently of the function itself. This decoupling of the model from the packaged and deployed Pulsar function provides us the opportunity to dynamically adjust our models on the fly, and, more importantly, allows us to change models based on external factors and conditions.

For example, we might require an entirely different delivery time estimation model for high-volume periods, such as lunch and dinner, than for non-peak hours. An external process would then be used to rotate in the proper model for the current time. In fact, the data science team could train the same model with time-specific datasets to produce different models based on the time of day or day of the week. For instance, training the time-estimation model with data from only 4–5 p.m. could produce a model for that specific timeframe.

The ML-enabled function then sends the completed feature vector along with the correct version of the ML model that it retrieved from Pulsar's internal state store to the ML execution engine (e.g., a third-party library), which produces both a prediction and an associated level of confidence in the prediction. For instance, the engine might produce a prediction of an ETA of seven minutes with an 84% degree of confidence. This information can then be used to provide an estimated time of arrival to the customer that placed the order.

While your Pulsar function might differ based on the ML framework you are using, the general outline remains the same. First, get the ML model from Pulsar's state store, and keep a copy in memory. Next, take the incoming precomputed features from the incoming message and map them to the expected input fields of the feature vector. Compute and/or retrieve any additional features that weren't already precomputed, and then call the ML library for your programming language to execute the model with the given dataset and publish the result.

11.3 Feature vectors

In ML, the term *feature* refers to an individual numeric or symbolic property that represents a unique aspect of an object. These features are often combined into an *n*-dimensional vector of numerical features, or a *feature vector*, that is then used as an input to a predictive model.

Every feature in the feature vector represents an individual piece of data that is used to generate the prediction. Consider the estimated time-to-delivery feature of the GottaEat food delivery service. Every time a user orders food from a restaurant, an ML model estimates when the food will be delivered. Features for the model include information from the request (e.g., the time of day or delivery location), historical features (e.g., the average meal prep time for the last seven days), and near real-time calculated features (e.g., the average meal prep time for the last hour). These features are then fed into the ML model to produce a prediction, as shown in figure 11.2. Many algorithms in ML require a numerical representation of features, since such representations facilitate processing and statistical analysis, such as linear regression.

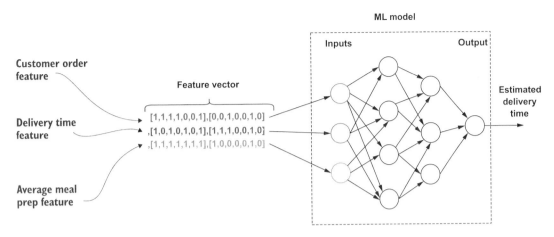

Figure 11.2   **The delivery time estimation model requires a feature vector comprised of features from multiple sources. Each feature is an array of numerical values between 0 and 1.**

Therefore, it is common that each feature is represented as a numerical value, as it makes them useful across various ML algorithms.

11.3.1 *Feature stores*

Models intended for deployment in near real-time mode have stringent latency requirements and cannot reliably be expected to compute features that require access to traditional data stores in a performant manner. You cannot consistently achieve sub-second query response times with a traditional relational database.

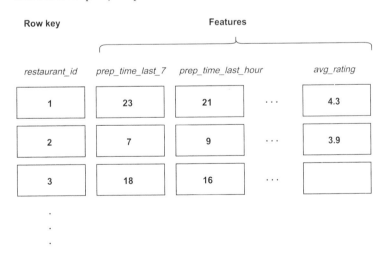

Figure 11.3   **The restaurant feature store uses the unique `restaurant_id` field as the row key, and each row contains several features for each restaurant. Some of the features are specific to the delivery time estimation model, while others are not.**

Therefore, it is necessary to establish ancillary processes to precompute and index these necessary model features. Once computed, these features should be stored in a low-latency datastore, known as a *feature store*, where they can be accessed quickly at prediction time, as shown in figure 11.3.

As I mentioned earlier, our feature store is kept inside a low-latency column-centric database, such as Apache Cassandra, which is designed to permit a large number of columns per row without incurring a performance penalty during the data retrieval process. This allows us to store features required by various ML models in the same table (e.g., delivery time estimation fields, such as average prep time, can be stored alongside features used by the restaurant recommendation model, such as the average customer rating). Consequently, we don't need to maintain a separate table for each model we want to use (`restaurant_time_delivery_features`, etc.). Not only does this simplify the management of the feature store database, but it also promotes the usage of features across ML models.

In most organizations, the design of the tables within the feature store falls squarely on the data science team, since they are the primary consumers of the feature store. Therefore, you will often only be provided the ML model along with a list of the features it requires as input when your company is ready to roll out the model to production.

11.3.2 *Feature calculation*

Typically, features are associated with an entity type (restaurant, driver, customer, etc.) because each feature represents a "has a(n)" relationship with each particular entity—for instance, a restaurant has an average meal preparation time of 23 minutes, or a driver has an average customer review of 4.3 stars. The feature store is then populated via an ancillary process that precomputes the various features, such as the average meal prep time for the last seven days for every restaurant or the average delivery time in the city for the last hour.

These processes need to be scheduled to run periodically to cache the results in the feature store and ensure that these features can be retrieved with sub-second response times when the order arrives. A batch-oriented processing engine is best suited for performing the pre-calculation of the features, as it can process a large volume of data efficiently. For instance, a distributed query engine, such as Apache Hive or Spark, can execute multiple concurrent queries against a large dataset stored on HDFS, using standard SQL syntax, as shown in figure 11.4. These jobs can asynchronously compute the average meal prep time for all restaurants over a specific period of time and can be scheduled to run hourly to keep these features up to date.

As you can see in figure 11.4, a scheduled job can kick off multiple concurrent tasks to complete the work in a timely manner. For example, the scheduled job could first query the restaurant table itself to determine the exact number of restaurant IDs, and then split the work by providing each instance of the restaurant feature calculation job with a subset of restaurant IDs. This divide-and-conquer strategy will speed up the process considerably, allowing you to complete the work in a timely manner.

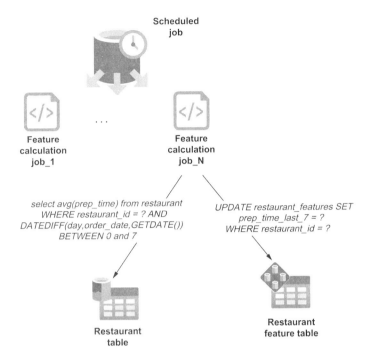

Figure 11.4 Feature calculation jobs will need to run periodically to update the features with new values based on the most recent data. A batch processing engine, such as Apache Hive or Spark, allows you to process many of these jobs in parallel.

It is also important that you coordinate with the proper team(s) to develop, deploy, and monitor these feature calculation jobs, as they are now business-critical applications that need to work continuously, or else the predictions made by your ML models will degrade if the feature data is not updated in a timely manner. Using stale data in your ML models will result in inaccurate predictions, which can lead to poor business outcomes and dissatisfied customers.

11.4 Delivery time estimation

Now that we have sufficiently covered the background and theory, it is time to see how to deploy an ML model that has been developed and trained by the data science team at GottaEat. A perfect candidate would be the delivery time estimation ML model we have been discussing throughout the chapter. As with any ML model that needs to be deployed to production, the data science team is responsible for providing us with a copy of the trained model to be used.

11.4.1 ML model export

Just like most data science teams, the data science team at GottaEat uses a variety of languages and frameworks to develop their ML models. One of the biggest challenges is finding a single execution framework that supports the models developed in different languages.

Fortunately, there several projects seeking to standardize ML model formats to support separate languages for model training and deployment. Projects such as the Predictive Model Markup Language (PMML) allow data scientists and engineers to export ML models developed from a variety of languages into a language-neutral XML format.

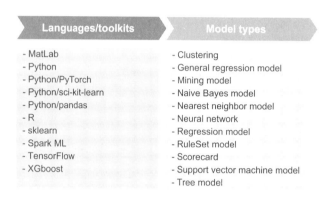

Languages/toolkits	Model types
- MatLab	- Clustering
- Python	- General regression model
- Python/PyTorch	- Mining model
- Python/sci-kit-learn	- Naive Bayes model
- Python/pandas	- Nearest neighbor model
- R	- Neural network
- sklearn	- Regression model
- Spark ML	- RuleSet model
- TensorFlow	- Scorecard
- XGboost	- Support vector machine model
	- Tree model

Figure 11.5   A list of programming languages, toolkits, and ML model types supported by the PMML. Any supported models developed in these languages can be exported to PMML and executed inside a Pulsar function.

As you can see from figure 11.5, the PMML format can be used to represent models developed in a variety of ML languages. Consequently, this approach can be used on any of the supported model types developed in one of the supported languages and/or frameworks.

In the case of the delivery time estimation model, the data science team used the R programming language to develop and train this model. However, since there isn't direct support for running R code inside Pulsar Functions, the data science team must first translate their R-based ML model into the PMML format, which can easily be accomplished using the r2pmml toolkit, as shown in the following listing.

Listing 11.1   Exporting an R-based model to PMML

Finalize the development of the ML model.

```
// Model development code

dte <-(distance ~ ., data = df)

library(r2pmml)
r2pmml(dte, "delivery-time-estimation.pmml");
```

Import the library that translates the R model into PMML.

Perform the translation from R to PMML.

The r2pmml library does a direct translation of the R-based model object into the PMML format and saves it to a local file named delivery-time-estimation.pmml. The PMML file format specifies the data fields to use for the model, the type of calculation to perform (regression), and the structure of the model. In this case, the structure of the model is a set of coefficients, which is defined as shown in the following listing. We now have a model specification that we are ready to productize and apply to our production data set to generate delivery time predictions.

Listing 11.2 The delivery time estimation model in PMML format

```
<?xml version="1.0" encoding="UTF-8" standalone="yes"?>
<PMML version="4.2" xmlns="http://www.dmg.org/PMML-4_2">
    <Header description="deliver time estimation">
        <Application name="R" version="4.0.3"/>
        <Timestamp>2021-01-18T15:37:26</Timestamp>
    </Header>
    <DataDictionary numberOfFields="4">
        <DataField name="distance" optype="continuous" dataType="double"/>
        <DataField name="prep_last_hour" optype="continuous"
          dataType="double"/>
        <DataField name="prep_last_7" optype="continuous" dataType="double"/>
            ...
    </DataDictionary>
    <RegressionModel functionName="regression">
      <MiningSchema>
        <MiningField name="distance"/>
            ...
      </MiningSchema>
      ...
      <NumericPredicitor name="travelTime" coefficient="7.6683E-4"/>
      <NumericPredicitor name="avgPreptime" coefficient="-2.0459"/>
      <NumericPredicitor name="avgDeliveryTime" coefficient="9.4778E-5"/>
            ..
  </RegressionModel>
</PMML>
```

Once the trained model has been exported to PMML, a copy of it should be published to the Pulsar state store so the Pulsar Function can access it at runtime. This can be accomplished by using the `pulsar-admin putstate` command, as shown in listing 11.3, which uploads the given file to a specified namespace inside Pulsar's state store. It is critically important that the namespace be the same as the one you will use to deploy the Pulsar function that will be using the model in order for it to have read access to the PMML file.

Listing 11.3 Upload machine learning model to Pulsar's state store

```
Using the pulsar-admin CLI
tool to upload the PMML file
 ⤷ ./bin/pulsar-admin functions putstate \
    --name MyMLEnabledFunction \
    --namespace MyNamespace \        You need to specify the correct tenant,
    --tenant MyTenant \        ◄────┘ namespace, and function name.
    --state "{\"key\":\"ML-Model\",
         \"byteValue\": <contents of delivery-time-estimation.pmml >}"    ◄┐
                              Upload the contents of the generated PMML file. ┘
```

Having the ability to automatically push model changes to production fits nicely within the emerging field of machine learning operations (ML ops), which applies the agile principles of continuous integration, delivery, and deployment to the ML process to accelerate and simplify ML model deployment. In this case, we use a script or CI/CD pipeline tool to check out the latest version of a model from source control and upload it to Pulsar using a simple shell script. Additionally, ancillary jobs can be scheduled to rotate different versions of the same model automatically based on a factor such as the time of day.

11.4.2 *Feature vector mapping*

The data science team must also provide us with a complete definition of the feature vector we need to provide to the ML model, along with a map of where these features reside inside the feature store(s), so we can retrieve these values at runtime and provide them to the model. The development team at GottaEat decided it would be easier to store the feature vector mapping information inside a protobuf object because of its built-in support for associated maps in the protocol. This allows us to store the data in the correct format and easily serialize/deserialize the data into a format that is compatible with the Pulsar state store (i.e., a byte array). The protobuf protocol is also language neutral, so it can be used by any of the programming languages supported by Pulsar Functions, including Java, Python, and Go. The definition of the protobuf object used to store the feature mapping information is shown in listing 11.4 and contains three elements: the name of the table to query inside the feature store, a list of all the features stored in the specified table that are required by the ML model, and an associated map that defines the mapping between the features in the feature store and the fields in the feature vector sent to the model.

> **Listing 11.4   The feature vector mapping protocol**

The name of the table inside the feature store that contains the fields specified

A list of all of the fields we need to retrieve from the feature store table

```
syntax = "proto3";

message FeatureVectorMapping {
  string featureStoreTable = 1;
  repeated string featureStoreFields = 2;
  map<string, string> fieldMapping = 3;
}
```

A mapping of each field name to its corresponding feature name inside the model's feature vector

The list of features is used to dynamically construct the SQL query used to retrieve the features to make the query as efficient as possible by returning only those values that we actually need instead of the entire row. The list also serves as a complete list of all the keys in the map data structure, which allows us to iterate over the list and retrieve all the feature-to-vector mappings contained in the map.

Once this information is captured inside a Protobuf object, it should be published to the Pulsar state store using the `putstate` command. However, the Pulsar function name will be that of the Pulsar function inside the feature collection pipeline that will perform the feature lookup for the deployed model. In the case of the delivery time estimation model, the feature extraction pipeline contains a Pulsar function named `RestaurantFeaturesLookup` that queries the restaurant table of the feature store using the ID of the restaurant that will be preparing the food for the customer.

Listing 11.5 The restaurant feature lookup function

```
public class RestaurantFeaturesLookup implements
  Function<FoodOrder, RestaurantFeatures> {

    private CqlSession session;
    private InetAddress node;
    private InetSocketAddress address;
    private SimpleStatement queryStatement;

    @Override
    public RestaurantFeatures process(FoodOrder input, Context ctx)
      throws Exception {
      if (!initalized()) {
        hostName = ctx.getUserConfigValue(HOSTNAME_KEY).toString();
        port = (int) ctx.getUserConfigValueOrDefault(PORT_KEY, 9042);
        dbUser = ctx.getSecret(DB_USER_KEY);
        dbPass = ctx.getSecret(DB_PASS_KEY);
        table = ctx.getUserConfigValue(TABLE_NAME_KEY);
        fields = new String(ctx.getState(FIELDS_KEY));
        sql = "select " + fields + " from " + table +
              " where restaurant_id = ?"
        queryStatement = SimpleStatement.newInstance(sql);
      }
      return getRestaurantFeatures(input.getMeta().getRestaurantId());
    }

    private RestaurantFeatures getRestaurantFeatures (Long id) {
      ResultSet rs = executeStatement(id);
      Row row = rs.one();
      if (row != null) {
        return CustomerFeatures.newBuilder().setCustomerId(customerId)
      .build();
      }
      return null;
    }

    private ResultSet executeStatement(Long customerId) {
      PreparedStatement pStmt = getSession().prepare(queryStatement);
      return getSession().execute(pStmt.bind(customerId));
    }
    private CqlSession getSession() {
      if (session == null || session.isClosed()) {
        CqlSessionBuilder builder = CqlSession.builder()
          .addContactPoint(getAddress())
          .withLocalDatacenter("datacenter1")
```

Annotations:
- **Get the feature store hostname from the configs.** → `hostName = ctx.getUserConfigValue(HOSTNAME_KEY).toString();`
- **Get the feature store port from the configs.** → `port = (int) ctx.getUserConfigValueOrDefault(PORT_KEY, 9042);`
- **Get the credentials for the feature store.** → `dbUser = ctx.getSecret(DB_USER_KEY);` `dbPass = ctx.getSecret(DB_PASS_KEY);`
- **Get the name of the table in the feature store to query.** → `table = ctx.getUserConfigValue(TABLE_NAME_KEY);`
- **Get all of the features we need to retrieve from the feature store.** → `fields = new String(ctx.getState(FIELDS_KEY));`
- **Construct an SQL statement using the specified fields and table name.** → `sql = "select " + fields + " from " + table + " where restaurant_id = ?"`
- **Construct a prepared statement using the specified fields.** → `queryStatement = SimpleStatement.newInstance(sql);`
- **There is only one record for any given ID.** → `Row row = rs.one();`
- **Execute the prepared statement for the given ID.** → `ResultSet rs = executeStatement(id);`
- **Map the fields to the outgoing schema.** → `... <`

```
        .withKeyspace(CqlIdentifier.fromCql("featurestore"));

      session = builder.build();
    }
    return session;
  }
}
```

The `RestaurantFeaturesLookup` function will connect to the feature store and retrieve only the features from the feature store that were specified by the data science team when they published them to the state store. Next, it maps those values to the outgoing schema type and publishes the message to the incoming topic of the Pulsar function that will execute the delivery time estimation model.

11.4.3 *Model deployment*

The final step in the process of deploying an ML model in near real-time mode is writing the Pulsar function itself. Fortunately, once an ML model is exported to the PMML format, it can be deployed to production using a wide variety of execution engines available in Java. In our case, we will use an open-source library called *JPMML*, which we can include in our Maven dependencies, as shown in the next listing.

Listing 11.6   The JPMML library dependency

```
<dependency>
  <groupId>org.jpmml</groupId>
  <artifactId>pmml-evaluator</artifactId>
  <version>1.5.15</version>
</dependency>
```

This library allows us to import PMML models and use them to generate predictions. Once the PMML model has been loaded into the JPMML evaluator class, we are ready to generate delivery time predictions on incoming food orders. Therefore, as you can see from listing 11.8, the very first step in the process is to retrieve the PMML model that is stored inside Pulsar's state store and use it to initialize the appropriate model evaluator. In this case, we need a regression model evaluator, since the delivery time estimation model uses linear regression.

Listing 11.7   The delivery time estimation function

```
import org.dmg.pmml.FieldName;
import org.dmg.pmml.regression.RegressionModel;
import org.jpmml.evaluator.ModelEvaluator;
import org.jpmml.evaluator.regression.RegressionModelEvaluator;    ◁——
import org.jpmml.model.PMMLUtil;

import com.gottaeat.domain.geography.LatLon;
import com.gottaeat.domain.order.FoodOrderML;

public class DeliveryTimeEstimator implements
```

Using the JPMML regression evaluator for the linear regression ML model

```
Function<FoodOrderML, FoodOrderML> {
```
> **The incoming message contains order details and retrieved features from the feature store.**

```
    private IgniteClient client;
    private ClientCache<Long, LatLon> cache;
    private String datagridUrl;
    private String locationCacheName;
```
> **The model requires information from the in-memory data grid.**

```
    private byte[] mlModel = null;
    private ModelEvaluator<RegressionModel> evaluator;
```
> **The JPMML model evaluator**

```
    @Override
    public FoodOrderML process(FoodOrderML order, Context ctx)
      throws Exception {

      if (initalized()) {
        mlModel = ctx.getState(MODEL_KEY).array();
        evaluator = new RegressionModelEvaluator(
         PMMLUtil.unmarshal(new ByteArrayInputStream(mlModel)));
      }
```
> **Retrieve the model from the Pulsar state store.**
>
> **Load the model into the regression evaluator class.**

```
      HashMap<FieldName, Double> featureVector = new HashMap<>();
```

Populate the feature vector with values stored inside the incoming message.
```
      featureVector.put(FieldName.create("avg_prep_last_hour"),
        order.getRestaurantFeatures().getAvgMealPrepLastHour());

      featureVector.put(FieldName.create("avg_prep_last_7days"),
        order.getRestaurantFeatures().getAvgMealPrepLast7Days());
```

> **Populate the feature vector with the driver location data from the IMDG.**

```
      ...

      featureVector.put(FieldName.create("driver_lat"),
        getCache().get(order.getAssignedDriverId()).getLatitude());

      featureVector.put(FieldName.create("driver_long"),
        getCache().get(order.getAssignedDriverId()).getLongitude());

      Long travel = (Long)evaluator.evaluate(featureVector)
      .get(FieldName.create("travel_time"));
```
> **Pass the feature vector to the model and retrieve the prediction.**

```
      order.setEstimatedArrival(System.currentTimeMillis() + travel);
      return order;
    }
```
> **Compute the estimated arrival time by adding the predicted travel time to the current time.**

```
  ...

}
```

Once the evaluator has been initialized, the DeliveryTimeEstimator constructs a feature vector and populates it with values contained inside the incoming message along with some values from other low-latency data sources, such as an in-memory datagrid. In this case, the model requires the driver's current location (latitude/longitude), which is only available from the IMDG.

11.5   *Neural nets*

While the PMML format is very flexible and supports a wide variety of languages and ML models, there are instances when you will need to deploy an ML model that isn't supported by PMML. Neural net models, which can be used to solve a variety of business problems, such as sales forecasting, data validation, or natural language processing, cannot be represented as PMML, and therefore a different approach is required for them to be deployed in near real-time mode.

Modeled loosely on the human brain, a neural net consists of thousands or even millions of artificial neurons (nodes) that are interconnected. Most of today's neural nets are organized into multiple layers of nodes, as shown in figure 11.6. Each node gets weighted input data that is fed into the computing node function and outputs the result of the function to the subsequent layer in the network. The data is fed forward through the network until a single value is produced.

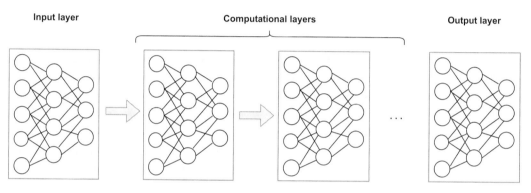

Figure 11.6   A neural net is comprised of an input layer, an output layer, and any number of hidden computational layers. The term deep learning refers to a neural network that is several computational layers deep.

The basic concept of layering is that each additional layer of the network increases the accuracy of the model itself. In fact, the term *deep learning* refers to the use of neural nets that are several layers deep. In this section, I will demonstrate the process of training and deploying a neural net using the popular high-level neural network API known as Keras, which is written in Python.

11.5.1   *Neural net training*

Neural nets are designed to recognize patterns in data, and they learn to do this by analyzing large training datasets. The process of training a neural net involves using a training dataset to determine the proper model weights for each node in the network. The training sets are often labelled, so the expected outputs are known in advance, and then the weights are adjusted until the model produces the expected results. Therefore, it is important to remember that these weights are critical to the performance and accuracy of the models.

The first step is to train a model using the Keras library in Python using your training data, as shown in listing 11.8. The input to the model shown is ten binary features that describe the various features of a food order, such as average order price of the customer, the distance between the customer's home address and the delivery address of the order, and other features. The output is a single variable that describes the probability that the order is fraudulent.

Listing 11.8 Training the neural net using Python

```
import keras                              │ Use the Keras libraries.
from keras import models, layers    ◁─────┘
# Define the model structure        ┌───── Define the model structure.
model = models.Sequential()         ◁─────┘
model.add(layers.Dense(64, activation='relu', input_shape=(10,)))
...
model.add(layers.Dense(1, activation='sigmoid'))
model.compile(optimizer='rmsprop',loss='binary_crossentropy',
              metrics=[auc])

history = model.fit(x, y, epochs=100, batch_size=100,    │ Compile and fit
              validation_split = .2, verbose=0)     ◁────┘ the model.

model.save("games.h5")       ◁─────── Save the model in H5 format.
```

As you can see in figure 11.7, each node inside a neural net takes in a feature vector as input along with a set of weights associated with each feature. These weights allow us to assign more importance to some features than to others when generating our prediction, such as the distance between the delivery address of the order and the customer's home address. If that feature is a good indicator of a fraudulent transaction, then it should have a higher weight. The process of training and fitting the model yields a set of optimal weights for each input node in the neural net.

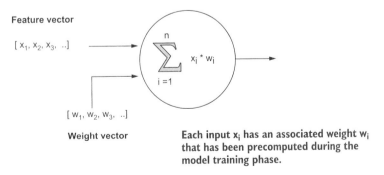

Each input x_i has an associated weight w_i that has been precomputed during the model training phase.

Figure 11.7 Each node in the neural net takes a feature vector as input along with a precomputed set of weights that are associated with each feature. These weights are calculated during the model training phase and are critical to the accuracy of the neural net.

Once the model has been properly trained (i.e., you have calculated the optimal weights for each input node) and is ready to deploy, you can save it in a specialized Keras-specific format known as H5. This format retains the complete models, including the architecture, weights and training configuration, whereas Keras models exported to JSON format only contain the model architecture but *not* the calculated weights. Therefore, be sure to always use the H5 format when exporting your Keras-based neural nets.

11.5.2 *Neural net deployment in Java*

To execute the Keras model within a Java runtime environment, we'll use the Deeplearning4J (DL4J) library. It provides functionality for deep learning in Java and can load and utilize models trained with Keras. One of the key concepts to become familiar with when using DL4J is *tensors*. Java does not have a built-in library for efficient tensor options, which is why I included the NDJ4 library in the Maven dependencies, as shown in the following listing.

Listing 11.9   Deeplearning4J library dependencies

```
<dependency>
    <groupId>org.deeplearning4j</groupId>
    <artifactId>deeplearning4j-core</artifactId>
    <version>1.0.0-M1</version>
  </dependency>
  <dependency>
    <groupId>org.deeplearning4j</groupId>
    <artifactId>deeplearning4j-modelimport</artifactId>
    <version>1.0.0-M1</version>
  </dependency>
  <dependency>
    <groupId>org.nd4j</groupId>
    <artifactId>nd4j-native-platform</artifactId>
    <version>1.0.0-M1</version>
  </dependency>
```

Now that we have the DL4J libraries set up, we can start using the neural net in near real-time mode by embedding it inside a Pulsar function, as shown in the following listing.

Listing 11.10   Deploying the neural net inside a Java-based Pulsar function

```
import org.deeplearning4j.nn.modelimport.keras.KerasModelImport;
import org.deeplearning4j.nn.multilayer.MultiLayerNetwork;      ◁         Using the DL4J
import org.nd4j.linalg.api.ndarray.INDArray;                              libraries
import org.nd4j.linalg.factory.Nd4j;

public class FraudDetectionFunction implements
   Function<FraudFeatures, Double> {               ◁          Input is a collection of features
                                                              used for fraud detection.
```

```
public static final String MODEL_KEY = "key";
private MultiLayerNetwork model;              ◁──── The ML model

public Double process(FraudFeatures input, Context ctx)
  throws Exception {                                        Retrieve the
  if (model == null) {                                      trained model from
    InputStream modelHdf5Stream = new ByteArrayInputStream(  the state store.
      ctx.getState(MODEL_KEY).array());            ◁─
    model = KerasModelImport.importKerasSequentialModelAndWeights(
      modelHdf5Stream);
  }
                                                    Create an empty
                                                    feature vector for
  INDArray features = Nd4j.zeros(10);        ◁──── 10 features.
  features.putScalar(0, input.getAverageSpend());
  features.putScalar(1, input.getDistanceFromMainAddress());
  features.putScalar(2, input.getCreditCardScore());
    . . .                                           Execute the model using
                                                    the given feature vector,
  return model.output(features).getDouble(0);  ◁── and return the predicted
  }                                                fraud probability.
}
```

Text annotations in the left margin:

Initalize the model with the HDF5 file. (points to `model = KerasModelImport.importKerasSequentialModelAndWeights(modelHdf5Stream);`)

Populate the feature vector with values. (points to `features.putScalar(2, input.getCreditCardScore());`)

The model object provides `predict` and `output` methods. The `predict` method returns a class prediction (fraud or not fraud), while the `output` method returns a numeric value representing the exact probability. In this case, we will return the numeric value, so we can evaluate it further (e.g., compare it to a configurable threshold used to define our threshold for fraud).

Summary

- Pulsar Functions can be used to provide near real-time machine learning on streaming data to produce actionable insights.
- Providing near real-time predictions requires an ML model that takes a predefined set of inputs, known as a feature set.
- A feature is a numeric representation of an individual aspect of an object, such as the average meal preparation time of a restaurant.
- Most features within a feature vector cannot be calculated using the data from a single message, nor can they be computed in a timely manner. Therefore, it is common to have ancillary processing compute these values in the background and store them in a low-latency data store.
- The predictive model markup language (PMML) is a standard format for representing ML models developed in a variety of languages, which helps make ML models portable.
- There is an open-source Java-based project that supports the evaluation of PMML models, which allows us to easily execute any PMML-supported model inside a Pulsar function.
- You can use other language-specific libraries to execute non-PMML models inside Pulsar Functions as well.

Edge analytics

12

This chapter covers

- Using Pulsar for edge computing
- Using Pulsar to perform edge analytics
- Performing anomaly detection on the edge using Pulsar Functions
- Performing statistical analytics on the edge using Pulsar Functions

If you are like most people, when you hear the term the *Internet of Things* (IoT), you tend to think of smart thermostats, internet-connected refrigerators, or personal data assistants, such as Alexa. While these consumer-oriented IoT devices tend to get a lot of attention, there is a subset of IoT called the *industrial internet of things* (IIoT), which focuses on the use of sensors that are connected to machinery and vehicles within the transport, energy, and industrial sectors. Companies use the information collected from sensors that are physically embedded inside industrial equipment to monitor, automate, and predict all kinds of industrial processes and outcomes.

The data collected from these IIoT sensors has several practical applications, including monitoring tens of thousands of miles of remote industrial equipment within the energy industry to ensure that there are no imminent failures that could lead to a catastrophic event resulting in a large environmental impact. Sensor data can also be gathered from non-stationary IIoT sensors, such as in a large fleet of refrigerated tractor trailers used to distribute a vaccine that must be kept below a certain temperature in order to remain effective across the globe. These sensors allow us to detect a gradual warming within any given refrigeration unit and reroute the cargo to a nearby maintenance facility for repairs.

In such a situation, it is important that we detect the change in temperature within the refrigeration units as soon as possible so we can react in time to preserve the heat-sensitive cargo. If we waited until the cargo arrived at its intended destination before we checked the temperature, it would be too late, and the vaccine would be useless. This phenomenon is often referred to as the *diminishing time value of data*, since the value obtained from the information is at its highest point immediately after the event occurs, and it rapidly diminishes over time. In the case of the refrigeration unit failure, the sooner we can react to that information, the better. If we are unaware of the failure for hours, the cargo is most likely going to spoil, and the information will no longer be actionable because it will be too late to do anything about it. As you can see in figure 12.1, the longer the response time to such a catastrophic event, the less impact any remedial action will have on the system.

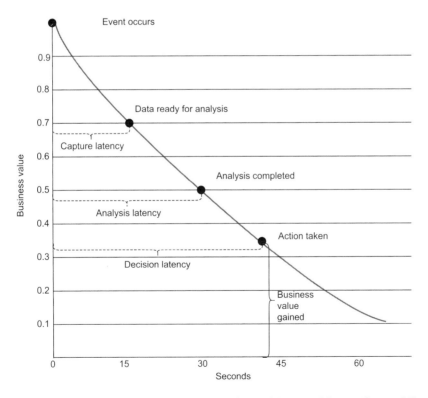

Figure 12.1 The value of any piece of information diminishes rapidly over time, and the goal of edge computing is to reduce the overall decision latency by eliminating the capture latency produced by transmitting the data from the sensor to the cloud for analysis.

The amount of time between when an event occurs and when a corresponding action is taken in response is known as the *decision latency* and is comprised of two components: the *capture latency*, which is the amount of time required to transfer the data to your analysis software, and the *analysis latency*, which is the amount of time required to analyze the data to determine what action to take.

From a technological perspective, the IIoT provides the same basic capability as any other "smart" consumer IoT device, which refers to the automated instrumentation and reporting capabilities of physical devices that previously did not have those capabilities. For example, the defining characteristic of a "smart" thermostat is that it can communicate its current reading and be adjusted remotely via a smartphone app. That being said, the scale of a typical IIoT deployment is significantly larger than a simple system that lets you adjust your thermostat from your phone.

With potentially millions of sensors spread across a single factory plant floor or a large fleet of tractor trailers, each of which is producing a new metric every second, one can easily see that these IIoT datasets are both high volume and high frequency. A common approach to processing these datasets is to collect all of the individual data elements, transfer them to the cloud, and use traditional SQL-based data analysis tools, such as Apache Hive, or more traditional data warehouses. This ensures that the analysis is done on a complete dataset from all of the sensors, so any inter-sensor reading relationships can be observed and used for analysis (e.g., the correlation between a temperature sensor and the overall plant humidity from a different sensor can be tracked and analyzed).

However, this approach has some serious disadvantages, such as significant decision latency (the time between when the event occurred and when it gets processed), cost inefficiencies associated with having to provision sufficient network bandwidth and computing resources to process such large datasets, and the storage cost of retaining all of this information.

From a practical perspective, the amount of the time required to transfer data from most IIoT platforms to a cloud computing environment for analysis makes it nearly impossible to perform any real-time reaction to a potentially catastrophic event. While some of the most dramatic examples of such an event include the detection of faults in power plants or airplanes before they explode or crash, the speed of data analysis in most IIoT applications is critical as well.

In order to overcome this limitation, some of the data processing and analysis of IIoT data can be performed on infrastructure that is physically located closer to the source of the data itself. Bringing computation closer to the source of the data decreases the capture latency and allows applications to respond to data as it's being created almost instantaneously rather than having to wait for the information to be transmitted over the internet before processing it. This practice of processing data near the edge of the network where the data is being generated, instead of in a centralized data collection point such as a data center or cloud, is often referred to as *edge computing*.

In this chapter, I'll demonstrate how we can deploy Pulsar Functions inside an edge computing environment to provide near real-time data processing and analysis to react more quickly to events within an IIoT environment and minimize the decision latency between the time a high-value event is perceived and when the appropriate response is made.

12.1 IIoT architecture

An IIoT platform acts as a bridge between the physical world of industrial equipment and the computational world of automated control systems used to monitor and react to it. As such, one of the primary goals of any IIoT system is the collection and processing of the data generated by all of the physical sensors distributed across various pieces of industrial equipment. While every IIoT deployment is different, they are all comprised of the three logical architectural layers, shown in figure 12.2, which play an important role in the data acquisition and analysis process.

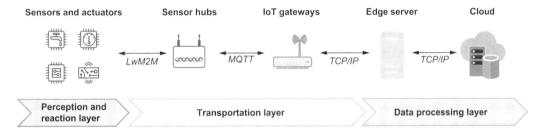

Figure 12.2 The three logical layers of an IIoT architecture ingest data, analyze it, and then present the information so that can be used by humans or by autonomous systems for making contextually relevant decisions in real time.

Within an IIoT environment, there can be millions of sensors, controllers, and actuators distributed across various pieces of industrial equipment within a single factory location. All of these sensors and devices collectively form what is commonly referred to as the *perception and reaction layer* because they allow us to perceive what is going on within the physical world.

12.1.1 The perception and reaction layer

The perception and reaction layer contains all of the hardware components (i.e., the things within the Internet of Things). As the basis for every IIoT system, these connected devices are responsible for perceiving the physical conditions of the industrial equipment and surrounding environment as sensed through numerous sensors that are either embedded in the devices themselves or implemented as standalone objects. These sensors emit a continuous, real-time stream of sensor readings either over lightweight machine-to-machine (LwM2M) protocols, such as Bluetooth, Zigbee, and Z-Wave, or longer-range protocols, such as MQTT or LoRa, if they have a wired connection.

In practice, most IIoT environments require multiple network protocols to support the various devices within the environment. Battery-powered sensors, for example, can only communicate over short distances using lightweight protocols designed for short-range use. In general, the larger the distance the signal needs to travel, the more power that is required by the device to send it. Battery-operated devices using a longer-range protocol to send their data aren't practical.

One of the primary responsibilities of the perception and reaction layer is to perceive the environment via the sensors by capturing their readings and relaying them up to the data processing layer. The other critical responsibility of this layer is reacting to the actionable insights produced by the processing layer and translating them into an immediate physical action when we detect a potentially dangerous condition. Being able to detect a potentially dangerous condition doesn't provide much business value if you can't respond to it in a meaningful way.

Several decades before the emergence of the IIoT, most large manufacturers invested large amounts of time and effort into specialized software systems known as *supervisory control and data acquisition* (SCADA) systems that allow them to monitor and control their industrial equipment. These systems contain control networks that permit the automated operation of the mechanical or electro-mechanical devices known as *actuators* that can perform a variety of manual operations, such as opening a pressure valve on a piece of equipment or completely turning off the power to a given machine.

By leveraging the existing control network within these SCADA systems, we are able to programmatically utilize these actuators from within our IIoT application by simply sending the correct command to activate the actuator. Where the sensors act as the "eyes" of this layer, the actuators serve an equally important role as the "hands" that allow us to respond to the data. Without them, our ability to react to a catastrophic sensor reading would be nonexistent. The information collected within the perception and reaction layer is sent over the *transportation layer* which, as the name implies, is responsible for the secure transmission of the sensor data up to a centralized data processing layer.

12.1.2   *The transportation layer*

The sensor readings that are generated inside the perception and reaction layer and transmitted over LwM2M protocols are detected by intermediary devices, known as sensor hubs, which sit at the outermost edge of the transmission layer. These specialized devices can receive the sensor readings being broadcast over the LwM2M protocols by low-power devices.

The primary purpose of the sensor hubs is to provide a bridge between short-range and long-range communication technologies. Battery-enabled IoT devices communicate with the sensor hubs, using short-range wireless transmission modes, such as Bluetooth LE, Zigbee, and Z-Wave. Upon receipt of the messages, the sensor hubs immediately relay the messages over a longer-range protocol, such as CoAP, MQTT, or LoRa, to a device known as an IoT gateway. Among these longer-range protocols, the *message queuing telemetry transport* (MQTT) specializes in low-bandwidth, high-latency environments, which makes it the one of the most commonly used protocols within the IIoT space.

An *IoT gateway* is a physical device that serves as the connection point between the cloud and the sensor hubs. These devices provide a communication bridge between the MQTT protocol and the Pulsar messaging protocol and are responsible for aggregating all of the incoming sensor readings sent over the lightweight, binary MQTT protocol and aggregating them before forwarding them to the data processing layer using Pulsar's messaging protocol.

12.1.3 *The data processing layer*

As you can see in figure 12.2, the *processing layer* spans two physical layers: the edge servers that are located close to the industrial equipment and the corporate data center or cloud infrastructure. The edge servers are used to aggregate, filter, and prioritize data from the massive volume of data that a large IIoT deployment typically generates to minimize the volume of information that needs to be forwarded to the cloud. This preprocessing of the data helps reduce transmission costs and response times. From a hardware perspective, the edge processing layer consists of one or more traditional computers or servers that are located within the industrial location itself (e.g., inside the factory). While the computing capacity at this layer might be constrained due to physical space limitations of the given location, these devices always have an internet connection that allows them to forward the data they have collected to the company's data center and/or cloud provider for further analysis and archival.

12.2 *A Pulsar-based processing layer*

Now that we have a basic understanding of an IIoT architecture, I want to demonstrate how we can use Apache Pulsar to enhance the processing capabilities of the architecture by extending the data processing layer in closer proximity to the sensors and actuators than in a traditional IIoT setting. First, let's review the computing resources that are available on each of the hardware devices within the IIoT platform. As you can see, figure 12.3 shows that there is an inverse relationship between the available computing resources and their proximity to the industrial equipment. The sensors, actuators, and other smart devices located within the perception and reaction layer are microcontroller based with limited memory and processing power. They are primarily battery operated and, therefore, are not good candidates for performing any sort of computation. While these wireless devices can be augmented with energy-harvesting devices that convert ambient energy into electrical energy, their power is best reserved for wireless communication with the sensor hubs rather than for computation.

Sensor hubs are typically hosted on slightly larger devices, referred to as *systems on a chip* (SoCs), that can have some or all of the components of a traditional computer, including a CPU, RAM, and external storage, although at a smaller scale. But given the sheer number of these devices, their specifications are kept to a minimum to be economically feasible to deploy in large number. Since these devices are primarily used to receive and transmit data, they only require a limited amount of memory to buffer the messages before retransmitting them over a different protocol.

Computing resources per device

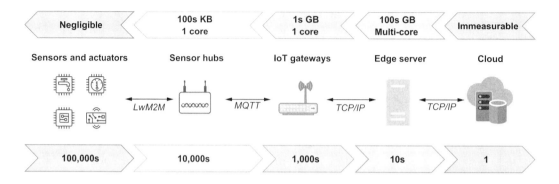

Figure 12.3   **There is an inverse relationship between the number of devices deployed at each layer and the computing resources found within each device.**

IoT gateways are also hosted on SoC hardware with one of the most popular platforms for these devices being the Raspberry Pi, which can have up to 8 GB of RAM, a quad-core CPU, and one MicroSD card slot for up to one terabyte (1 TB) of storage. These devices can also run traditional operating system software, such as Linux, which makes them an ideal candidate for running complex software applications, such as Pulsar.

The last physical piece of hardware is edge servers, which are an optional feature within the IIoT architecture. Depending on the nature of the industrial environment, these devices can range in size from multiple servers with terabytes of RAM, multiple cores, and terabytes of disk storage residing inside a server closet on a factory floor, to a single desktop computer on a remote drilling site. Just like the IoT gateways, devices at this layer run more traditional operating systems and resemble what most people think of when using the term *computer*.

From a computing perspective, any device that has sufficient computing resources (8 GB of RAM and a multi-core x86 CPU) to run a traditional operating system and an internet connection is a potential hardware platform for hosting a Pulsar broker. Within an IIoT architecture, this would include not only the edge servers and the IoT gateway devices, but also any sensor hub that is running on a sufficiently equipped SoC device as well.

Installing a Pulsar broker on these devices enables us to deploy Pulsar functions directly on them to perform the analysis much closer to the source of the data. Doing so effectively extends the data processing layer closer to the origin of the sensor data, as shown in figure 12.4. We are effectively extending the edge closer to the industrial equipment, and doing so creates a large distributed computational framework where Pulsar functions can be deployed across two tiers of the architecture to perform parallel computation on the data.

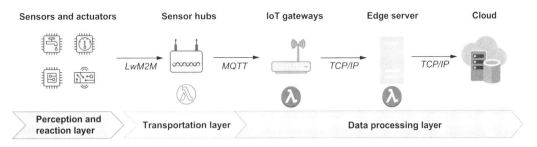

Figure 12.4 By installing Pulsar brokers on the IoT gateways and edge servers, we can extend the data processing layer closer to the source of the data itself, which will enable us to react to it much quicker.

The key takeaway from this is the fact that we can deploy our Pulsar functions on any of the devices inside the IIoT environment that are capable of hosting a Pulsar broker and have them perform complex data analysis on the edge, rather than just collecting the events and forwarding upstream for processing, as is done in a more traditional IIoT environment.

To be fair, some IIoT vendors do provide software packages that can be used to process data on IoT gateway devices as well, but the features are typically limited to more rudimentary capabilities, such as filtering and aggregation. Furthermore, these software packages are closed source and do not allow for you to extend the framework to add your own data processing functions. However, with Pulsar Functions, you can easily create and use your own functions to perform more complex data analysis.

It is also worth noting that Apache Pulsar provides support for the MQTT protocol via a plugin, which allows devices using the MQTT protocol, such as the sensor hubs, to publish messages directly to a topic on a Pulsar broker. This allows us to use Pulsar as an IoT gateway device without the need for another piece of software to act as the MQTT message broker to consume and process the sensor data directly on the gateway itself, as you can see in figure 12.5. A Pulsar-based IoT gateway supports bidirectional communications over the MQTT protocol, which allows the Pulsar functions to send messages to the actuators in response to potentially catastrophic events they detect.

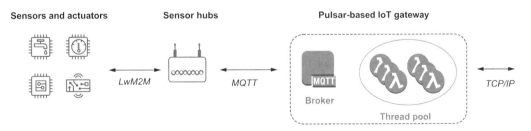

Figure 12.5 The complete functionality of an IoT gateway can be performed using a Pulsar broker that has the MQTT plugin enabled, which allows it to receive messages from the sensor hubs, while the Pulsar functions can be administered via the TCP/IP connection.

The TCP/IP connection not only enables users to deploy, update, and administer Pulsar Functions directly on the IoT gateway device, but it also allows the Pulsar broker to communicate with an Apache BookKeeper-based storage layer hosted in a remote location. Last, and certainly not least, the TCP/IP connection allows us to communicate with other Pulsar clusters within the IIoT architecture—particularly ones that have been deployed on the edge servers. This allows us to forward data generated on all of the IoT gateways up to a centralized location for additional edge processing before finally being sent to the cloud for archival.

12.3   Edge analytics

The practice of performing some or all of the data analysis on infrastructure outside of a traditional data center or cloud computing environment is commonly referred to as *edge analytics* and differs from traditional analytics in a few other key ways that must be kept in mind when you are designing your overall analytics strategy. For starters, the analysis must be done on streaming datasets, where each piece of information will be provided to your Pulsar function only once. Since there is very limited physical disk space in an edge environment, these sensor values are not retained, and thus cannot be reread at a future point in time. If you wanted to determine the average reading of a sensor over the previous hour in a cloud environment, for example, you could simply execute an SQL query to calculate it for you from the historical data. This is not an option with edge analytics. Another big difference is that the closer you move the processing to the sensors, the less information you have in your dataset, which makes the detection of patterns between sensors that are not co-located within the range of the same IoT gateway impossible.

12.3.1   Telemetric data

In order to get a better understanding of the term *edge analytics* and what we are trying to accomplish by performing some of the data analysis on the edge, it is best to start with a basic understanding of the type of data we are processing in an IIoT environment. The overarching function of any IIoT system is the collection of sensor data so it can be used to monitor and manage the company's industrial infrastructure. Once the data is collected, it can then be analyzed for any potential events of interest that might need to be addressed.

These sensors are constantly emitting a stream of observations obtained through repeated measurements of the same variable over time, such as a sensor that sends the temperature reading of a specific piece of equipment every second. These sequences of numerical data points taken at fixed intervals in chronological time order are referred to as *time-series data*. The entire process of collecting this time-series information in the form of measurements or statistical data and forwarding it to remote systems is often referred to as *telemetry*. Like nearly all time-series datasets, this telemetric data will often have one or more of the following characteristics:

- *Trend*—When referring to the *trend* in time series data, we are referring to the fact that the data has a pronounced trajectory in one direction (either up or down) over a specified timeframe. A good example of a trend would be a steady long-term increase in network traffic.

- *Cycles*—Repeating and predictable fluctuations in the data that are not at a fixed frequency and, thus, cannot be correlated to any specific time period or interval.

- *Seasonality*—If there are regular and predictable cycles within the data that are correlated with the calendar (e.g., daily, weekly, etc.), the data has a seasonality characteristic. This differs from a trend because the cycle fluctuates for a short period of time and is usually driven by outside factors, such as a spike in network traffic to a popular e-commerce site during Cyber Monday.

- *Noise*—This refers to randomness in the data points that cannot be correlated with any explained trends. Noise is unsystematic and short-term, and needs to be filtered out to minimize its detrimental impact on our predictions. Consider a temperature sensor that has consistently reported a value of 200 degrees Fahrenheit over the past hour. Any sensor reading that is significantly different than the previous values we have received is most likely just noise and should be ignored. For instance, a single sensor reading of 25 degrees Fahrenheit is mostly likely not an accurate reading and should be ignored.

In the context of IIoT, edge analytics are used to detect these characteristics of the data so they can then be used to predict future values based on previously observed values, as shown in figure 12.6. The real observed values can then be compared to the predicted values to determine whether some sort of action needs to be taken. For instance, if a pressure reading is trending downward, this might indicate a loss of pressure in the line, and a maintenance team should be dispatched to investigate.

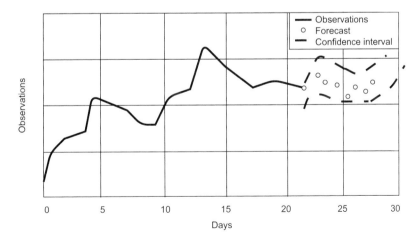

Figure 12.6   Time series forecasting is the use of time-series data to predict future values based on previously observed values.

12.3.2 *Univariate and multivariate*

The other aspect of telemetric datasets is the number of variables that are being tracked within them. The most common scenario is when the data contains a set of observations of a single variable (e.g., the readings from the exact same sensor). The more formal term for this type of dataset is *univariate,* and for our purposes we will assume that all of the datasets collected at the IoT gateway layer are univariate. As you may have guessed, any dataset that tracks more than one variable is known as *multivariate* and allows us to track the relationship between multiple sensor readings over the same timeframe. Rather than containing a single value at a given point in time, these datasets contain several values. Within a Pulsar-enabled IIoT architecture, multivariate datasets are generated using Pulsar Functions by combining several univariate datasets together, as shown in figure 12.7, where the values from each sensor taken at the same time are combined into a tuple of three values.

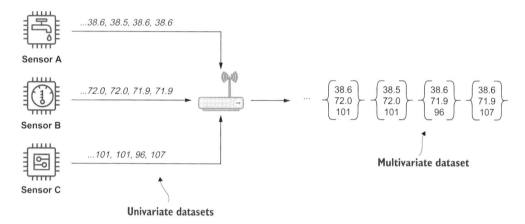

Figure 12.7   Each sensor emits a sequence of readings at a predetermined interval. Upon receipt on the IoT gateway, these univariate datasets are combined into a multivariate dataset that contains the values of all three sensors at a given point in time. This allows us to detect patterns and correlations between these sensor values.

Multivariate datasets can be used to perform more complex and accurate analysis by including data from multiple sources that is strongly correlated. Since there is no limit to the number of variables that can be contained within these datasets, any number of readings may be combined as needed. In fact, these datasets are well suited to serve as feature stores for any ML model you wish to deploy on the edge. As you may recall from chapter 11, feature stores contain a set of precalculated values required by ML models. These feature sets are populated by external processes that rely on historical data to calculate the values. In a Pulsar-enabled IIoT environment, these multivariate datasets are populated from the univariate datasets being collected on the edge, which ensures that your ML models are using the most-recent data to make their predictions.

12.4 Univariate analysis

The endless streams of readings taken from the same sensor are the foundation of edge analytics. These univariate datasets represent the raw data used to perform the analysis of the IIoT data as a whole. Therefore, it is best to start by covering the type of analysis that can be performed on these univariate datasets. A summary of the various types of analytic processing commonly performed is depicted in figure 12.8.

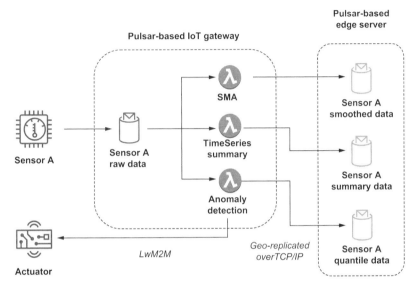

Figure 12.8   The sensor publishes its readings to the `Sensor A Raw Data` topic that is used as input to three Pulsar functions. Two of the functions, `SMA` and `TimeSeriesSummary`, use the values to compute statistical values from the raw data before publishing these statistics to local topics that are configured to be geo-replicated to the Pulsar cluster running on the edge server. The third function determines whether the sensor value is anomalous and should activate an actuator in response to any potentially catastrophic event it detects.

This processing is accomplished using Pulsar functions deployed on the IoT gateways closest to the source of the data. Therefore, it is important that these functions minimize the amount of memory and CPU required to perform their analysis.

12.4.1 Noise reduction

I previously mentioned how there can be noise (i.e., randomness) within the sensor data. In order to better forecast future data values, an important preprocessing step is the reduction of the noise in these univariate datasets. A common technique used to smooth out these fluctuations of the data is to simply compute the mathematical average of the data points within a predefined time window to produce a value. This computed moving average is then retained rather than the raw values. Doing so minimizes the impact that any individual sensor reading has on the reported value (e.g., if you have 99 sensor readings with the same value of 70 and one with a value of 100, then using a computed average of 70.3 would effectively smooth out the data and provide a value that is more indicative of the sensor reading over that interval).

While there are many different moving average models, for the sake of brevity, I will only cover the *simple moving average* in this chapter. A simple moving average is calculated by retaining the most recent subset of the time-series data, such as the last 100 sensor readings. When a new reading arrives, it is used to replace the oldest value in the collection. Once the newest value has been added, the mathematical average of these remaining values is computed and returned.

Listing 12.1   A Pulsar function to calculate the simple moving average

```
public class SimpleMovingAverageFunction implements Function<Double, Void> {

    private CircularFifoQueue<Double> values;          The circular buffer of values
    private PulsarClient client;                        that automatically removes
    private String remotePulsarUrl, topicName;          the oldest item
    private boolean initalized;
    private Producer<Double> producer;                 A Pulsar client for the Pulsar cluster
                                                        running on the edge servers
    @Override
     public Void process(Double input, Context ctx) throws Exception {
       if (!initalized) {
         initalize(ctx);
       }                          Add the sensor reading
                                  to the list of values.
       values.add(input);                              Calculate the simple
       double average = values.stream()                moving average.
         .mapToDouble(i->i).average().getAsDouble();
       publish(average);
       return null;              Publish the computed value
    }                            to a topic on the edge server.

    private void publish(double average) {
      try {
        getProducer().send(average);
      } catch (PulsarClientException e) {
        e.printStackTrace();
      }
    }

    private PulsarClient getEdgePulsarClient() throws PulsarClientException {
      if (client == null) {
        client = PulsarClient.builder().serviceUrl(remotePulsarUrl).build();
      }
      return client;
    }

    private Producer<Double> getProducer() throws PulsarClientException {
      if (producer == null) {
            producer = getEdgePulsarClient()
                    .newProducer(Schema.DOUBLE)
              .topic(topicName).create();
```

```
      }
      return producer;
   }

   private void initalize(Context ctx) {
      initalized = true;
      Integer size = (Integer) ctx.getUserConfigValueOrDefault("size", 100);
      values = new CircularFifoQueue<Double> (size);
      remotePulsarUrl = ctx.getUserConfigValue("pulsarUrl").get().toString();
      topicName = ctx.getUserConfigValue("topicName").get().toString();
   }
}
```

Fortunately, it is relatively straightforward to implement the calculation of moving averages using Pulsar Functions. As you can see from listing 12.1, the key is using a circular buffer to retain the last *n* values required to calculate the moving average. You can then use this Pulsar function to preprocess the individual sensor readings and publish the calculated SMA rather than the raw value itself. This ensures that all downstream analysis is performed on less-noisy data.

12.4.2 *Statistical analysis*

Moving averages aren't the only meaningful statistic that can be calculated from univariate datasets. In fact, it is quite easy to calculate just about any of the statistics that are commonly used in statistical analysis using a Pulsar function. Take, for example, the function code shown in the next listing, which computes the following statistics in a single function: geometric mean, population variance, kurtosis, root mean square deviation, skewness, and standard deviation.

Listing 12.2 A Pulsar function to calculate multiple statistics

**Convert the data from a collection
to a two-dimensional array.**

```
import org.apache.commons.math3.stat.descriptive.DescriptiveStatistics;
import org.apache.commons.math3.stat.descriptive.SummaryStatistics;
import org.apache.commons.math3.stat.regression.*;
import org.apache.pulsar.functions.api.Context;
import org.apache.pulsar.functions.api.Function;

public class TimeSeriesSummaryFunction implements
   Function<Collection<Double>, SensorSummary>  {

   @Override
   public SensorSummary process(Collection<Double> input, Context context)
      throws Exception {

      double[][] data = convertToDoubleArray(input);
      SimpleRegression reg = calcSimpleRegression(data);
      SummaryStatistics stats = calcSummaryStatistics(data);
      DescriptiveStatistics dstats = calcDescriptiveStatistics(data);
      double rmse = calculateRSME(data, reg.getSlope(), reg.getIntercept());
```

This function relies on external libraries to perform the statistical calculations.

The input collection contains all of the sensor readings within the specified window.

```
SensorSummary summary =
  SensorSummary.newBuilder()
    .setStats(TimeSeriesSummary.newBuilder()
      .setGeometricMean(stats.getGeometricMean())
        .setKurtosis(dstats.getKurtosis())
        .setMax(stats.getMax())
        .setMean(stats.getMean())
        .setMin(stats.getMin())
        .setPopulationVariance(stats.getPopulationVariance())
        .setRmse(rmse)
        .setSkewness(dstats.getSkewness())
        .setStandardDeviation(dstats.getStandardDeviation())
        .setVariance(dstats.getVariance())
        .build())
  .build();

  return summary;
}

private SimpleRegression calcSimpleRegression(double[][] input) {
  SimpleRegression reg = new SimpleRegression();
  reg.addData(input);
  return reg;
}

private SummaryStatistics calcSummaryStatistics(double[][] input) {
  SummaryStatistics stats = new SummaryStatistics();
  for(int i = 0; i < input.length; i++) {
    stats.addValue(input[i][1]);
  }
  return stats;
}

private DescriptiveStatistics calcDescriptiveStatistics(double[][] in)
{
  DescriptiveStatistics dstats = new DescriptiveStatistics();
  for(int i = 0; i < in.length; i++) {
    dstats.addValue(in[i][1]);
  }
  return dstats;
}

private double calculateRSME(double[][] input, double slope, double
 intercept) {
  double sumError = 0.0;
  for (int i = 0; i < input.length; i++) {
    double actual = input[i][1];
    double indep = input[i][0];
    double predicted = slope*indep + intercept;
          sumError += Math.pow((predicted - actual),2.0);
            }
        return Math.sqrt(sumError/input.length);
}
```

Use the various computed statistics to populate the result.

```
    private double[][] convertToDoubleArray(Collection<Double> in)
      throws Exception {
        double[][] newIn = new double[in.size()][2];
        int i = 0;
        for (Double d : in) {
        newIn[i][0] = i;
        newIn[i][1] = d;
        i++;
        }
        return newIn;
    }
  }
```

Obviously, these statistics cannot be computed from a single data point in the time-series data, but rather need to be computed from a larger collection of data elements. Attempting to calculate the geometric mean of a single number makes no sense. Therefore, we need to specify a strategy for splitting the endless stream of metric data into finite sets of data, known as *windows*, which we will use to calculate these statistics. So how do we go about defining the boundaries of a data window? Within Pulsar Functions, there are two policies used to control window boundaries:

- *Trigger policy*—Controls when our function code is executed. These are the rules that the Apache Pulsar Functions framework uses to notify our code that it is time to process all of the data collected in the window.
- *Eviction policy*—Controls the amount of data retained in the window. These are the rules used to decide if a data element should be retained or evicted from the window.

Both of these policies are driven by either time or the quantity of data in the window and can be defined in terms of time or length (number of data elements). Let's explore the distinction between these two policies and how they work in concert with one another. While there are a variety of windowing techniques, the most prominent ones are tumbling and sliding windows.

Tumbling windows are contiguous, non-overlapping windows that are either of fixed-size, such as 100 elements, or taken at fixed intervals, such as every five minutes. The eviction policy for tumbling windows is *always* disabled to allow the window to become completely full. Therefore, you only need to specify the trigger policy you want to use as either count-based or time-based. Figure 12.9 shows the behavior of a tumbling window with a length-based trigger policy set to 10, which means that at the point in time at which 10 items are in the window, the Pulsar function code will be executed, and the window will be cleared. This behavior is irrespective of time; whether it takes five seconds or five hours for the window count to reach 10 items doesn't matter—all that matters is when the count reaches the specified length. Therefore, the first window takes approximately 15 seconds to become full, while the last one requires 25 seconds to elapse before the window fills up.

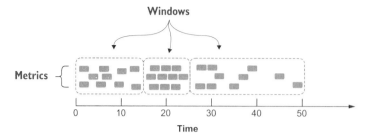

Figure 12.9   When using a count-based trigger, each tumbling window will contain the exact same number of metrics, but may span different durations of time.

The sliding window technique, on the other hand, utilizes a combination of a trigger policy that defines the sliding interval and an eviction policy that limits the amount of data retained within the window for processing. Figure 12.10 shows the behavior of a sliding window with the eviction policy configured to be 20 seconds, meaning that any data older than 20 seconds will not be retained or used in the calculation. The trigger policy is also configured to be 20 seconds, which means that every 20 seconds the associated Pulsar function code will be executed, and we will have access to all of the data within the entire window length to perform our calculation.

Thus, in the scenario shown in figure 12.10, the first window contains 15 events, while the last one contains only two. In this example, both the eviction and trigger policies are defined in terms of time; however, it is also possible to define one or both of these in terms of length instead. Additionally, the window length and sliding interval don't have to be the exact same value. For instance, if you wanted to perform the SMA using this technique, you could achieve that by setting the window length to 100 and the sliding interval to 1.

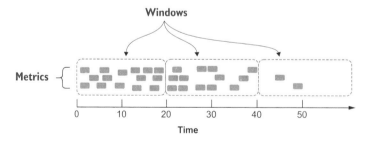

Figure 12.10   When using a time-based sliding window, each window will span the exact same amount of time and will most likely contain different numbers of metrics.

Once these statistical summaries have been calculated, they can be sent upstream to the edge servers to be compared to the stats computed for similar equipment within the industrial infrastructure to detect potential problems, or they could be forwarded to a database within the cloud for longer-term storage and future analysis. Performing the calculations before storing the data in the database will save us from having to recalculate these values during the analysis phase, which can be an expensive operation. Pulsar Functions provides the four different windowing configuration parameters shown in table 12.1, which enables you to implement all four variations of the windows discussed in this section when used in the proper combination.

Table 12.1 Configuring windowing for Pulsar functions

Time-based tumbling window	`--windowLengthDurationMS==xxx`
Length-based tumbling window	`--windowLengthCount==xxx`
Time-based sliding window	`--windowLengthDurationMS==xxx` `--slidingIntervalDurationMs=xxx`
Length-based sliding window	`--windowLengthCount==xxx` `--slidingIntervalCount=xxx`

Implementing either of these types of windowing functions in Pulsar Functions is straightforward and only requires that you specify a `java.util.Collection` as the input type. Therefore, if we wanted to run the Pulsar function shown in listing 12.2 to perform the statistic calculation on a sliding window of data, then all that we would have to do is submit it using the command shown in the following listing, and the Pulsar Functions framework would handle the rest for us.

Listing 12.3 Performing the statistical calculation on a sliding window of data

```
$ bin/pulsar-admin functions create \
    --jar edge-analytics-functions-1.0.0.nar \
    --classname com.manning.pulsar.iiot.analytics.TimeSeriesSummaryFunction \
    --windowLengthDurationMS==20000 \
    --slidingIntervalDurationMs=20000.
```

Defines a trigger policy of 20 seconds

Defines an eviction policy of 20 seconds

This makes it easy to utilize either of these windowing techniques without having to write the significant amount of boilerplate code necessary to perform the collection and retention of the individual events. Instead, it allows you to write clean code that focuses solely on the business logic you are trying to implement.

12.4.3 Approximation

When analyzing streaming data, there are certain types of queries that cannot be computed on the edge because they require huge amounts of both computing resources and time to generate exact results. Examples include count distinct, quantiles, most-frequent items, joins, matrix computations, and graph analysis. Therefore, these types of calculations are typically not performed on these streaming datasets at all. However, if an approximate answer will suffice, there is a specialized category of streaming algorithms for providing approximate values, estimates, and data samples for statistical analysis when the event stream is either too large to store in memory or the data is moving too fast to process.

These streaming algorithms utilize small data structures, known as *sketches*, which are usually only a few kilobytes in size, to store the information. Sketch-based algorithms perform *one-touch processing*, meaning they only need to read each element in the stream once. Both these properties make these algorithms ideal candidates for deployment on edge devices. There are four families of sketching algorithms, each focused on solving a different type of problem:

- *Cardinality sketches*—Provides approximate counts for each distinct value in the stream, such as the number of page views across a number of different web pages in a given timeframe.
- *Frequent item sketches*—Provides a list of the most frequently seen values in the stream, such as the top 10 web pages viewed in a given timeframe.
- *Sampling sketches*—Uses reservoir sampling to provide a uniform random sample of data from the stream that can be used for analysis.
- *Quantile sketches*—Provides a frequency histogram that contains information about the distribution of the data stream values that can be used for anomaly detection.

There is an open source library called Apache DataSketches that contains implementations of these algorithms in Java, which makes them easy to use inside a Pulsar function, such as the one shown in listing 12.4, which uses the quantile sketch to detect anomalies in the sensor data.

QUANTILES

The word *quantile* is derived from the word *quantity* and simply refers to equal-sized groupings of something—typically a probability distribution or a series of observed values. You are already familiar with some of the more common quantiles that are referred to by their more common names, such as halves, thirds, quarters, etc. In statistics and probability, quantiles are more formally defined as cut points that divide a probability distribution into continuous, adjacent intervals with an equal number of elements.

For example, in figure 12.11 there are three values—Q1, Q2, and Q3—which splits the dataset into equally weighted sections. The areas under the graph between each of these points are the quantiles, in this case thirds, which contain an equal number of data points.

For our use case, we will be processing an endless stream of metric data values and using them to dynamically construct a quantile. This

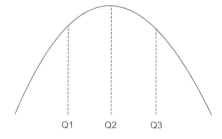

Figure 12.11   A dataset that is divided into three equal-sized sections known as quantiles. Values less than or equal to Q1 are considered part of the first quantile; values between Q1 and Q2 are part of the second quantile; and those greater than or equal to Q3 are part of the third quantile.

allows us to make our decisions based solely on the actual observed values when determining whether or not a value is anomalous by comparing it to previous values of the same metric. When a new metric reading comes into our Pulsar function, we will first add it to the quantile to update the distribution model, and then we will calculate the *rank* of the metric reading. The rank is best described as the proportion of values in the distribution that the given value is greater than or equal to. For instance, if a metric reading is higher than 79% of the previously observed values, then its rank would be 79. Ranking a value helps us determine whether a given metric reading is commonplace or not, and we have decided to use a configurable value to define the threshold that we consider anomalous.

Listing 12.4 A Pulsar function for anomaly detection

```
import org.apache.datasketches.quantiles.DoublesSketch;
import org.apache.datasketches.quantiles.          ◁──── This function relies on the DataSketches
[CA]UpdateDoublesSketch;                                  library to perform the statistical calculations.
. . .
public class AnomalyDetector implements Function<Double, Void> {

    private UpdateDoublesSketch sketch;
    private double alertThreshold;
    private boolean initalized = false;

    @Override
    public Void process(Double input, Context ctx) throws Exception {
      if (!initalized) {
        init(ctx);
      }                                       Add the metric
      sketch.update(input);     ◁─┘           reading to the sketch.       Get the metric reading's
                                                                           rank value, and compare
      if (sketch.getRank(input) >= alertThreshold) {  ◁─┘                  that to the alert threshold.
        react();       ◁─
      }                        If the metric is above the
      return null;             configured threshold, then react.
    }

    protected void init(Context ctx) {
      sketch = DoublesSketch.builder().build();
      alertThreshold = (double) ctx.getUserConfigValue ("threshold");
      initalized = true;
    }

    protected void react() {
      // Implementation specific    ◁─       This will vary based on the LwM2M
    }                                         protocol being used by the actuator.
}
```

The logic for the function is fairly straightforward. First, we update the quantile sketch by adding the data element to it. Then, we request the relative rank of the value in the overall distribution. Next, we determine whether the value is an outlier or not by comparing the metric reading's rank to the preconfigured alert threshold. If an outlier is detected, then we use an LwM2M client to send a message to an actuator in the perception and reaction layer to perform some sort of preventative action, such as turning off a machine or opening a pressure valve. The logic of the react function shown in listing 12.4 will vary based on the LwM2M protocol being used and the command(s) we need to send in response to the event.

12.5 *Multivariate analysis*

Thus far we have implemented various analytical techniques on data from a single sensor. While this univariate analysis does enable us to perform anomaly detection and trend analysis on a single sensor, much more interesting analysis can be performed once we have combined the data from multiple sensors, as was shown previously shown in figure 12.7. In this section, I will provide an outline of the steps required to combine data collected from different IoT gateways, analyze it, and respond to these new insights.

12.5.1 *Creating a bidirectional messaging mesh*

Creating a messaging framework that can be used to transmit messages up from the IoT gateways to the edge servers involves an initial configuration phase to add all of the Pulsar clusters to the same Pulsar instance. As you may recall from chapter 2, a Pulsar instance can contain multiple Pulsar clusters. Being part of the same Pulsar instance is also a prerequisite for enabling geo-replication of data between Pulsar clusters, which, as you saw in figure 12.8, is the preferred mechanism for forwarding the calculated statistical sensor data from the IoT gateways to the edge server.

The first phase of this configuration is adding each of the individual IoT gateway-based Pulsar clusters to the same Pulsar instance as the Pulsar cluster running on the edge server. This can be easily achieved using the `pulsar-admin` command line interface or REST API, as shown in the following listing, which shows the command used to add a single IoT gateway cluster to the Pulsar instance.

> **Listing 12.5 Adding an IoT gateway cluster to the Pulsar instance**

Each name has to be unique.

```
$ pulsar-admin clusters create iot-gateway-1 \          URL address of the TCP
    --broker-url http://<IoT-Gateway-IP>:6650 \         broker on the gateway
    --url http://<IoT-Gateway-IP>:8080
                                                         Confirm that the cluster
$ pulsar-admin clusters list                             was added to the list.
```

Service URL for the gateway

This command has to be run just once for every IoT gateway-based Pulsar cluster in your IIoT environment. Once a cluster has been added to the Pulsar instance, it is able to have messages delivered to it asynchronously via Pulsar's geo-replication mechanism rather than having to write additional code to perform the data replication.

The next step in establishing geo-replication between the IoT gateways and the edge servers is to define a tenant that can be used for bidirectional communication. This can be easily achieved using the `pulsar-admin` command line interface or REST API, as shown in the following listing, which shows the command to create a new Pulsar tenant that can be accessed by all of the IoT gateway clusters as well as the Pulsar cluster running on the edge servers.

Listing 12.6 Creating a geo-replicated tenant

```
$ pulsar-admin tenants create iiot-analytics-tenant \
    --allowed-clusters  iot-gateway-1, iot-gateway-2, ...  \
    --admin-roles analytics-role
```

Provide a complete list of all the IoT gateway clusters you created.

Specifies the admin role for this namespace

The last step of the configuration process is the creation of a namespace that can be used specifically for the geo-replication of the data between the IoT Gateways and the edge servers. This can be easily achieved using the `pulsar-admin` command line interface or REST API, as shown in listing 12.7, which shows the command to create a new Pulsar namespace that can be accessed by all of the IoT gateway clusters as well as the Pulsar cluster running on the edge servers. Please note that this replicated namespace has to be within the tenant we created previously. (See appendix B for details on configuring geo-replication between Pulsar clusters.)

Listing 12.7 Creating a geo-replicated namespace

```
$ pulsar-admin namespaces create \
    iiot-analytics-tenant/analytics-namespace \
    --clusters iot-gateway-1, iot-gateway-2, ...
```

Provide a complete list of all the IoT Gateway clusters you created.

Once you create a geo-replicated namespace, any topics that producers or consumers create within that namespace are automatically replicated across all of the clusters. Therefore, any messages published to topics within the geo-replicated namespace on the IoT gateways will automatically be sent asynchronously to the edge server. Unfortunately, this would also result in the message being replicated to all of the other IoT gateways within the IIoT infrastructure, which is not what we want at all. Not only would this inter-gateway replication waste precious network bandwidth, but it would also waste disk space on the gateways themselves, as they would have to store the messages they receive. Since these messages will never be consumed on the other gateways, storing them just wastes disk space.

Therefore, we need to enable selective replication to ensure that the outbound messages that are only intended to be consumed by the edge server are only replicated to the edge server and not across all of the IoT gateways. This can be accomplished by writing a simple Pulsar function that consumes from a local, non-geo-replicated topic on the gateway and publishes it to a geo-replicated topic but restricts the replication to only the edge servers, as shown on the left side of figure 12.12.

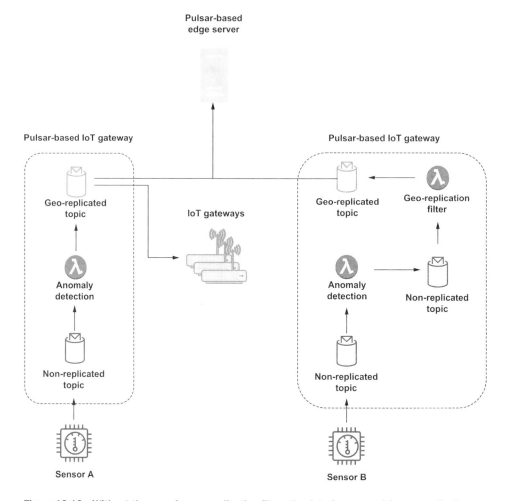

Figure 12.12 **Without the use of a geo-replication filter, the data for sensor A is automatically replicated to all of the IoT gateway clusters in addition to the edge server, whereas data for sensor B is only replicated to the Pulsar cluster running on the edge servers.**

As you can see in listing 12.8, the Pulsar function used to forward these messages would use the existing producer Java API to restrict the replication of the messages to only the edge cluster, resulting in the message flow shown on the right side of figure 12.12, where the message first goes to a local topic before getting forwarded to a geo-replicated topic, but only to the edge server rather than all of the clusters.

Listing 12.8   Geo-replication message filter function

```
public class GeoReplicationFilterFunction implements Function<byte[],Void> {

    private boolean initialized = false;
    private List<String> restrictReplicationTo;
```

```
private Producer<byte[]> producer;
private PulsarClient client;
private String serviceUrl;
private String topicName;

@Override
public Void process(byte[] input, Context ctx) throws Exception {
  if (!initialized) {
    init(ctx);
  }
  getProducer().newMessage()
        .value(input)
        .replicationClusters(restrictReplicationTo)
        .send();

  return null;
}

private void init(Context ctx) {
   serviceUrl = "pulsar://localhost:6650";
  topicName = ctx.getUserConfigValue("replicated-topic").get().toString();
   restrictReplicationTo = Arrays.asList(
      ctx.getUserConfigValue("edge").get().toString());
   initalized = true;
}

private Producer<byte[]> getProducer() throws PulsarClientException {
   if (producer == null) {
      producer = getClient().newProducer()
              .topic(topicName)
              .create();
   }
   return producer;
}

private PulsarClient getClient() throws PulsarClientException {
   if (client == null) {
     client = PulsarClient.builder().serviceUrl(serviceUrl).build();
   }
   return client;
}
}
```

Create a new message using the input bytes.

Restrict the clusters that the message will be replicated to.

We are publishing to a local geo-replicated topic.

The destination topic should be in the replicated namespace.

This should be the name of the Pulsar cluster running on the edge servers.

The Pulsar function is writing to a geo-replicated topic on the local machine to allow the Pulsar geo-replication mechanism to handle the forwarding of the message rather than sending it directly to the edge server to avoid the synchronous call over the network for each message. Now that we have covered the up direction of the messaging mesh, let's focus on the down direction of the bidirectional mesh, which is focused on delivering the insights discovered on the edge servers through the analysis of data from multiple sensors back down to the Pulsar functions running on the IoT gateways. In reality, this process is fairly straightforward because all that is required is for the edge servers to publish to a geo-replicated topic and have the interested parties subscribe to the topic to have the messages delivered. Even though the topics are geo-replicated, the messages will *not* be sent to the IoT gateways unless there is an active consumer of the topic on the gateway node.

12.5.2 *Multivariate dataset construction*

Consider the scenario in which you have multiple temperature sensors measuring the ambient temperature across your entire data center. Rather than comparing the current reading of a given individual sensor to its previous readings, you want to see how it compares to the previous readings of all of the other temperature sensors deployed across your data center. Obviously, this would provide a much more meaningful comparison, particularly in the case where the sensor readings gradually drifted higher or lower rather than suddenly, such as if one of your pieces of equipment was gradually overheating, and the temperature readings slowly rose from a safe range to a more dangerous level. In such a scenario, there might not be any single reading that is significantly large enough to be considered an anomaly, but compared to other similar sensors, all of the readings would be considered high.

To perform a comparison across a much broader set of data would require the combination of data from potentially hundreds of different sensors. Therefore, we must first gather all of the data into a single location to calculate the statistics for the sensor group as a whole rather than individually. Fortunately, the data sketches used inside the `AnomalyDetector` function can be merged together rather easily to provide these types of statistics. A data sketch generated from a series of readings from a single sensor can be used to determine the ranking of any given sensor reading relative to all of the readings recorded in the sketch thus far. But if you combine 100 sketches, then you can use the resulting sketch to determine the ranking of any given sensor reading relative to all the readings across 100 sensors. This is a much more meaningful value and would solve the issue we are trying to address because we are comparing each sensor reading to all others across the entire factory.

To achieve this, we must first modify the existing `AnomalyDetector` function, as shown in the following listing, to periodically send a copy of its sketch to the edge servers so it can be merged with the sketches from all the other `BiDirectionalAnomaly-Detector` function instances running on different IoT gateways.

Listing 12.9 Update `AnomalyDetection` function

Property that defines how often the local data sketch gets published (in minutes)

Property that defines the topic name used to send the local data sketch to the edge server

Property that defines the topic name used to receive the updated alert threshold from the edge server

Calculated alert threshold provided by the edge server

The URL for the Pulsar broker running on the edge server

```
public class BiDirectionalAnomalyDetector
    implements Function<Double, Void> {

    private boolean initialized = false;
    private long publishInterval;
    private String reportingTopic;
    private String alertThresholdTopic;
    private double alertThreshold;
    private String remotePulsarUrl;
```

Consumer for receiving updated alert threshold values from the edge server

Producer for sending the data sketched to the edge server

Local thread pool where the consumer thread can run in the background

```
    private PulsarClient client;
    private Producer<byte[]> producer;
    private Consumer<Double> consumer;
    private ExecutorService service = Executors.newFixedThreadPool(1);
    private ScheduledExecutorService executor =
      Executors.newScheduledThreadPool(1);
    private UpdateDoublesSketch sketch;

    @Override
    public Void process(Double input, Context ctx) throws Exception {
      if (!initialized) {
        init(ctx);
        launchReportingThread();
        launchFeedbackConsumer();
      }

        synchronized(sketch) {
          getSketch().update(input);

          if (getSketch().getRank(input) >= alertThreshold) {
            react();
          }
        }
      return null;
    }

    private void launchReportingThread() {
      Runnable task = () -> {
        synchronized(sketch) {
          try {
            if (getSketch() != null) {

    getProducer().newMessage().value(getSketch().toByteArray()).send();
              sketch.reset();
            }
          } catch(final PulsarClientException ex) { /* Handle */}
        }
      };
      executor.scheduleAtFixedRate(task,
        publishInterval, publishInterval, TimeUnit.MINUTES);
    }

    private void launchFeedbackConsumer() {
      Runnable task = () -> {
        Message<Double> msg;
        try {
          while ((msg = getConsumer().receive()) != null) {
            alertThreshold = msg.getValue();
            getConsumer().acknowledge(msg);
          }
```

Local thread pool that invokes the publishing thread at a fixed interval (e.g., every five minutes)

Create an exclusive lock on the data sketch when writing the data.

Start the data sketch publishing thread just once.

Start the alert threshold consuming thread just once.

Create an exclusive lock on the data sketch when publishing the data.

Clear all of the data from the sketch.

Schedule the publishing task to run at the fixed interval specified by the configuration properties.

Wait for incoming alert threshold messages.

Update the alert threshold with the provided value.

```
        } catch (PulsarClientException ex) {*/ Handle */ }
      };
      service.execute(task);
    }
```
Launch the alert threshold consuming thread in the background.

```
  private UpdateDoublesSketch getSketch() {
    if (sketch == null) {
      sketch = DoublesSketch.builder().build();
    }
    return sketch;
  }

  private Producer<byte[]> getProducer() throws PulsarClientException {
    if (producer == null) {
      producer = getEdgePulsarClient().newProducer(Schema.BYTES)
        .topic(reportingTopic).create();
    }
    return producer;
  }

  private Consumer<Double> getConsumer() throws PulsarClientException {
    if (consumer == null) {
      consumer = getEdgePulsarClient().newConsumer(Schema.DOUBLE)
        .topic(alertThresholdTopic).subscribe();
    }
    return consumer;
  }

  private void react() {
    // Implementation specific
  }

  private PulsarClient getEdgePulsarClient() throws PulsarClientException {
    ...
  }

  protected void init(Context ctx) {
    ...
  }
}
```

The BiDirectionalAnomalyDetector function still listens for incoming sensor readings and adds them to a local data sketch object before comparing the sensor reading to the anomaly threshold to determine whether immediate action must be taken. However, it also creates two additional background threads to communicate with the SketchConsolidator function running on the edge server. This function relies on the Java ScheduledThreadExecutor to ensure that the local data sketches are published at a periodic interval (e.g., every five minutes), while the other thread is used to continuously monitor the feedback topic for any updates to the alert threshold value. Next, we must create a new Pulsar function, like the one shown in listing 12.10, that will run on the edge servers and will receive these inbound sketches and merge them together to produce a larger, more accurate sketch that encompasses data from all of the sensors within a given sensor family.

Listing 12.10 Data sketch merging function

```
import org.apache.datasketches.memory.Memory;
import org.apache.datasketches.quantiles.DoublesSketch;
import org.apache.datasketches.quantiles.DoublesUnion;
import org.apache.pulsar.functions.api.Context;
import org.apache.pulsar.functions.api.Function;

public class SketchConsolidator implements Function<byte[], Double> {

    private DoublesSketch consolidated;      ◁——— Data sketch that contains data
                                                   from all of the sensors
    @Override
    public Double process(byte[] bytes, Context ctx) throws Exception {
        DoublesSketch iotGatewaySketch =
            DoublesSketch.wrap(Memory.wrap(bytes));   ◁——| Convert the incoming
                                                           bytes to a data sketch.
        DoublesUnion union = DoublesUnion.builder().build();   ◁——— Build a new
        union.update(iotGatewaySketch);                              object used to
        union.update(consolidated);          ◁——— Add the existing consolidated    merge multiple
        consolidated = union.getResult();          data sketch to the union object.  data sketches.
        return consolidated.getQuantile(0.99);   ◁———
    }                                                   Publish the newly calculated
}                                                       threshold value for the 99th
                                                        percentile.
```

Add the incoming data sketch to the union object. (annotation pointing to `union.update(iotGatewaySketch);`)

Update the consolidated data sketch to be equal to the result of the merge. (annotation pointing to `consolidated = union.getResult();`)

The interaction between these two Pulsar functions is depicted in figure 12.13, which shows both of the communication channels used to send data up from the BiDirectionalAnomalyDetector functions running on all of the IoT gateways to the SketchConsolidator function running on the edge servers, and the channel used to send the newly calculated threshold from the SketchConsolidator function back down to the BiDirectionalAnomalyDetector function instances running on the IoT gateways.

The SketchConsolidator function should be configured to listen to the geo-replicated topic where all of the BiDirectionalAnomalyDetector functions will be publishing their respective sketches. As you can see from the code in listing 12.10, once the data sketches have been merged, we use the newly created object to determine the exact value that represents the threshold of the 99th percentile of all sensor readings. We then send this value back to the BiDirectionalAnomalyDetector functions rather than the entire sketch (to save space and bandwidth) so they can use this newly calculated value as their alert threshold instead of the locally calculated threshold.

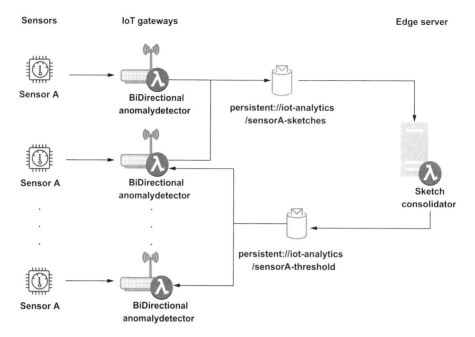

Sensors   IoT gateways   Edge server

Sensor A   BiDirectional
                  anomalydetector   persistent://iot-analytics
                                         /sensorA-sketches

Sensor A   BiDirectional
                  anomalydetector   Sketch
                                                                          consolidator

                                         persistent://iot-analytics
                                         /sensorA-threshold

Sensor A   BiDirectional
                  anomalydetector

Figure 12.13   A copy of the `BiDirectionalAnomalyDetector` function will run on each IoT gateway and publish its locally calculated data sketches to the same geo-replicated topic. The `SketchConsolidator` function will consume these sketches and merge them together before publishing the cutoff value for the 99th percentile value to a different geo-replicated topic. The `BiDirectionalAnomalyDetector` functions will consume messages from this topic and use the published value as the new anomaly threshold for the sensor reading.

12.6   *Beyond the book*

As I wrap up this final chapter of the book, I hope you have enjoyed reading it and have found it to be informative, enlightening, and thought-provoking. It has been a pleasure to interact with many of you throughout the MEAP process via the online discussion forum, and I've appreciated all of the feedback you have provided. It's great to know not only that so many of you have found the book to be of use, but more importantly, how you intend to use Apache Pulsar to harness the power of streaming data within your organizations.

As with all technologies, Apache Pulsar will continue to evolve rapidly thanks to its growing and vibrant developer and user communities. In fact, several new features have been added since I started writing this book, such as support for transactions. It is a testament to Pulsar's technological strength that it is so widely adopted across a diverse set of companies and industries. However, this evolution will inevitably make the content of the book become increasingly dated over time, so you should refer to the following resources for the most up-to-date information and new features:

- The Apache Pulsar project page (https://pulsar.apache.org/) and documentation (https://pulsar.apache.org/docs/en/standalone/).

- The Apache Pulsar slack channel, apache-pulsar.slack.com, which I and several of the project committers monitor on a daily basis. The heavily used channel contains a wealth of information for beginners and a concentrated community of developers who are actively using Apache Pulsar on a daily basis.
- Several blog posts, including those on the StreamNative web site (https://streamnative.io/en/blog/), that are written by many of the committers to the Apache Pulsar project.

For those of you who are looking to introduce stream computing into your organization or considering using a message-based microservices architecture for future applications to take advantage of the emerging cloud computing paradigm, let me offer the following advice on how to go about convincing your company to consider adopting Apache Pulsar: focus on the benefits of using Pulsar, such as the fact that it is a cloud-native technology designed to scale the computing and storage layers independently, which leads to more efficient use of expensive cloud resources. Another advantage is the fact that it can serve as both a queue-based messaging system, like RabbitMQ, and a streaming messaging platform, like Kafka, in a single system.

Another approach is to bring Apache Pulsar in as an underlying technology for a brand-new initiative within your organization, such as microservices. You can begin your organization's foray into microservices application development using Apache Pulsar Functions as the underlying technology. Your development team will benefit from the simplicity of the programming model Pulsar Functions provides without having to use a proprietary API. If your company is using one of the cloud vendor serverless computing technologies, such as AWS Lambda, you can stress the fact that Pulsar Functions provides the same functionality at a fraction of the cost and without vendor lock in. Furthermore, all application development and testing can be done locally for free rather than on costly AWS computing resources.

If your organization has an incumbent technology already in place, such as Apache Kafka, then you would be wise to heed the advice of Mark Twain when he said, "It's easier to fool people than to convince them that they have been fooled." This sentiment succinctly captures people's reluctance to accept the fact that may have made a bad choice. So rather than framing the conversation as a competition between the incumbent technology and Pulsar, in which you must convince your organization that they made a bad decision, you should instead focus on the positives that Pulsar brings to your organization that the other technology cannot. In this way, Pulsar can be seen as a supporting technology that can co-exist within the organization, rather than a replacement technology that would require a significant amount of change across the entire organization. Such a wholesale replacement strategy will be met with a large amount of resistance by those who decided upon the incumbent technology and those who invested a lot of time and effort in developing solutions based on it. You will have a greater chance of success by focusing on Pulsar's strengths (which were covered in chapter 1) than the incumbent technology's weaknesses.

Thank you again for your interest in Apache Pulsar. I hope this book has inspired you to start using Apache Pulsar in some of your projects, and I look forward to interacting with you in one of the many forums within the Pulsar open source community!

Summary

- The amount of time between when an event occurs and when you respond to it is known as the time value of data. This time value decreases rapidly over time, so being able to respond quickly is important.
- Pulsar Functions can be used to provide near real-time analytics on IoT data within an edge computing environment that consists primarily of resource-constrained devices, such as IoT gateways.
- Running Pulsar Functions on these IoT gateways maximizes the time value of the data.
- Pulsar's geo-replication mechanism can be used to create a bidirectional communication network between Pulsar clusters running on the IoT Gateways and Pulsar clusters running on the Edge Servers.

appendix A
Running
Pulsar on Kubernetes

Kubernetes is a popular open source platform for deploying and running containerized applications at scale. It originated inside Google as a solution for managing their extensive infrastructure by automating many of the manual processes involved in deploying, managing, and scaling their applications across multiple hosts. For more information on Kubernetes, I highly recommend *Kubernetes in Action* by Marko Lukša (Manning, 2017).

The primary purpose of Kubernetes is to schedule containers to run on a cluster of physical or virtual machines based on the available computing resources and the resource requirements of every container. A container is simply a ready-to-run software package that contains everything needed to run an application. As we saw in chapter 3, Docker is one of the most popular container technologies. So, naturally, Kubernetes can be used to schedule and run Docker containers, including those generated by the Apache Pulsar project. This allows you to run an entire Pulsar cluster and all of its components, such as Zookeeper, BookKeeper, and the Pulsar Proxy, entirely on a Kubernetes cluster. This appendix walks you through the process of doing this.

A.1 Create a Kubernetes cluster

A cluster is the foundational base for running your containerized applications. In Kubernetes, a cluster consists of at least one *cluster master* and multiple worker machines, called *nodes*, as shown in figure A.1. The cluster master machine hosts the Kubernetes control plane, which performs all the administrative functions for the cluster, while the nodes are the machines that will host the containers themselves.

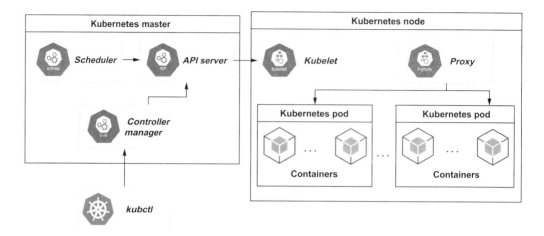

Figure A.1   The Kubernetes master node is used to control all of the Kubernetes nodes in the node pool. Each Kubernetes node can host multiple pods, which in turn can host one or more application containers.

The computing resources from all of the nodes are registered with the cluster master and form a *resource pool* from which all the containers draw. For instance, if your particular container is hosting a database application, and it requires 8 GB of RAM and four CPU cores, the cluster master would have to find a node with sufficient resources available to meet this request and run the container on it. These claimed resources would then also be subtracted from the resource pool to indicate that they are already committed to a container. Once the cluster resource pool is exhausted, no more containers can be hosted until more resources are available.

With Kubernetes, resources can be easily added by adding more nodes to the cluster. This effectively allows you to scale your cluster up based on your needs in a seamless manner. This feature is so appealing that nearly all cloud vendors offer some sort of Kubernetes option for hosting your applications. In addition, there is a large open source implementation of Kubernetes, known as OpenShift, which allows you to host a Kubernetes cluster on your own physical hardware. While both of these options are good choices for production applications, they do impose a rather high barrier for local development. Most people don't want to pay the cost of hosting a large Kubernetes cluster simply for development or testing purposes, which is why `minikube` is a popular option for developers. Pulsar was designed specifically to run in a containerized environment, such as Kubernetes, where you can easily increase or decrease the number of Pulsar broker containers and/or BookKeeper bookies based on your demand.

A.1.1   Install prerequisites

As a prerequisite for working with Kubernetes, you will need to install the Kubernetes command-line tool called `kubectl`, which allows you to run commands against Kubernetes clusters. You will need this tool to deploy applications, inspect and manage cluster resources, and view logs. If you don't already have `kubectl` installed, you should download it (https://kubernetes.io/docs/tasks/tools/#before-you-begin) and follow the instructions for your operating system.

Listing A.1 Installing `kubectl` on a MacBook

```
brew install kubectl    ⟵── Using Homebrew to install kubectl
. . .
==> Downloading https://homebrew.bintray.com/bottles/
    ➥ kubernetes-cli-1.19.1.catalina.bottle.tar.gz    ⟵──┐ Downloading and
==> Pouring kubernetes-cli-1.19.1.catalina.bottle.tar.gz     installing version
==> Caveats                                                  1.19.1
Bash completion has been installed to:
  /usr/local/etc/bash_completion.d

zsh completions have been installed to:
  /usr/local/share/zsh/site-functions
==> Summary
    /usr/local/Cellar/kubernetes-cli/1.19.1: 231 files, 49MB
```

If you have a Mac, you can use the Homebrew package manager to install it using a single line, as shown in listing A.1. If you are using a different operating system, please consult the online documentation for installation instructions specific to your OS. You must use a `kubectl` version that is within one minor version difference of your cluster. Therefore, it is best to use the latest version of `kubectl` to avoid any compatibility issues.

A.1.2 *Minikube*

Once `kubectl` has been installed, the next step is to create a Kubernetes cluster to host the Pulsar cluster. While all of the major cloud vendors provide Kubernetes environments that are well-suited for production use, in this appendix I will use a more cost-effective alternative known as `minikube`, which allows me to run a Kubernetes cluster on my development machine.

    `minikube` is a tool that runs a single-node Kubernetes cluster on your personal computer. It is well suited for day-to-day development tasks that require access to a containerized application, such as Pulsar. It is a good choice if you want to develop and test your application inside a Kubernetes environment to familiarize yourself with the Kubernetes API.

Listing A.2 Installing `minikube` on a MacBook

```
brew install minikube    ⟵── Using Homebrew to install minikube
. . .                                                          Downloading and
==> Downloading https://homebrew.bintray.com/bottles/minikube-  installing version
    ➥ 1.13.0.catalina.bottle.tar.gz    ⟵──                     1.13.0
Already downloaded: /Users/david/Library/Caches/Homebrew/downloads/
➥ b4e7b1579cd54deea3070d595b60b315ff7244ada9358412c87ecfd061819d9b--
➥ minikube-1.13.0.catalina.bottle.tar.gz
==> Pouring minikube-1.13.0.catalina.bottle.tar.gz
```

```
==> Caveats
Bash completion has been installed to:
  /usr/local/etc/bash_completion.d

zsh completions have been installed to:
  /usr/local/share/zsh/site-functions
==> Summary
🍺  /usr/local/Cellar/minikube/1.13.0: 8 files, 62.2MB
```

If you don't already have `minikube` installed, you should download it (https://minikube
.sigs.k8s.io/docs/start/) and follow the instructions for your operating system. If you
have a Mac, you can use the Homebrew package manager to install it using a single line,
as shown in listing A.2. If you are using a different operating system, please consult the
online documentation for installation instructions specific to your OS. After `minikube`
has been installed, the next step is to create a Kubernetes cluster using the commands
shown in the following listing. The first command creates the cluster itself and specifies
the resources it will claim from my laptop for its resource pool.

> **Listing A.3   Creating a Kubernetes cluster using `minikube`**

```
    minikube start \          Reserve 8 GB of RAM for the cluster.
  --memory=8192 \   ◁
  --cpus=4 \          ◁      Reserve four cores for the cluster.
  --kubernetes-version=v1.19.0   ◁
                                    Specify the version of
                                    Kubernetes we will be using.
▷ kubectl config use-context minikube

Set kubectl to use minikube.
```

In order for the `kubectl` tool to find and access a Kubernetes cluster, it must first be
configured to point to the Kubernetes cluster you wish to interact with. This association
is controlled by a kubeconfig file, which is created automatically when you deploy a
`minikube` cluster and is located at `~/.kube/config`. You can use the `kubectl config
use-context <cluster-name>` command, as shown in listing A.3, to configure the
kubectl tool to point to the newly created minikube cluster. You can confirm that the
`kubectl` is properly configured by running the kubectl `cluster-info` command,
which will return basic information about the Kubernetes cluster.

A.2   *The Pulsar Helm chart*

Now that we have a Kubernetes cluster up and running, we can deploy containerized
applications on top of it. This can be accomplished with a deployment configuration
file that contains all the information needed to create all the containers required by
your application. These deployment configuration files are simple YAML files that
conform to a specific structure, as shown in the following listing, which shows the configuration for a single Ngnix-based web server that listens on port 80 for incoming
requests.

Listing A.4 A Kubernetes deployment configuration file

**Specifies the API version
of the configuration file**

```
apiVersion: apps/v1        Specifies the resource type
kind: Deployment           defined in the configuration file
metadata:
  name: mysite        ◁—— The application name
  labels:
    name: mysite
spec:
  replicas: 1        ◁—— The number of pods to create
  template:
    metadata:
      labels:
        app: mysite
    spec:                 Specifies all of the
      containers:         containers inside each pod
        - name: mysite
          image: ngnix   ◁—— The Docker image name to use
          resources:
            limits:
              memory: "128Mi"
              cpu: "500m"
          ports:
            - containerPort: 80      ◁—— The exposed port for the container
```

**The resources
required for
the nginx
container**

Once you have created this file, you can then use the `kubectl apply -f filename` command to deploy it to your Kubernetes cluster. While this approach is relatively straightforward, it is a bit tedious to have to create and edit all of these verbose files manually. As you can see, the deployment file for a simple, single-container application requires 22 lines of YAML. You can just image how big and complex the deployment file is going to be for an application as complex as Pulsar, which requires multiple instances of multiple containers (brokers, bookies, ZooKeeper, etc.).

Kubernetes-orchestrated container applications can be complex to deploy. Developers can use incorrect inputs for configuration files or not have the expertise to roll out these apps from YAML templates. Therefore, a deployment tool known as Helm was created to simplify the deployment of containerized applications to Kubernetes.

A.2.1 What is Helm?

Helm is a package manager for Kubernetes that allows developers to easily package, configure, and deploy applications and services onto Kubernetes clusters. It is analogous to Linux package managers such as YUM or APT because they all allow you to deploy a software package, along with all its dependencies, with a simple command.

We will be using Helm to install our Pulsar cluster, so if you don't already have Helm installed, you should install it now. If you have a Mac, you can use the Homebrew package manager to install it using a single line, as shown in the following listing. If you are using a different operating system, please consult the online documentation (https://helm.sh/docs/intro/install/) for installation instructions specific to your OS.

Listing A.5   Installing Helm on a MacBook

```
brew install helm        ⊲——— Using Homebrew to install Helm        Downloading and
. . .                                                                installing version
==> Downloading https://homebrew.bintray.com/bottles/               3.3.1
    ⧎ helm-3.3.1.catalina.bottle.tar.gz        ⊲
Already downloaded: /Users/david/Library/Caches/Homebrew/downloads/
⧎ 77e13146a8989356ceaba3a19f6ee6a342427d88975394c91a263ae1c35a3eb6--helm-
⧎ 3.3.1.catalina.bottle.tar.gz
==> Pouring helm-3.3.1.catalina.bottle.tar.gz
==> Caveats
Bash completion has been installed to:
  /usr/local/etc/bash_completion.d

zsh completions have been installed to:
  /usr/local/share/zsh/site-functions
==> Summary
🍺  /usr/local/Cellar/helm/3.3.1: 56 files, 40.3MB
```

Helm allows us to package Kubernetes applications into packages of preconfigured Kubernetes resources, known as *charts*. Helm charts provide push button deployment and deletion of apps, making development and deployment of Kubernetes applications easier for those with little or no container or microservices experience.

ANATOMY OF A HELM CHART

A Helm chart is basically a collection of files inside a directory. The directory name is used as the name of the chart. Within this directory, the Helm chart directory contains a self-descriptor file named chart.yaml, a values.yaml file, and one or more manifest files that are stored in the chart's template folder, as shown in the following listing.

Listing A.6   The Helm chart directory layout

```
package-name/
    charts/
    templates/        ⊲——————— Folder of manifest files
    Chart.yaml        ⊲——————— The self-descriptor file
    values.yaml       ⊲
  ⊳ requirements.yaml           Default values used in the templates

Optional list of dependencies
```

The Helm chart uses the YAML templates for application configuration with a separate value.yaml file to store all the values, which are injected into the template YAML at the time of installation. Essentially, Helm charts can be thought of as Kubernetes files that can be parameterized.

When your chart is ready for deployment, you can use the `helm package <chart-name>` command to create a tar-gzipped file containing all the files. Once all this is packaged into a Helm chart, anyone can use it, using the `helm install` command and providing custom values to the configurations via an external values file or as an argument to the `helm install` command, and those values are used while creating the Kubernetes application by running the `helm install <chartname>` command.

A.2.2 *The Pulsar Helm chart*

I have covered what Helm charts are and how they can be used to deploy an entire application. You will be glad to know that there is a Helm chart for Apache Pulsar that is included in the open source distribution, and you can easily access the chart by cloning the repo, using git, as shown in the following listing.

Listing A.7   Downloading the Pulsar Helm chart

```
git clone https://github.com/apache/pulsar-helm-chart   ⟵ Clone the Helm chart repo.

cd pulsar-helm-chart   ⟵┐ Change into the folder that
                        │ the repo was cloned into.
```

Once you have cloned the repo, you can examine the contents of the Helm chart inside the chart's subfolder, as shown in the next listing. As expected, the directory structure conforms to the Helm directory structure we saw earlier in listing A.6 with Chart.yaml and values.yaml files at the base level along with a directory of template files.

Listing A.8   The Pulsar Helm chart directory layout

```
ls ./charts/pulsar/                              ⟵┐ Examine the structure of the generated
Chart.yaml    templates    values.yaml            │ Pulsar Helm chart directory.

ls ./charts/pulsar/templates/*.yaml              ⟵┐
./charts/pulsar/templates/autorecovery-configmap.yaml     │ List all of the
./charts/pulsar/templates/autorecovery-service.yaml       │ generated templates.
./charts/pulsar/templates/autorecovery-statefulset.yaml
./charts/pulsar/templates/bookkeeper-cluster-initialize.yaml
./charts/pulsar/templates/bookkeeper-configmap.yaml
./charts/pulsar/templates/bookkeeper-pdb.yaml
./charts/pulsar/templates/bookkeeper-podmonitor.yaml
./charts/pulsar/templates/bookkeeper-service.yaml
./charts/pulsar/templates/bookkeeper-statefulset.yaml
./charts/pulsar/templates/bookkeeper-storageclass.yaml
./charts/pulsar/templates/broker-cluster-role-binding.yaml
./charts/pulsar/templates/broker-configmap.yaml
./charts/pulsar/templates/broker-pdb.yaml
./charts/pulsar/templates/broker-podmonitor.yaml
./charts/pulsar/templates/broker-rbac.yaml
./charts/pulsar/templates/broker-service-account.yaml
./charts/pulsar/templates/broker-service.yaml
./charts/pulsar/templates/broker-statefulset.yaml
./charts/pulsar/templates/dashboard-deployment.yaml
./charts/pulsar/templates/dashboard-ingress.yaml
./charts/pulsar/templates/dashboard-service.yaml
./charts/pulsar/templates/function-worker-configmap.yaml
./charts/pulsar/templates/grafana-admin-secret.yaml
./charts/pulsar/templates/grafana-configmap.yaml
```

```
./charts/pulsar/templates/grafana-deployment.yaml
./charts/pulsar/templates/grafana-ingress.yaml
./charts/pulsar/templates/grafana-service.yaml
./charts/pulsar/templates/keytool.yaml
./charts/pulsar/templates/namespace.yaml
./charts/pulsar/templates/prometheus-configmap.yaml
./charts/pulsar/templates/prometheus-deployment.yaml
./charts/pulsar/templates/prometheus-pvc.yaml
./charts/pulsar/templates/prometheus-rbac.yaml
./charts/pulsar/templates/prometheus-service.yaml
./charts/pulsar/templates/prometheus-storageclass.yaml
./charts/pulsar/templates/proxy-configmap.yaml
./charts/pulsar/templates/proxy-ingress.yaml
./charts/pulsar/templates/proxy-pdb.yaml
./charts/pulsar/templates/proxy-podmonitor.yaml
./charts/pulsar/templates/proxy-service.yaml
./charts/pulsar/templates/proxy-statefulset.yaml
./charts/pulsar/templates/pulsar-cluster-initialize.yaml
./charts/pulsar/templates/pulsar-manager-admin-secret.yaml
./charts/pulsar/templates/pulsar-manager-configmap.yaml
./charts/pulsar/templates/pulsar-manager-deployment.yaml
./charts/pulsar/templates/pulsar-manager-ingress.yaml
./charts/pulsar/templates/pulsar-manager-service.yaml
./charts/pulsar/templates/tls-cert-internal-issuer.yaml
./charts/pulsar/templates/tls-certs-internal.yaml
./charts/pulsar/templates/toolset-configmap.yaml
./charts/pulsar/templates/toolset-service.yaml
./charts/pulsar/templates/toolset-statefulset.yaml
./charts/pulsar/templates/zookeeper-configmap.yaml
./charts/pulsar/templates/zookeeper-pdb.yaml
./charts/pulsar/templates/zookeeper-podmonitor.yaml
./charts/pulsar/templates/zookeeper-service.yaml
./charts/pulsar/templates/zookeeper-statefulset.yaml
./charts/pulsar/templates/zookeeper-storageclass.yaml
```

As we can see from listing A.8, there are quite a few templates that encapsulate the bulk of the chart logic. Let's examine the templates associated with the Pulsar brokers to get a better understanding of the details these templates contain.

Listing A.9   The Pulsar broker deployment configuration file

```
cat ./charts/pulsar/templates/broker-service.yaml        ◁─┐  The file containing the Pulsar
...                                                          │  Broker service definition

{{- if .Values.components.broker }}
apiVersion: v1
kind: Service
metadata:
  name: "{{ template "pulsar.fullname" . }}-{{ .Values.broker.component }}"
  namespace: {{ .Values.namespace }}
  labels:
    {{- include "pulsar.standardLabels" . | nindent 4 }}
    component: {{ .Values.broker.component }}
```

```
    annotations:
{{ toYaml .Values.broker.service.annotations | indent 4 }}
spec:
  ports:
  # prometheus needs to access /metrics endpoint
  - name: http
    port: {{ .Values.broker.ports.http }}         ◁────── The HTTP port to use
  {{- if or (not .Values.tls.enabled) (not .Values.tls.broker.enabled) }}
  - name: pulsar
    port: {{ .Values.broker.ports.pulsar }}       ◁────── The data port to use
  {{- end }}
  {{- if and .Values.tls.enabled .Values.tls.broker.enabled }}  ◁──┐
  - name: https                                    ┌─────────────┐  │  Whether the
    port: {{ .Values.broker.ports.https }}  ◁──── │ The secured │  │  Broker should
  - name: pulsarssl                                │ HTTPS port to use │  use TLS or not
    port: {{ .Values.broker.ports.pulsarssl }}  ◁──┘
  {{- end }}                                        │ The secured data port to use
  clusterIP: None
  selector:
    app: {{ template "pulsar.name" . }}
    release: {{ .Release.Name }}
    component: {{ .Values.broker.component }}
{{- end }}
```

As you can see in listing A.9, the Pulsar broker definition file depends on parameterized values for configuration. As you may suspect, these values are provided in the values.yaml file that was generated for us when we ran the script to produce the Pulsar Helm chart. The following listing shows the corresponding section of the values.yaml file that contains the definitions for the Pulsar broker.

Listing A.10 The Pulsar broker-related values in values.yaml

```
## Pulsar: Broker cluster
## templates/broker-statefulset.yaml
##
broker:
  # use a component name that matches your grafana configuration    ┌──────────┐
  # so the metrics are correctly rendered in grafana dashboard      │ Specifies │
  component: broker                                                 │ a total of │
  replicaCount: 3                                    ◁────────────  │ three broker │
  # If using Prometheus-Operator enable this PodMonitor to discover broker │ instances │
    scrape targets
  # Prometheus-Operator does not add scrape targets based on k8s annotations
  podMonitor:
    enabled: false
    interval: 10s
    scrapeTimeout: 10s
  ports:              ◁────────┐ Section that specifies
    http: 8080                 │ the various port values
    https: 8443
    pulsar: 6650
    pulsarssl: 6651
  # nodeSelector:
```

```
      # cloud.google.com/gke-nodepool: default-pool
   ...
      resources:       ◁──────  Section that specifies
      requests:                 the pod resources
        memory: 512Mi
        cpu: 0.2
   ## Broker configmap
   ## templates/broker-configmap.yaml  ◁────  The associated broker
   ##                                          configuration map
   configData:
     PULSAR_MEM: >
       -Xms128m -Xmx256m -XX:MaxDirectMemorySize=256m  ◁──  The JVM memory settings
     PULSAR_GC: >                                           for the broker pods
       -XX:+UseG1GC
       -XX:MaxGCPauseMillis=10
       -Dio.netty.leakDetectionLevel=disabled
       -Dio.netty.recycler.linkCapacity=1024
       -XX:+ParallelRefProcEnabled
       -XX:+UnlockExperimentalVMOptions
       -XX:+DoEscapeAnalysis
       -XX:ParallelGCThreads=4
       -XX:ConcGCThreads=4
       -XX:G1NewSizePercent=50
       -XX:+DisableExplicitGC
       -XX:-ResizePLAB
       -XX:+ExitOnOutOfMemoryError        The JVM garbage collection
       -XX:+PerfDisableSharedMem  ◁────   settings for the broker pods
     managedLedgerDefaultEnsembleSize: "2"
     managedLedgerDefaultWriteQuorum: "2"  ◁───  The write quorum size
     managedLedgerDefaultAckQuorum: "2"          for the Pulsar ledger
```

The ensemble size for the Pulsar ledger

The ack quorum for the Pulsar ledger

As you can see from listing A.10, these settings are on the small side in terms of resources. This is because the default Pulsar Helm chart is designed specifically for minikube-based deployment. You can modify these values to suit your own needs.

A.3   Using the Pulsar Helm chart

Now that we have downloaded and examined the Pulsar Helm chart, the next step is to use it to provide our Pulsar cluster. The first step in this process is to add the Pulsar Helm chart to your local Helm repository and initialize it, as shown in the following listing. This will allow your local Helm client to locate and download the Pulsar Helm chart.

Listing A.11   Adding the Pulsar Helm chart to your Helm repository

Add the Pulsar Helm repo to your local Helm repo.

```
 ─▷ helm repo add apache https://pulsar.apache.org/charts
```
Instruct Helm to create the
Kubernetes namespace.
```
    ./scripts/pulsar/prepare_helm_release.sh \
      --create-namespace \
      --namepsace pulsar \       ◁────  The name of the Kubernetes
 ─▷   --release pulsar-mini             namespace to create
```
The Pulsar release name

```
namespace/pulsar created
generate the token keys for the pulsar cluster          ⊲─┐
The private key and public key are generated to /var/folders/zw/
➥ x39hv0dd7133w9v9cgnt1lvr0000gn/T/tmp.QT3EjywR and
➥ /var/folders/zw/x39hv0dd7133w9v9cgnt1lvr0000gn/T/tmp.YkhhbAyG
➥ successfully.
secret/pulsar-mini-token-asymmetric-key created
generate the tokens for the super-users: proxy-admin,broker-admin,admin
generate the token for proxy-admin
secret/pulsar-mini-token-proxy-admin created
generate the token for broker-admin
secret/pulsar-mini-token-broker-admin created
generate the token for admin
secret/pulsar-mini-token-admin created          ⊲───────┐
------------------------------------

The jwt token secret keys are generated under:          ⊲────
    - 'pulsar-mini-token-asymmetric-key'

The jwt tokens for superusers are generated and stored as below: ⊲──
    - 'proxy-admin':secret('pulsar-mini-token-proxy-admin')
    - 'broker-admin':secret('pulsar-mini-token-broker-admin')
    - 'admin':secret('pulsar-mini-token-admin')
```

Generating the public and private token files

Generating the tokens for the various admin users

Generating the JWT secret

Generating the JWT access tokens

The final step in the process is to use Helm to install the Pulsar cluster, as shown in the following listing. It is important to specify `initialize=true` when installing a Pulsar release for the first time because it will ensure that the cluster metadata for both BookKeeper and Pulsar is properly initialized.

Listing A.12 Install Pulsar using the Helm chart

The unique name for this cluster

Request that the cluster metadata be initialized.

```
helm install \
--set initialize=true \          ⊲
--values examples/values-minikube.yaml \          ⊲
pulsar-mini \
apache/pulsar          ⊲─── The Helm chart to use
```

The values file to use

```
kubectl get pods -n pulsar -o name          ⊲
pod/pulsar-mini-bookie-0
pod/pulsar-mini-bookie-init-94r5z
pod/pulsar-mini-broker-0
pod/pulsar-mini-grafana-6746b4bf69-bjtff
pod/pulsar-mini-prometheus-5556dbb8b8-m8287
pod/pulsar-mini-proxy-0
pod/pulsar-mini-pulsar-init-dmztl
pod/pulsar-mini-pulsar-manager-6c6889dff-q9t5q
pod/pulsar-mini-toolset-0
pod/pulsar-mini-zookeeper-0
```

List all the pods created for the Pulsar cluster.

After Helm has completed the installation process, you can use the `kubectl` tool to list all of the pods created for the Pulsar cluster and validate that the necessary services are up and running, get the IP addresses, etc.

A.3.1 *Administering Pulsar on Kubernetes*

Once you have deployed a Pulsar cluster to a Kubernetes environment, one of your first concerns will be deciding how to administer the pulsar cluster. Fortunately, the Pulsar Helm chart creates a pod named `pulsar-mini-toolset-0` that contains the `pulsar-admin` CLI tool, which is already configured to interact with the deployed Pulsar cluster. Consequently, all that is required to administer the cluster is to use the `kubectl exec` command to access the pod and execute the commands directly against the cluster, as shown in the following listing.

Listing A.13   Administering Pulsar on Kubernetes

```
kubectl exec -it -n pulsar pulsar-mini-toolset-0 /bin/bash

bin/pulsar-admin tenants create manning

bin/pulsar-admin tenants list

"manning"
"public"
"pulsar"
```

Since the `pulsar-admin` CLI tool is the same for both the Kubernetes cluster and the Docker standalone container, the `docker exec` and `kubectl exec` commands can be used interchangeably throughout this book if you choose to follow the examples using Kubernetes rather than Docker. For more details on the `pulsar-admin` CLI, please refer to the documentation.

A.3.2 *Configuring clients*

The main challenge with connecting to a Pulsar cluster inside a K8s environment is finding the ports that the cluster is listening on. The default binary port, 6650 and HTTP admin port, 8080 are not exposed outside of the K8s environment. Therefore, you first need to determine where these node ports are mapped to.

By default, the Pulsar Helm chart exposes the Pulsar cluster through a Kubernetes load balancer. In `minikube`, you can use the command shown in listing A.14 to check the proxy service. The output from this command will tell us which node ports the Pulsar cluster's binary port and HTTP port are mapped to. The port after `80:` is the HTTP port, while the port after `6650:` is the binary port.

Listing A.14   Determining the Pulsar Client ports

Command to determine port mappings

```
$kubectl get services -n pulsar | grep pulsar-mini-proxy

pulsar-mini-proxy            LoadBalancer    10.110.67.72      <pending>
  80:30210/TCP,6650:32208/TCP    4h16m

$minikube service pulsar-mini-proxy -n pulsar --url
  http://192.168.64.3:30210
  http://192.168.64.3:32208
```

The output tells us port 80 is mapped to port 30210, and port 6650 is mapped to port 32208.

The proxy's HTTP URL

The proxy's binary URL

Command to find the IP address of the exposed ports inside minikube

At this point, you have service URLs you need to connect your clients to the Pulsar cluster running inside minikube, and you can use them, along with required security tokens that we generated earlier when configuring your Pulsar clients to interact with the cluster.

appendix B
Geo-replication

Geo-replication is a common mechanism used to provide disaster recovery in multi-datacenter deployments. Unlike other pub–sub messaging systems that require additional processes to mirror messages between data centers, geo-replication is automatically performed by Pulsar brokers and can be enabled, disabled, or dynamically changed at runtime. Traditional geo-replication mechanisms typically fall into one of two categories: synchronous or asynchronous. Apache Pulsar comes with multi-datacenter replication as an integrated feature that supports both of these geo-replication strategies. In the following examples, I will assume that we are deploying our Pulsar instance across the three cloud provider regions: US-West, US-Central, and US-East.

B.1 Synchronous geo-replication

A *synchronous* geo-replicated Pulsar installation consists of a cluster of bookies running across multiple regions, a cluster of brokers also distributed across all regions, and a single global ZooKeeper installation to form a single global logical instance across all available regions, as shown in figure B.1. The global "stretched" Zoo-Keeper ensemble is critical to supporting this approach because it is used to store the managed ledgers.

In the synchronous geo-replication case, when the client issues a write request to a Pulsar cluster in one geographical location, the data is written to multiple bookies in different geographical locations within the same call. The write request is only acknowledged to the client when the configured number of the data centers have issued a confirmation that the data has been persisted. While this approach provides the highest level of data guarantees, it also incurs the cost of the cross-datacenter network latency for each message.

Synchronous geo-replication is actually achieved by Apache BookKeeper in the storage layer for Pulsar and relies on a placement policy to distribute the data

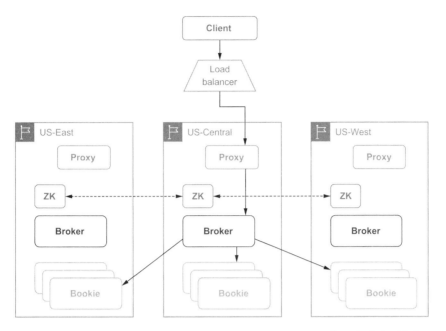

Figure B.1 Clients access a synchronously geo-replicated cluster via a single load balancer, which forwards the publish request to one of the Pulsar proxies. The Proxy routes the request to the broker that owns the topic, which then publishes the data across the regions based on the placement policy that is configured.

across multiple data centers and to guarantee availability constraints. You can enable either the rack-aware or region-aware placement policy, depending on whether you are running in a bare metal or cloud environment, respectively, by modifying the broker configuration file (broker.conf), as shown in the following listing.

Listing B.1 Enabling the region-aware policy

```
# Set this to true if your cluster is spread across racks inside one
# datacenter or across multiple AZs inside one region
bookkeeperClientRackawarePolicyEnabled=true

# Set this to true if your cluster is spread across multiple datacenters or
# cloud provider regions.
bookkeeperClientRegionawarePolicyEnabled=true
```

When you enable the region-aware placement policy, for example, BookKeeper will choose bookies from different regions when forming a new bookie ensemble, which ensures that the topic data will be distributed evenly across all of the available regions. Note that only one of these settings will be honored at runtime with region awareness taking precedence if both are set to true.

The use of a single ZooKeeper cluster to implement synchronous geo-replication also requires some additional configuration changes in order for the geographically dispersed broker and bookie components to work together as a single cluster. Configuring ZooKeeper for such a scenario involves adding a `server.N` line to the conf/zookeeper.conf file for each node in the ZooKeeper cluster, where *n* is the number of the ZooKeeper nodes, as shown in the following listing, which uses one ZooKeeper node per region.

Listing B.2   Single ZooKeeper configuration for synchronous geo-replication

```
server.1=zk1.us-west.example.com:2888:3888
server.2=zk1.us-central.example.com:2888:3888
server.3=zk1.us-east.example.com:2888:3888
```

In addition to modifying the conf/zookeeper.conf file in the conf directory of each Pulsar installation, you will also need to modify the `zkServers` property in the conf/bookkeeper.conf file to list each of the ZooKeeper servers, as shown in the following listing.

Listing B.3   BookKeeper configuration for synchronous geo-replication

```
zkServers= zk1.us-west.example.com:2181, zk1.us-central.example.com:2181,
zk1.us-east.example.com:2181
```

Similarly, you will need to update the `zookeeperServers` property in both the conf/discovery.conf and conf/proxy.conf files to be a comma-separated list of the ZooKeeper servers as well, since both the Pulsar proxy and service discovery mechanism depend on ZooKeeper to provide them with up-to-date metadata about the Pulsar cluster.

Synchronous geo-replication provides stronger data consistency guarantees than asynchronous replication, since the data is always synchronized across the datacenters, making it easier to run your applications independent of where the messages are published. A synchronous geo-replicated Pulsar cluster can continue to function like normal even if an entire datacenter goes down, with the outage being entirely transparent to the applications that are accessing the cluster via a load balancer. This makes synchronous geo-replication good for mission-critical use cases that are able to tolerate a slightly higher publish latency.

B.2   *Asynchronous geo-replication*

An *asynchronous* geo-replicated Pulsar installation consists of a two or more independent Pulsar clusters running in different regions. Each Pulsar cluster contains its own respective set of brokers, bookies, and ZooKeeper nodes that are completely isolated from one another. In asynchronous geo-replication, when messages are produced on a Pulsar topic, they are first persisted to the local cluster and are then replicated asynchronously to the remote clusters. This replication process occurs via inter-broker communication, as shown in figure B.2.

With asynchronous geo-replication, the message producer doesn't wait for a confirmation from multiple Pulsar clusters. Instead, the producer receives a response

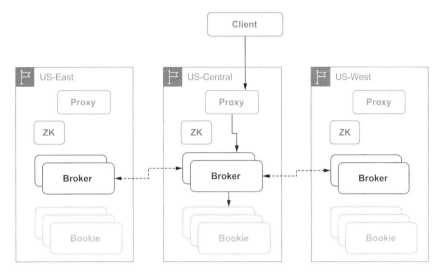

Figure B.2   Clients access an asynchronously geo-replicated cluster via the closest proxy, and the proxy routes the request to the broker that owns the topic, which then publishes the data to the bookies in the same region. The broker then replicates the incoming data to the brokers in the other regions.

immediately after the nearest cluster successfully persists the data. The data is then replicated to the other Pulsar clusters in an asynchronous fashion in the background. Under normal conditions, messages are replicated at the same time that they are dispatched to local consumers.

While asynchronous geo-replication provides lower latency because the client doesn't have to wait for responses from the other data centers, it also provides weaker consistency guarantees due to asynchronous replication. Given that there is always a replication lag in asynchronous replication, there will always be some amount of data that hasn't been replicated from source to destination at any given point in time. Therefore, if you choose to implement this pattern, your application must be able to tolerate some data loss in exchange for lower publish latency. Typically, the end-to-end replication latency is bounded by the *network round-trip time* (RTT) between the remote regions.

It is worth noting that asynchronous geo-replication is enabled on a per-tenant basis in Pulsar rather than a cluster-wide basis, allowing you to configure replication only for those topics for which it is needed. This allows each individual department or group to maintain control over its data replication policies. Asynchronous geo-replication is managed at the namespace level, which provides more granular control over the datasets that get replicated. This is particularly useful for cases in which you are not permitted to allow data to leave a particular region due to regulatory and/or security reasons.

B.2.1   *Configuring asynchronous geo-replication*

As you may recall from chapter 2, a Pulsar instance is comprised of one or more Pulsar clusters that act together as a single unit and can be administered from a single location, as shown in figure B.3. In fact, one of the biggest reasons for using a Pulsar instance is to enable geo-replication, and only clusters within the same instance can be configured to replicate data amongst themselves. Therefore, enabling asynchronous geo-replication requires us to first create a Pulsar instance.

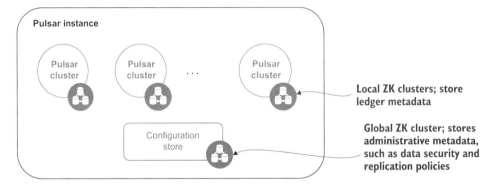

Figure B.3   A Pulsar instance can consist of multiple, geographically dispersed clusters.

A Pulsar instance employs an instance-wide ZooKeeper cluster called the *configuration store* to retain information that pertains to multiple clusters, such as geo-replication and tenant-level security policies. This allows you to define and manage these policies in a single location. While the complete documentation is available online, I wanted to highlight a few of these steps in the next section.

It is worth noting that the instance-wide ZooKeeper instance should be deployed in such a manner as to make it completely independent from the individual Pulsar clusters so that, in the event of a failure on the part of the instance-wide ZooKeeper ensemble, the individual clusters will be able to continue to function without interruption.

DEPLOYING THE CONFIGURATION STORE

In addition to installing the individual clusters, creating a multi-cluster Pulsar instance involves deploying a separate ZooKeeper quorum to use as the configuration store. This configuration store should be implemented with its own dedicated ZooKeeper quorum spread across at least three regions. Given the very low expected load on the configuration store servers, you can share the same hosts used for the local ZooKeeper quorum, but will have to do so as either separate ZooKeeper processes or K8s pods, depending on your deployment environment. You will also have to use a different TCP port to avoid port conflicts.

Listing B.4 ZooKeeper configuration for the configuration store quorum

```
tickTime=2000
dataDir=/var/lib/zookeeper
clientPort=2185
initLimit=5
syncLimit=2
server.1=zk2.us-west.example.com:2185:2186
server.2=zk2.us-central.example.com:2185:2186
server.3=zk2.us-east.example.com:2185:2186
```

Use a different location for storing the transaction log.

Use a different port than the local ZK instance.

The quorum consists of servers from across three regions listening on the same port.

Setting up a separate ZooKeeper quorum is fairly straightforward and well documented on the Apache ZooKeeper documentation page. Each ZooKeeper server is contained in a single JAR file, so installation consists of downloading the jar, unpacking it, and creating a configuration file. The default location for this configuration file is conf/zoo.cfg. All of the servers in the new ZooKeeper quorum should have the exact same configuration file, as shown in listing B.4.

INITIALIZING CLUSTER METADATA

Now that the secondary ZooKeeper quorum is up and running, the next step is to populate the configuration store with information about all the clusters that will be included in the Pulsar instance. This metadata can be initialized by using the `initialize-cluster-metadata` command of the Pulsar CLI tool, as shown in the following listing.

Listing B.5 Initializing the cluster metadata

The name of the cluster that will be used when setting up replication

The local ZK connection string

```
$ /pulsar/bin/pulsar initialize-cluster-metadata \
    --cluster us-west \
    --zookeeper zk1.us-west.example.com:2181 \
    --configuration-store zk1.us-west.example.com:2184 \
    --web-service-url http://pulsar.us-west.example.com:8080/ \
    --web-service-url-tls https://pulsar.us-west.example.com:8443/ \
    --broker-service-url pulsar://pulsar.us-west.example.com:6650/ \
    --broker-service-url-tls pulsar+ssl://pulsar.us-west.example.com:6651/
```

The connection string for the configuration store

The command associates all the various connection URLs to a given cluster name and stores that information inside the configuration store. This information is used when replication is enabled to connect the brokers that need to exchange data between them (e.g., replication data from US-West to US-East). You will need to run this command for every Pulsar cluster you are adding to the instance.

CONFIGURE THE SERVICES TO USE THE CONFIGURATION STORE

After you have populated the configuration store with all the metadata associated with the Pulsar clusters in your instance, you will need to modify a couple of configuration files on every cluster to enable geo-replication. Since geo-replication is accomplished via broker-to-broker communication, the most important one is the conf/broker.conf configuration file, as shown in the following listing.

Listing B.6   Updated broker.conf for asynchronous geo-replication

```
# Local ZooKeeper servers
zookeeperServers=zk1.us-west.example.com:2181,zk2.us-
    west.example.com:2181,zk3.us-west.example.com:2181
```
Use the local ZK
quorum as before.

```
# Configuration store quorum connection string.
configurationStoreServers=zk2.us-west.example.com:2185,zk2.us-
    central.example.com:2185,zk2.us-east.example.com:2185
```
Use the second
ZK quorum for
the configuration
store.

```
clusterName=us-west
```
Specify the name of the cluster
that the broker belongs to.

Make sure that you set the `zookeeperServers` parameter to reflect the local quorum and the `configurationStoreServers` parameter to reflect the configuration store quorum. You also need to specify the name of the cluster to which the broker belongs using the `clusterName` parameter, taking care to use the value you specified in the `initialize-cluster-metadata` command. Finally, make sure that the broker and web service ports match the values you provided in the `initialize-cluster-metadata` command as well. Otherwise, the replication process will fail because the source broker will be attempting communication over the wrong port.

If you are using the service discovery mechanism included with Pulsar, you need to change a few parameters in the conf/discovery.conf configuration file. Specifically, you must set the `zookeeperServers` parameter to the ZooKeeper quorum connection string of the cluster and the `configurationStoreServers` setting to the configuration store quorum connection string using the same values used in the broker configuration file. Once you have finished updating all of the necessary configuration files, all of these services will need to be restarted after these changes are made for the new properties to take effect.

B.3   *Asynchronous geo-replication patterns*

With asynchronous replication, Pulsar provides tenants a great degree of flexibility for customizing their replication strategy. That means that an application is able to set up active–active and full-mesh replication, active-standby replication, and aggregation replication across multiple data centers. Let's take a quick look at how to implement each of these patterns inside of Pulsar.

B.3.1   *Multi-active geo-replication*

Asynchronous geo-replication is controlled on a per-tenant basis in Pulsar. This means geo-replication can only be enabled between clusters when a tenant has been created that allows access to all of the clusters involved. To configure *multi-active geo-replication*, you need to specify which clusters a tenant has access to via the `pulsar-admin` CLI, as shown in the following listing, which displays the command to create a new tenant and grant it permission to access the US-East and US-West clusters only.

Listing B.7 Granting a tenant access to clusters

Create a new tenant named customers.

Grant the tenant permission to access these two clusters only.

```
$ /pulsar/bin/pulsar-admin tenants create customers \
    --allowed-clusters us-west,us-east \
    --admin-roles test-admin-role
```

Now that the tenant has been created, we need to configure the geo-replication at the namespace level. Therefore, we will first need to create the namespace using the pulsar-admin CLI tool and then assign the namespace to a cluster—or multiple clusters—using the set-clusters command, as shown in the following listing.

Listing B.8 Assigning a namespace to a cluster

```
$ /pulsar/bin/pulsar-admin namespaces create customers/orders

$ /pulsar/bin/pulsar-admin namespaces set-clusters customers/orders \
    --clusters us-west,us-east,us-central
```

By default, once replication is configured between two or more clusters, as shown in listing B.8, all of the messages published to topics inside the namespace in one cluster are asynchronously replicated to all the other clusters in the list. Therefore, the default behavior is effectively full-mesh replication of all the topics in the namespace with messages getting published in multiple directions, as shown in figure B.4. When you only have two clusters, the default behavior can be thought of as an active–active cluster configuration where the data is available on both clusters to serve clients, and in the event of a single cluster failure, all of the clients can be redirected to the remaining active cluster without interruption.

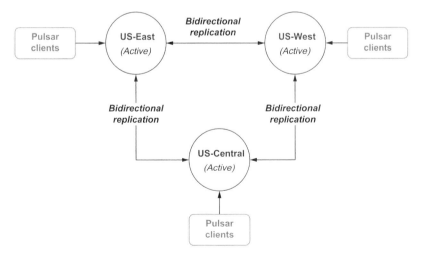

Figure B.4 The default behavior is full-mesh geo-replication between all clusters. Messages published to a topic inside a replicated namespace in the US-East cluster will be forwarded to both the US-West and US-Central clusters.

Besides full-mesh (active-active) geo-replication, there are a few other replication patterns you can use. Another common one for disaster recovery is the *active-standby replication pattern.*

B.3.2   *Active-standby geo-replication*

In this situation you are looking to keep an up-to-date copy of the cluster at a different geographical location, so you can resume operations in the event of a failure with a minimal amount of data loss or recovery time. Since Pulsar doesn't provide a means for specifying one-way replication of namespaces, the only way to accomplish this configuration is by restricting the clients to a single cluster, known as the active cluster, and having them all failover to the standby cluster only in the event of a failure. Typically, this can be accomplished via a load balancer or other network-level mechanism that makes the transition transparent to the clients, as shown in figure B.5. Pulsar clients publish messages to the active cluster, which are then replicated to the standby cluster for backup.

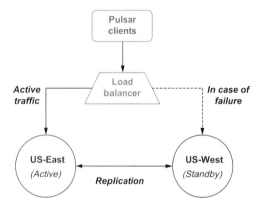

Figure B.5   **You can use asynchronous geo-replication to implement an active-standby scenario in which all of the data within a given namespace is forwarded to a cluster that will be used only in the event of a failure.**

As you may have noticed, the replication of the Pulsar data will still be done bi-directionally, which means that the US-West cluster will attempt to send the data it receives during the outage to the US-East cluster. This might be problematic if the failure is related to one or more components within the Pulsar cluster or the network for the US-East cluster is unreachable. Therefore, you should consider adding selective replication code inside your Pulsar producers to prevent the US-West cluster from attempting to replicate messages to the US-East cluster, which is most likely dead.

You can restrict replication selectively by directly specifying a replication list for a message at the application level. The code in listing B.9 shows an example of producing a message that will only be replicated to the US-West cluster, which is the behavior you want in this active-standby scenario.

Listing B.9 Selective replication per message

```
List<String> restrictDatacenters = Lists.newArrayList("us-west");

Message message = MessageBuilder.create()
    ...
    .setReplicationClusters(restrictDatacenters)
    .build();

producer.send(message);
```

Sometimes you want to funnel messages from multiple clusters into a single location for aggregation purposes. One such example would be gathering all the payment data collected from across all the geographical regions for processing and collection.

B.3.3   *Aggregation geo-replication*

Assume we have three clusters all actively serving the GottaEat customers in their respective regions and a fourth Pulsar cluster named *internal* that is completely isolated from the web and only accessible by internal employees, and that is used to aggregate the data from all of the customer-serving Pulsar clusters, as shown in figure B.6. To implement aggregation geo-replication across these four clusters, you will need to use the commands shown in listing B.10, which first creates the E-payments tenant and grants access to all the clusters.

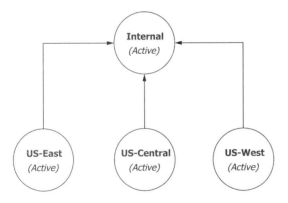

Figure B.6   An aggregation geo-replication configuration to funnel messages from three customer-facing Pulsar clusters to an internal Pulsar cluster for aggregation and analysis

Next, you will need to create a namespace for each of the customer services clusters (e.g., E-payments/us-east-payments). You *cannot* use one such as E-payments/payments because that would lead to full mesh replication if you attempted to use it, since every cluster would have that namespace. Thus, a per-cluster namespace is required for this to work.

Listing B.10   Aggregator geo-replication

Create the global tenant for Payments.

Create the cluster-specific namespaces.

```
/pulsar/bin/pulsar-admin tenants create E-payments \
  --allowed-clusters us-west,us-east,us-central,internal

/pulsar/bin/pulsar-admin namespaces create E-payments/us-east-payments
/pulsar/bin/pulsar-admin namespaces create E-payments/us-west-payments
/pulsar/bin/pulsar-admin namespaces create E-payments/us-central-payments

/pulsar/bin/pulsar-admin namespaces set-clusters \
  E-payments/us-east-payments --clusters us-east,internal

/pulsar/bin/pulsar-admin namespaces set-clusters \
  E-payments/us-west-payments --clusters us-west,internal

/pulsar/bin/pulsar-admin namespaces set-clusters \
  E-payments/us-central-payments --clusters us-central,internal
```

Configure US-East to internal replication.

Configure US-West to internal replication.

Configure US-Central to internal replication.

If you decide to implement this pattern and you intend to run identical copies of an application across all the customer-servicing cluster, be sure to make the topic name configurable so the application running on US-East knows to publish messages to topics inside the us-east-payments namespace. Otherwise, the replication will not work.

index